Young lives on the Left

Manchester University Press

Young lives on the Left

Sixties activism and the liberation of the self

Celia Hughes

MANCHESTER
UNIVERSITY PRESS

Published by Manchester University Press
Altrincham Street, Manchester M1 7JA
www.manchesteruniversitypress.co.uk

British Library Cataloguing-in-Publication Data
A catalogue record for this book is available from the British Library

Library of Congress Cataloging-in-Publication Data applied for

ISBN 978 0 7190 9194 0 hardback

First published 2015

The publisher has no responsibility for the persistence or accuracy of URLs for any external or third-party internet websites referred to in this book, and does not guarantee that any content on such websites is, or will remain, accurate or appropriate.

Typeset 10.5/12.5pt Sabon
by Graphicraft Limited, Hong Kong
Printed in Great Britain
by CPI Group (UK) Ltd, Croydon, CR0 4YY

Contents

Acknowledgements

I wish to express my sincere gratitude to the women and men who have trusted me with their stories for this book. Sharing memories, reflections and hospitality, opening address books and sometimes cajoling friends for interviews, all have warmly assisted my work and inspired my thinking about the possibilities for political, social and subjective change. I only hope they feel I have done justice to their histories.

I would also like to thank individuals who generously allowed me access to their personal papers, and who entrusted me with their material memories often for months at a time. I am grateful to staff at the Modern Records Centre at Warwick University, the Women's Library in London and the British Library Sound Archive for their help during my research.

This work began as a doctoral thesis at the University of Warwick (2008–11), for which I thank the Arts and Humanities Research Council for funding. During my time in the History Department I benefited from the reflections, constructive criticism and encouragement staff and students offered. Special thanks go to my supervisor, Gerd-Rainer Horn, and my doctoral examiners, Carolyn Steedman and Sally Alexander. I completed the book as an *adjunkt* in the Department for English, Germanic and Romance Studies at the University of Copenhagen. My thanks go to the department for generously funding further field trips and to my colleagues for providing a supportive and stimulating environment in which to develop my work.

Finally, I express heartfelt thanks to my family and dear friends, whose unfailing love has enabled me to complete this book.

Abbreviations

AEU	Amalgamated Engineering Union
CAST	Cartoon Archetypal Slogan Theatre
CCC	Birmingham Centre for Cultural Studies
CMPP	Camden Movement for People's Power
CND	Campaign for Nuclear Disarmament
CPGB	Communist Party of Great Britain
CVSC	Camden Vietnam Solidarity Campaign branch
DPA	Di Parkin Archive
GCA	Geoffrey Crossick Archive
GLF	Gay Liberation Front
GRA	Geoff Richman Archive
IMG	International Marxist Group
IS	International Socialists
JHA	John Hoyland Archive
LSE	London School of Economics
LWLW	London Women's Liberation Workshop
MNA	Mica Nava Archive
MRC	Modern Records Centre, Warwick University
NAC	National Abortion Campaign
NLF	National Liberation Front
RSSF	Revolutionary Socialist Student Federation
SDS	Students for a Democratic Society/*Sozialistische Deutsche Studentbund*
SMA	Socialist Medical Association
SLL	Socialist Labour League
SW	Socialist Woman
VSC	Vietnam Solidarity Campaign
VSO	Voluntary Service Overseas
WLM	Women's Liberation Movement
YCL	Young Communist League
YCND	Youth Campaign for Nuclear Disarmament
YS	Young Socialists

Introduction

This book tells the story about the making of a post-war radical self. It presents the early life histories of women and men who came of age in radical left circles in 1960s England. As teenagers, apprentices and undergraduates, these individuals immersed themselves in a New Left landscape that grew up around Britain's anti-Vietnam War movement, the Vietnam Solidarity Campaign (VSC). Initiated in June, 1966 by individuals around the Bertrand Russell Peace Foundation and the International Marxist Group (IMG), from 1967 until 1969 the VSC was the heart of a growing activist scene, fuelled by the student movement and the expanding membership of the two far left groups, the International Socialists (IS) and the IMG. At the height of the anti-war campaign, young activists belonged to a minority network which enabled them to move freely between leftist groupings inside metropolitan and provincial universities and local urban neighbourhoods through to the counter-cultural scene and the old working-class world of labour inside the docks, factories and the tenants' movements. Within this fluid scene, they found possibilities for transcending the boundaries of nationality, class, gender and sexuality that continued to define post-war English life.

Young Lives on the Left is a history of modern radical subjectivities. It explores the English experience of activist life previously neglected in histories of 1968 focused on Western Europe and North America. One might ask what historical value is to be gained from studying a minority of radical young people who in their politics, social attitudes and behaviours stood at odds with the moderate, conservative patterns that commentators noted continuing to define their contemporaries.[1] Social historians emphasise the importance of attending to the everyday experiences and perceptions of 'ordinary' people, whose lives offer the most potential for measuring real change over time. Nowhere is this more the case than with histories of the sixties. The period remains a contested historical landscape, and yet studies of post-1945 society remain in their infancy. In recent years historians have begun to challenge what Frank Mort has termed 'the progressive' reading of the sixties, which sees the uninterrupted transition from fifties conformity and Victorian 'puritanism' to 'permissive' social and sexual attitudes and behaviours that triumphed in the high sixties.[2] Instead they have stressed the existence of continuity alongside change that comes from reframing the post-war period to allow for a longer-term chronology.[3] They have shown the complicated, sometimes contradictory ways in which old and new social patterns co-existed, and the tension and sheer messiness with which individuals sought to negotiate these.[4] As part of this shift in the historiography, memoirs of radical youth by writers and historians seeking to shape the historical script are criticised for contributing to the false progressive picture.[5] Yet the search for more nuanced narratives should not discount the value that dissenting lives offer the post-war historian. *Young Lives on the Left* seeks to offer new understanding about the complex and contested relationship between young post-war subjects and the shifting social and cultural landscape of mid-century England. Over the course of five chapters this account follows the life stories of approximately twenty men and women from childhood to early adulthood, charting the process of activist self-making over time. Attention is given to how life in the far left and non-aligned left milieux intersected with specific experiences of social class, family relations, gender and changing post-war English society. It explores how radical left cultures shaped everyday experiences of university, political activism, work, family life and political and personal, social and sexual relations.

The book takes a biographical approach and aims to make an informative contribution to the unfolding subjective turn in social history. This acknowledges the value of examining individual lives and subjectivities to illuminate some of the complex ways individuals in the past have used available cultural resources to find meaning in their lives and to form a coherent sense of self.[6] The approach reflects a concern to understand individuals as emotional or affective subjects in dialogue with their material and discursive environments. This book does not always support some historians' faith in the human-directed shape of historical change;[7] the narratives informing this account suggest that, on occasions, men and women were, in fact, at pains to override the cultural power of gendered discourses operating in mainstream society and in radical circles.

Young Lives on the Left explores the historical relationship between the young post-war self and the social, the emotional and the political. It makes no attempt to claim that the stories told here represented typical growing-up and early adult experiences for most higher-educated young people. However, it does argue that their experiences merit attention, not least because they provide telling insight into the felt complexities of negotiating shifting cultural norms and expectations. On the cusp of adulthood at a breaking moment of New Left liberation politics, these young men and women were key agents in shaping a new language of gendered subjectivity that would leave a powerful mark, initially on the Left, and later more widely, on the increasingly egalitarian heterosexual relationships prevailing at the century's end. They came to political consciousness in a left world on the point of transition, part of the Western European post-war generation that created a new democratic left project.[8] Yet, as activists they continued to maintain important political and emotional attachments to the old labour Left. Politically, socially and emotionally, then, young activists straddled old and new cultural models. Their contested relations with the post-war landscape offer a unique dissenter's perspective of what it meant to mediate between 'discourses and representations on the one hand' and the social and emotional 'trials' of becoming young adults and political beings on the other.[9]

Young sixties activists were a group of citizens uneasy with their modernity. In the late 1960s their New Left politics railed against the atomising, alienating effects of work, culture and social relations in the post-industrial society. Building on the grass-roots, do-it-yourself campaigns inherited from the Campaign for Nuclear Disarmament (CND), they added their voices to a host of other post-war dissidents challenging the individualising, dehumanising impulses of capitalist consumption in the affluent society. Yet, as social and psychological as well as political subjects, they were inherently modern. Championing the struggle of the subjective, theirs was a politics predicated on an understanding of human selfhood rooted in the project of modernity. From CND at the start of the decade, to the tenants' and race campaigns, and the anti-Vietnam War movement of the late 1960s, through to the new politics of Women's Liberation in the early 1970s, underlying all these struggles was the conviction that the human agent was free, self-made and authentic. This was a politics that called for the realisation not only of the dignity and basic material entitlement of the modern labouring self, but for the post-materialist values of self-expression, self-fulfilment and self-development that emerged as new modes of selfhood from the mid-century onwards. Privileging the lived experience of oppressed people, young activists actively contributed to the expanding range of possibilities for realising this postmodern self. Along with underground community newspapers, do-it-yourself agitprop street politics and radical street-theatre groups, the consciousness-raising practice of the Women's Liberation Movement (WLM) operated on the assumption that, as Carolyn Steedman has argued, 'the subaltern *could* speak, that through articulation in spoken or written words, the dispossessed could come to an understanding of their own story'.[10]

This focus on the subjective needs to be understood in the context of the 'valorisation of the self' that occurred in Britain following the war.[11] The young men and women of this book grew up at a time of increasing possibilities for constructing and experiencing the self. Since the late nineteenth century, meanings of selfhood had been reformulated according to new psychological modes of thinking. Mathew Thomson has highlighted the range of psychological perspectives disseminated via popular culture in the inter-war years.[12] More recently, Matt Houlbrook has shown how self-fashioning in this period became inter-twined with new modes of consumer culture that harnessed the imagination through dreaming and fictionality.[13] Such developments all supported the interior, individual and developing sense of self that had emerged by the Second World War, what Steedman refers to as 'a quite richly detailed sense of self' within.[14] But it was the post-war period when, many scholars argue, the pursuit of modernity created the truly self-reflexive individual. Thomson has shown how the Second World War spread new thinking about the psychology of everyday life amongst wartime citizens. The emotional intensity of the crisis created the cir-cumstances for psychology to gain popular appeal, whether for answers and explanation or merely distraction.[15] The social instability associated with the challenges of reconstruction created favourable conditions for psychological thinking to remain an influential force after 1945. In the late 1940s and 1950s affluence, commercialism, mass popular culture, education and state welfare institutions presented ever more complex social identities for men and women to realise themselves as social, psychological, gendered and embodied subjects. Just as early twentieth-century modernity had provoked anxieties as well as opportunities, the mid-century confronted governments and citizens with a range of new questions and concerns that promoted an intensive mapping of the social and psychological self. The shifting contours of Britain's imperial mission, uncertainty about her role in post-war Europe, the demise of the nation as a world power, the escalating Cold War and the threat of the Bomb, concern about the effects of American culture on social stability, and the social anxieties generated by the affluent society – such fears not only provoked intense questioning, as Chris Waters has argued, about what it meant to be British, but also generated intensive scrutiny about subjectivity in relation to social citizenship.[16]

Scholars like Nikolas Rose and Mike Savage have argued that managing the personal and interior lives of citizens became a specific focus of government planning after 1945. Whereas for Rose the 'psy-sciences' were central to new concepts of the self-governing and self-regulating self, Savage has emphasised the influence of an expanding professional social science apparatus that also became harnessed to projects of governmentality.[17] The voices of both professions could be heard loudly amongst the range of experts claiming a role in Britain's moral and social reconstruction.[18] In the increasingly competitive media environment of the 1950s, journalists too had their own 'ethical mandate' for social renewal. According to Frank Mort, broadsheet editors promoted discourses of scientific objectivity to manage open discussions of controversial social and sexual questions. In contrast, many tabloid editors saw their papers as active moral and social agents with the task to liberalise national values and attitudes.[19] Building on the late nineteenth-century convention of social investigative reporting, in the post-war period the press continued to be an influential body disseminating psychological and social scientific discourses and informing popular modes of thought about social selfhood in relation to contested issues such as homosexuality, race, the family and social and sexual change associated with affluence, class and youth.[20] Privileging the views of psychological experts, the popular press promoted the ideal of the self-reflective and self-developing independent subject. Quizzes and questionnaires that encouraged the practice of self-reflection were designed to enable self-discovery and to aid self-improvement. Chapters 2 and 3 showcase the important role that newspapers and television played in shaping young individuals' sense of self in the world. Reports of foreign conflicts and visual images of faraway, exotic landscapes generated alternative, imaginative spaces for belonging. For working-class individuals rooted in immobile communities, descriptions of unfamiliar areas of Britain had the same effect. From the confines of their localities, as school children, adolescents and young adults, sixties activists projected private feelings of otherness onto social groups engaged in political and social struggles. Stories of oppressed peoples and marginalised cultures provided alternative social identities that suggested new ways of being.

In their search for more expansive geographic horizons and social opportunities, the men and women of this book reflected desires more widely expressed by post-war higher-educated youth. Yet, unlike most of their contemporaries, this radical cohort also expressed unease with the institution of the post-war family and the models of selfhood it offered. Such sentiments reflected the mid-century shift towards an increasingly home-centred, individualised society that created more explicit demarcations between public and private life. The New Left personal politics of the early 1970s emerged out of an intimate national site that had become 'a testing ground' for models of selfhood that 'prioritized self fulfilment' and 'privileged authenticity but struggled to verify it'.[21] Discourses of love, marital roles and social and sexual relations surrounding the family gave young activists a language for conceptualising an authentic, reflexive and autonomous self liberated from the constraints of Victorian social practices, attitudes and values. A central argument of this book is that the creation of New Left spaces represented the quest for a construction of self that could accommodate the range of contradictions concerning class, gender, religion, race and sexuality that young activists experienced growing up. Despite the increasing possibilities for social identity, the inadequacy of the models available to these young people propelled their journeys on the Left. They sought a mode of self-understanding that would enable them to make sense of themselves in relation to the instabilities and shifts occurring across Britain and the wider world.

From the mid- to late 1950s this was a world in the midst of social, cultural and political transformation. The booming western economies facilitated rising material affluence that generated new social freedoms and cultural expressions for youth and supported the postmodern project of the independent, entitled self. In Britain young people's assurance of their right to existence was fed by the material nutrients of welfare-state orange juice and free school milk, and by the educational opportunities made possible by the 1944 Butler Education Act that accorded free secondary education to all. Reflecting on her fifties childhood, Steedman considered: 'I think I would be a very different person now if orange juice and milk and dinners at school hadn't told me, in a covert way, that I had a right to exist, was worth something.'[22] Sixties youth was not only encouraged to pursue self-fulfilment as a mode of being, but given the time and material conditions in which to realise this goal. The majority of this radical cohort was amongst the growing, though still small, proportion of mainly middle-class young men and women attending university in the 1960s. The experience provided many with a series of life-defining moments in their journeys towards radical selfhood. Although frustrated by outmoded, authoritarian teaching regimes and *in loco parentis* rules, in the late 1960s universities became hubs for the protest network growing round the VSC. Against the international context of 1968, student life represented a time when many young activists began seriously to experiment with alternative social identities. Many subsequently took advantage of postgraduate funding opportunities and early 1970s social security to extend the time available for pursuing self-actualisation.

Expanding possibilities for social selfhood occurred in a world that was also visibly expanding. Rapid advances in communication and media technology brought sites of foreign cultures, races, religions, as well as international conflicts, closer to home via radio and television sets in the living rooms and common rooms of young people. Young activists also saw sites of social and cultural difference at first hand through travel to Europe, North America and the newly independent colonial countries. For many of this book's interviewees, early experiences of overseas travel occurred in the context of fathers serving in the armed services or as civil servants in far-flung quarters of the decolonising Empire. Many later travelled as teenagers and students, for leisure, through Voluntary Service Overseas (VSO) or via the international protest networks that developed amongst young activists in the late 1960s. Individuals often remembered such experiences as processes of mapping themselves in relation to this wider social, cultural and political landscape. The post-colonial setting provided an important context for conceiving self-autonomy. New concepts of universal human rights, enshrined in the charter and resolutions of the United Nations, were taken up by Afro-Asian nationalist movements, and, by the 1960s, the western world had seen a decisive shift in public opinion and state policies that made it difficult for nations to defend policies that openly endorsed colonial subjugation and racial inequality.[23] Yet, at odds with this discursive climate of equal human rights, images of white violence against civil rights campaigners in the United States and South Africa provided disturbing evidence that attitudes of racial superiority continued to prevail. In Britain too, government policies, everyday instances of discrimination and discourses of race and immigration pointed to the survival of colonial mentalities at a time when black and Asian migrants were framed as racial others outside a socially cohesive nation.[24]

Young sixties activists shaped understandings of self in a nation that was also inherently unsure about its relationship to modernity. Scholars repeatedly highlight the conflicting social dynamics of permissiveness, progressivism and Victorian conservatism that characterised post-war institutions and cultural practices. Running through social and cultural practices, discourses of gender were also in flux. Feminist scholars have shown how conflict between new social and educational opportunities for young sixties women and traditional representations of femininity created internal tension for a cohort of university-educated young wives and mothers that would find expression in the WLM at the end of the decade.[25] More recently, historians have noted the conflict between the identity of the home-centred family man and the imaginative 'flight from domesticity' discernible in social and cultural images. However, with the exception of feminist histories, few have considered individual responses to changing socio-economic, cultural and political patterns and post-war discourses at the level of the interiority of selfhood. Through careful attention to spoken and visual memories, this book focuses attention on some of the complex ways in which young individuals engaged with the contradictions they confronted while growing up in post-war Britain. It offers suggestions about the role that childhood and early adult feeling, fantasy and thought played in shaping subjectivities. An important theme of the book is the psychic conflict young activists faced in their efforts to negotiate new and existing models of social, political and gendered selfhood. As they struggled to recreate themselves as autonomous, far-left, New Left, feminist and pro-feminist selves, many individuals found it hard to relinquish older ways of being as men, women, parents and social and sexual subjects. This book tells the story of what it meant for a young sixties cohort to create new political cultures and to pursue visions of liberated modes of life and subjectivity.

1968

Young Lives on the Left lies at the intersection of several bodies of post-war historiography. The stories told here belong to the collection of radical voices of 1968 activists – that global generation of young political actors who tell recognisable yet individual stories of journeys to change the world. Theirs are all stories of self-transformation amidst political struggle. Scholarship on 1968 comprises an ever-expanding, now global field. Yet English voices occupy an ambiguous and marginal place within this global collection of life histories. The recent study of *Europe's 1968* is one of the few collections to include stories of English activists since Ronald Fraser's 1988 collaborative oral history study.[26] In her assessment of British student protest during the Vietnam War, Sylvia Ellis offers a possible explanation for the dearth of studies on the British experience of 1968: 'The British student movement during the 1960s was undoubtedly less violent, less radical and more easily controlled than those in continental Europe and the United States of America. There were no barricades, no petrol bombs, no fire hoses, no tear gas, no heavy rioting, no national university strikes or general strikes, no mass destruction of property and no shootings.'[27] When they are understood in these terms, it is all too tempting for internationally framed studies to disparage the actions and rhetoric of British activists as insignificant in comparison to the national power struggles played out elsewhere across the globe.[28] However, assessing protest movements merely in terms of their impact made upon the national body politic and society overlooks the more subtle questions transnational scholars are increasingly asking about the dynamics at work within the international activist networks.[29] Any attempt to understand the social and technological modes of political and cultural transfer operating across porous national boundaries calls for attention to the individuals who were both recipients and transmitters[30] – to reposition the voices behind the movements and to acknowledge the legitimacy of their experiences.

England stands apart from Europe and North America, where scholars have applied an ever innovative range of historical methods and approaches to understand how cultures of grass-roots activism took shape in individual countries.[31] These scholars have also traced the imprint that memories of activism continue to make on those contemporary societies.[32] The few studies of political and social protest in sixties Britain have shown little attention to the nuanced relationship between political culture and subjectivity. Accounts of England's extra-parliamentary Left have focused almost exclusively on the political narratives at the expense of the social, cultural and emotional.[33] Others have considered the student protest, overlooking the larger, more socially nuanced left network that emerged around the VSC, with its interpersonal connections to the labour movement, Communist Party intellectuals, the first New Left and the counter-culture.[34] Only recently have revisionist histories of post-1945 Britain begun to acknowledge the significance of protest movements, grass-roots civil activism and voices of dissent as sites for scrutinising and challenging the 'consensus' picture that historians inherited from contemporaries, and which for many years dominated post-war histories.[35] Influenced by the cultural and affective turns, studies of post-war political culture have also cast new perspectives on the social, emotional and gender codes and attitudes prevailing in these years.[36] Together with recent social histories of the post-Second World War period, they complicate the 'progressive' narrative that saw the war as a significant watershed in social and cultural life.[37] *Young Lives on the Left* offers to further refine the more nuanced picture that is emerging of British society after 1945. The stories presented here show a complex, multi-layered landscape where old and new social identities of class, gender, sexuality, ethnicity and nationality co-existed and sometimes competed.

Sources

The book is based on oral history interviews with fifty men and women, conducted at intervals between 2009 and 2012. However, it focuses in depth on approximately twenty individual stories. Such a small number could never claim to speak for the lives of all young sixties activists. In any case it is perhaps a misnomer to use the word 'typical' in this context. As Rebecca Clifford, Robert Gildea and James Mark have noted, 'there are as many stories of journeys into activism as there are activists themselves'.[38] The book is concerned with exploring the rich individual subjectivities that only a small range of stories make possible. However, as previously explained, it also draws attention to selected cultural patterns and themes which offer new perspectives on the social landscape in which these young radicals came of age. The small selection of interviewees allows for a more in-depth exploration of the complex relationship between cultural patterns, discourses and experience. The life stories were selected not for their representativeness but because the individuals had strong connecting currents to each other; all were closely interwoven with the radical network that grew up around and out of the metropolitan-based VSC. After 1969 they went on to be heavily involved in either of the two main far-left organisations, or in the non-aligned circles that emerged out of this network. As a result, the book has a strong metropolitan bias. However, it does include stories of provincial activity that span the early and later parts of the decade. The reference to northern regions such as Newcastle-on-Tyne, Middlesbrough and Leeds to some extent reflects individuals' movement to these places following the fragmentation of the VSC after 1969; some settled in these areas following their departure from northern universities, while a few grew up and remained active nearby. Stories of provincial activism reflect a regional hinterland of radical protest cultures and left networks that existed in cities and towns across the country in the 1950s, and which expanded in the late sixties with the new liberation movements and the expansion of far-left organisations.[39]

The close interpersonal network at the heart of the VSC influenced how interviewees were selected. The historian and socialist-feminist Sheila Rowbotham provided the initial starting point by suggesting possible interviewees; notwithstanding her prominence in the WLM, her heavy involvement in a range of left projects, campaigns and groups concentrated in the capital throughout the sixties and seventies made her well placed to guide initial contacts. From Sheila's address book the 'snowball' effect took place, leading to other interviewees, who provided further contacts.[40] Interviewees encompassed men and women who, during the late 1960s and 1970s, had either been active members of IS and IMG or been involved in 'non-aligned' libertarian milieux that grew out of the VSC and the early north London Women's Liberation groups. The latter included artistic and theatrical groups,

Agitprop, the Cartoon Archetypal Slogan Theatre (CAST), Red Ladder and grass-roots community groups, including the Camden Movement for People's Power (CMPP), which held close connections with the Tufnell Park Women's Liberation group.

In selecting interviewees, I was mindful of the dangers already apparent in previous studies of 1968; of historians returning repeatedly to narratives of individuals who at the time and since have become publicly associated with movements and campaigns. In the case of Britain, Fraser's 1988 study has, to date, remained the authoritative account upon which historians have drawn upon for first-hand testimonies. However, when placed alongside the few memoirs written by individuals who were publicly at the forefront of campaigns, the result has been to shape a dominant narrative of Britain's '68 activism as an entirely student affair.[41] The sensitivity surrounding historical representation and typicality is a concern not only of historians, but also of former movement participants themselves.[42] The powerful emotional investment that young radicals made in groups, organisations and campaigns left a lasting imprint on their sense of self in the world. Unsurprisingly, many continue to express claims and desires over the official histories. Nowhere has this perhaps been more evident than with the case of the WLM, as witnessed at the fortieth-anniversary conference at Oxford's Ruskin College, held in March 2010, when tension emerged between movement historians and women who feel that their local and regional activities continue to be overlooked.[43]

This book aims to tell less-familiar stories of young radical life that go beyond experiences of student activism alone. It is structured across the life-cycle, from childhood to young adulthood, up to the mid-1970s. Considering the private as well as the public lives of young activists, it shows how the mundanity and everydayness of young adult life cut across the thrills of demonstrating and organising. Attention is given to the cultural texture of activists' homes, to front-room meetings and to paper sales in working-men's clubs and public houses. It is how young individuals mediated themselves through these cultures as political, emotional and gendered beings with which this book is primarily concerned. It considers the psychological spaces that radical cultures provided for young sixties men and women.

Young Lives on the Left includes the voices of men and women who, in contrast to more prominent members of organisations and campaigns, remained active at the grass roots in local and regional far-left branches or 'non-aligned' radical community projects. Although most interviewees did participate in university protests and VSC demonstrations as students in the mid- to late 1960s, a smaller number had been recruited into far-left organisations earlier in the decade. Their experiences have received little historical attention. These members came mainly from working-class – manual, though occasionally white-collar – homes and, through activity often firstly in CND, followed a political pathway through the Young Socialists (YS) into the IS and IMG. The book includes the stories of five men and one woman who followed parental employment patterns into non-skilled or semi-skilled manual labouring jobs and whose entry into the extra-parliamentary left continued older histories of Communist Party and labour movement activism.

Following pioneers Alessandro Portelli and Luisa Passerini, oral historians have shown the rich 'horizon of possibilities' this distinctive practice allows for privileging and interrogating subjectivities.[44] Yet, as sources for selfhood, oral narratives retain their sceptics. In 1996 James Hinton reiterated the problematic nature of oral history as a source for the construction of identity, precisely because the process of '"remembering" how we became who we are now' involves a narrative construction in which what might at the time have been significant experiences are forgotten or reinterpreted in the light of more recent ones.[45] Mark Freeman has described the 'process of self-understanding that involves gathering together the various dimensions of selfhood that have heretofore gone unarticulated, or been scattered, dispersed or lost'.[46] All forms of memory, even apparently spontaneous, everyday spoken or unspoken memories, are constructions, mediated 'by complex psychical and mental processes'.[47] Yet, as sources of intimate lives, oral history narratives are ultimately no more problematic than any others. In many respects the life-history approach of oral history interviewing particularly lends itself to the study of activist subjectivities because it allows the historian to understand something of the political and emotional imprint that years of intensive activity left on individuals. Interviewees elicited strong signals of past subjectivities through the past and present selves they composed. The book discusses individuals' stories by focusing close attention on how and why interviewees told and selected particular memories of activist life; careful consideration is given to the specific temporal, spatial and social, political and cultural contexts in which interviewees articulated their memories, and to the significance of recurring tropes and emotional registers. Bill Schwarz reminds us that historians 'needn't be frightened of phantoms', of understanding the 'symbolic, psychic means by which the past is *represented* in the present'.[48] The book illustrates the complex place of the past and present that was involved in the composition of the activist self.

Alongside the interviews the book draws upon a range of printed primary material: internal bulletins, leaflets, campaign pamphlets, posters and ephemera as well as newspapers and monthly newssheets. A considerable body of literature derives from personal archives belonging to interviewees, which in a few rare cases included personal diaries and correspondence.

Young Lives on the Left

Young Lives on the Left tells the story of activist self-making over the long 1960s. It is also a history of young post-war subjects growing up and seeking to find new ways of being. It considers what it meant to try to shape a liberated self on the extra-parliamentary left in the late sixties and early seventies. It does not pretend to deliver a comprehensive *political* narrative of the major left campaigns of these years. Instead, it concentrates on the individual lives as they were felt and experienced, illuminating the joys as well as the tensions that came from negotiating post-war society and new-left cultural spaces. The idea of these cultures as liberating spaces became challenged with the arrival of adulthood. In the first half of the 1970s the arrival of Women's Liberation and the shifting political shape of the activist network coincided with new social experiences, of parenthood, work, full-time activism and life on the dole. As such, chapters 4, 5 and 6 focus on the complex ways in which far and 'non-aligned' left activists attempted to incorporate these changes into their everyday lives and to negotiate the multiple, sometimes fractured identities that the new political and personal worlds created. Throughout this book the term 'New Left' will be used to refer to the left cultures that up to 1969 cohered in a fluid interpersonal network around the VSC. Chapter 3 will illustrate how this sinuous landscape coincided with a developmental moment in adult life when men and women's openness to new ideas encouraged freedom of movement across the multiplicity of far and new-left groups. After the VSC's demise the term 'New Left' acquired an altered meaning, as 'non-aligned' left activists embraced a new pre-figurative politics that imposed a cultural gulf between them and the industrial labour focus of far-left organisations, the IS and IMG. The result of this political and cultural shift was to solidify the boundaries between the Trotskyist and 'non-aligned' milieux as part of a transition that saw the network taking on an increasingly demarcated shape. Between 1969 and 1971 this process of political realignment was given added impetus by the emergence of the new politics of Women's Liberation, which, in politics and personnel, shared many connections with the 'non-aligned' left. Chapters 4 and 5 will examine the political, cultural and social points of continuity and departure between the post-VSC pre-figurative politics and Women's Liberation that contributed to a new libertarian, socialist feminist left.

The book is structured into six chapters which explore individuals' involvement with the English new-left network over the course of the life journey. Chapter 1 starts by introducing the key protagonists. It addresses their stories of childhood and early adolescence, situating them against existing studies of post-war family life in order to show how they fit into prevalent patterns of social continuity and change, and to emphasise their role as agents challenging the post-war social and domestic consensus. It considers how their experiences distinguished them from familiar narratives of post-war childhood and adolescence. Through attention to early structures of feeling or underlying feeling, it shows how encounters and experiences in the family home, school and local community intersected with the wider national and international world, to forge often uneasy and disputatious relationships with the landscape.

Post-war culture performed an important role for young individuals starting to critically question the prevailing consensus by mediating relationships between selfhood and society. Chapter 2 explores the political, social and gendered dynamics of the activist left cultures that preceded the extra-parliamentary scene surrounding the VSC. It shows how young activists' initial steps into these cultures invariably began with encounters with late-fifties and early-sixties subcultures, including 'Angry Young Men' and French existential movements, and CND. The chapter encompasses individuals' radical reading, dramatic, musical and other cultural and political experiences, to consider the meaning these held for youngsters in the context of their childhood histories. The gendered dimension of activist selfhood is an important theme running through this book. This found political expression from 1968, when Women's Liberation threatened to disrupt the prevailing culture and subjectivities for men and women. This chapter addresses the gendered dimension of radical subcultural experiences in the early to mid-1960s, including young women and men's experiences inside the YS and the Trotskyist groups, the IS and the International group (later known as the IMG). It shows the complex ways in which masculine radical cultures added to the contradictory discourses constituting 'woman' and 'man' that visibly prevailed throughout the post-war society in which interviewees were shaping identities.

Interviewees' attendance at university coincided with the tumultuous global events surrounding 1968. Chapter 3 examines the political, cultural and socio-psychological experiences students underwent within the fluid left milieux (encompassing Labour clubs, socialist societies, Marxist societies and Trotskyist groups) at metropolitan and provincial universities across England in the mid- to late 1960s. Attention is given to the common cultural patterns running across interviewees' memories of student activism, which denote the enduring psychic power of the liberated self they forged during these years. Interrogating the relationship between memory, identity and cultural representations of 1968, this chapter discusses how and why individuals constructed their stories within particular frameworks of time and space. It assesses what the composition of remembered narratives reveals about the key factors shaping activism as a liberating subjective condition. Discussion includes students' interactions with left groups on university campuses, radical reading experiences and activism in docks, strikes and student protests, which opened up new possibilities of being. The radical open spaces often served as sites in which young activists began to work out a sense of self in relation to everyday patterns of home and university as well as radical politics and international liberation struggles. The chapter explores the growth of the VSC and its place at the heart of a bourgeoning activist scene. From the mid- to late 1960s the libertarian cultures of the network permitted young men, and notably young women too, to push further against the social boundaries governing their freedom. Yet this was an ambiguous gendered landscape, and alongside new opportunities for social and sexual agency female students sometimes also experienced emotional tensions, as perceptions of gendered social difference lay hidden beneath other, more prominent registers of selfhood that prevailed during these years – class, intellectual identity and international solidarity.

The period 1969–71 heralded a political transition on the Left following the disintegration of the VSC. The first reference to the 'new politics' came from activist and feminist Sheila Rowbotham, to distinguish the politics of Women's Liberation from the alienating revolutionary culture she and other women had encountered around the Trotskyist groups in the VSC. But in 1968 the emotive tenets and psychological hallmarks of Rowbotham's new-left politics echoed elsewhere around the VSC. Chapter 4 focuses on a north London VSC branch, based in Camden Town, which in 1969 reformed away from the VSC to become a new-left collective, the CMPP. The middle-class membership included a contingent of American scientists and scholars who had been active in American New Left student politics and who helped to shape the group's new-left political culture, which placed emphasis on subjective experience, equal participation and community engagement. At the end of 1968 American female members took CMPP's discourse of personal politics into the Tufnell Park Women's Liberation group, one of the first four groups composing the London Women's Liberation Workshop (LWLW), when it began in mid-1969. The story of CMPP and the

Tufnell Park Women's Liberation group presents a new perspective of English activist life at a breaking political moment. This is a rarely told account of women and men's political and personal experiences of the 'New Left' women's politics in its very early days.

Chapters 5 and 6 address adulthood in the activist milieux in the first half of the 1970s. During this decade members with the organisations IS and the IMG and the loose collectives of the 'non-aligned' Left committed themselves to realising different visions for grass-roots socialist agitation. Trotskyists devoted themselves to building revolutionary parties oriented to industrial working-class struggle, whilst the 'non-aligned' Left embraced the personal politics of Women's Liberation, endeavouring to live their politics through collective living, childcare, activism in their local communities and experiments with more open and honest social and sexual relations between men and women. Chapter 5 considers the subjective experience of the new liberation politics in the north London 'non-aligned' Left. It explores the complex social and emotional impact on individual activists and their sense of self as activists, mothers, fathers, friends, husbands and wives and lovers. Chapter 6 mirrors the themes of the previous chapter by exploring the specific social and psychological demands young Trotskyists faced in adapting their political language and social behaviour to the landscape of militant labour politics at a high point of trade union struggles. Discussing the gendered dimension of revolutionary identity, it shows the challenges and contradictions of trying to reconcile everyday social and emotional life to a fraternal political culture that denied space for the personal. As men and women who were not directly committed to the sexual politics of the 'non-aligned' Left, but who were close enough to the movement to be aware of its politics, the stories of this far-left cohort provide insight into the impact of Women's Liberation on the everyday private life and subjectivity of individuals beyond the immediate vicinity of socialist feminist circles.

Notes

1 P. Abrams and A. Little, 'The Young Voter in British Politics', *British Journal of Sociology*, 16:2, June (1965), pp. 95–110; F. Musgrove, *Youth and the Social Order* (London: Routledge, 1968); M. Schofield, *The Sexual Behaviour of Young People* (Harmondsworth: Penguin, 1965); F. Zweig, *The Student in the Age of Anxiety: A Survey of Oxford and Manchester Students* (London: Heinemann, 1963), pp. 42–5.

2 F. Mort, *Capital Affairs: London and the Making of the Permissive Society* (London: Yale University Press, 2010), p. 3.

3 N. Thomas, 'Will the Real 1950s Please Stand Up: Views of a Contradictory Decade', *Cultural and Social History*, 2, June (2008), pp. 227–36. See also D. Sandbrook, *Never Had It So Good: A History of Britain from Suez to the Beatles* (London: Abacus, 2005), pp. xx–xxv.

4 C. Langhamer, *The English in Love: The Intimate Story of An Emotional Revolution* (Oxford: Oxford University Press, 2013); C. Langhamer, 'Love, Selfhood and Authenticity in Post-War Britain', *Cultural and Social History*, 9:2 (2012), pp. 277–97; C. Langhamer, 'Adultery in Post-War England', *History Workshop Journal*, 62:1 (2006), pp. 86–115.

5 M. Donnelly, *Sixties Britain: Culture, Society and Politics* (Harlow: Pearson, 2005), pp. 12–13; Sandbrook, *Never Had It So Good*, p. xxiii.

6 J. Hinton, *Nine Wartime Lives. Mass-Observation and the Making of a Modern Self* (Oxford: Oxford University press, 2010), p. 18; C. Feely, 'From Dialectics to Dancing: Reading, Writing and the Experience of Everyday Life in the Diaries of Frank P. Forster', *History Workshop Journal*, 69, Spring (2010), pp. 90–110.

7 Hinton, *Nine Wartime Lives*, p. 18.

8 G. Eley, *Forging Democracy: The History of the Left in Europe, 1850–2000* (Oxford: Oxford University Press, 2002), p. 328.

9 M. Tebbutt, *Being Boys: Youth, Leisure and Identity in the Inter-War Years* (Manchester: Manchester University Press, 2013), p. 1.

10 C. Steedman, 'The Peculiarities of English Autobiography: An Autobiographical Education, 1945–1975', in *Plurality and Individuality. Autobiographical Cultures in Europe* (ed. Christa Hammerle), IFK Internationales Forschungzentrum, Kulturwissenschaften, Vienna, 1995, p. 90.

11 C. Waters, 'Disorders of the Mind, Disorders of the Body Social: Peter Wildeblood and the Making of the Modern Homosexual', in B. Conekin, F. Mort and C. Waters (eds), *Moments of Modernity: Reconstructing Britain 1945–1964* (London: Rivers Oram Press, 1999), p. 150.

12 M. Thomson, *Psychological Subjects: Identity, Culture and Health in Twentieth Century Britain* (Oxford: Oxford University Press, 2006), pp. 27–40.

13 M. Houlbrook, '"A Pin to See the Peepshow": Culture, Fiction and Selfhood in Edith Thompson's Letters, 1921–1922', *Past and Present*, 207 (2010), pp. 223–4.

14 C. Steedman, *Strange Dislocations: Childhood and the Idea of Human Interiority 1780–1930* (London: Virago, 1995), p. 4.

15 Thomson, *Psychological Subjects*, pp. 209–11.

16 C. Waters, '"Dark Strangers in Our Midst": Discourses of Race and Nation in Britain, 1947–1963', *Journal of British Studies*, 36:2 (1997), pp. 207–8.

17 N. Rose, 'Assembling the Modern Self', in R. Porter (ed.), *Rewriting the Self: Histories from the Renaissance to the Present* (London: Routledge, 1997), pp. 224–49. N. Rose, *Governing the Soul: The Shaping of the Private Self* (London: Routledge, 1989); M. Savage, *Identities and Social*

Change in Britain Since 1940 (Oxford: Oxford University Press, 2010); M. Savage, 'Affluence and Social Change in the Making of Technocratic Middle-Class Identities: Britain, 1939–55', *Contemporary British History*, 22:4 (2008), pp. 457–76.

18 Waters, 'Disorders of the Mind', p. 141.

19 F. Mort, 'The Ben Pimlott Memorial Lecture 2010: The Permissive Society Revisited', *Twentieth Century British History*, 22:2 (2011), p. 278.

20 See also A. Bingham, *Family Newspapers? Sex, Private Life, and the British Popular Press 1918–1978* (Oxford, 2009) and L. King, 'Hidden Fathers? The Significance of Fatherhood in Mid-Twentieth-Century Britain', *Contemporary British History*, 26:1 (2012), p. 29.

21 Langhamer, 'Love, Selfhood and Authenticity', p. 278.

22 C. Steedman, *Landscape for a Good Woman: A Story of Two Lives* (London: Virago, 1986), p. 122.

23 A. G. Hopkins, 'Rethinking Decolonisation', *Past and Present*, 200 (2008), pp. 233–4.

24 Waters, '"Dark Strangers in our Midst"'; W. Webster, *Englishness and Empire, 1939–1965* (Oxford: Oxford University Press, 2007), chapter 6.

25 A. Coote and B. Campbell, *Sweet Freedom* (Oxford: Blackwell, 1982); S. Rowbotham, *Promise of a Dream: Remembering the Sixties* (London: Verso, 2000); L. Segal, *Making Trouble: Life and Politics* (London: Serpent's Tail, 2007); Birmingham Feminist History Group, 'Feminism as Femininity in the Nineteen Fifties', *Feminist Review* 3 (1979), pp. 48–65; M. Wandor, *Once a Feminist: Stories of a Generation* (London: Virago, 1990).

26 R. Gildea, J. Mark and A. Warring (eds), *Europe's 1968: Voices of Revolt* (Oxford: Oxford University Press, 2013); R. Fraser (ed.), *1968: A Student Generation in Revolt* (New York: Random House, 1988).

27 S. Ellis, '"A Demonstration of British Good Sense?" British Student Protest during the Vietnam War', in G. J. DeGroot (ed.), *Student Protest: The Sixties and After* (Essex: Longman, 1998), p. 54.

28 G. DeGroot, *The 60s Unplugged: A Kaleidoscopic History of a Disorderly Decade* (London, 2008), pp. 356–63, and Marwick, *The Sixties*, p. 634.

29 B. Davis, W. Mausbach, M. Klimke, and C. MacDougall (eds), *Changing the World, Changing Oneself: Political Protest and Collective Identities in West Germany and the U.S. in the 1960s and 1970s* (Oxford: Berghahn Books, 2010); C. Fink, P. Gassert, and D. Junker (eds), *1968. The World Transformed* (Cambridge: Cambridge University Press, 1998); G-R. Horn, *The Spirit of '68 Rebellion in Western Europe and North America, 1956–76* (Oxford: Oxford University Press, 2007); R. I. Jobs, 'Youth Movements: Travel, Protest and Europe in 1968', *American Historical Review*, 114:2 (2009), pp. 376–404.

30 Davis, Mausbach, Klimke, 'Introduction', p. xi.

31 For recent examples, see Bhambra and Demir (eds), *1968 in Retrospect*; I. Cornils and S. Waters (eds), *Memories of 1968*; L. J. Frazier and D. Cohen (eds), *Gender and Sexuality in 1968: Transformative Politics in the Cultural*

Imagination (New York, 2009); Davis, Mausbach, Klimke, and MacDougall, 'Introduction', in (eds), *Changing the World, Changing Oneself*.

32 K. Ross, *May '68 and its Afterlives* (Chicago: University of Chicago, 2002).

33 J. Callaghan, *British Trotskyism: Theory and Practice* (Oxford: Basil Blackwell, 1984), and P. Shipley, *Revolutionaries in Modern Britain* (London: Bodley Head, 1976).

34 Fraser (ed.), *1968*; N. Thomas, 'Challenging Myths of the 1960s: The Case of Student Protest in Britain', *Twentieth Century British History*, 13:3 (2002), pp. 277–97.

35 A. Beckett, *When the Lights Went Out: What Really Happened to Britain in the Seventies* (London: Faber, 2009); S. F. Browne, 'A Veritable Hotbed of Feminism'? Women's Liberation in St Andrews, Fife, c. 1968–c. 1979', *Twentieth Century British History* 23:1 (2012), pp. 100–23; Donnelly, *Sixties Britain*; E. Setch, 'The Face of Metropolitan Feminism: The London Women's Liberation Workshop, 1969–79' *Twentieth Century British History* 13:2 (2002), pp. 171–90; J. Rees, 'Are you a Lesbian?': Challenges in Recording and Analysing the Women's Liberation Movement in England', *History Workshop Journal*, 69, Spring (2010), pp. 177–87; J. Rees, 'A Look Back at Anger: the Women's Liberation Movement in 1978', *Women's History Review*, 19:3 (2010), pp. 337–56; L. Robinson, *Gay Men and the Left in Post-War Britain: How the Personal Got Political* (Manchester: Manchester University Press, 2011).

36 L. Black, *Redefining British Politics: Culture, Consumerism and Participation 1954–70* (London: Palgrave Macmillan, 2010); M. Francis, 'Tears, Tantrums and Bared Teeth: The Emotional Economy of Three Conservative Prime Ministers, 1951–1963', *Journal of British Studies* 41:3 (2002), pp. 354–87; K. Gildart, 'From Dead-End Streets to "Shangri Las": Negotiating Social Class and Post-War Politics with Ray Davies and the Kinks', *Contemporary British History*, 26:3 (2012), pp. 273–98.

37 P. Thane, 'Introduction: Exploring Post-War Britain', Cultural and Social History, 9:2 (2012), p. 271.

38 R. Clifford, R. Gildea and J. Mark, 'Awakenings', in Gildea, Mark and Warring (eds), *Europe's 1968*, p. 21.

39 For accounts of regional activism and left culture, see, for example, D. J. Douglass, *Geordies – Wa Mental* (Hastings: Read 'n' Noir, 2002); D. J. Douglass, *The Wheel's Still in Spin: A Coal miner's Mahabharata* (Hastings: Read 'n' Noir 2009); J. Charlton, *Don't You Hear the H-Bomb's Thunder? Youth and Politics on Tyneside in the Late 'Fifties and Early 'Sixties* (Pontypool: Merlin, 2010).

40 Rees, '"Are You a Lesbian?"', p. 183.

41 See, for example, T. Ali, *Street Fighting Years: An Autobiography of the Sixties* (2nd edn., London, 2005); S. Rowbotham, *Promise of a Dream*.

42 I. Birchall, 'Working-Class Power: What is really worth remembering about May '68 – a talk by Ian Birchall', '1968 and All That conference', Conway Hall, London, 10 May, 2008.

43 D. Philips, 'The Women's Liberation Movement at Forty (review)', *History Workshop Journal*, 70, Autumn (2010), pp. 293–7. See also B. Caine, 'Feminist Biography and Feminist History', *Women's History Review*, 3:2 (1994), p. 258.

44 A. Portelli, *The Battle of Valle Giulia: Oral History and the Art of Dialogue* (Madison: University of Wisconsin, 1997), p. 276, cited in A. Thomson, *Moving Stories: An Intimate History of Four Women Across Two Continents* (Manchester, 2011), p. 183.

45 J. Hinton, 'Middle-Class Socialism: Selfhood, Democracy and Distinction in Wartime County Durham', *History Workshop Journal*, 62, Autumn (2006), p. 116.

46 M. Freeman, *Rewriting the Self: History, Memory, Narrative* (London: Routledge, 1993), p. 29.

47 S. Radstone, 'Reconceiving Binaries: the Limits of Memory', *History Workshop Journal*, 59, Spring (2005), p. 135.

48 B. Schwarz, 'Not Even Past Yet', *History Workshop Journal*, 57, Spring (2004), p. 103.

1

Post-war childhood and adolescence

Young sixties activists grew up in a historically distinct landscape. Allowing for the social and psychological dislocations of war, post-war Britain remained a stable and conservative place to be. Simon J. Charlesworth explained the importance of understanding place as a 'natural starting point for understanding being'.[1] Autobiographies of fifties middle- and working-class childhood have commonly identified the psychological security deriving from the stable social and economic conditions of the post-war boom.[2] These are the retrospective narratives of British 'baby-boomers', the generational cohort who escaped the privations of inter-war depression, the disruptions of war, and who were still infants during the austerity years. This experiential and psychic gulf between post-war parent and child formed a key component of the generation gap that social commentators began to pay attention to following the student protests of the late 1960s.[3]

Self-belief for fifties and early-sixties youngsters was intertwined with the fabric of the landscape. It came packaged in the bottles of free school milk and the grammar school education that instilled expectations of academic achievement and hopes of social advancement. This post-war subjectivity may be seen as an outcome of the social citizenship rights that 1940s welfare and educational policies conferred upon children. Shaped by authorities concerned about the child's subjective development and the universal human rights enshrined in the charter and resolutions of the United Nations, state services had extended to the child what Cambridge sociologist Thomas Marshall called 'a kind of basic human equality associated with the concept of full membership of a community'.[4] These policies were part of the material building blocks for the modern, entitled self.

As children, young sixties activists exhibited belief in their material and emotional entitlement. Yet from within their homes and communities they saw the actions of a benevolent state cut through with inequalities that told some citizens they were worth more than others.

Early memories railing against the unfairness of material and emotional distribution provide insight into the psychic structures moulded by post-war welfare and education. Childhood outrage at human inequality was the subjective response of the young citizen speaking as a member of an equally entitled community. From an early age the men and women of this book exercised claims, as 'citizens *in potentia*', to improve everyday social and emotional life for themselves and others.[5]

The relationship between place and selfhood is an important component of this study and a useful starting point for thinking about how young sixties activists began to live out a sense of who and what they were. This chapter considers how interviewees started out on their journeys towards life on the Left. It addresses the role of childhood and adolescent experience in shaping radical subjectivity. Through attention to childhood memory, it seeks to understand the structures of feeling underlying youngsters' encounters within particular social, cultural and political sites. The chapter argues that, as agents challenging the social and domestic consensus, young activists' desire for new ways of seeing and being on the Left can be found rooted in their experiences in the family, school and local community. It situates their stories against existing studies of post-war family life in order to show how they fit into prevalent patterns of social continuity and change. The chapter shows how sensitivity to class dynamics, social injustice, racism and emotional and intellectual affinity for the Left developed, and how and when the local, national and international world began to collide. It argues that close attention to the 'shifting reciprocal relationship' between 'psychic life' and individual histories provides the key to understanding why young men and women became drawn towards particular left spaces and why they began to carve out new cultural channels within them.[6]

The post-war family

Stories of sixties activism began in the family. Sally Alexander has shown how 'iconic moments in spoken and written [London] childhood memories reveal the (remembered) child's self-awareness in relation to the outside world and to the child's own place within it'.[7] These moments of self-awareness often arose through the child's feelings as they observed and communicated with family members. Childhood memories, mediated through the trope of the mother and father, illuminate the emotional signals and unfulfilled, even unconscious dreams children picked up from parents and relatives, all of which helped to foster an early relationship to the wider world. Paul Thompson has shown how the family transmits 'social values and aspirations, fears, world views, domestic skills, and taken-for-granted ways of behaving'.[8] Fragments of childhood memory redolent with 'primitive' and 'visceral feeling' suggest possibilities for understanding the relationship between the childhood landscape and subjectivity.[9] Thinking about how children come to form relationships with the world around them is fundamental to thinking about how structures of feeling or 'underlying feeling' came to be shaped into critical and even political thought. Raymond Williams and Carolyn Steedman offer insight into childhood cognition and its connection to the social world. Williams wrote of the 'real . . . physical and material relational processes' which occur as an 'activation of specific relations' when poems are read, stories told, plays enacted and watched.[10] Although he was discussing a specific interaction with culture, his reflections might be extended to children's interactions with parents' social and political behaviour and emotional signals. These were individual and collective 'means of cognition, ways of thought' which then moved into social worlds.[11]

Young activists grew up in a home-centred society in which the family was widely understood to be at the heart of national life. Following on from wartime, the family was the subject of unprecedented psychological and social scientific investigation, and a contemporary preoccupation. It was the place where individually and as a collective body the nation invested its hopes, desires and fears. The view that a happy home and family life were the secrets to national stability and wellbeing informed the post-war reconstruction project. In dialogue with social and cultural discourses, men and women looked to the home and family as the centre of their lives; their roles as husbands, wives, fathers and mothers became highly important in shaping their sense of self. Whilst Claire Langhamer has acknowledged that the aspiration and reality of the private home was 'never a uniform experience',[12] Laura King has suggested that, overall, increasing material and emotional investment in the family home made it for many 'a pleasant place to spend one's time'.[13] However, the narratives of the individuals in this book show that for a minority of children the family home was far from a self-contained private site and not always conducive to a secure identity. It frequently provided connections to wider political and social communities where parents and relatives provided models of engaged and dissident citizenship. The home was often the starting point for children thinking about themselves in relation to a wider social and gendered body: a problematic experience for some that led to journeys outside it for explanations and alternative sites for belonging. Social and emotional dislocations inside the home raised complex questions about social norms, justice, democracy and identity.

The narratives of young sixties activists show that material circumstances of family life continued to shape uneasy relationships with the social landscape. Their experiences contested descriptions of the post-war working class that emphasised new patterns of everyday life and relationships rooted in affluence and welfare legislation. Recent histories of the 1950s and early 1960s emphasise the continuing dominance of class as a relational social identity.[14] The testimonies underlying this study confirm the complexities of this identity, as class differences increasingly interacted with affluence, consumption and teenage culture as well as with new tenets of gender and sexuality to create new subjectivities. Yet, as Pat Thane has argued, economic boom and the welfare state did not herald a total transformation, and relative deprivation continued to be an important subjective marker for many working-class children in this book. Consciousness of having or not having continued to define early life experiences and social relations, arousing in the child their first sense of awareness that they existed in relation to other people who had more or less than themselves. From such awareness often came the realisation that 'their lives were controlled by more powerful people' who acted seemingly without care for those below them.[15]

Sue Bruley grew up in a newly built Surrey council estate close to Epsom Downs race course. The working-class estate was part of the extensive post-war urban redevelopment that included council housing programmes financed from government subsidies paid to local authorities. Sue's parents took part in the working-class migration from inner cities to suburbs situated in the New Towns constructed after 1946. Yet the estate's leafy surroundings failed to disguise her parents' weekly struggle to make ends meet. The sight of the Friday money pile denoted the family's hand-to-mouth existence where 'every penny had to be justified'.[16] Sue's memory confirmed the findings of post-war sociologists that, despite welfare-state provision and high labour demand, working-class families remained vulnerable to poverty in the suburbs as well as the inner cities.[17] As in many working-class households, her mother combined part-time work with family management. Elizabeth Roberts has argued that this period saw a weakening of women's traditional control over the family finances.[18] However, Sue's mother was one of the minorities of working-class women who retained control over the household budget. The household's traditional gender balance gave Sue close insight into the strain this weekly responsibility placed on her mother:

My father would get paid on a Friday and there would be piles of money on the table to sort out the bills, and it was weekly pay, you know, and so they would have these conversations about what they could afford . . . then on Tuesday she would get the family allowance, which was I think seventeen or eighteen shillings . . . I had to go down the shops with her . . . because we didn't have a car or anything like that . . . she was waiting for that money on a Tuesday to feed us on Wednesday, Thursday, Friday, until my Dad got paid on a Friday. It was hand to mouth stuff.

Childhood lived 'on the borderlands' could invoke an early sense of injustice towards social authorities whose intervention in their lives added humiliation to hardship.[19] Alan Woodward remembered how first-hand experiences of near 'abject poverty' in Broadstairs, Kent fuelled his early antagonism towards society. Before leaving school at sixteen, he undertook four part-time jobs to supplement his parents' meagre wages. The endless round of newspaper deliveries and car washing induced weariness with a life barely begun, but, as for Sue, it was the distress of witnessing his mother's daily suffering that angered him. He expressed this towards the most visible source of social authority: 'It was a religious society. There was a Catholic church you could see from my back garden and I went to a Church of England school, so it became a natural focus of my . . . resentment.'[20] The connection made sense because Alan knew his mother had been an active Salvation Army member in her youth. Sue's and Alan's testimonies show that before working-class children were able to articulate coherent ideas about the social order and their place within it, material conditions of domestic life, daily patterns and a child's sensitivity to parental feeling shaped an early relationship with the world; they often grasped early the unfairness of the social system their parents negotiated every day.

Post-war Britain remained indelibly imprinted by class and class consciousness. Social surveys of the 1950s and especially the 1960s showed a preoccupation with class. In a 1950–51 *People* questionnaire, 90 per cent of respondents assigned themselves to a social class, without hesitation.[21] Sociological surveys charting the impact of working-class affluence revealed that rising living standards, consumer goods and commercial culture had done little to erode entrenched working-class values and identities. John Goldthorpe and Martin Lockwood's study of Luton's affluent workers (1962) showed that their sense of class continued to be rooted in older patterns of social relationships. Comparing their findings with Richard Brown's north-east study of Wallsend shipbuilders, Mike Savage has noted how both groups defined themselves in relation to a visible, powerful and moneyed upper class.[22] This had changed little from the previous decade. Raphael Samuel remembered how, in the 1950s, the 'vertical division between "us" and "them" was the dominant idiom in the perception of social life, informing not only politics and culture but also personal comportment'.[23] It was class as a relationship and a determinant of identity rather than simply as a hierarchical social structure that registered in the child's consciousness and marked interviewees' memories.

As children, sixties activists developed an awareness of class from impressionistic, emotional responses to parents' interactions with the local community and state. Parents could inculcate a sense of the meanings of class by expressing firm ideas about their place in the social order. Joanna Bourke has argued that by the early 1960s 'historical construction' played a powerful role in shaping working-class identity whereby individuals drew upon 'an identity based not only on their current position within society, but also on a position inherited from their parents and their grandparents'.[24] Interviewees' testimonies illustrated how this began with childhood perception and feeling. In rare cases it was working-class deference they first heard. In 1950s north Leeds, Sheila Hemingway's father lived 'according to the rule'.[25] He was a laundry worker at the local St James' Hospital, her mother a Hoffman presser in the nearby tailoring factory, and they lived with Sheila's three siblings in a two-up, one-down, back-to-back house. Her father told her, '"You know your place. Your place is here. It's them at the top who know how to rule . . . We were born to work"'.[26] But a strike at the tailoring factory made eleven-year-old Sheila aware that her mother was not as compliant. She recalled the conversation between mother and daughter: '"Why aren't you at work?" "I'm not at work today 'cos I'm on strike." "What does that mean?" "Well, I'm not going to work today." And it was set off like that.' Although it was not until she met her husband that Sheila began to understand labour politics, the conversation brought momentary consciousness about the contested relations between and within classes.

Family stories contributed to a long tradition of working-class culture to help inculcate these children with a sense of class. In Newcastle-on-Tyne John Charlton came from a line of men and women employed in private service. After wartime service as an RAF motor mechanic his father had been a bus driver, and later a chauffeur for a local shipping owner. John recalled a childhood full of stories that were part of family legend. One particularly vivid tale came from his maternal uncle, 'about 1931 and the Great Crash when his father, my grandfather, had been taken aside by his employer and told we must all make sacrifices, and had his pay cut'.[27] Before he came to formulate tangible political ideas as a teenager, stories like this became 'embedded in' John's 'thoughts'. John understood that the 'we' excluded his grandfather's employer, and the blatant injustice provoked an antagonism towards society which became sharpened when, in the late 1940s, the family moved as tenants to the owner-occupied suburb of Kenton. The family was surrounded by predominantly lower middle-class families, and John explained how 'summer holidays delineated social difference'. His family had operated an open house, but when calling on friends, at two houses at least, he would be kept waiting on the doorstep. Alive to his social unacceptability as a working-class boy, the shame of being made to feel an outsider had stung sharply.

The working class and the Labour Party

The political as well as the cultural implications of class were learned inside the family. Men and women spoke of becoming almost intuitively left as a logical extension of their working-class lineage. Again, family stories fostered emotional and cultural attachment to the Labour Left. Judith Milner recounted her father's tales about her maternal grandfather, who had been active in the Amalgamated Engineering Union (AEU) during the war. Before he met Judith's mother, her father knew of his future father-in-law from his reputation in the shipyards: 'My grandfather was very keen on unionising everybody and there was a great backlash against him and his comrades.'[28] Judith's respect for her grandfather's politics was nurtured by the story of the police escort accompanying him to work each day. Roger Cox's father had been a lorry driver for British Railways' eastern region Cartage Department at London's Liverpool Street station. As a boy he too heard repeated stories of his father defending Bishopgate members of the National Union of Railwaymen. He made an emotional connection with these to form a vague feeling that 'something was not quite right with the world'.[29]

For young activists who went on to develop new political expressions of solidarity, post-war political patterns framed a particular relationship between them and the landscape. Loyalty to the Labour Party was in this period often 'a hereditary affair'.[30] Working-class children learned about longstanding political and cultural ties between the working-class and Labour through familial relationships. In the early 1950s the Labour Party was a mass organisation with extensive ties to workingmen's and labour clubs, and to the Co-Operative stores marking working-class communities. Samuel noted that '"Labour" homes and "Labour families" could be numbered in tens of thousands; there would be at least one in any working-class street.'[31] Sandy Irving understood that even though his Huddersfield 'parents weren't particularly left-wing . . . they voted Labour because it was just assumed, because I grew up on a council house estate and everybody on the estate voted Labour'.[32] The 'mental horizons' of class seemed to have altered little since Richard Hoggart noted the social divisions between 'us' and 'them' characterising inter-war working-class Leeds.[33] Bob Light described the 'tribal class' in which he and his brothers grew up in London's East End.[34] From within this tightly knit neighbourhood he accepted that people like himself, his family and neighbours voted for the Labour Party and identified with the Labour Left. Household patterns were formative in transmitting this understanding. His paternal uncles visited on most Sundays throughout the year; all 'were socialists of one sort or another', though only his father was a card-carrying Communist. The brothers' 'violent' political arguments comprised part of the 'verbal furniture' of Bob's childhood, along with discussions about football. Children's sense of working-class identity, felt as family bonds, could extend to the local community. Attachment to the Labour Left was strengthened through games and childhood talk. At the 1955 general election Bob was six years old, yet he and his school friends were 'aware that we were Labour, and I don't mean just me, but everybody in the class was aware of that'.

For some interviewees memories of these bonds became interwoven with nostalgic constructs of lost working-class communities to enrich the child's [remembered] psychic connection to the parental landscape. Laurie Flynn grew up in 1950s class-conscious Edinburgh, alive to his parents' Glaswegian socialist roots. His father was a bookbinder, who taught his son to revere education and its possibilities for exploring the world. Both parents had imparted humanistic socialist ideals and Laurie made a direct psychic connection between childhood feelings of nurture, parental displays of kindness and the community spirit sustaining Glasgow's slum districts:

> We are talking about this free thinking, non-commercial place. Looking back I came from a very generous-hearted [single] socialist class, and one of the things I remember is the tenets of the Socialist Sunday School of 1920 which is when Christians and non-Christians attempted to teach kids a humanistic set of commandments.[35]

It was unclear how far Laurie may have imposed his adult values onto this remembered place. Yet as a boy he had glimpsed something of his father's harsh childhood when visiting the Irish market at Shipbank Lane. In one of Glasgow's poorest areas he learned that poverty meant second-hand shoes and spectacles. These remembered images signalled the subjective significance of this place: here Laurie began applying childhood values to his surroundings along a trajectory that took him from his family's new council house to the London School of Economics (LSE) in 1965: 'Its radical tradition attracted me . . . Coming to LSE from my parents' background and their love of education, we knew the world needed to be changed.'

In middle-class families too, children inherited the values of Labour-supporting parents. Martin Shaw's mother was the daughter of a greyhound stadium manager. Along with her siblings, she had broken from the family's Conservative Party roots to become a firm Labour voter. His father had worked in a butcher's shop until a grammar school education had taken him into a career in adult education. In the late fifties he had joined the Adult Education department at Leeds University alongside New Left historian Edward Thompson and sociologist John Rex. Although Communism always 'remained at a distance', he and Martin's mother had both adhered to the liberal Catholicism that identified them as Labour voters. Similarly to working-class children, Martin was sensitive to the left-wing politics shaping his parents' moral values and everyday conversation. In 1956 news of the Suez crisis and Hungarian uprising so upset the nine-year-old that he organised his first activity for the Left: 'We didn't have a television so it must have been in the newspapers, and I organised a jumble sale outside the gate of our house.'[36] Wenda Clenaghen was raised on the Isle of Sheppy, off the northern coast of Kent, the daughter of two teachers. Her mother came from a long line of Labour supporters and even voted Communist a few times, though as a small-town teacher this was not something she publicly admitted: from 1947 to 1948, the start of the Cold War had seen the Labour government purging Communists from the civil service and the teaching profession.[37] Within the family, however, her mother's left-wing views were known and endorsed. Wenda explained: 'we all went along with that', and remembered 'crying when Labour lost the election in 1951, because my Mum was crying you see, and she thought it was going to be back to the 1930s and all the rest of it'.[38] As a child, Wenda was unaware that her mother's fears had likely been provoked by the populist fascism re-emerging between 1945 and 1951. Whilst Labour failed to take any decisive action against Oswald Mosley and his supporters' street campaigns, its presence in government had probably reassured her mother that the threat would be contained as long as the Left held power.[39] Wenda saw in her mother's tears the instability that Labour's defeat posed to her childhood world, and in 1960, aged fourteen, she joined the Labour Party Young Socialists as a logical response.

The Communist Party family

If family socialisation patterns fostered emotional and cultural ties to
the Labour Left, this was most overt in Communist Party homes. In the
early 1950s the Communist Party of Great Britain (CPGB) occupied a
marginal position in political life. Both its membership and influence
had declined considerably since the peak of its power at the end of the
war. Whereas in the 1945 general election twenty-two Communist Party
candidates had stood and won a total of 102,780 votes, by 1950 the
Party had dwindled as an electoral force; in that year's general election
it stood 100 candidates, who between them won only 91,815 votes.[40]
As the Cold War encroached, the Labour government's rightward shift
limited the Party's room for manoeuvre on the Left and created a climate
in which to be a Communist was once again to be a national pariah.

Communism suffused day-to-day domestic life and conversation in
all-encompassing, often subtle ways, transferring to children attitudes
and beliefs pertaining to the Left, almost without question. Stories of
Communist Party childhood echo Samuel's evocative description of the
British Communist world as a 'complete society' accompanied by 'a
complete social identity' transcending 'the limits of class, gender and
nationality'.[41] Michael Rosen described how culture, Party and politics functioned as one.[42] Children born into this world followed the
example set by their parents; they grew up to consider political activism
and discourse normative behaviours. Raised to be critical thinkers, they
often became critically conscious of established authority through direct
encounters with its manifest unjustness. Through situations involving
family members they came to see themselves as social 'outsiders' or
'other'.

In 1949 thirteen-year-old Sarah Cox became entranced by tales of
fellow school pupils recently returned from a youth rally in Eastern
Europe. Eager to join in their Communist activities, she was dissuaded
by her father, who had left the Party in 1940 when he joined the civil
service. He urged her: '"Please don't", because it would have put his
job at risk. He got investigated by a really quite nasty guy . . . he got
put through the mill and it nearly drove him to a nervous break-down,
but he would still go on and talk about Marxism.'[43] John Cowley
learned about the bitter feelings Communist Party membership could
arouse from stories of a family rift prior to his birth. In 1933 revisions
to the Labour Party constitution had stopped CPGB members from
joining the Party. John's mother came from avowedly Labour-supporting
parents, and when her younger brother joined the Communist Party
his action was seen as a betrayal to the family. John vividly recounted

the 'painful' tale he often heard about how 'my mother's father had to eject his son from the party meeting'.[44]

Although Britain escaped the worst excesses of America's McCarthyism, amidst Cold War paranoia anti-Communist investigations remained cruel in the personal devastation they wrought upon victims and their families.[45] Steve Jefferys was first attacked as a member of a dissident collective in 1962. The secret service made an application to his head-master to investigate Communist Party members at the school. In the wake of the William Vassall spy case that year, the threat came closer to home after Steve's uncle was blacklisted and dismissed as a civil service union officer. After questions were raised in the House of Commons about why the headmaster should be exposing the political affiliation of his pupils, Steve felt a sense of 'who' and 'we' being defined.[46]

Communist culture instilled in children distrust of established author-ity. Interviewees raised within this background learned to question the opinions and actions of authority where they contravened their own moral framework. Steve Jeffrey's brother was suspended indefinitely in October 1962 after daring as head boy to announce a meeting to morning assembly about the Cuban missile crisis. The suspension was eventually lifted after their mother visited the headmaster. Steve remembered the experience for 'being defined as a collective, as a net-work, in part by the dominant authorities'. Yet his mother had also confirmed the legitimacy of challenging official opinion. This manner of thinking would be vital in encouraging him to challenge university, state and government authorities when he went to the LSE in 1965: 'This was a period in which you were not expected to question author-ity. You were expected just to sit down and do what you were told, and here, largely because of the political ideas we had, which were running counter to the system, we were most likely to be saying, well what about this, what about that?'

Yet, for this cohort Communism was never a serious choice. At the start of the decade revelations of Stalinism and the legacy of 1956 remained imprinted on the collective memory of the Left. Although the Young Communist League (YCL) was active around the VSC, the Communist Party remained largely outside the late-sixties network. Most interviewees were still children when images of Soviet tanks rolling into Budapest had appeared on television screens, and awareness of the political and emotional significance of this year varied, depend-ing on individuals' age and political trajectory. Yet, as will be shown in later chapters, connections with individual Communists and their families remained variously influential throughout the decade. Dissident

Communist intellectuals, notably individuals associated with the 'first' New Left, hovered on the horizons of the network, and made an important impression on the intellectual contours of young activists. The Communist Party father also presented an image of political masculinity that remained etched in young men's memories. As activists they strove to live up to this ideal, an effort complicated by contradictions between cultural images and received lived experiences of masculinity which they often negotiated silently. The next section will turn to the post-war family as a site of gendered selfhood.

Family and the gendered self

Critiques of the nuclear family were central to the Women's Liberation politics that suffused New Left communities from 1968 onwards. Socialist feminists saw women's oppression rooted in the capitalist ideology of the nuclear family that isolated them within a closed domestic unit, overwhelmingly responsible for childcare and housework. In the early 1970s social and sexual relations between men and women took on unprecedented focus as a personal site of political struggle. As left women began to speak out against the phallic culture of the revolutionary Left, the clarion call for comrades, husbands and lovers to discover new ways of being men imbued deeper questions of masculinity and femininity, and their relationship to post-war patterns of socialisation. In early Women's Liberation groups women employed consciousness raising as a new political tool to explore the roots of their own oppression. Socialist feminists encouraged men to do the same, and by 1972 in 'non-aligned' left circles some men took up the challenge as they sought to discover new forms of masculine identity to transform relations between the sexes. Childhood experiences featured heavily in women's and men's discussions in early consciousness-raising groups, as individuals sought to understand wider social questions behind specific experiences on the Left. Questions surrounding the roots of early feminist consciousness have traditionally focused on the experience of girls growing up in 1950s and early 1960s society and culture.[47] Yet little attention has been given to men's 'defensive solidarity' that caused these women such confusion.[48] This section scrutinises the subjectivity of the post-war 'scholarship boy' whose sense of left self was accompanied by his own specific experiences of social and sexual relations.

In this study I have followed Steedman's anachronistic practice of using the terms 'scholarship boys' and 'girls' in the context of the 1950s when, following the introduction of compulsory, free secondary education, the only remaining scholarship pupils were those who won local authority scholarships to attend public day schools or the previously endowed fee-paying grammar schools.[49] I have loosely adopted these terms to denote the intellectual pathway of a particular cohort of activist men and women that started in the grammar or public day school and followed through into mid-1960s radical subcultures and late-sixties university left circles. The narratives of this cohort reveal contested journeys towards modern selfhood that began with uneasy relations with fathers and mothers.

Fathers and sons

The scholarship boys who populated the left milieux uneasily negotiated the shifting mid-century social and emotional landscape. Memories and images of fathers provide particular signals of boyhood subjectivity. Just as narratives of fifties scholarship girls feature the post-war mother, those of young left men are punctuated with the leitmotif of the father whose social values had been indelibly shaped by an inter-war realm of experience. Stories of boyhood insecurity, alterity and the adolescent's search for a tangible sense of self began with memories of the boy's otherness in relation to the father. As generational narratives the stories form a familiar picture of divisions between parents and children that testified to the ever-expanding forms of modern selfhood available to the post-war child and adolescent. But for these men and women stories of self were inextricably interwoven with political ideology and conservative and radical cultures. Clues to understanding the new political subjectivities lie in young activists' encounters with parents' socially prescribed rules.

Sally Alexander has argued that Virginia Woolf's concept of thinking back through the mother offers the historian a deeper understanding of twentieth-century female subjectivity by interrogating individual life histories for 'metonymic signs of femininity'.[50] To the extent that the masculine subject may be understood as a partial, ongoing construction, her ideas offer useful transference to the masculine realm of experience and identity. The metaphor of the father and its relation to generational memory and masculine subjectivity suggests a valuable framework for remapping mid-century male life. In the men's earliest memories visual markers of the childhood landscape were interwoven with relationships to fathers who were dominant figures literally, but also figuratively. Their powerful presence is suggestive of the male authority structuring post-war society, politics, culture and domesticity. Conflict between fathers and sons provides insight into the social and emotional disjuncture of the scholarship boy trying to find a place amidst conflicting social messages fed to him by the patterns of his class and education. It speaks of a larger chasm within the masculine post-war realm in which the reconfiguration of middle-class masculinity, ongoing since the First World War, took on new political and social expression amongst young activist men.[51] Intellectually and emotionally, they stood at odds with the established middle-class conservatism of the inter-war era that harked back to a Victorian age of class-bound institutions, colonialism, imperialism and Christian moral fibre, as embodied in the public schools. The 1950s scholarship boy confronted contradictory meanings about what it meant to be a young middle-class man.

Historians are in general agreement that the mid-twentieth century saw the transition of gender roles and relations, in which men and women began to work out 'new ways of living within a historically-distinct family framework'.[52] In this period men were presented with images of a 'family-oriented' masculinity which stressed involved fatherhood and a happy home life in ways that were compatible with the preservation of male authority.[53] Yet, alongside the ideal of the involved family man, post-war culture continued to provide a psychic space that accommodated an imaginative male 'flight from domesticity'.[54] Martin Francis has argued that popular culture provided a continuing outlet for an older, nineteenth-century imperial masculinity to co-exist with a post-Empire vision of modern male heroism and adventurism. Neither of these manly cultural trends disrupted the early post-war triumph of the companionate marriage and home-loving family man, because the two were interrelated, and perhaps key to the successful reintegration of men to the home front following the Second World War.[55] However, the boyhood narratives of male interviewees suggest a more complicated picture than this interpretation allows. They suggest that contradictions between cultural images and received lived experiences of masculinity were in tension and problematic for the individuals concerned. In the new climate of self-expression, meanings about legitimate emotional male expression were far from uniform. For these middle-class boys, there was, it seems, a disjuncture between representations of masculinity received in the home, grammar and public school, in 1950s and early-1960s popular culture, and in their own developing sense of masculine selves. As the male adolescent strove to assemble more egalitarian, just social narratives, the turbulent experience of reconfiguring new codes of selfhood came to be felt at the level of father–son relations.

The emotional distance between fathers and sons often began by physical separation during or immediately after the war. The return of demobilised fathers was often a disorienting process for children and fathers alike. For children too young to have conscious memories of their fathers before they departed for war 'the concept of "Daddy" had by 1945 often reached the levels of the purest abstraction'.[56] Mike McGrath's father returned home in 1949, a virtual stranger to his eight-year-old son. The freedom defining Mike's early childhood in Bishops Stortford came to an abrupt end when his father's arrival saw the family move away from the Hertfordshire fields: 'So he came back and we left there and went and lived in a series of RAF stations starting at Fazakerley in Liverpool, which is barbed wire and armed guards and dogs. It was awful.'[57] This visual imagery compounded Mike's memories of his father's remoteness. Juxtaposing the stark metallic barriers of the RAF camps with memories of playing in the surrounding fields, he remembered this boyhood freedom as 'a golden age' and lamented, 'there was never that again'.

Influenced by Kleinian analytic theory, Graham Dawson has highlighted the role narrative fantasies provide as 'a screen through which the social world and social relations are experienced' to inform explanations of self. Events can become interwoven with the narrator's fantasies in which imaginary scenarios or scenes 'represent a range of possible selves situated in the social world'.[58] The role of imagination is to enable the subject to achieve a composed sense of self or psychic coherence. Read in this way, the metaphorical power of Mike's narrative derives from the underlying structure of boyhood feeling expressed through the imagery in the landscape. Memories of freedom and play apart from his father evoked mythic images of a lost golden age that frequently accompany popular representations of fifties childhood. They suggested a moment of psychic security before his RAF father brought a disruptive and threatening authoritarian presence into his childhood world. Memories of his father's return were interwoven with his entry to Dulwich College, the all-male, south-east London boarding school to which he won a scholarship in 1952. The harsh metallic images of war denoted the alienating elite masculine culture Mike associated with his father and the school. The pastoral idyll of the boy playing in open fields signalled an inner rupture and the turning-point which his father's return represented in his masculine self.

In adolescence the emotional chasm between father and son often assumed political and social meaning around the issue of race. Young middle-class men learned to read social alterity through their fathers. Disputes over race symbolised how young men's experiential gulf from the inter-war man became internalised and found expression in early political and moral values. It was no coincidence that anti-racism formed a core tenet of their early politics. The gulf from fathers propelled their vision for a humane and free society, leading to deeply felt outrage against the inhumanity of South African apartheid, the segregation of American blacks and America's offensive in Vietnam. Mike McGrath remembered his distance from his father's right-wing views: 'He was a racist and an extreme right-wing Tory.'[59] Uneasy relations between Dave Lyddon and his father took a similar focus: 'My father was a Labour supporter . . . but was also quite racist. That was the aspect of his politics I didn't like. There was an ingrained racism against blacks in a more general sense, so I suppose, really, if I was anything, I was anti-racist.'[60]

Interweaving between the immediacy of childhood and interconnecting patterns of class and paternal politics conjured the prejudicial taste the men's fathers had aroused. Interviewees renewed this distaste in the course of retelling, suggesting the place perception of prejudice held in the formation of adult identity, and the point at which the father lost some of his power and became a figure within a wider world of class and politics. Chris Rawlence's early memories of his father as RAF hero were disturbed by impressionistic recollections of his anti-Semitic quips and ditties. Even as an adult he was unable to reconcile his father's anti-fascist stand on 1930s Cable Street with 'the Jew-hating rhyme' that 'had the city slickers guffawing in their youth'.[61] His views gave Chris an uncomfortable understanding of otherness that held implications for his own moral framework as a relational social subject: 'My grandfather had an accountant called Le Voye, which is a kind of Francophile version of Levi, and there was always a feeling that, you know, he was other. The gypsies are the main other I was brought up with, always . . . first in line to be accused of nicking stuff if it went missing . . . I mean you couldn't imagine doing anything as naughty as that, basically.'[62] Ian Birchall remembered his father's jocular but pejorative references to Labour Party supporters. He recalled these in the same context as the mild anti-Semitism common amongst his parents' lower middle-class circles. One day when his mother mentioned in passing her Jewish dentist, her friend exclaimed, 'I don't think I could have a Jew inside my mouth.'[63] Ian's inability to relate to his parents' middle-class world of trivialities and hypocrisies echoed the disjuncture proclaimed by Mike, Dave and Chris. However, distance between him and his father was not a complete estrangement: 'My father, for someone who had left school at fifteen, was a very well read man. So I would occasionally discuss books with my father. He read Thomas Mann, for example.' His recollections reflected the way in which distance from conservative values, material symbols and associated patterns of behaviour could be simultaneously tempered by momentary emotional affection and a son's respect for his father's actions.

Luisa Passerini noted how the paternal figure nullified any simple rupture between the Italian left generations. Tension between continuity and discontinuity was borne out in the ambivalent father whose values were the source of conflict as well as liberal renewal in their children.[64] Similar tensions underlined paternal relations for English activists. David Widgery identified the contradiction between his father's nonconformist politics and authoritarian sense of discipline, which as an adolescent he found hard to reconcile with the surrounding climate of leniency and indulgence. He admired his father's deep social conscience: his concern for attractive London County Council housing and the democratic provision of art for ordinary people. He showed interest in his son's politics, and the young medical student felt free to discuss his political feelings.[65]

Memories of sporadic affection between fathers and sons reflected wider shifts in parenting patterns discernible during the 1940s and 1950s. By the mid-century popular newspapers were presenting 'a clear normative standard of fatherhood', encouraging men to be emotionally involved parents, even potential 'friends' or 'pals' to their children.[66] Social surveys focusing on fatherhood and the family confirmed that changes in the perceived norms of fatherhood were being reproduced in certain contexts. Michael Young and Peter Willmott's study of Bethnal Green and Debden suggested that working-class fathers were more involved in their children's lives than had been the case in previous generations.[67] From their study of over 700 Nottingham families John and Elizabeth Newson confirmed that increasing paternal investment in the family was evident in all social classes.[68] Conflict between father and son occurred because the middle- and lower middle-class father stood at a juncture of normative masculinity, half-way between Victorian puritanism and moralism, and the reflexive, authentic selfhood embodied by the post-war son.

Occasionally a father left an imprint through his absence. Martin Tompkinson spoke of the shadow his father's death cast over his childhood from the age of four:

> Wrongly, but understandably, I got the notion [that] it was my fault he had died. . . . To all and intents and purposes I had a happy childhood, but that whole experience left me with a life view that the world isn't fair . . . and made me want to get on to terms with the world.[69]

His father's Left Book Club specials provided a comforting, tangible presence in the house when, aged nine, he started to become aware of political events like the Suez crisis. Before long he became interested in Marx and subscribed to *Soviet Weekly*. John Hoyland's father had been killed in the war when John was just three. As an anti-fascist activist and military hero, this Communist father was a phantom to revere, but not always easy to emulate. At Reading's Leighton Park, the same boarding school his father had attended, John 'sweated blood trying to live up to his expectations'.[70] His socialist, Quaker grandfather provided the connection between his father's politics and authoritative masculine presence: 'My grandfather, with his idealism and high-mindedness, reinforced the powerful sense of duty – the duty to achieve great things, preferably for the sake of others, that my absent father had instilled in me.' In the late 1950s he was a chairman of the Friends Peace Committee, touring the country speaking out against the H-bomb. A decade later, John followed his grandfather's example by becoming active in Youth CND, and the weight of this paternal presence remained: 'I felt throughout my life that I had to live up to him [my father] and so it was very easy for me to feel throughout my life that I wasn't good enough, doing enough, worthy enough, you know. Certainly I did feel that about my politics very often.'[71]

Mothers and daughters

The maternal leitmotif occupied an equally prominent place in women's narratives. It signalled the way in which common experiences of post-war femininity and girlhood, of contradictory images of what it meant to be a woman, crossed over with specific experiences concerning class and politics, shaping the left consciousness of activist women. Stories of difficult relations with mothers told of girls' social relationships to the wider female realm and to normative values they encountered as young women. These narratives resonated with other post-war female voices; those secondary, often higher-educated women, born in Britain between 1943 and 1951.

During the 1970s the theme of mother–daughter relations began to be taken up for exploration by sociologists and psychologists alike. Key texts like Nancy Friday's *My Mother/My Self: The Daughter's Search for Identity* inspired feminist discussion of mothers and daughters. These narratives belong to the collective voice of post-war women journeying to modern female selfhood. Their experiences informed a new model of female morality away from the conservative values their mothers embodied. In the 1950s and early 1960s the young female generation saw in their mothers a continuation of the 'conservative' discourse of female respectability surviving from the pre-war era. As Lynn Abrams has noted, 'this was a discourse of respectability, self-sacrifice or self-abnegation, and service (inflected by social class) . . . which in effect told girls and women that freedom and choice came with a condition

– to be a good girl or a good woman'.[72] Rooted in Christian doctrine, it acted as a strong moral force guiding women's behaviour. What distinguished these left women's voices from those of the wider female generation was alertness to and rejection of contradictions and hypocrisies their mothers' lives seemed to represent. Attention to these women's interactions with their mothers reveals particular interpretations of female social duty, femininity and class, which they would carry into left circles from the mid-1960s. For women who formed identities within these circles the process of redefining moral values away from their mothers was not simply part of an unconscious social and cultural shift, expanding the boundaries of post-war female freedom. Rather, the process entailed a more extensive change in the way in which they came to inhabit their own class and left identities. Young left women came to establish an antagonistic relationship to wider social structures and became alert to political events which had at their heart acts of hypocrisy or injustice. At root of this 'left' female morality stood the image of their mothers as the 'good woman', and the unhappiness she exuded. Mothers emitted powerful understandings of female 'goodness', which daughters came to see bound up with class patterns, and the meanings they took added to the contradictions inhabiting the social body of post-war femininity. Like other women of their generation, many of these young girls were attuned to the subterranean channels of resentment running deep within their mothers; unspoken regrets for opportunities lost through their marital roles.[73] Class experience was integral to their mothers' frustrations because it was through submitting to dominant middle-class discourses of what marriage and motherhood entailed that they subordinated imagined identities and dreams. Caroline Bond reflected on her mother's wartime freedom when she had been evacuated to Kent as a physical education teacher. It had marked an all too brief interlude disrupted by a 'good' middle-class marriage to Caroline's father, whose technical film profession had given the family material comfort in Hampstead Heath:

> My mum was a very frustrated woman ... We used to have rows all the time. 'If you are a Communist why didn't you send us to a comprehensive school?' She wasn't really a Communist I don't think ... She was worthy, nice, dutiful, always helping other people and everything. My mum was always helping anyone in the street who needed help filling in forms or she was very active helping other households, so [there was] a huge sense of duty.[74]

The women's narratives suggest how daughters reacted against the contradictions of their mothers' lives to reinvest their social consciences towards what they saw as genuine causes. Caroline reflected on her mother's imprint: 'We did very early stay at the grass roots, but it was very much an ought rather than a desire I felt . . . I was driven by duty.'

Prue Chamberlayne's conceptions of 'duty' and 'goodness' were similarly framed by her rural middle-class upbringing and a Christianity she retained into her late teens. Her teenage diaries reveal an inward struggle as exposure to social injustice prompted a crisis of faith in her conservative moral values. In 1966, whilst undertaking VSO in Southern Rhodesia, she reflected on the racial prejudice she observed in relation to earlier European travels, questioning whether she would have had sufficient courage to denounce Nazi atrocities. Her diaries illustrate how she, too, interpreted 'duty' within the class expectations of her gender. Following sexual relations with a boyfriend, Prue became preoccupied with the tension between marriage and a successful relationship as she faced the social implications of pre-marital sex, the possibility that she could be pregnant and the inevitable disquiet the union would cause her parents. She expressed dislocation from her parents' class preoccupations and antagonism towards her father's conservative attitudes. On 20 September, 1964 she wrote that having adopted 'the Labour role' to annoy him, she now took it 'for granted that I shall vote Labour – it is as if he decided it for me!'[75] Yet, as long as she was immersed within this middle-class environment she felt unable to escape its norms and expectations. She worried that her parents would discover the boyfriend she had met in Bratislava was the son of a postman, and caught herself scrutinising his table manners. Prue's diary, read together with her oral narrative, presents a portrait of earnest social conscience intertwined with uncertain modern selfhood. From one perspective her anxieties reflected the transition teenage girls underwent from the early sixties in their attitudes towards religion and sexual morality: she stood at the edge of women's revolt against the 'respectability' and 'puritanism' shaping early to mid-twentieth-century sexual restraint.[76] Yet, her disquiet also betrayed the inner turmoil accompanying her emerging socialist values, feeling caught between Christianity and Marxism as codes for moral and social duty. Her diary showed her rationalising, though never quite reconciling these: 'Christianity teaches us how to live on the personal level; Marxism on the social level . . . Marxism should help us towards Christianity; it tells us that the state must help people if they are to be good – it is asking too much of people who are always grovelling in hunger and humiliation not to become cynical and despairing and be given to pleasures of the flesh.'

Other women remembered their mothers as models of confident female selfhood. The experience tempered their early socialist consciences and fed into a critical engagement with the world. Judith Herren's mother was a doctor and formative role model as a professional working mother. Judith's father had been killed in the war, and as a girl she had adapted to the routines of her mother's working life, growing up knowing what it meant to be a thinking woman: 'We were an all-female household so I had an instinctive understanding of what it was to be a woman and to be independent, and to think for yourself.'[77] The social assuredness her mother imparted fed into confident interactions with male students Judith met in Cambridge's New Left circle in the early 1960s.

Jane Storr's mother had trained as a Norland nanny. She raised her daughter according to progressive childcare, thinking to foster an independent-spirited child. Jane's father held socialist values and encouraged Jane to believe that 'You can be anything you want'.[78] Emphasising education as a route to intellectual and social freedom, he encouraged her to think critically about the world. She grew up preoccupied with questions of social justice and equality: 'You know we were always, well what if that happened, what would have been the outcome if you'd have done that or, if it's a political situation, what could another outcome of this have been if so and so had done that ... you know that was a way of thinking and talking.' As a fourteen-year-old she began attending YS meetings in her Hemel Hempstead home town, but it was CND, civil rights and the Vietnam War which fired her social conscience and left her unable to ignore the moral atrocities newspapers and television showed. Her mother set the tone for Jane's self-assertion within this wider social and political world, but the contradictions she embodied led to a tumultuous relationship between them. In her mother's wifely devotion she saw the opposite to the ambitious, free-thinking womanhood her father presented:

> My mum was totally enthralled by my father so deferred to him in terms of all intellectual opinions: how you ran the house, the money. They had on the surface a pretty idyllic marriage, never argued, but I think I was probably about eleven when I thought you know what? This I do not want ... to have a marriage like this, and I had a very sort of tumultuous relationship with my mother through my adolescence based on the perception that she was trying to hold me back. I was trying to fly.

The diasporic family

Children of immigrant or refugee parents felt the deep emotional and psychological imprint of their parents' displacement as the subjectivity of alterity. Sensitive to the plight of 'outsiders', they grew up with an instinctive need to correct injustices they observed. In the 1950s children of Jewish refugees struggled to live up to the task of belonging bestowed upon them from birth. They inhabited an imagined image of 'other' conjured from unspoken signals parents and older relatives transmitted. For this wartime generation, becoming English offered the protection of belonging, and adopting the social and cultural tenets of their new homeland was a method of survival in a society in which to be a Jew was not an invitation to social acceptance. Tony Kushner has argued that in the immediate post-war years, austerity and the retreat from Empire resulted in a loss of esteem that contributed to a new, inward-looking English national identity.[79] The government's immigration policies carried a clear message as to which outsiders could or could not become British. As David Cesarani has noted, 'East Europeans were deemed worth this exertion [to integrate], but Jews, Blacks and Asians were not'.[80] The Jewish terrorism that arose over the 'British-Jewish' Palestine conflict, and the August 1947 riots targeting Jews in several British towns, made British Jews uneasily conscious about their marginality.[81] This sense of insecurity was heightened by revelations about the nature and scale of the Holocaust in Western and Eastern Europe. Surrounded by unexplained contradictions, children of refugees lived with an unspoken legacy of trauma which adults tried to conceal. Victor Seidler's parents were refugee Jews who had fled from Vienna in the late 1930s. He was born in 1945, at 'a catastrophic moment of realisation', and his parents named him 'as a claim' for Englishness, safety and 'belonging'.[82] News that all of his father's relatives and his mother's father had perished in the camps came in 1947–48. When he began to ask questions about his family, Victor's mother strove to protect him and his brothers from the truth. Yet silences within the north London family home carried meaning:

> I don't know what or how I knew it, but I knew something *bad* or dramatic or catastrophic had happened . . . I knew there was no family . . . but you couldn't ask about it, it was kind of unspeakable . . . [this] meant that often we were in rooms where people were talking and we did understand, but we were told that we didn't. But we did.

Insecurity could be expressed in different social, cultural and psychological forms, but a common effect was to make children uneasily conscious of their marginality. Mica Nava discerned her parents' foreignness through observing their deliberate, awkward efforts to belong. The family lived in the middle-class, Tory Home Counties, near Newbury, where assimilation meant a particular kind of Englishness. Her mother impressed upon her daughter the important relationship between social behaviour and belonging; she dressed in the conservative fashions worn by local women, and encouraged Mica to participate in the pony club and gymkhanas. Yet she also clung to radical tenets that had marked her Viennese teenage years, breaking Home Counties political-gender norms by standing as a Labour Party parish candidate. She also imparted to Mica radical ideas about sex. 'She said basically sex is okay, you know. You just have to make sure you don't have a baby . . . That was completely different from most mothers in the fifties.'[83] The Weisselbergs' unconventional household, its train of 'non-Jewish Jews' from Holland, Austria and France, distinguished it in the neighbourhood, and Mica was acutely conscious of the 'otherness' her parents' progressive, free-thinking lifestyle signalled. 'I grew up feeling completely different from most people around me . . . They were liberal. They were definitely liberal parents.' As an older teenager she discovered freedom away from English cultural norms, gravitating to radical cosmopolitan corners from London to Paris. Her rebellious self-expression seemed to be a specific response to her parents' half-hearted assimilation: 'My aunt said [of Nava's mother] she was much more of a bohemian when she arrived in Vienna, and so she became more conservative, and I maybe took up the banner on her behalf.' Along with her parents' unconventional moral codes, Mica echoed their 'boldly-expressed political views and emotions' that spoke of a 'need to protect others and correct injustice'.[84] When sixteen she sent packing the decorator in her parents' London flat after she heard him expressing derogatory views about West Indian immigrants in nearby Notting Hill. By the end of the 1960s Mica returned from New York and Mexico's bohemian quarters to find a home within underground, radical enclaves around the London VSC.

As they began to be conscious of wider societies and international politics, the insecurity that children had picked up from refugee parents coloured their engagement with Cold War conflicts. The legacy of persecution sometimes inculcated an early anti-Communist stance. Even before they became aware of the significance of 1956, children responded to stories of family experiences in the Soviet satellite states. Lee Comer's mother was a Czech Jew who had escaped from Prague at sixteen, leaving behind her sister to complete her education. Lee recalled the difficulties the Iron Curtain created for them to keep in touch: 'We travelled there and she came over to see us but under such constant supervision; it was pretty horrible. She had constantly to report to the police, and when we went there we knew we were being followed.'[85] Anna Paczuska's parents had come to Britain during the 1940s to escape the worst excesses of Communist-controlled Poland. Before the war her mother had been interned in Russian and Polish prisoner camps, and Anna remembered learning about the meaning of Communism from her stories:

> My mum and Dad always talked about Britain as a land of opportunity, my mum in particular. They saw what was happening in Poland as vicious and nasty, which it was, and it kind of left an impact on me growing up that Communism was something very nasty, and this was reinforced by letters arriving from my grandparents with bits censored and various bits cut out of them . . . There were stories of people who disappeared or were never heard of again, of poverty, well, of repression and oppression at every level.[86]

Anti-racist tenets were often transmitted through liberal-minded parents. James Swinson's mother was 'staunchly anti-apartheid'.[87] She was a cook at the LSE and often invited South African students to join them for Christmas. The anti-fascism of Bob Light's father had distinguished him as an East End dock worker. Bob had grown up in Bethnal Green in the 1930s, when his parents had made a deliberate decision to support the Left. Bob recounted one memorable incident in which his father had profoundly impressed upon him the need to counter racial prejudice:

> My Dad and I used to go up the Lane . . . Petticoat Lane is an open street market which runs on a Sunday and that was also the period of the 1950s when Mosley was trying to revive the British Union of Fascists . . . I can remember one Sunday; we must have come on the fringes of one of the Fascist meetings, and we got there and the next thing I know my Dad is thumping people, and fighting, and rolling on the ground, and I didn't know what to do. I was trapped between being a child and a man. A couple of years later I would probably have joined in, but at that stage I was embarrassed and frightened.[88]

The moment stood out because the embarrassing feelings it evoked signified the chasm between childhood helplessness and adult responsibility. Yet, the memory was also significant because the lessons it imparted fed into Bob's early activism. In 1967 he joined his local YS, suffused with Hackney's working-class Jewish culture. Anti-fascism still prevailed in the local labour movement and Bob's and other left groups eagerly championed anti-racist causes when they arose.

Religion and subjectivity

Scholars are in general agreement that the 1960s represented a significant turning-point in the decline of Britain's established Christian churches. From the late 1950s religion had to contend with alternative sources for selfhood. For young people, women especially, expanding possibilities for social and cultural expression seem to have increasingly supplanted the injunctions of Christianity as a framework for moral and social comportment.[89] Situated against this background, narratives of young activists provide valuable insight into some of the ways in which this cohort was engaging with Christian faith and established Anglican culture. These youngsters were inquisitive, morally attuned to and, not least, highly perceptive of acts of hypocrisy and injustice. Rejecting the Anglicanism of their parents and schools was often the earliest way in which they came to position themselves against the prevailing orthodoxies of middle-class culture and social practice. However, Christian faith remained a highly individual affair, complicated by issues of class, politics, gender and social conscience, and the histories of religious engagement presented a far from uniform picture.

Although the practice of weekly church attendance was in decline by the early sixties, Anglican culture remained embedded within the national fabric. Its imprint ranged from Sunday observance to religious broadcasting, and the churches' continued involvement in organisational life that started with the Girl Guides and Boys' Brigades and extended to the Women's Institute and working-class brass bands.[90] Anglicanism particularly suffused middle-class life. Willmott and Young noted that in the London suburb of Woodford the local church denoted 'a quintessential middle-class club, a way of meeting new neighbours and mixing with the right sort'.[91] Above all, Anglican piety left its trace in the culture of respectability continuing to pervade 1950s society. Sheila Rowbotham explained that for a northern, lower middle-class child Anglicanism provided 'the first vehicle for general thoughts about existence'.[92] Anglican ways seemed to her altogether at odds. She failed to understand the school minister's explanation that grace could only be received. She was also puzzled when her apparently secular father quite violently defended this Anglicanism following her announcement that she wanted to be received as a Methodist. The relationship between social belonging and conscience became clearer when Rowbotham's mother explained that in her father's south Yorkshire village Methodists had been looked down upon.

Rejection of childhood faith was often the earliest way for young activists to express their disjuncture from established middle-class patterns of home and school. At Birkenhead Boys Grammar School on the Wirral, Fred Lindop briefly absorbed his school's Christian teaching and developed a sense of faith. However, the middle-class authoritarianism of his school masters dissolved this as his growing sense of working-class identity conflicted with his Anglican observance:

When I was fourteen or fifteen, I decided to become a . . . Christian because I was . . . I suppose in a sense the only reading I had available apart from conventional school textbooks was the Bible, and it was a Church of England day school, and so we used to argue about the significance of things like, it will be easier for a camel to pass through the eye of a needle, so I became a Christian but rapidly discovered that most Christians were extremely reactionary Tories, including most of the masters who were in charge, and so by the fifth year I had become an agnostic or atheist.[93]

Ian Birchall reacted against middle-class Anglican hypocrisy in his West Riding home town of Shipley. His grandfather and uncle were Methodist preachers, and as a teenager he regularly attended the Anglican church, but doubts about Christianity's ethical tenets started to encroach when he uneasily registered anti-Catholic and anti-Semitic anecdotes common in the neighbourhood. Briefly he considered himself a Christian socialist, but his decision to reject his faith represented a final break from hypocrisies he associated with his background:

I was still going to church for the first couple of years I was at Oxford, but I was more and more struck that actually so-called religious people didn't take seriously what they supposedly believed in. I mean a thing, for example, that sticks with me. I had read the Bible right through, but I had read things, for example, where Jesus says it is easier for a camel to go through the eye of a needle than for a rich man to enter the king-dom of heaven. I loved that. I thought let all the rich go to hell, let's watch them fry, and I started quoting this to people in my home town.[94]

In 1958 Ian met Oxford Labour Club members who seemed 'to be actually putting their money where their mouth was', doing vast amounts of political activity without the prospect of reward. Over time, the experience confirmed that his conscience fitted most comfortably with socialism without the moral taint of Christianity.

However, other young people grew up in Christian families where New Testament teachings of love were interwoven with their parents' socialism and civic engagement. Wisty Hoyland was one of five daughters raised by a Church of England vicar in draughty Cambridge vicarages. The family's modest circumstances kept the trappings of affluence at a distance; her father encouraged his daughters to look outward to social injustice and human suffering, and his teachings were influential: 'A big influence on me was the sort of side of Christianity that promoted love thy neighbour, that bit, and my father definitely was associated with, he voted Labour all his life, so there was sort of awareness of these sort of values, very much in our house.'[95]

In their attempts to make sense of themselves and the surrounding world some youngsters embraced Christian discourses independently from their families. Brian Jackson noted Huddersfield grammar school girls who 'mentioned private thinking into religion' as a way of coping with the turbulence of adolescence and perplexities about the self, social roles and existence.[96] Although neither of her parents was particularly religious, Gilda Peterson had an intermittent relationship with God until her early twenties: 'I'd been a sort of Christian, and then I decided it was all a bit of rubbish at about fourteen, and then at about sixteen I decided to be saved . . . because again I wanted answers. I wanted a theory that made sense of things really.'[97]

Secondary education, scholarship boys and girls

Childhood encounters with Anglicanism illuminate the enquiring minds with which young activists forged defiant relationships with post-war society. Christianity stood alongside parental and school authority as the most immediate frames of reference determining a common code of ethics and defining standards of behaviour. The life histories reveal the longevity of established conservative discourses in interviewees' psychic structures. Some found it hard to relinquish the cultural and spiritual underpinnings of middle-class upbringing from their social and moral conscience well into early adulthood. Prue Chamberlayne's diaries have already shown the hold rural middle-class Christianity retained over her social conscience. It suggests that the Christian moral compass was not always so easily discarded, and the result could be troubling for the young person's composure in the modern world at a time when sexual and moral codes were understood to be shifting. Later chapters will show how conservative discourses sometimes complicated young activists' efforts to live out new, liberated behaviours and subjectivities. The educational establishment forms an important component of individual stories of sixties activism. Images of scholarship boys and girls haunted the [remembered] activist landscape of the late 1960s and 1970s. The identity of the intellectual activist was variously held up for admiration and critique, informing the subjectivity of left men and women. Often it was only once at university that many interviewees came to connect with Marx and to understand themselves as being of the Left in any organisational sense. However, this section argues that the secondary school provided the early groundwork, sowing the seeds for critical engagement with politics, culture and society.

Historians have long seen the hopes of the post-war settlement embedded in the Education Act of 1944, which made free education available to children through to university.[98] However, little attention has been given to the lived experience of secondary education in its relation to individual subjectivity. Interviewees' narratives show how secondary schools fostered critical enquiry about contemporary social and political issues and introduced interviewees into a milieu of children who shared radical sensibilities over class, culture and politics. Children often positioned themselves against their schools' Anglicanism as an early gesture against middle-class social practices and hypocrisies they discerned; through such acts they implicitly defined themselves as 'other' against prevailing norms. Unsurprisingly, the atheism of many Communist Party children brought them into conflict with school authorities. James Hinton's father was an entomologist and a Communist: 'atheism was in the blood'.[99] In 1958 at Bristol's Colston Boy's School, sixteen-year-old James 'took off' intellectually and 'began arguing with this vicar about God because I got hold of Bertrand Russell's *Western Philosophy*, and his book on power and atheism was crucial'. At Dulwich College, Mike McGrath refused to kneel for Sunday prayers. This everyday act of resistance occurred just beneath the surface, and spoke less of religious conscience than of his need to express individuality away from the established mould of the public school boy as state servant.

However, interviewees' stories also showed the capacity of the Anglican grammar school to foster powerful concepts of social duty amongst pupils. This represented several discursive examples of wartime citizenship evident after 1945.[100] For young women these discourses were interwoven with older notions of female goodness already identified with post-war mothers. Many female interviewees also highlighted the influence of female teachers who nurtured instincts of social conscience. Anglican notions of female civic virtue lived on in the self-service ethic that continued to circulate in girls' grammar and independent public schools, part of a longer Christian tradition that had seen Victorian women practising evangelical social philanthropy. Gilda Peterson recalled the ethos of social duty prevailing at Hartlepool Girls' Grammar School. Symbols of heroic Edwardian women stressed the importance of serving one's community: 'We were all in houses, you know, called Nightingale and all of that . . . Cavell, Nurse [Edith] Cavell, where, you know, you were kind of feeling that it was good to do good.'[101] This message of service was reinforced through outside organisations that formed part of her daily childhood pattern and inculcated tenets of the established faith. Church, Sunday school and the Girl Guides all carried the message of service to God and the Queen, whilst stories of missionaries in Africa and China gave Gilda a glimpse of a world beyond Hartlepool.

Pupils attending Quaker and Methodist schools felt the profound sense of personal responsibility that had informed the English radical tradition of religious and political dissent. Hilary Wainwright attended York's Mount School. Her Methodist father had worked in the Friends Ambulance Unit during the war and had been impressed by the values of many Quakers he met. He had also learned that Quakers tradition-ally provided the sort of 'good' education he wished for his daughter. Hilary recalled the school's ethos of social service, which had encour-aged its pupils to take an interest in life outside the school, particularly, from 1966, to attend student Christian meetings held against the Vietnam War.[102] Sheila Rowbotham remembered the independent and tolerant spirit of inquiry embodied in her Methodist history teacher.[103]

Olga Wilkinson was one of many female teachers women mentioned as influential for imparting educative understandings of female social duty. Inside grammar and independent schools, girls had often been taught by teachers who encouraged them to believe that education offered the route to female social advancement. Many teachers had attended university in the 1920s and 1930s where they had fought hard to gain intellectual acceptance by deeply patriarchal institutions. The British Home Civil Service abolished the marriage disqualification for women only in 1948, and even then the middle-class assumption that marriage and teaching were not compatible governed grammar schools. Consequently, the female educational community had filled many of these teachers' lives with the meaning that marriage and their own children might otherwise have done.[104] They translated fierce aspirations to their surrogate offspring and left girls in no doubt that the price of post-war female privilege was duty to go out into the world and to be achieving women. Bronwen Davis explained the expectations she felt as a middle-class grammar school girl in north London: 'You didn't think of going into something like nursing for instance or secretarial work, you know, you were being educated for something more than that.'[105]

Alongside the social and psychological gulf defining mother–daughter relations, teachers symbolised subterranean points of continuity between the female generations. Caroline Bond and Gilda Peterson spoke with reverence of inspirational female teachers who had encouraged them to imagine futures beyond their mothers' constricted lives. Caroline had attended Camden's prestigious Collegiate School, whose founder Frances Buss had left a powerful legacy of female excellence. She particularly remembered her English teachers, Carole Hanley and Margo Heinemann. The latter was active in the same Communist Party circles as Caroline's parents, but both women had impressed upon the girls aspirations to 'go out and live boldly in the world'.[106] Spiritually and intellectually, the voices of women like Hanley and Heinemann penetrated the often defiant restlessness of fifties female adolescence. Some teachers encouraged young women to think critically about contemporary political and social issues, whilst others even introduced them to Marxist thinking. Joan Smith remembered that when she left Harrow Girls' Grammar School in 1964 her history teacher gave her a copy of *Das Kapital* 'on the grounds I might read it'.[107] Val Graham recalled, as a fourteen-year-old, asking her geography and economics teacher 'if she had a copy of *Das Kapital*, and she actually gave me a copy of Volume One'. She was one of two 'very, very powerful' female teachers whom Val later discovered were lesbians.[108] She emphasised their importance as models of independent and critically thinking womanhood: 'They struck me very differently, and one of the lesbian couple had very strongly anti-racist views, and she did talk to us about things like that, so I was genuinely influenced.'

However, secondary schools also confronted scholarship girls with contradictory messages about female identity. Whilst female education offered new opportunities for higher education and professional paid work, it also left them in little doubt that womanhood carried social restrictions. Young activist women sometimes found themselves at odds with female teachers when, as figures of authority, they upheld rules and values the girls perceived to be hypocritical or unjust. Hilary Wainwright highlighted the tension between, on the one hand, the rhetoric of teachers who encouraged pupils to invest themselves in worthwhile causes and, on the other, social restrictions hampering their ability to participate in anti-war campaigns. Restrictions on whom they could talk to after meetings and the sort of young men they were permitted to share coffee with betrayed contradictions between the openness with which the school encouraged them to be active citizens and petty restrictions emphasising their childlike status. In a burgeoning climate of energetic youth culture, messages of democratic citizenship supported young people's increasing social presence and consumer power and were hard to ignore, whereupon illogical rules over coats and shoes became authoritarian symbols for resistance. Hilary employed her own tools of direct action, from passive acts of defiance to outright support for friends threatened with expulsion for accompanying boys to coffee bars.[109]

The role of class is central to post-war secondary education shaping a particular kind of dissident selfhood. This was a period in which the issue of class 'impelled enlightened educational reform and practice'.[110] Concerns about social justice motivated studies such as J. Floud,

A. H. Halsey and F. M. Martin's *Social Class and Educational Opportunity* (1956), Jackson and Marsden's *Education and the Working Class*, and official surveys like the *Newsom Report* (1963) and the *Plowden Report* (1967).[111] New taught and learned practices of the self particularly informed the progressive educative methods that were concerned to address the economic and cultural deprivation of working-class children. Generally, however, the spirit of progressivism was designed to target the working-class majority who did not respond to the traditional pedagogical orthodoxies at the core of grammar school education. Beyond the context of Jackson and Marsden's study, as Paul Long has noted, historians have paid little attention to the subjectivity of working-class children in terms of how they and others identified themselves as working class inside the secondary school.[112] The testimonies of working-class men and women show that grammar and independent direct grant schools left a powerful imprint on children and adolescents that had important implications for their sense of self and their social and political relationships. Many remembered how political engagement prior to university often developed out of friendships with likeminded youngsters who came from similar backgrounds. These relations were rooted in common ways of thinking and feeling about class, and the social, cultural and political authorities moulding their psychic structures. By the time Harold Wilson became Prime Minister in 1964, Rab Butler's tripartite system of grammar schools, secondary moderns and selection through the Eleven Plus had long been subject to profound criticism. As early as 1951, Hilde Himmelweit showed that in Greater London 'children from lower working-class homes, despite their numerical superiority in the population as a whole, continued to be seriously under-represented' in the grammar schools – constituting only 15 per cent of the sample.[113] Middle-class boys also consistently outperformed working-class boys academically. Despite the social acclaim that working-class children gained from entry to grammar school, these could be uncomfortable places, arousing awareness of social difference and even inferiority in relation to middle-class pupils and teachers. Jackson and Marsden described the confusion afflicting many working-class children when the schools' middle-class ethos displaced the 'mesh of securities, expectations, [and] recognitions' that comprised children's 'neighbourhood'.[114]

Interviewees from working-class homes repeatedly recalled the social isolation that followed separation from neighbourhood friends. Sandy Irving had attended King James Grammar School from 1950 and, as a Huddersfield boy, knowingly situated his experiences against Jackson and Marsden's high-profile study: 'It was very striking when I went to

grammar school how different it was, and how different the people
were compared to the people on our council estate. In fact one lad with
whom I became friends owned the factory where my father worked.'[115]
During these years Sandy had continued the regular Sunday visits to
his great uncle to 'read the *Daily Worker* and to listen his opinions'.
He gradually came to connect his early experiences of social alterity
with his uncle's Communism and to see 'it in terms of a system rather
than just a random thing'. Val Graham remembered how the Eleven
Plus raised questions about Chesterfield's patterns of social organisation
and who she was: 'What I saw was that there was this division that
some children were sent off to schools in town, right, in Chesterfield,
and other children had to go to the local school and that's what I
couldn't understand. I couldn't understand how I could be separated
from my friends at that time.'[116] Working-class children managed the
strangeness or 'haze' of grammar school in different ways. Jackson and
Marsden noted that where antagonism arose against 'the formal school
orthodoxies', this usually occurred when children chose to align their
loyalties to the neighbourhood rather than the school.[117] Fred Lindop
retained a sense of himself as a 'neighbourhood' boy by negotiating 'hated'
authoritarian middle-class structures.[118] His 'conservative atheism' represented one dimension of his alienated self, and his intellectual identity
became another:

> School was very much about competition and one of the ways in which
> I survived and became simultaneously integrated and drawn in was
> through academic competition ... that became one way of establishing
> myself as having some kind of value in comparison with the people who
> came from better-off backgrounds than me.

Absorbing himself within his studies offered Fred an identity that was
simultaneously 'within' and 'against' the school, and a way of coping
with the discomfort he felt within its dominant middle-class culture.
Like other working-class children, his school friendships displayed his
neighbourhood loyalties. The boys expressed 'pretty reactionary ideas'
against hypocrisies and injustices they too saw in the community.
Fred remembered one notable incident 'in the lower sixth, being very
angry about the way in which the local girls' direct grant school, which
was just down the road, the way the girls there related to the better-off
boys'. This resentment echoed the angry working-class masculinity
redolent in 'Angry Young Men' literature and films circulating at the
time. John Charlton described how, at Newcastle Boys' Grammar
School, his circle of working-class friends also introduced him to ways
of thinking about himself and the world through a socialist perspective:

'I gravitated towards other boys who probably felt the same as I did [about class] . . . one or two boys who were from socialist homes and Labour homes, and I think I was in the sixth form when the Suez event occurred, and I absolutely clearly remember myself starting off actually by myself supporting the government, but being ridiculed by other boys who were just totally antagonistic to it.'[119]

It was not only grammar schools that had the capacity to arouse class consciousness and antagonism towards the social order. The male boarding school also held a prominent place in the coming-of-age narratives of men from lower middle- or middle-class origins. The emotionally stilted ethos of the public school was a common source of hostility amongst sensitive, critically thinking adolescent boys. Antagonism towards middle-class fathers often fed into expressions of resistance against the authoritarian masculinity of Victorian institutions which for generations had supplied the military personnel and civil servants intended to run the British Empire. Despite the national retreat from Empire, narratives of imperial manliness remained at large in 1950s culture, inscribed especially in the values of elite all-male institutions overwhelmingly populated by boys of the upper and middle classes. The minority of lower middle-class boys who won direct grant scholar-ships identified a double sense of exclusion that combined class identity with emotional alienation from the schools' colonial masculine codes. Mike McGrath spoke of loneliness and a search for self at Dulwich College, one of the more prestigious direct grant schools that sought to perform a socially conditioning role. With the expansion of the social catchment of grammar and independent schools, teachers' fears that 'parity of esteem' would weaken 'every part of national life' led to efforts to strengthen traditionalism. Initiatives like cadet schemes and military training were designed to support imperial masculine codes that had dominated the schools since their late-Victorian heyday.[120] Mike's consciousness of 'difference' from the relative privilege of Dulwich's pupils compounded the isolation of his boyhood in RAF camps. He explained 'it less [in terms] of being conscious of an insecurity, but more so defining myself against them, and just not being like them, so being different from them'.[121] But his unhappiness derived more from the emotional codes of manliness which institutions like Dulwich demanded of their pupils, the public/private divide denying any public space for expressing social or psychic vulnerability.

The schools' codes did not promote identities to allow young men to incorporate and make sense of feelings associated with their pasts. Consequently, where boys had experienced emotionally turbulent child-hoods they entered adolescence feeling displaced and in search of a language that might offer clues for self-discovery. Dave Lyddon won a scholarship to Christ's Hospital School in Horsham, West Sussex in 1958. His entry coincided with his mother's arrival home following her long stays in psychiatric hospitals since his birth. As in Mike's case, his boyhood years had also been marked by remote parental relations, having been raised primarily by his father and yet apart from him emotionally. His own memories of isolation showed the loss of early sustaining friendships with working-class boys from his neighbourhood:

> I was eleven years old, what the hell do I know, you know? [I was] a kind of very naive little lad, so I end up going to this strange place, where you are incarcerated I suppose for thirty-nine weeks of the year. There were quite long holidays . . . but you are kind of torn away from your peer group who you gradually loose contact with because they only see you in the holidays, whatever, and they develop new friendships.[122]

The interweaving between first- and second-person pronouns denoted the painful loneliness of Dave's boyhood self. As an adult he expressed the anger he had been unable to register or articulate as a vulnerable child.

The men's narratives point to the complex range of responses they developed to define themselves against the masculine rituals which fathers and the public school tried to instil. During the self-searching of adolescence these young men adopted modes of selfhood primarily to signify who or what they were not. Individually, and collectively with other boys, cultural and political symbols of alterity opened up imaginative sites of alternative masculinity. At Dulwich Mike found a brief public space for individuality in the chapel, by refusing to kneel for prayers. Dave Lyddon's sensations of class identity saw him forming intense friendships with boys from similar backgrounds sustained by ties of hostility towards the elitist culture of Christ's Hospital. He also began to rebel against his father when at home during the holidays. Resentment against the injustice of suffering found expression against a parent who visibly embodied the school's authoritarian values. At Liverpool College Max Farrar imaginatively countered the emotional closure that marked constructions of admirable masculinity. In 1962 he returned from the summer vacation with a new collection of reading: Ernest Hemingway's *For Whom the Bell Tolls*, John Steinbeck's *The Grapes of Wrath* and J. D. Salinger's 1951 account of teenage angst and alienation, *The Catcher in the Rye*, and projected onto the male protagonists his own private confusions of self. In these novels he met characters who were striving to inhabit an emotionally deeper world; identifying with them, he surreptitiously reclaimed 'the forbidden feminine' that the Victorian system sought to expunge.[123] He explained:

'I suddenly realised there was a whole world out there . . . something like the Spanish Civil War in *For Whom the Bell Tolls* was opening me to a whole new world of ideas, culture, and of course whatever else you say about Hemingway it is emotionally charged.'[124] Simultaneously, he embarked on friendships with boys who helped him to give social form to his internal dissident narratives. Consciousness of race, otherness and the struggle for civil rights came within his adolescent purview during whispered, prohibited conversations after lights out, when his half-Trinidadian friend revealed his discomfort in his father's middle-class, Liverpool medical circles: 'He said, "When I go home at the holidays everybody goes silent when I walk into the room." And I said, "Why would they?" . . . he said . . . I remember it like a bolt from the blue, "Because I'm black".' Surrounded by perverse, unjust authorities, and in the context of the schools' imperial codes, the American civil rights movement became a common point for introjective identification, and the boys began to read the novels of civil rights activist James Baldwin. The image of the non-white male struggling for self-determination provided a sort of self-distancing from their own immediate troubles. It gave their internal narratives a political edge and an imaginative social selfhood that felt empowering.

Through another friend Max became drawn into the bohemian youth subculture that by the early sixties had evolved around a cohort of writers and intellectuals that American commentators labelled 'Angry Young Men' and whose critical opposition to 'the Establishment' provided a collective voice for socially discontented youth. This dissident subculture, which found a moral cause in the Bomb and political expression in CND, imbued what Kenneth Tynan termed 'instinctive Leftism': with its 'kitchen sink' drama and provincial writers of working-class origin, it decried the class hierarchy of British society.[125] Criticism of 'the Establishment' focused on the informal power structure or 'old boy network' whose moral hypocrisy and political ineptitude were pilloried over the Eden government's handling of the Suez crisis in 1956. Other cultural components included jazz, folk song, American beatnik and French existentialist literature, along with an affinity for new-wave films and American rhythm and blues. From jazz to Sartre, Kerouac, Camus and Colin Wilson's philosophical examination of *The Outsider*, all seemed to speak for the first adult wave of working-class grammar school graduates coming through the Butler Education Act. Max 'lapped up' subcultural currents that encouraged his developing class dissidence as well as his willingness to resist unjust acts. By the time he read Alan Sillitoe's *The Loneliness of the Long Distance Runner* at sixteen, he was ready to display his own great act of refusal by rejecting the school's weekly officer training course. He recalled his identification with Sillitoe's Smith and how he integrated the narrative into his own sense of self: 'I very quickly realised that what in fact I was doing, which was always getting into trouble, always telling people what I thought of them, and then getting caned for it.' For public school boys like Max, Mike and Dave, the dissident subculture offered opportunities to assume the modern reflexive selfhood that the Victorian 'Establishment' constrained. It offered temporary relief from uneasy class consciousness and emotional hunger that spoke of 'a still existent division between "athletes" and "aesthetes"' dating back to the 1870s.[126]

Max's story offers a useful perspective for understanding the meaning early youth subcultures acquired for young activists. There was no predetermined path between these and the late-sixties network. Adolescents who found strong affinity with early radical subcultures did not necessarily follow this through into fully fledged activism. Often what radical subcultures offered was quite mundane, relief from the embrace of everyday conformity. But for young individuals who in the sixth form, at university or shortly thereafter began to gravitate towards New Left spaces, the dissident subcultures of the late fifties and early sixties marked signposts along their leftward journeys. They provided *ways of coping* with the uncertainty of adolescence and the social and political dislocations this entailed, whether at home, at school or in the wider world.[127] The early subcultures provided alternative, subversive yet psychologically safe spaces in which to discover an early sense of social and political self.

Notes

1 S. J. Charlesworth, *A Phenomenology of Working-Class Experience* (Cambridge: Cambridge University Press, 2000), p. 20.

2 C. Steedman, *Landscape for a Good Woman: A Story of Two Lives* (London: Virago, 1986), p. 121; A. Carter, 'Truly It Felt Like Year One', in S. Maitland (ed.), *Very Heaven: Looking Back at the 1960s* (London: Virago, 1988), pp. 209–16; L. Heron (ed.), *Truth, Dare or Promise: Girls Growing Up in the Fifties* (London: Virago, 1985).

3 D. G. Macrae, 'The Culture of a Generation: Students and Others', *Journal of Contemporary History*, 2:3 (1967), pp. 1–11; M. Mead, *Culture and Commitment: A Study of the Generation Gap* (London: Bodley Head, 1970); G. I. M. Robertson, 'The Generation Gap and the Defence of Britain', *Contemporary Review*, 242 (1983), pp. 71–7.

4 T. H. Marshall, 'Citizenship and Social Class', in *Sociology at the Crossroads* (London: Heinemann, 1963), p. 72, cited in Rose, *Governing the Soul*, p. 124.

5 Rose, *Governing the Soul*, p. 124.

6 C. Kaplan, *Sea Changes: Culture and Feminism* (London: Verso, 1986), pp. 4–5.

7 S. Alexander, 'Memory Talk: London Childhoods', in S. Radstone, and B. Schwarz (eds), *Memory: Histories, Theories, Debates* (New York: Ford University Press, 2010), p. 236.

8 P. Thompson, 'Family Myths, Models and Desires in the Shaping of Individual Life Paths', in D. Bertaux, and P. Thompson (eds), *International Year Book of Oral History and Life Stories: Between Generations: Family Myths, Models and Memories*, Vol. 2 (Oxford: Oxford University Press, 1993), pp. 14–37.

9 Alexander, 'Memory Talk', p. 236.

10 C. Steedman, *Strange Dislocations: Childhood and the Idea of Human Interiority, 1790–1930* (London: Virago, 1995), p. 19; R. Williams, 'Culture is Ordinary', reprinted in A. Gray and J. McGuigan (eds), *Studying Culture: An Introductory Reader* (London: Arnold, 1993), pp. 5–6.

11 Ibid.

12 C. Langhamer, 'The Meanings of Home in Post-war Britain', *Journal of Contemporary History*, 40:2 (2005), p. 361.

13 King, 'Hidden Fathers?', p. 38.

14 S. Brooke, '"Slumming" in Swinging London? Class, Gender and the Post-War City in Nell Dunn's *Up the Junction* (1963)', *Cultural and Social History*, 9:3 (2012), pp. 429–49; S. Brooke, 'Gender and Working Class Identity in Britain during the 1950s', *Journal of Social History*, 34 (2001), pp. 773–95; Langhamer, 'The Meanings of Home', pp. 341–62; Savage, 'Affluence and Social Change'; S. Todd, 'Affluence, Class and Crown Street: Reinvesting the Post-War Working Class', *Contemporary British History*, 22:4 (2008), p. 510.

15 P. Thane, 'Introduction. Exploring Post-War Britain', *Cultural and Social History*, 9:2 (2012), p. 273.

16 Interview with Sue Bruley, London, 14 May, 2010.

17 Todd, 'Affluence, Class and Crown Street', p. 502.

18 E. Roberts, *Women and Families: An Oral History, 1940–1970* (Oxford: Blackwell, 1995), p. 93.

19 Steedman, *Landscape for a Good Woman*, p. 144.

20 Interview with Alan Woodward, London, 2 January, 2009.

21 Cited in D. Kynaston, *Family Britain 1951–57* (London: Bloomsbury, 2009), p. 135.

22 Savage, *Identities and Social Change*, p. 219.

23 R. Samuel, *The Lost World of British Communism* (London: Verso, 2006), p. 10.

24 J. Bourke, *Working-Class Cultures in Britain 1890–1960* (London: Routledge, 1994), p. 25.

25 F. Mort, 'Social and Symbolic Fathers and Sons in Postwar Britain', *Journal of British Studies*, 38:3 (1999), p. 364.

26 Interview with Sheila Hemingway, Leeds, 7 June, 2009.
27 Interview with John Charlton, Newcastle-upon-Tyne, 2 June, 2009.
28 Interview with Judith Milner, London, 2 December, 2008.
29 Interview with Roger Cox, London, 24 March, 2009.
30 Samuel, *The Lost World*, p. 63.
31 Ibid.
32 Interview with Sandy Irving, Newcastle-upon-Tyne, 2 June, 2009.
33 R. Hoggart, *The Uses of Literacy* (Harmondsworth: Penguin, 1961), p. 72.
34 Interview with Bob Light, London, 28 March, 2009.
35 Interview with Laurie Flynn, London, 23 December, 2008.
36 Interview with Martin Shaw, Brighton, 15 January, 2009.
37 P. Hennessy and G. Brownfeld, 'Britain's Cold War Security Purge: The Origins of Positive Vetting', *Historical Journal*, 25:4 (1982), pp. 966–7.
38 Interview with Wenda Clenaghen, London, 22 January, 2009.
39 J. Eaden and D. Renton, *The Communist Party of Great Britain since 1920* (Basingstoke: Palgrave Macmillan, 2002), pp. 106–7.
40 Ibid., p. 109.
41 Samuel, *The Lost World of British Communism*, p. 14.
42 M. Rosen, 'All in the Family', in P. Cohen (ed.), *Children of the Revolution: Communist Childhood in Cold War Britain* (London: Lawrence and Wishart, 1997), pp. 52–4.
43 Interview with Sarah Cox, London, 24 March, 2009.
44 Interview with John Cowley, London, 22 January, 2009.
45 P. Waterman, 'Hopeful Traveller: The Itinerary of an Internationalist', *History Workshop Journal*, Spring, 35 (1993), p. 171.
46 Interview with Steve Jefferys, London, 13 November, 2008.
47 M. Wandor, *Once a Feminist: Stories of a Generation* (London: Virago, 1990).
48 S. Rowbotham, *Woman's Consciousness, Man's World* (Harmondsworth: Penguin, 1973), p. 43.
49 C. Steedman, 'Writing the Self: The End of the Scholarship Girl', in J. McGuigan (ed.), *Cultural Methodologies* (London: Sage, 1997), p. 109.
50 S. Alexander, 'Two Women's Lives in the Inter-War Year', in *Becoming a Woman: and Other Essays in 19th and 20th Century Feminist History* (London: Virago, 1994), p. 234.
51 M. Roper, 'Between Manliness and Masculinity: The "War Generation" and the Psychology of Fear in Britain, 1914–1950', *Journal of British Studies*, 44:2 (2005), pp. 343–62.
52 Langhamer, 'The Meanings of Home', p. 356.
53 King, 'Hidden Fathers?', p. 27.
54 M. Francis, 'A Flight from Commitment? Domesticity, Adventure and the Masculine Imaginary in Britain after the Second World War', *Gender and History*, 19:1 (2007), pp. 163–85.
55 M. Francis, *The Flyer: British Culture and the Royal Airforce 1939–1945* (Oxford: Oxford University Press, 2008), pp. 97–105.

56 A. Allport, *Demobbed: Coming Home after the Second World War* (London: Yale, 2009), pp. 68–74.
57 Interview with Mike McGrath, Leeds, 3 June, 2009.
58 G. Dawson, *Soldier Heroes: British Adventure, Empire and the Imagining of Masculinities* (London: Routledge, 1994), p. 22.
59 Interview with Mike McGrath.
60 Interview with Dave Lyddon, Keele, 15 July, 2009.
61 C. Rawlence, 'Stokowski's Socks', in J. Hoyland (ed.), *Fathers and Sons* (London: Serpent's Tail, 1992), pp. 77–9.
62 Interview with Chris Rawlence, Chipping Norton, 29 August, 2012.
63 Interview with Ian Birchall, London, 4 November, 2008.
64 L. Passerini, *Autobiography of a Generation*, Italy 1968 (translated by Lisa Erdberg, Middletown: Wesleyan University Press, 1996), p. 26.
65 Ronald Fraser interview with respondent C896/18, April 1984, 9 October, 1984, pp. 9–10, Ronald Fraser Interviews: 1968 – A Student Generation in Revolt, British Library Sound Archive.
66 L. King, 'Fatherhood and Masculinity in Britain, c. 1918–1960' (Unpublished PhD thesis, University of Sheffield, September, 2011), p. 161.
67 M. Young and P. Willmott, *Family and Kinship in East London* (London: Pelican, 1957), pp. 28–9.
68 J. Newson and E. Newson, *Patterns of Infant Care in an Urban Community* (Harmondsworth: Penguin, 1965), pp. 133–4.
69 Interview with Martin Tompkinson, London, 6 November, 2008.
70 J. Hoyland, 'The Man with the Bright Red Trousers', in J. Hoyland (ed.), *Fathers and Sons* (London: Serpent's Tail, 1992), p. 150.
71 Interview with John Hoyland, London, 4 March, 2009.
72 L. Abrams, 'Mothers and Daughters: Negotiating the Discourse on the "Good Woman", in 1950s and 1960s Britain', p. 74.
73 M. Ingham, *Now We Are Thirty: Women of the Breakthrough Generation* (London: Eyre Methuen, 1981).
74 Interview with Caroline Bond, Leeds, 5 June, 2009.
75 The diary of Prue, 20 September, 1964, p. 43, in the private papers of Prue Chamberlayne.
76 C. G. Brown, 'Sex, Religion and the Single Woman, c. 1950–75: The Importance of a "Short" Sexual Revolution to the English Religious Crisis of the Sixties', *Twentieth-Century British History*, 22:2 (2011), pp. 189–215.
77 Interview with Judith Herren, London, 5 March, 2009.
78 Interview with Jane Storr, Leeds, 4 June, 2009.
79 T. Kushner, 'Anti-Semitism and Austerity: The August 1947 Riots', in P. Panayi (ed.), *Racial Violence in Britain 1840–1950* (Leicester: Leicester University Press, 1993), p. 159.
80 D. Cesarani, *Justice Delayed: How Britain became a Refuge for Nazi War Criminals* (London: Phoenix, 1992), p. 81.

81 Kushner, 'Anti-Semitism and Austerity', pp. 159–60.

82 Interview with Victor Seidler, London, 13 December, 2011.

83 Interview with Mica Nava, London, 20 November, 2010.

84 M. Nava, *Visceral Cosmopolitanism: Gender, Culture and the Normalisation of Difference* (Oxford: Berg, 2007), pp. 138–9.

85 Interview with Lee Comer, Leeds, 3 June, 2009.

86 Interview with Anna Paczuska, London, 4 January, 2010.

87 Interview with James Swinson, London, 2 February, 2010.

88 Interview with Bob Light.

89 Brown, 'Sex, Religion and the Single Woman', pp. 189–215.

90 Kynaston, *Family Britain*, p. 536.

91 P. Willmott and M. Young, *Family and Class in a London Suburb* (London: New English Library, 1960), pp. 82–3.

92 S. Rowbotham, 'Revolt in Roundhay', in L. Heron (ed.), *Truth, Dare or Promise* (London: Virago, 1985), p. 199.

93 Interview with Fred Lindop, Wareham, 13 January, 2009.

94 Interview with Ian Birchall.

95 Interview with Wisty Hoyland, London, 21 January, 2009.

96 B. Jackson, *Working Class Community* (London: Routledge, 1968), pp. 136–7.

97 Interview with Gilda Peterson, Leeds, 4 June, 2009.

98 C. Steedman, 'State Sponsored Autobiography', in B. Conekin, F. Mort and C. Waters (eds), *Moments of Modernity: Reconstructing Britain 1945–1964* (London: Rivers Oram Press, 1999), pp. 41–55.

99 Interview with James Hinton, Coventry, 20 November, 2008.

100 M. Grant, *After the Bomb: Civil Defence and Nuclear War, 1945–68* (Basingstoke: Palgrave Macmillan, 2010), pp. 64–7.

101 Interview with Gilda Peterson.

102 Interview with Hilary Wainwright, London, 26 November, 2009.

103 Rowbotham, *Promise of a Dream*, p. 9.

104 M. Evans, *A Good School: Life at a Girl's Grammar School in the 1950s* (London: Women's Press, 1991), p. 56.

105 Interview with Bronwen Davis, Llanishen, 17 June, 2009.

106 Interview with Caroline Bond and Gilda Peterson, Leeds, 5 June, 2009.

107 Interview with Joan Smith, London, 20 March, 2009.

108 Interview with Val Graham, Chesterfield, 17 October, 2009.

109 Interview with Hilary Wainwright.

110 P. Long, *Only in the Common People: the Aesthetics of Class in Post-War Britain* (Newcastle: Cambridge Scholars, 2008), p. 217.

111 J. Floud, A. H. Halsey and F. M. Martin (eds), *Social Class and Educational Opportunity* (London: Heinemann, 1956); B. Jackson and D. Marsden, *Education and the Working-Class: Some General Themes Raised by a Study of 88 Children in a Northern Industrial City* (Harmondsworth: Penguin, 1966); Ministry of Education, *Half Our Future: A Report of the Central Advisory Council for Education (England)* (London, Her Majesty's

Stationery Office, 1963) (The Newsom Report); *Children and their Primary Schools: A Report of the Central Advisory Council for Education (England)* (London, Her Majesty's Stationery Office, 1967) (The Plowden Report).

112 P. Long, *Only in the Common People: the Aesthetics of Class in Post-War Britain* (Newcastle: Cambridge Scholars, 2008), p. 217.

113 H. T. Himmelweit, 'Social Status and Secondary Education since the 1944 Act', in D. Kynaston (ed.), *Austerity Britain 1945–51* (2nd edn London: Bloomsbury, 2008), p. 575.

114 B. Jackson and D. Marsden, *Education and the Working Class* (Harmondsworth: Penguin, 1969), p. 110.

115 Interview with Sandy Irving.

116 Interview with Val Graham.

117 Jackson and Marsden, *Education and the Working Class*, p. 122.

118 Interview with Fred Lindop.

119 Interview with John Charlton.

120 R. Lowe, *Education in the Post-War Years: A Social History* (London: Routledge, 1988), p. 109.

121 Interview with Mike McGrath.

122 Interview with Dave Lyddon.

123 P. M. Lewis, 'Mummy, Matron and the Maids: Feminine presence and absence in male institutions, 1934–63', in M. Roper and J. Tosh (eds), *Manful Assertions: Masculinities in Britain since 1800* (London: Routledge, 1991), p. 182.

124 Interview with Max Farrar, Leeds, 5 June, 2009.

125 A. Sinfield, *Literature, Culture and Politics in Postwar Britain* (Oxford: Basil Blackwell, 1989), p. 240.

126 G. Stedman Jones, 'History and Theory: An English Story', in *Historien: European Ego-histoires: Historiography and the Self, 1979–2000*, vol. 3 (2001), p. 108.

127 Sinfield, *Literature, Culture and Politics*, p. 108.

2

Youth subcultures

The New Left cultures that emerged around the VSC in the mid-1960s grew from radical subcultures young activists shaped earlier in the decade. Encounters with these subcultures often occurred in adolescence, the transitional period contemporaries generally regarded as spanning the years between fourteen and twenty-one, between childhood and legal adult age. For most young activists entry into the network around the VSC coincided with the first years of university, so that early-sixties subcultures bridged the social and psychological uncertainties of youth. The final section of the previous chapter began to consider the significance of radical literature and drama for a cohort of public school boys struggling to express subjectivities away from their schools' elite, upper middle-class culture. This chapter develops this theme to explore how early subcultural encounters and national and international politics interacted with childhood structures of feeling and seeing.

Sixties contemporaries have testified to the appeal youth culture exercised as a resource for selfhood, whether to enact imaginative scenarios or to inhabit alternative real spaces away from the adult generation.[1] However, historians have shown little interest in pursuing this further to understand the relationship between youth culture, post-war society and individual subjectivities. This chapter offers to address this gap by examining some of the complex ways in which young sixties activists embraced dissident cultures in efforts to make sense of themselves and their place in the world. It argues that radical subcultures performed specific social and psychological roles for young men and women starting to critically question the post-war 'consensus'. It shows how childhood histories and daily adolescent experience gave individual meaning to 'angry' literature and theatre, new-wave films and the radical Bomb culture surrounding CND to provide new ways of seeing social norms, relationships and Cold War politics. In the late 1950s and early 1960s dissident subcultures spoke to youngsters' concern with the tangible and the present that the unfairness and instability of the surrounding world provoked. Hearing calls for autonomous action, they attempted to resolve their uncertainties about class, gender and politics, and discovered possibilities for living out individual subjectivities of alterity. The chapter explores the political, social and gendered dynamics of the left cultures preceding the late-sixties extra-parliamentary scene. Specific attention is focused on the YS and the IS and IMG as milieux that bridged the collapse of CND and the growth of the student movement and the VSC in the mid-1960s.

Selfhood in the sixth

Many interviewees first encountered radical cultural movements during the sixth form. Their testimonies highlight the relationship between expanding secondary education and the increasing opportunities sixties youth had for thinking about subjectivity. Central to the attitudinal changes associated with post-war teenagers was recognition of the individual agency young people were exercising in their working and social lives. Historians of social youth movements have noted that in order to compete with the new commercial youth cultures, older-established movements recognised the need to redefine their Victorian philosophies away from character building towards self-discovery and self-development.[2] Post-fifteen education supported social understandings of youth as a time of personal growth. Teachers were often active in this process. The previous chapter showed female teachers encouraging intellectual endeavour among sixties girls. Mary Ingham recalled the 'oasis of stimulation' marking her sixth-form days: 'our minds were being tuned and primed, travelling around the world, back in time, communicating in foreign languages, conducting experiments, making calculations'.[3] More generally, by the sixth form teachers' assumptions that pupils staying on at school would be heading for university or training colleges often fostered less restrictive intellectual environments. Pupils studying the arts experienced a change in the style of learning from a 'mechanical', knowledge-based model to one that emphasised understanding and discussion.[4] John Charlton has noted how in Newcastle grammar schools 'superior class attitudes heard from teaching staff to pupils miraculously disappeared', in the expectation that pupils heading for university or college would be 'joining a club to which the masters and mistresses already belonged'.[5] Teachers occasionally became more open in their political opinions. It was in the sixth form that Joan Smith's history teacher handed her a copy of *Das Kapital*. General studies lessons encouraged pupils to develop opinions about the world. Sandy Irving remembered general studies lessons as 'quite a forum . . . The teacher just used to sort of mention something and . . . there was enough people in the class who were happy just to talk, to spend the lesson talking.'[6] John Charlton reflected that 'the sixth form at grammar school was critically important to me. That was the narrowing down of people who thought, talked, talked about ideas . . . We were interested in history and literature and current affairs. There was lots of argument, lots of discussion going on all the time.'[7]

For the minority of working- and middle-class young people staying on to take A levels, the sixth form offered space in which to make or postpone decisions about the future. For some it was an opportunity for introverted dreaming, but for most it represented a time in which to explore the self in relation to the outside world. Gilda Peterson supposed that by the time she entered the sixth form in 1966, she had 'some kind of sense of Europe, and who am I, because I . . . spent a lot of time in the public library, because we had very few books in the house'.[8] She also enrolled in a philosophy class: 'I suppose my main aim there was, what's the meaning of life? What's it all about? What's consciousness about, and in that sense I suppose a wider political thing.' At King William's College, on the Isle of Man, David Carter remembered how 'in the sixth form, we used to get the newspapers delivered and there was a reading room, and I'd just read them voraciously for news of what was going on elsewhere'.[9] Contradictions between personal choices open to educated youth and the authoritarian restrictions associated with age, class, race and gender often made the sixth form a time in which individuals strove for more authentic models of selfhood. David's appetite for current affairs reflected his intense dislike for the stiff-upper-lip ethos that public school boys in the previous chapter objected to. Cut off from the cultural and political developments happening on mainland Britain, reading news reports and cultural reviews offered him an avenue into the permissiveness associated with 'Swinging London'.

Other individuals remembered personal conflicts beginning to be interwoven into wider political and cultural narratives. In 1966, Bronwen Davis' entry into the sixth form coincided with her mother's return from Nigeria, where Bronwen's father was a civil servant. She and her younger brother had spent the previous year in England supervised by family and friends. She remembered the profound effect of the separation: 'It made me very angry with my mother. I really, really . . . I hated her when she came back.'[10] Confused sensations of abandonment and the pressures of defining herself against the expectations of school and peers fed into angry protests against American imperialism through CND marches and demonstrations against the Vietnam War. Bronwen's activism at seventeen denoted a quest for self. Hers were independent ventures, conducted apart from school friends and complemented by hours searching bookshelves and the noticeboards below CND's King's Cross office.

Self-searching, profuse reading experiences and intellectual discoveries characterised stories of these years. Scholarship boys and girls repeatedly journeyed to the library in search of answers; mapping the world through radical reading experiences offered to offset the uncertainty youngsters felt about the future, who they were and what to make of adult society. As sixth-formers they began to make connections between childhood structures of feeling and an intellectual framework of ideas, developing ways of seeing that, by university, saw them affiliating to the radical Left.

'Angry Young Men' and women: radical literature and drama

Despite the cultural and social significance scholars have attributed to the new wave and 'Angry Young Men' movements, little attention has been given to the individual ways in which working- and lower middle-class sixties youngsters were reading these social realist genres. Feminists have critiqued the aggressive hostility which male protagonists exhibited towards female characters associated with conspicuous consumption patterns thought to be eroding traditional working-class communities and cultures.[11] However, young men's engagement with these heroic masculine models needs to be understood in the specific context of their individual histories. In novels, on stage and on screen, the 'Angry Young Man' spoke directly to the vital experiences of class that working-class grammar school boys had been struggling to make sense of. John Charlton's memories of his halcyon sixth-form days saw him relating the bond of identity which 'Angry Young Men' literature gave him to his Newcastle cohort. Sharing the movement's cultural 'effervescence' around class, John had felt himself 'floating' in its antagonistic spirit because the authors' revolt echoed his own embarrassed discomfort as a chauffeur's son denied entry to neighbouring genteel middle-class households. Kingsley Amis' *Lucky Jim* (1954) was 'an absolute' favourite: 'We loved it, we absolutely loved it. In our sixth-form common room we might even read out chunks of it. It was a big giggle . . . They were a bit older than us those angry young men . . . but I guess they were sharing the same kind of assault, really, on the establishment, on establishment outlooks.'[12] The boys also read avidly the reviews of John Osborne's 1956 seminal play *Look Back in Anger*, too far from London to see it on stage. The play spoke to John, as it did to a wider cohort of working- and lower middle-class scholarship boys, because he heard within it 'lessons in feeling' which Osborne had intended to evoke as a means of breaking down class barriers.[13] Tynan noted that the 'salient thing about Jimmy Porter was that we – the under-thirty generation in Britain – recognised him on sight. We had met him; we had shared bed-sitting rooms with him.'[14] Whilst John and his friends were, in 1956–57, too young to have shared Porter's seminal experiences, as adolescents they spoke his and Jim Dixon's provincial class idiom; the anger which the protagonists exuded towards the established order was rich in the same vital engagement that the Newcastle boys were beginning to make in relation to domestic Labour and international politics.

As mentioned briefly in the previous chapter, the 'Angry Young Man' spoke equally to middle-class boys whose experiences of home and school placed them at emotional odds with the hypocrisies and trivialities of conservative middle-class society and culture. In 1958 eighteen-year-old Ian Birchall saw Osborne's play performed by a provincial repertory company and found it 'absolutely electrifying'.[15] His hostility to Suez had by now confirmed him as a 'Labour man' and, like other scholarship boys, his identification with the class-conscious working man was coupled with an intellectual persona that extended his reading to French existentialist literature, Marxist histories and seminal Marxist publications. The 'Angry Young Men' movement fed a heroic working-class male mythology that began with earlier literary encounters and reached a crescendo during his Oxford undergraduate years, when he came across influential left men from working-class backgrounds. He particularly remembered the future dramatist Dennis Potter, whose critiques of the decaying establishment he heard in the Labour Club and read in *Isis* (Oxford's university magazine):

> I hero-worshipped him . . . He had come from a mining family and then he had come to Oxford, and he used to come out with this sense of [. . .] the division of the values of where he had come from, and the values of Oxford . . . He was a very fine speaker, a good writer, and very much this sense of class loyalty and so on . . . this just hit me very powerfully.

Simultaneously *Clarion*, the magazine of the National Association of Labour Students, introduced him to the writings of the Marxist Ken Coates. Ian recalled how his admiration for this Trotskyist sympathiser grew after he discovered that Coates had opted to work as a miner rather than to fight as a conscript against Communist and Nationalist guerrillas in Malaya. His idealised image of Coates as a real-life radical labourer may well have been coloured by his own recent exemption from national service: 'I think I probably romanticised this a bit, because again, in the fifties, national service was compulsory. I had just missed this by about six months which I was delighted about. Later on I felt slightly guilty and thought as a revolutionary [I] should have learned to fire a gun.'

Ian's earliest introduction to an 'aggressively "working-class hero"' had come in the form of Alf Tupper, the central character in the boys' comic *Rover*, which he read between the ages of seven and fourteen. Tupper was a welder and amateur athlete who trained in his spare time by running around the gasworks, his fish-and-chip diet identifiably working class. Hilary Young has highlighted the character model that Tupper served as a working-class anti-hero set against 'the official discourse of middle-class respectability and ideal middle-class masculinity, and exemplified in other boy's [*sic*] publications such as *Eagle* and *Boy's Own Paper*'.[16] Tupper's adventures provided an affective reading experience for working-class boys because they felt able to identify with his poor living conditions. Removed from Tupper's harsh environment, Ian gained a different sort of identification, but one which provided a similar imaginative experience. He read the stories while hearing his parents' conservative attitudes and moral judgements, and becoming aware that something about these made him feel uneasy. For both middle- and working-class boys Tupper's triumph over adversity offered a means of escaping from the uncomfortable reality of everyday life. The social recognition boys found in Tupper related to the contested power relations they saw at home and school, as well as the desirable physical attributes he embodied as an image of 1950s sporting masculinity.

Literature that resonated with young men's felt dislocations helped to frame their experiences collectively and swathed their understandings of class and identity with several layers of meaning. Bob Tressell's *The Ragged Trousered Philanthropists* and its 1967 television adaptation enabled seventeen-year-old Sandy Irving to make sense of his boyhood anger towards his uncle's employers. The novel's biting Marxist analysis gave him a political language with which to relate his inner experiences to a wider community of social relationships. He realised, 'there were different groups and one group perhaps gained at the expense of other groups, and you might begin to use words like capitalism to describe what kind of society . . . it was and that it wasn't just that people were different. There was the notion of exploitation that I got from . . . books like that'.[17] He too read it as a sixth-former when, in 1967, an extra year of study allowed him intensive reading time in the public library. The discovery of 'people like Marx' occurred partly 'just out of curiosity, because some of my friends we used to argue about politics', but it was

only when he read some of Marx's shorter pamphlets in conjunction
with left-wing publications such as *Tribune*, *Labour Worker* and *International Socialism* that Marxism began to acquire contemporary
meaning. Together these texts equipped Sandy with a Marxist framework with which to make sense of formative political events around
1968: the Prague Spring, the May events in Paris and the televised
images and reports of the Vietnam War. He explained their role in
countering the initial allure of his uncle's Communism:

> I very much knew about Prague, and just looking at the Soviet Union,
> as you saw it on the television, it didn't look that much different from
> America. You had a Party elite with massive military power rather than
> anything different. I wasn't struck by a lot of what the *Daily Worker*
> said. Just somehow it didn't ring true to me ... The point is, I suppose,
> I was already predisposed to organisations that might advance different
> ideas on the subject.

Sandy's account illustrates the kaleidoscopic political and cultural
strands he and others absorbed during formative years of social and
intellectual maturation. The social recognition he found in left-wing
texts was complemented by other cultural mediums critiquing ruling
authorities. At a friend's house he heard Bob Dylan's protest lyrics,
which 'seemed to confirm what you were suspecting [about official
authority] already', and honed his critical voice by watching the popular
satirical television programme *That Was The Week That Was* (TW3).
This and *Private Eye* pilloried an elite establishment run by out-of-
touch, colonially shaped leaders. He heard their critiques as part of a
wider repertoire of political and cultural images out of which he constructed a dissenting male identity, culturally desirable and connected
to male images recognisable from his past. However, Sandy's testimony
also confirmed the gulf that other contemporaries have referred to
between the modernising impulses of sixties subcultures and the conservative local contexts in which they were sometimes received.[18] In
provincial settings old and new cultures added to the complexity with
which daily experience and individual histories coloured young men's
self-images, values and conduct. Sandy reflected on his engagement
with Huddersfield's working-class cultural traditions: 'There wasn't an
alternative counter-cultural scene in Huddersfield. It was quite a drab
place. In fact, I went to more classical music concerts because I was a
volunteer at the door of the Huddersfield Choral Society at the town
hall. Musically, I would have listened to more Wagner than Dylan.'
Alongside the brass band of the pit, the long-established choral tradition made classical music a feature of Huddersfield culture. In this

setting Sandy's musical tastes were not, as they were for others, a revolt against respectability and upper-class culture; rather, they affirmed an already discernible, locally rooted class identity combined with a socially critical conscience.

Scholarship boys' rebellious male heroes denoted 'cultural imaginaries', interrelated discursive themes, images, motifs and narrative forms that exist within a culture and are inhabitable by a community at a given time independently of an individual imaginer.[19] At a time when they were searching for identities to make sense of collective experiences, narratives of dissenting working-class men brought order to their social worlds by providing a common cultural framework for seeing. However, the men's testimonies also show the individual psychic investment they made within these imaginaries in accordance with their particular histories. Each saw different possibilities for being as working- or lower middle-class dissidents. As an eighteen-year-old David Carter projected his rebellious fantasies onto a range of film and musical male icons to construct an imaginative counter-cultural identity. They empowered him because he saw the men's anti-social behaviour at a real-life moment of personal release. In January 1969 York University offered him an unconditional place to read Politics, promising freedom from King William's College, the Isle of Man and the social conformity of a future centred on Athol Street's lower middle-class professionals. Immediately, the school's authority ceased to have any hold over him, and he 'had this real feeling of freedom':

> I remember going into Douglas, hitch-hiking in I think because we tended to do that, not that you were supposed to, not that I could've cared less, and going to see the Lindsay Anderson film *If*, and that was just like, I was traumatised by it in a quite positive way, because . . . it ends up with the boy, Malcolm McDowell, machine gunning most of the establishment in the school, and I remember coming back to the establishment in the school and saying 'God, you've got to see this film. It's unbelievable. It's like it's us. It's all our fantasies coming true.' You know, and that was a real formative thing. You know, there's hope beyond conformity.[20]

Some young men inhabited several cultural forms at any one time because of the range of possibilities each offered for psychic life. In 1957 twelve-year-old Victor Seidler saw himself mirrored in Colin Wilson's outsider. The artistic lives Wilson drew upon echoed the multiple social spaces and identities in which Victor sought belonging. The model spoke to his sense of exclusion at home, where his mother denied him the Jewish masculinity he associated with his deceased father. Her emphasis on the importance of practising Englishness placed pressure on him to embody a middle-class masculinity that created tensions in the mixed class world of his north London, Burnt Oak Grammar School: 'I played football a bit, not a lot, but a bit. I wasn't unsporty, so I wasn't the kind of nerd, and you moved between different worlds. So the masculinity of school, which was kind of working-class and opposition between the Catholic secondary modern school . . . and being able to defend yourself and fight, and knowing how to create alliances.'[21] Possibilities for expressing sensations of marginality came when Victor discovered a local youth club near to his Hendon home. Members were sons and daughters of Jewish families, many of them working class with a range of migration experiences. However, the fact that the youth club was a Jewish space gave Victor the belonging that his middle-class male peer group at school was unable to. The group introduced him to intellectual writings such as those of Martin Buber, whose work provided a route back to the Jewish cultural tradition Victor's father had introduced him to in the synagogue.

Women and early radical subcultures

Alternative subcultures presented more problematic meanings for young sixties women. Sheila Rowbotham noted that in 1961, when the 'idyllic working-class hero' was just arriving, there was no equivalent romantic literary genre for women.[22] Female icons accorded powerfully to the fifties reassertion of traditional femininity in an atmosphere when female emancipation was taken as given.[23] There was no female equivalent of Marlon Brando. Rowbotham's 'rag-bag' of ideal women, Mary Wollstonecraft, Olive Schreiner, Simone de Beauvoir and Doris Lessing, either were ensconced in the past or their lives seemed far removed from hers. Yet in the late 1950s and early 1960s young women were involved in youth subcultures that marked them out as dissident subjects. Angela McRobbie has highlighted the presence of teddy and 'mod' girls, noting their complementary but different patterns of behaviour from male peers.[24] How did young women make sense of their experiences of gender and class in relation to dissident masculine subcultures? One of the difficulties of trying to understand this question concerns the complexity of how they thought about themselves as gendered subjects. Rowbotham drew attention to this when she reflected that 'When I saw myself able to live as I wanted I didn't have any specific idea of myself as a woman doing whatever I would be doing. I would simply be doing things.'[25] For female interviewees, remembering how they had felt in relation to subcultures where female representations were few was a challenging and multilayered experience. They looked back through a feminist framework which had left a powerful imprint on their sense of selfhood. The women's feminist identities shaped their memories and thoughts about how they had related to cultural forms that had been influential for young left men. In certain instances this created problems for subjectivity and composure, especially where the women's memories failed to accord with representations of sixties femininity they had since encountered. Bronwen Davis showed the potential threat her own memories faced when held up against feminist discourses. Prior to our interview she had attended a workshop of Cardiff women who had all been active in the WLM. She mentioned feminist discussions she had heard about women's traditionally passive role in sixties culture. However, she became quite frustrated when unable to articulate her own sense of self in relation to these discourses. Her words 'I was just me' denoted the asexual terms in which she experienced herself as a teenager:

> I didn't identify myself as a woman at all. I was just me and you know ... when people talk about the impact of role models and media, cultural influences, and feminists talk about the fact, when we were growing up you would have just the representation of women in books and on television, it was in those days in the fifties and sixties all the people doing anything interesting, action, were men and the women ... and so that clearly wasn't going to be me, so I was going to be a man I suppose, except clearly I wasn't a man. I was just going to be me.[26]

Bronwen's interweaving between first- and third-person pronouns denoted the difficulty of situating her [remembered] adolescent sense of self in a temporal and cultural setting that could accommodate her individual and collective feminist identities. Her testimony illustrates how masculine, radical cultures added to the contradictory discourses constituting 'woman' that visibly prevailed when these women were shaping identities. For girls growing up in the 1950s, the fragile female dimension of their world presented a host of dualisms. They were exposed to contradictory images from their mothers, teachers and wider culture about what it meant to be a woman and what constituted appropriate feminine behaviour.[27] Whilst expanding education seemed to be opening up opportunities for them to take a more prominent part in public life, few of their mothers worked in full-time paid employment, they equated female teachers – their most immediate images of professional women – with spinsterhood and many of their mothers continued to voice hopes that university would provide opportunities to meet a 'good' husband. It is unsurprising that the world these women aspired to inhabit was masculine.

Gilda Peterson's unstable adolescent identity derived partly from the educational and social aspirations her grammar school teachers heaped on her, at odds with the model of working-class deference her mother presented. Far less confusing was the masculine realm she occupied as a girl: '[I] just wanted to be a boy, was in the guides and went camping, had two brothers, and so I didn't have much girly identity as a young child at all.'[28] The uncertainty of Gilda's female world was intertwined with the class dislocations school and home exuded. School elocution lessons taught her the unacceptability of her Hartlepool accent. Yet she never expressed the angry class consciousness several of her male counterparts displayed, adhering more closely to her mother's working-class deference:

> You knew what you couldn't do . . . a group of the girls, I was in a sort of gang and we did a lot of youth hostelling together . . . We had a lot of freedom, really. But I didn't do horse riding, for instance, like a few of them did, because it just wasn't in the question.

The cultural narrowness of Hartlepool precluded possibilities for seeing her situation in more critical terms. Before she went to Birmingham University in 1964, for example, Gilda had rarely seen a play. 'The odd thing you would see in Hartlepool was *Annie Get Your Gun,* or the *Wizard of Oz* might have been out by then, or something like that . . . Our biggest excitement, culturally, was to go to the local Chinese take-away, which had just opened, and have something and chips followed by banana fritters.' Yet newspaper and television reports did arouse awareness of a world beyond northern England. News of Suez and the French Algerian crisis added to earlier missionary notions of far-off countries, raising questions of consciousness and Gilda's relationship to this wider world.

Like Rowbotham, other young women immersed themselves more readily into radical subcultural movements. Di Parkin saw the 'angry' working-class protagonists as deeply influential in shaping her teenage rebellion. In 1962 she joined the Labour Party Young Socialists in Wimbledon as a disaffected fifteen-year-old: 'I was bored so my mother thought it would be a good activity for me because she was in the Labour Party.'[29] The memory of attending her first meeting remained imprinted on her sense of adolescent self. After hearing IS speaker John Palmer arguing the merits of workers' control, Di had felt herself converted into a revolutionary: 'He explained about workers' control and I got it. I bought it and I became a revolutionary there and then.' It was in this context that she internalised the 'Angry Young Men' motif. Her 'angry' radical self was rooted in the same teenage friendships that her male contemporaries described: 'My friendship with Jill Curry was based on the fact that we were both socialists . . . our identity was mainly in terms of being culturally alternative, and so we went to see *Look Back in Anger*.' Di identified with this 'angry' culture because, like other middle-class young men and women, she was sensitive to 'my own privilege', unable to identify 'with my own class'. To offset this discomfort, she had conjured an idealised working-class image that was to all intents and purposes male, informed by the aggressive, active masculinity embodied by northern realist film heroes.[30] She absorbed their celebratory cultural and political messages because *Saturday Night and Sunday Morning*, *The Loneliness of the Long Distance Runner* and *The L Shaped Room*, *A Kind of Loving* and *A Taste of Honey* were 'all films about working-class life and I wished I had been working-class'.

Yet, Rowbotham has shown how rebellious subcultures could sometimes become spaces for young women to consider themselves as female subjects. Gender equality was most likely to be addressed as individual questions of subjectivity. Rowbotham immersed herself within these subcultures in search of a 'sense of release' from the profound ambiguity she saw in all cultural representations of post-war womanhood. In *Promise of a Dream* she drew upon Simone de Beauvoir's term *dépayser* (to change scenery or disorientate) to describe her own adolescent reading experience. As a girl, de Beauvoir had read books much in the same fashion as Rowbotham and Gilda: to transport herself away from her surroundings and to transform herself. Subcultures promised 'extreme inner experiences'.[31] Carrying such hopes, Rowbotham shared something in common with young men she would meet around the VSC network who had sought the same 'profound disorientation' from 'the petty customs' of home and school. This radical reading experience offered intellectual inner retreat and the freedom of fantasy. However, scrutinising the meaning of life did not, for young men, entail the confusion surrounding female social and sexual conduct. The 'mystical nihilism' of Allen Ginsberg's *Howl*, Jack Kerouac's *On the Road* or Sartre and Brecht provided partial private release from the 'knotted' tensions she and other young women encountered between freedom and restrictive morality. What the subcultures failed to supply was the heightened sense of awareness that might have illuminated the muddled contradictions she 'exhaustingly' straddled.[32] Just like Di, Rowbotham 'simply switched sex', unconscious of the 'rough ride' girls got, even though her own sense of self as a thoughtful girl contradicted the living doll that pop singers like Cliff Richard sang about.

'Don't you hear the H-bomb's thunder?' CND

In the early to mid-1960s, entry into left subcultures often began with CND. Young activists identified with and became involved in the movement against the Bomb for various moral, political and personal reasons. Above all, participation in CND occurred in the context of growing political awareness as well as in relation to individual questions of subjectivity. As the largest extra-parliamentary organisation in early post-war Britain, the Campaign became the first radical space in which socially aware youngsters could invest an uncertain teenage identity, at odds with the conservative customs of home, school and state institutions. Drawing upon the anti-modern, socially engaged tone of the 'Angry Young Men', CND provided the first 'brave cause' through which to hone a critical voice against the moral bankruptcy of state power. What distinguished young CND activists from teenagers who wore the upturned 'Y' CND badge or who drifted to marches to annoy adults was their 'propensity to identify themselves with certain remote events' most of their peers were 'less keenly sensitized to'.[33] James Hinton identified the Bomb as the issue which 'started [me] off'.[34] His discovery of CND coincided with his intellectual awakening, the formation of moral certainties and the strengthening of atheist convictions that challenged his school's conservative Anglicanism. For him at the age of sixteen the timing of CND coincided with formative psychological changes:

> I was appointed a Prefect, but I was de-prefected because the house master discovered in my locker a pile of leaflets I had had printed calling on the youth of Bristol to set up an YCND [Youth Campaign for Nuclear Disarmament]. This must have been '58–59 . . . I cashed in my post office savings to get this leaflet printed. My mother came from the lower edges of landed gentry and was educated; my father colonial. I had this sense of belonging to an elite, an intellectual class, and there was [in] my family background, people who were intellectual achievers, and I had this coming intellectually alive after being disapproved of by my father for being stupid.

The 'magnificent [moral] simplicity' of the Bomb offered James a means of demarcating himself from the archaic ruling powers he associated with home and school. The Campaign provided a safe social and political space in which to orientate away from the uncomfortable feelings of childhood and to negotiate autonomy in his upper middle-class family. He had discovered a new identity: in late-fifties and early-sixties society CND was part of a subterranean litany to which young people subscribed in order to be marked out as dissidents. According to Jenny Diski, 'Our parents, and the papers they read, hated the marchers with their long hair, jeans, resistance songs and clashes with the police. What more could an angry fifteen-year old want?'[35] Just as Communist Party upbringing marked out children as outsiders, so CND provided a similar mantle: to wear desert boots and Levi jeans was 'to be CNDish'.[36]

Cultural representations of CND complemented the anti-establishment youth subculture that supplied an oppositional teenage identity, often interwoven with enthusiasm for the beatnik movement, jazz, folk music, French existentialist and 'angry' literature and drama. Contrary to press claims, teenagers formed only a small contingent of the marchers. Yet the new youth culture injected a festival spirit into each march that would precede the agitprop New Left protest around the VSC. According to Jeff Nuttall, it was the 'wild public festival spirit that spread the CND symbol through all the jazz clubs and secondary schools in an incredibly short time', and granted to young marchers 'a new feeling of licence', enhanced by their 'obvious' humanitarianism.[37] David Widgery explained the forbidden appeal: 'It was terribly enticing. At school we were told to be aware of them, not to fraternize.'[38]

Meredith Veldman described CND as 'an avenue of psychological freedom', a means for protesters to mentally escape Cold War culture and to articulate their disappointments and dreams.[39] The stories of youth CND activism echo this depiction. For many interviewees the CND badge became a motif for the social and psychic meaning they had found in the movement at important moments of self-development. Max Farrar distinctly recollected 'the joy I had when . . . my little metallic CND badge arrived in the post . . . pinning it on my blazer, and not really doing very much else apart from going to CND meetings'.[40] The moment coincided with a wider political awakening in the sixth form at Hemel Hempstead Grammar School, where the town's lively left enclaves brought new opportunities for social freedom after the restrictions of his public school. The memory stood out because of its associations with friendships he remembered as politically and socially formative, including his first girlfriend, who would go on to be his lifelong partner. Max's involvement in CND and Hemel Hempstead's radical politics were intimately interwoven with the discovery and excitement of adolescent friendship, love and sex:

> So we [Max and his girlfriend] joined that milieu and then we met other sort of bohemians and hippies some of whom were in the IS. There was a . . . [IS member] I remember him so affectionately. He was one of the few . . . because Hemel Hempstead, because it had these very good grammar schools, sent lots of working-class kids to university, and then they'd come back in the holidays, and we knew their younger brothers or we went to political and cultural events.

For Bronwen Davis the CND badge represented 'the start of me being fairly intolerant of interference by institutions and what I think is right'.[41] Initially, the Campaign seemed to signify the passionate moral example her father's activism had set; she began the interview by recounting childhood memories of his anti-nuclear campaigning. As with many other interviewees, both of Bronwen's parents had been active CND supporters and the threat of nuclear weapons had been openly discussed at home. In 1961 her father had taken eleven-year-old Bronwen on her first Aldermaston march. Combined with her parents' discussions about the Bomb, the marchers' urgent moral language left her in little doubt about the importance of her own participation in the cause: 'When you are a child you see the world in much more black and white terms, so to me it [the Bomb] was a real threat . . . you know my father went and campaigned about it, so therefore I was going to do that, because it was clearly the right thing to do.' In 1963 she attended her second march, this time with a female school friend. It coincided with the mass circulation of the Spies for Peace document disclosing the Regional Seat of Government 6 near Reading, and Bronwen recalled the girls' enthusiasm for diverting the march away from the official route.[42] However, when she later came to speak about this in greater detail, she by-passed the marches and the familial ties they had signified. The memory of wearing her CND badge brought a new set of emotional associations: in the mid-1960s Bronwen had officially joined CND just prior to her family's departure for Nigeria. By this time her isolation and the resentment she would express upon her parents' return were already beginning to find expression in political and moral convictions that distanced her from home and school. Unexplained feelings of unhappiness combined with antagonism towards her left-wing parents after they chose to pay for her to attend a girls' public day school: 'I thought they should have sent me to a comprehensive school, which as I said they believed in, and the friend I went on the Aldermaston march with was at a comprehensive school.' In this context Bronwen's memories of wearing her CND badge conjured up defiant feelings of adolescent outrage. Within the Campaign she found momentary belonging as a member of a dissenting collective, set apart socially, morally and emotionally from her middle-class world:

> I became a member of CND and I don't remember going to any meetings, but always wearing a CND badge on my coat, and selling them to other people at school for six pence each . . . I thought it was very wrong that the school should think that it was meaningful and appropriate to fuss about whether you wore a badge on your uniform. I thought it was right

to be in CND and to wear the badge because it was a way of spreading the message, and also what business was it of the school's what you wore on your uniform?

Lee Comer's story confirmed how complex questions of adolescent subjectivity were interwoven with the Campaign's cultural symbolism and moral appeal. She joined the movement in 1959, when, aged sixteen, she discovered one of the main nerve centres close to home, and became membership secretary of the 'Hampstead branch of CND no less'.[43] As for many radical youngsters following international affairs, moral conscience was crucial to Lee's commitment to the unilateralist cause: 'We were deep in the Cold War; it was self-evident.'[44] Yet, her own particular engagement with CND reflected a much more private struggle for selfhood that was intimately tied to the story of separation between her Czech mother and aunt. Lee saw in the Iron Curtain the ideological struggle bearing down on her family. The two sisters had become separated in 1938 after Lee's mother escaped to England 'with money sewn into her coat, alone, aged sixteen', the only member of the family to escape the camps. As for so many second-generation Holocaust survivors, Lee's adolescence had been coloured by the burden of her mother's survival guilt: 'My mother's mental health was very fragile and very difficult.' Her attempt to make sense of this trauma and of herself as a young English woman had been complicated by the female model her mother aspired to for Lee: 'My mother and step-father were trying to turn me into a nice Jewish girl, and I refused to be a nice Jewish girl. I didn't go to the nice Jewish youth clubs and all that, and get off with [the sons of] lawyers and solicitors, and go to university. It wasn't me at all. I was deep into existentialism and Simone de Beauvoir and Earnest Hemingway.' Against this background, CND facilitated retreat into an inner intellectual world, supplying a moral and political framework to make sense of her family history, and a radical identity to distinguish her from it. Visceral revolt became a symbol of a deeper psychic struggle for a future free from the weight of the past.

Morally and psychologically, as well as politically, then, the shadow of the Bomb profoundly shaped the consciences of young activists. The testimonies show the wealth of meanings which youngsters read into the nuclear threat. Victor Seidler's own story of Jewish adolescence revealed that behind the Bomb's shadow activists saw hidden shapes that carried echoes of darker pasts. In the early 1960s the discourse of nuclear holocaust dominated the Campaign's publications and the speeches of its leading figures. For Victor, printed images of Hiroshima evoked memories of the BBC newsreels of Bergen Belsen he had watched with his mother in the early 1950s:

> It was the way that the Jewish and the injustice [of Hiroshima] for me went together. And it was hidden . . . the stories around Passover were always the same time as the Aldermaston march . . . You listened to Bertrand Russell and you listened to Canon Collins and you were aware that this was a life and death . . . It was about slavery and oppression, and some of the images that were coming through that we had seen were the Belsen liberation images that came in 1950 . . . shown on BBC and watching with my mother and she saying 'Look what Hitler did to the Jews' . . . and not knowing who we were seeing, so you were imagining you could be seeing your uncle.[45]

Whether or not they participated in CND, few interviewees escaped the full psychological impact of the Bomb; it suffused moral and political values they formed during this period. In 1958 a chance encounter with the Aldermaston march prompted thirteen-year-old Chris Ratcliffe to question received parental opinion on the movement:

> I remember once being in the centre of London and we went into Lyons Corner House for lunch, and as we went in we saw a mass demonstration . . . as far as the eye could see there were thousands and thousands. We had quite a long lunch and when we came out they were still coming past. Subsequently, we know this is how demonstrations work, but for a young boy I just thought they can't all be louts as my dad referred to them, and it was just kind of wow, what's going on? This is something I wanted to know about.[46]

Before institutional politics featured in childhood landscapes the eccentric appeal of the marches struck a chord with the diffuse anxieties with which individuals responded to media reports on the nuclear threat. Chris explained, 'I was a reasonably bright young lad and I did follow the news. It was quite worrying, especially the Cuban missile crisis.'

Interviewees' memories of the 1962 Cuban missile crisis shared an eve-of-destruction mood. The narratives suggested something of the Bomb's impact on the psychology of post-war children and adolescents. Depending on age and political understanding, the crisis inspired a myriad of sentiments that anticipated a critical relationship with governing authorities and a desire for youngsters to engage themselves in assertive action for political change. Before they were able to articulate political outrage at the recklessness of international leaders, adolescent feelings most often expressed personal resentment at experiences, especially sexual experiences never to be. For Di Parkin, 15 November, 1962 appeared like any other except that, as she stood at the school bus stop, world war and annihilation seemed certain. The threat of war had sat on her shoulders from her earliest memories, informing childhood games: 'You have to lie still in the cooling bath water and count, or else the plane flying overhead will turn out to be a bomber and that will be that.'[47] But as a sixteen-year-old she was able to shape an opinionated response: '"I'm going to die a virgin!" I am deeply angry.' Other women's memories highlight the sexual preoccupations of adolescent girls faced with the threat of extinction. As to the question Gilda Peterson posed, 'what are you going to do with your last four minutes? Will we all have sex?' few were in doubt.[48] Ingham recalled how, at her Midlands girls' high school, 'the consensus of opinion was to rush out into the street and grab a man'.[49] Adolescents' instinctive understanding that 'the world was a mess' may have been emotionally charged and clumsily expressed, but the cognition, discussions and activities that followed these feelings suggested a logical progression into action. Elaine Connell's memories of the three o'clock deadline suggested how the terror of the nine-year-old child – 'I was scared, scared, scared' – later coalesced into awareness of her vulnerable lack of agency: 'My childhood resumed but . . . I never forgot how my little life was at the mercy of people I didn't know and couldn't control.'[50] Her response signalled the capacity of CND to provide an early model for direct action as a means to assuage childhood terrors: 'I was going to become one of those people Dad called "beatniks" and "layabouts" who marched every year.' Marching offered Elaine security in the faith that CND activists 'seemed to be the only ones who cared about children like me'.

Many young activists became involved in CND because of their parents' own support for or active involvement in the movement. Wisty Hoyland's Anglican father, the Chairman of Cambridge CND, 'was quite outspoken to the extent that he'd even stand up in the pulpit and . . . express his views much to the annoyance of the hierarchy in the Church of England'.[51] At her independent Cambridge school, The Perse, affiliation to CND served as a defiant response to teachers who publicly voiced their disapproval of her father's radicalism.

Activism in CND commonly featured in Communist Party families. Steve Jefferys' activism in YCND and the Committee of 100 followed a seamless political trajectory that began at the age of four. One of his first recollections was of 'being pushed in a wheel chair in a demonstration the Communist Party organised [against German rearmament] in Downing Street. We were charged by police horses.'[52] Unlike the children of other Communist families she knew, Caroline Bond never showed any interest in joining the YCL. However, CND marches were a family affair as well as an occasion for friendship. The Aldermaston marches were 'quite near to us and my mum was very active in CND more than in the Communist Party. My mum was always very anti-war . . . and she took me on the marches.'[53]

The social ethos of CND was fundamental to its appeal in fostering a new, dynamic model of grass-roots activism. Marches created energy, community and fun. Phil Hearse remembered his first Aldermaston march, in April, 1962: 'An amazing experience . . . kids with long hair, duffle coats and guitars singing protest songs.'[54] The resounding sentiment, aside from the sense of community, was the Campaign's capacity to engender spontaneous action and individual initiative. For twenty-one year old John Charlton, 'CND was action' and he was 'very comfortable with the idea of doing things'.[55] CND established the foundations for grass-roots canvassing that would characterise the do-it-yourself politics of the VSC. The method had struck a chord early on among CND youths. In 1962 YCND members participated in 'Flying Columns', intensively campaigning door to door. Participants spoke of the improvements the experience had made to their effectiveness as campaigners. Peter Latarche, YCND chairman, had propounded the merits of this method in the YCND newspaper, *Youth Against the Bomb*, advocating the simple idea of 'Let's talk to the people'.[56] Reflecting back, he enthused about 'a kind of naive socialism' the Easter marches provided: 'Everybody mucked in, everybody suffered the same discomforts, everybody shared, supported everybody else. This, I thought, was how a civilised society would behave towards its members.'[57] The direct action young activists tasted in the Committee of 100 sit-downs ruined many for 'committee meetings and points of order' for ever more.[58] Already influenced by his parents' involvement with the *New Reasoner* group, Steve Jefferys identified the Committee's protests as marking a 'key turning-point' in his left libertarian politics.[59] In September 1961 the Committee of 100 protested after the Russians exploded an atomic bomb in the atmosphere above Central Asia:

> I went on the Committee of 100 core demonstration outside Knightsbridge, and found to my genuine shock and horror that the numbers were down by half or three quarters of what they normally were because the Communist Party and fellow travellers were not protesting against the Russian Embassy, so I suppose that was formative in shaping my political thinking . . . It was all very civilised sitting down in the street, and people would kind of lift you up and throw you quite brutally in police wagons, and try to intimidate you, and so I had experiences of dealing with the police and being arrested . . . those sorts of experiences meant I was open for lots of different things.

CND imprinted an enduring legacy in the intellectual and emotional tenets young activists developed in the left milieux they joined from the mid-1960s. The New Left politics that coalesced around the VSC encompassed various left traditions: Communism, the 'first' New Left, the Labour Party and the labour movement as well as international New Left protest movements. By the mid-1960s young activists' encounters with the full range of these traditions had inspired attachment to a new energetic form of grass-roots engagement. Like many of his LSE cohort, Steve eventually found affinity with the IS politics of 'Neither Washington nor Moscow', rejecting the binary logic of the Cold War in favour of an internationalism that advocated an alliance with the workers of Europe, Asia, Africa and the rest of the world. CND was a vital staging-post preparing the cultural terrain for the left milieux of the late 1960s and, together with the New Left, marking out an international framework that envisioned close connection with the Third World. In the late 1960s the positive neutralism of CND and the New Left was to transmute into Third World radicalism as young activists sought to align themselves with national liberation movements, most prominently in Vietnam.

Socialist youth culture in the early 1960s

In the early to mid-1960s CND remained part of a wider, though still small, fluid left scene that provided a cohort of young activists with political education and space for social belonging. These radical circles aided members to make intellectual sense of international and domestic politics and to reflect on their own sense of self within this framework. Interviewees' testimonies reveal how permeable boundaries between left groups facilitated the transfer of ideas and political forms, often through memorable meetings with older Marxists whose own politics had been shaped prior to the war. In the early 1960s the British Left was in transition following the wake of the 1956 Communist Party split. By 1962 the New Left was in decline and many of its activists had begun to drift away into more promising milieux such as CND and the Labour Party.[60]

CND provided a rite of passage into socialist politics inside the YS, the IS, the Socialist Labour League (SLL) and *The Week* (from 1968 the IMG), or involvement in a variety of anarchist or libertarian groups that had sprung up in the vicinity. On CND's 1966 Easter march, Phil Hearse saw 'a group of people carrying red flags and banners, stating the National Liberation Front'.[61] The marchers were an early contingent of VSC supporters whose declaration of solidarity with the Democratic

Republic of Vietnam and the National Liberation Front (NLF) repre-
sented a radical departure from the Left's moderate stance over the
Vietnam War. As a sixth-former at Ealing Boys' Grammar School,
Phil joined *The Week* group and began organising pupils onto early
VSC demonstrations.

Some young activists who joined the two far-left contingents in the
VSC (IS and IMG) first encountered speakers around these groups
through Labour Party and YS circles. In February 1960 the decision
of the Labour Party to launch a new national youth organisation,
the YS, had prompted Trotskyist groups, notably the Socialist Review
group (the name of the IS group prior to 1964) and the SLL, to use
the opportunity for recruitment. Through CND, YS meetings and the
Socialist Review's youth paper, *Young Guard*, YS men and a few women
were absorbed into a youthful revolutionary culture that combined beer
drinking and folk singing with activity in the labour movement. As the
main youth organisation on the Left, the YS attracted a predominantly
working-class base from manual, though occasionally white-collar homes
and involved a specifically working-class political culture. As a result
those working- and lower middle-class adolescents who first became
active within this milieu already had an experience with industrial
labour politics that often came later for middle-class university students.
Part of its appeal derived from the cultural and emotional connection
which working-class youngsters made between membership, politics
and their own personal histories. Continuity between the childhood
and activist landscape was mediated through a working-class identity
grounded in a specific locality, cultural patterns and memories, all of
which nurtured an emotional attachment between interviewees and the
labour Left. In 1963 Joan Smith joined the Kenton IS branch after being
active in the Harrow YS. Situated half-way between home and school,
the branch was a familiar landmark along her daily route, but she also
'felt very comfortable at their meetings because it was actually a very
working-class group. It was very like my background; it was people
who worked on the Park Royal industrial estate; there were engineers,
a couple of post office engineers, a secretary at one of the universities,
a primary school teacher, another teacher, it was a mix of people that
was just okay.'[62] Impressed by her friend's participation in CND, Val
Graham followed her into the Chesterfield YS. In the early 1960s her
Labour-supporting school friends mirrored her parents' own Labour
Party circles so that the girls' break-time discussions echoed the political debates Val heard emanating from her living room.[63]

In 1959 John Charlton was slightly older than most adolescents
joining the YS and CND. As a twenty-one-year-old secondary modern

teacher he was one of the founding members of Newcastle's unofficial young socialist group, the 59 Society. Members met on Friday evenings, came from a range of independent, direct grant and grammar schools as well as from Newcastle University, and worked and socialised under the 'umbrella of CND'.[64] John's recollections of this time showed how a broad spectrum of socialist activities moved him towards an intellectual understanding of his disordered feelings and experiences. In a period when ideas were in a 'fluid state' he moved between the 59 Society, CND, Newcastle's Labour Party and the New Left.[65] He reflected that what 'I was probably doing was seeking for an explanation for the world I lived in'. The socialist literature he read from across this spectrum (*Tribune*, *New Left Review*, the *New Statesman*) excited his interest in a range of issues being debated: housing, nationalisation and workers' control. This fluid landscape also brought him into contact with leading members of Trotskyist groups working on the edges of the labour Left. In Easter 1961 John was a delegate at the London YS conference, which 'turned out to be a sort of bear garden of factions, of youth factions, of Trotskyist factions ... At that conference I came into contact with people from the Socialist Labour League. But my friend Jim met people from the IS.' Such occasions moved him closer to understanding what kind of socialist he felt himself to be, partly by clarifying what he was not. Like many young people who came across the SLL, John knew instantly that leader Gerry Healy's 'hysteric bullying approach' was not for him. This intensive wealth of left ideas and forms exposed him to new ways of seeing his country and transformed how he saw himself a social subject: 'In a way I think I'd stopped thinking about it [class] in terms of my feelings, and it became a more cerebral concern with class. We were now working. I was now working for the working class, if you like.' Whilst CND satisfied John's youthful desire for action, it pushed him further to the labour Left. Meanwhile, New Left meetings grounded his earlier emotional hostility to Soviet Communism in reasoned argument:

What you got in New Left meetings was a much harder argument, an argument laid out by a speaker about different aspects of the world ... I knew I wasn't interested in the Communist Party ... I remember sitting with the radio glued to my ear during Hungary. I was very keen on football and in 1953 ... it was the first time the England team had been beaten on their own soil by the Hungarians ... I watched it on the newsreels at the cinema and there were some absolutely brilliant players, and when the Hungarian revolution broke out my main interest was to find out what had happened to them ... I was absolutely appalled by the Russian tanks pouring in, so I was never going to go that way.

Although John valued New Left speakers for expanding his international horizons, the activism and easy sociability of the 59 Society held more ready appeal. The New Left's cultural solemnity stood too close to the Labour Party's bureaucratic formality, whereas the 59 Society felt more 'exciting, an opportunity to meet people, you see, particularly girls . . . it was an opportunity for drinking in friendly company, of meeting people, of arguing with people, of laughing with people. All those things were really, you know, were what you kind of needed.'

The appeal of early left cultures often derived from the release, friendship and fun their lively sociability offered adolescents. The social community fostered by CND marches, demonstrations, pub meetings and parties only added to youngsters' feeling that they had become 'political in a different kind of way'.[66] Pop music, dancing and sexual desire characterised many early-sixties left spaces where teenagers found a sense of belonging. Alongside folk and jazz clubs, skiffle and beat cellars, coffee bars and pubs, these could bring young people together from different social classes. Victor Seidler's socialist youth club included middle- and working-class Jewish children from across Hendon. The club became a melting pot for political and cultural transfer where members explored Jewish intellectual writings alongside CND politics, the American civil rights movement, sexology and existentialism against the background of popular music. Victor recalled the club's appeal: 'It was an enormous amount of freedom and liberation . . . there was music and there was dance, and there were women and there were girls and desire and rating girls, and there was sex.'[67] Discussions around protest, class and race created a shared intellectual culture through which he could begin to situate his hidden past against contemporary international affairs. Free social mixing away from parental control offered him opportunities for escaping the war's shadow and his mother's hold on the past. Dancing focused attention on sensations of the body and, alongside other girls and boys, affirmed his sense of identity as a member of a youthful generation grounded in the present.

The YS and IS

The stories of several male apprentices particularly illustrate the close relationship between class, gender, sociability and subjectivity inside mid-sixties socialist youth cultures. For a small number of working-class London men, experience inside the YS/IS milieu related to their earliest childhood efforts to understand themselves in relation to their families and localities. Their accounts echo the findings of LSE-trained sociologists whose surveys of working-class life suggested a complex, multilayered society with tensions between older patterns of class and modernising impulses of affluence and youth culture. Also pertinent is the work of the Birmingham Centre for Cultural Studies (CCC), notably that of Phil Cohen, who interpreted post-war youth subcultures as specific yet contradictory responses to social disruptions which had affected the entire East End community. Cohen saw the styles of mods, teddy boys and skin heads as attempts to 'express and resolve, albeit magically, the contradictions which remain hidden or unresolved in the parent culture'.[68] Such findings illuminate the cultural expression of working-class YS men; their styles informed the wider responses of working-class youth growing up in communities deeply embedded in class feeling, especially where caught up in real social shifts.

The political cultures of the YS/IS milieu reflected the very sociocultural identity that informed the young men's Marxism. Slightly later than other members, in 1967 Bob Light encountered 'a group of young kids' from the East London YS.[69] After leaving school in 1965 he had travelled across Western Europe and North America, working in youth hostels, exploring black music and enjoying opportunities for sexual freedom: 'I was a young, good-looking working-class kid who had grown up in a working-class community where working class is about marriage and formal shit, and all of a sudden we are kind of marching in parallel with international developments. It was a mind-blowing experience to have at sixteen.' By 1967 Bob had returned home, determined to involve himself in politics, but keen to find an alternative to his father's Communism: 'I knew how much I detested Russia even though I respected my father's politics. But I knew I wanted something different, and I trawled left book shops looking for different things, and I quite quickly came across *Labour Worker*, and I wrote to them and someone [from the IS] came to my house.'

The branch appealed to Bob because of members' shared background. When he joined there were a dozen or so predominantly East End working-class young men as well as a few women, but by 1968 it had expanded to integrate Walthamstow, Leyton and Hackney. Like Bob, several members came from left-wing families, carried a history of political interest and shared his enthusiasm for football, non-mainstream music, especially blues and folk, and held some very good parties. The group reflected the almost tribal youth culture in which he had grown up and attracted him largely because it felt so familiar: 'My experience is almost self-defining. Walthamstow was very self-contained. People didn't travel and so it was very much kids from the local area . . . The guys would be all working-class background, but somewhere with a dissident gene; so Roy, for example, Jimmy, people like that came like me from a political family and politics was a natural area of interest.' This localised youth culture echoed portraits of teenage mod culture originating from communities such as Croyden, Tottenham and Hackney outside the centre of 'Swinging London'.[70] Despite the internationalism of the branch's socialism, central to its appeal was its ability to accommodate a local working-class youth culture that encompassed a vibrant rhythm 'n' blues music scene based in pubs like the Britannia, the YS haunt next to the Hackney Empire.

Four years older than most members, LSE postgraduate Fred Lindop was an exception in the branch. He was married, and his Oxford education, extensive book collection and serious manner distinguished him from the laddish persona of Bob and 'the guys' who shared a flat, a 'den of iniquity and excess', near to Walthamstow Central. Nevertheless, Fred's deprived Birkenhead background reinforced the branch's inclusive working-class character. Memories of discomfort and antagonism at his grammar school translated into an assertive class consciousness that brought acceptance from younger members.[71] In this localised setting fierce factional divisions between 'tendencies' enhanced cultural expressions of class. As a branch member, Rowbotham recalled how 'accusations of petty bourgeois status abounded'. Conformity to the tendencies extended even to the men's dress. While IS men were 'predominantly donkey-jacketed', 'Militant – a deep-entrist lot – wore brown suedette jackets with fur collars'.[72] Yet, at the level of subjectivity, ties between members rested heavily on shared childhood patterns and emotions. With his background and his Jewish Hackney wife Fred added his own social and psychic imprint to the overall working-class ethos enveloping the membership.

Fred related to the intensity of the branch in a way that Rowbotham did not. Whilst she endured the weekly trial by meeting, the solemn sectarian strife and the Militant men's taste for outdated fifties music, he understood the otherness of the Trotskyist identity because it seemed to speak for his own adolescent alterity. Thriving off sectarian arguments with Militant members like Peter Taff and Brian Smith, his class antagonism found a home and acquired an anti-racist edge from encounters with Ridley Road's West Indian community. In the mid-1960s the Trotskyism that prevailed in the East End remained tinged with the legacy of political failure, and for youngsters bearing the weight of class injustice the bitterness of the politics chimed with their experiences. Bob explained his own sense of class hostility: 'We had a ceremonial cricket match every year and there is this documentary by Lindsay Anderson, *We Are the Lambeth Boys*, and they go and play cricket against the public school, and we would do this. The level of venom, we would try and hurt them. There was a strong sense of injustice.'[73]

The men's stories echo the suffusion of class and cultural attachment to Labour present in other working-class testimonies. They were often drawn to the YS/IS milieu initially for social reasons. Alan Watts grew up in Tottenham, the son of a factory engineer. His early political awareness came from the small circle of male friends with whom he joined the Tottenham YS:

> I knew I was socially aware and then Gordon, a mate of mine, was big into reading war stories, and I remember having an argument with him about this . . . [it was] 1958 and I said 'Why do we need nuclear weapons?' He said, 'Well, we've got to protect ourselves.' I said 'Well if we got rid of them and so did they' . . . but none of this went anywhere, and later on several of us who knocked around together, the guy we hung around with, Mel Norris, asked us to go to a YS meeting, and we went there and came across these people just pouring out these ideas and stuff I had never heard before, and it was absolutely brilliant.[74]

Roger Cox's entry into Tottenham IS occurred through similar friendships. His activism began when, in 1953, he joined the Labour Party's Shoreditch branch:

> When I was in secondary school my best friend was the son of a London County Councillor and therefore he was in the Labour Party, and so from the age of twelve or thirteen I was active in the Labour Party, and you had lots of different views, and in terms of friendships and ties you had got this . . . I was in the YS . . . but the other thing was that the old Trotskyist organisations began to grow around these circles, and we bumped into people from the SLL, and the other people who came round was the IS.[75]

Roger's testimony shows how activism within YS circles brought bright, socially enquiring and class-conscious youngsters into contact with leading IS members whose political ideas and energetic delivery style struck a chord with their social and political experiences. These core members would exercise a decisive influence on the development of their thinking as well as their sense of self. By 1964 the Labour Party Young Socialists had begun to move progressively leftwards as discontent with Labour Party headquarters increased. They had also come under the increasing influence of the SLL, IS and the Revolutionary Socialist League, which lent activists a willingness to defy the party line.

Active around the YS and CND, the IS had emerged in the 1950s as the Socialist Review Group, following the orientation of its leader, Tony Cliff. In 1960 the group had launched a theoretical magazine,

International Socialism, whose title asserted the state-capitalist position Cliff had embraced. According to Martin Shaw, the group provided an anti-Stalinist, freethinking alternative to the intimidating 'orthodoxy' of the SLL and, in the early sixties, began to attract 'refugees' from the latter and from the declining New Left, as well as a few young workers and students from CND and the YS.[76]

For working-class activists like Alan Watts and Roger Cox the striking impact of IS ideas came in the way in which they seemed to resonate with their experiences of the local workaday world. Cliff emphasised, for example, the concept of 'substitutionism', substituting the revolutionary party for the working class to advocate a party which discussed and decided openly in front of workers. Alan remembered the electrifying ideas he heard on Tuesday evenings when IS speakers, Cliff and Palmer, spoke to his YS group:

> What was exciting about it to me was that it was the beginnings of an explanation of what was going on around me . . . On the one hand I was working in this factory everyday with loads of working-class people, obviously, toolmakers, and so there was a union organisation because they were all craftsmen, and on Tuesday evenings going to these meetings, and I can distinctly remember going to work in the mornings and work-ing my drill, and my head was just spinning with all these ideas. It was just fantastic . . . I just thought what about this, what about that?[77]

Alan's narrative confirms how, regardless of background or education, for politically and class-conscious youngsters in the early 1960s, the uncertainty and angst of the early adult self often became intertwined within a wider framework of national and international politics and social developments. He encountered the IS at a crucial moment of frustration with his work and family. Having gained an apprenticeship at Enfield's Stockholm Metal Works, he had recently been dismissed after accusing his foreman of responsibility for a serious accident crush-ing a worker's fingers in a ten-ton press. Simultaneously, his hopes of travelling to Southern Rhodesia had been dashed after his brother but not he was accepted for VSO: 'David went when he was nineteen and my mother always thought he was the dog's bollocks and I was the son who was the Commie. It was all a bit of a nightmare really.'

For Alan the moral and political issue of the Bomb seemed to sym-bolise his lack of agency. Week by week, as he listened to the speakers, the ideas he heard equipped him with explanations that felt empower-ing because they enabled him to situate feelings of injustice within the class framework Cliff and others presented. Why it was necessary to build the Bomb suddenly became clear through IS theoretician Michael

Kidron's theory of the 'permanent arms economy', and he began to feel he had a grasp on the way the world worked. As he relived the exciting revelations Cliff's explanations of Russia and the Bomb had brought, Alan showed how the subjectivity of the frustrated young apprentice came to speak through the language of International Socialism:

> What was being explained to me over quite a long period of time was really how we all fitted together. The Bomb, for instance, was a bit of an issue, it was ongoing ... The explanations that were being presented for why it was necessary to build the bomb was explained by the politics of IS at the time with the permanent war economy ... So that was quite exciting that suddenly I had a grasp on the Bomb and why they needed to have it ... when you explain Russia ... it was a black hole ... There was an iron curtain in our heads, and so when Tony Cliff and the IS group were explaining the class nature of Russia I began to get a grasp of the way the world worked.

Bob Light confirmed how, for these young men, politics was from the outset inextricably personal because their encounters with the YS/IS occurred at pivotal moments of transition in their young lives. In the summer of 1964 he was leaving school, had just signed to play professional football and was involved in an intensive relationship with a fellow schoolgirl. Dreams of the future seemed to be unfolding when Bob's girlfriend discovered she was pregnant and committed suicide. Bob was shocked and guilt-ridden; unsurprisingly, his outlook changed: 'It was horrible beyond belief and there was a sense in which I grew up in a weekend ... I didn't want to kick a ball around anymore. I didn't want to prove myself running.'[78] He followed other young boys from his neighbourhood in the revolt into style, immersing himself in the vibrant mod scene around East End pubs. Subsequent years of travel, black music and sexual experimentation suggested a psychic response to his girlfriend's death, but the international style awakened his interest in a political and cultural world beyond East London.

Roger Cox showed how the captivating appeal of IS speakers occurred at a critical juncture of these men's relations with the Left, when they were seeking a new, dynamic political space to accommodate their own contradictory experiences of affluence and Cold War politics. Apart from CND, few radical options appealed to jocular East End youngsters, who were likely to greet the brittle orthodoxy of SLL activists with cynicism and teasing. Whilst the Communist Party was politically irrelevant as the party of Russia and the Bomb, its members tired and authoritarian, the Labour Party represented bingo sessions in Shoreditch. Roger was instantly captivated by the first IS members he met, Robyn Fiore and Michael Kidron, whose ability to relate ideas to him with humour and sincerity contrasted with the austere culture he had met elsewhere on the Left:

> Then arrived on the scene two contrasting characters and the impact they had was quite unimaginable really. One was Robyn Fiore and the other was Mike Kidron. These two toffs, gents, spoke very posh. They came and had these arguments with us, do you know this, and they were incredibly unpatronising and quite funny, and again they were from this different world, a world which was more sophisticated, and again there was this opportunity to actually have a better understanding of the world, and they used to go around various groups of youngsters talking to them to lure them into Tony Cliff's front room where he gave these lectures on Marxism.[79]

The captivating personality of Cliff, and his ability to nurture, engage, yet banter with and challenge the apprentices, was central to the organisation's appeal. Once Fiore and Kidron had successfully 'lured' Roger into Cliff's front room, he was enraptured by this 'funny old man', his Marxism heavy with amusing idiosyncrasies. In stark contrast to the officialdom of the Communist Party and the labour movement, Roger explained how 'suddenly there is this Marxism and Cliff is going to do it, and it was in someone's front room so you didn't have the intimidation'. The domesticity of meetings in the Cliff's Stoke Newington home created a reassuring familiarity and intimacy. Before long Roger and Bob found themselves baby-sitting for Cliff and his South African wife, Chanie, at home in a familial circle that fluidly encompassed the organisation's tiny membership.[80] Chanie also played a nurturing role to the young workers who came into Cliff's circle. She was a teacher, and Roger's wife, Sarah, recalled her attentiveness to her young husband, setting him tests on the group's politics.[81] For Bob, Cliff played an important role in helping him to negotiate his love for his father and distance from his Communism, and confirmed Bob's commitment to Cliff's organic socialist ideas:

> You cannot imagine the influence. He was in so many respects a parallel to my father . . . My father was ten years older or so, and my father was the product of a troubled home, and he came out of it as really fine people, he and my mum, and for all I didn't agree with my father, and he and I used to have really intense political arguments at this stage, especially about Russia because [of] the invasion of Czechoslovakia, but it was vicious at this time, but you meet Cliff, he was an intellectual in this sense.[82]

For Bob, Roger and Alan, the IS provided a Marxist education that in other circumstances they might have gained from Oxford's Ruskin

College or the Workers' Educational Association. Cliff's was a small and intimate circle, but a hothouse of intellectual debate and activity. Cliff, Kidron, Palmer, Paul Foot and others nurtured these youngsters, took a personal interest in their political education and encouraged them to pursue their own ideas through challenging Marxist texts. Their limited secondary education made this a sometimes difficult experience, but the young men persevered because the leadership instilled confidence in their intellectual abilities, where school teachers had dismissed them. From the moment he joined IS in 1958, Roger's receptiveness to self-education resulted from the importance he saw the organisation attach to him as a worker. Cliff devoted time to grilling him on the life of the factory, its politics and union practices, as well as daily minutiae like the tea break. In such areas workers like seventeen-year-old Roger were experts and Cliff made them feel so. The self-determination he gained from the organisation opened up new possibilities for how to counter the alienation of the industrial world:

> Right from the start I was told by the organisation, when I was doing my apprenticeship, you must work hard and pass your exams, and then you can get a good job and really begin to operate. Education is of the utmost importance. You had to read . . . For a working-class boy like me the organisation was your university. It was where you learned everything and where you were expected to teach yourself. If you talk to a kid of my generation I was probably exceptional in a way. You stood head and shoulders above people around you in terms of ideas, you know . . . The best conversations I had were with my mates when I was on the railways because some of these guys had travelled the world a bit and [had also left behind] the narrowness I didn't have any longer.

In 1968 global political and cultural transfer offered young activists new ways of thinking and being in the world. Yet, in East End working-class communities early IS culture drew upon recognisable patterns of work, family and leisure which affluence and consumption were reframing. For young men like Alan, Roger and Bob, belonging in the organisation was rooted in consciousness of class and its relationship to locality. It brought alternative education, identity and the opportunity to engage in this transnational moment of intellectual mobility and political exchange.

YS culture and masculine sociability

The culture of the YS/IS milieu was defined by male sociability. Young socialist men were bound together by a shared identity of class, enthusiasm for newly discovered Marxist ideas, political debate, activity and cultural tastes. The process of being collectively active and learning how to be activists fostered the bonds of comradeship. In the run-up to the 1964 general election Alan Watts attended a meeting at Finsbury town hall where he and his friends clashed with far-right supporters:

> I thought whatever happens I'm going to go in. So we got into this meeting, but we kept thinking we knew which side we were on. We had had meetings on Russia and Germany, and all that sort of stuff, and the Spanish Civil War, and so we knew what the story was, and so we acted collectively to oppose people with like views over here so this drew us together as friends and comrades.[83]

This combative politics cultivated a socially buoyant, yet intellectually rooted masculinity which in the late 1960s became subsumed into the street politics around the VSC. Bob Light was drawn further into the East End YS/IS branch by members' involvement in the VSC just as it began to move its politics out of Transport House and onto the street. His participation in the anti-Vietnam War demonstration on 22 October, 1967 enhanced his attachment because the protest signalled a discernible shift towards a militant, activist politics that connected to his East End roots:

> I began to form a loyalty and the first big demo was in October '67 . . . and there was a part of me that really liked being able to smack the police right in the mouth, exerting all that resentment built up over the years being a working-class kid, and Red Riding is the thin version, but they were little Nazis, and it added up to a really nice day out to me, and you consolidate the sense of identification, and I think I got arrested at that one. I didn't mind, no great stigma, I got fined and then I went away.[84]

Alan Woodward joined Tottenham YS around 1962. After completing national service in 1959, he had trained as a secondary school teacher and become active in the Labour Party, CND and the YS, first in Notting Hill Gates and then in Islington, where he and his wife lived around the corner from Cliff. Alan's wife was also an active YS member, but soon after they moved to Tottenham he remembered how the branch's frenetic pace seemed to leave the young women behind. The social bonds of comradeship exuded a collective self-assertion that derived from the energy the young men generated through shared activities. Within the Tottenham group members supported the tenants' struggle, went on CND marches, were arrested in the Committee of 100 sit-downs, wrote, leafleted a factory ('A Blow Against the Bomb is a Blow Against the Boss') attended countless meetings, sold the IS paper, *Labour Worker*, and later joined the anti-Vietnam War marches.

All this activity occurred alongside continual, heated discussions; 'people saying I have read this book. Have you read that book?'[85] Implicit within these earnest but friendly debates was the intellectual competition on which the men's bonds rested.

The language of the milieu reinforced fraternal and comradely ties. Before they were able to feel fully part of the group, YS men had to learn the Trotskyist code employed by longstanding members. Alan Woodward acquired this fairly rapidly because he shared a house with an older IS activist from Notting Hill Gate: 'We were always arguing about things, going to meetings, intervening as the expression is, and seeing where that got us, and so I developed that basic socialist consciousness fairly quickly . . . If you didn't know you would think the person was talking rubbish, but once you knew the code, the vanguard, the proletariat, etcetera, there was a cohesion behind it all.' Shared leisure pursuits added to an intense home life to strengthen comradeship. In 1966 Alan accompanied his comrades on a wet camping trip to Aviemore: 'We were a little group who went around together . . . on holiday together, once to Scotland hitchhiking and sleeping in railway trains . . . so there was this group who in a sense carried out an intense rescheduling of my thinking into revolutionary socialist lines.'

Through integrated social and political patterns YS developed their own vibrant youth culture in which boundaries between politics, work, home and leisure blurred. This picture of a lively IS subculture complements the earlier portrait of CND as a 'culturefest' for the young, highlighting the role these milieux performed as cultural staging posts for the VSC.[86] Symbolic of the close interaction between subculture and activist politics was 65 Bishop's Close, the fulcrum of Bob Light's East End IS branch. By 1968 the household was drawing in an ever-growing number of working-class youths from Walthamstow. Attracted by the legendary parties the flat hosted, young party-goers were recruited and branch meetings, held in the Britannia Pub, increased in frequency as Bob and his comrades, heavily keen on blues and San Francisco music, started up a band, playing to the pub's young audience. The libertarian politics of IS fitted easily alongside the mod subculture shaping the young men's musical tastes, dress and sexual conduct:

> We were simultaneously young men, yeah, doing young men things. We were really into music and we had a band associated with the flat . . . in many ways it was the DNA of our politics, the exploration of new kinds of music . . . There was no party line on what music you liked . . . The sense of sexual freedom was important because in an earlier generation you couldn't have done it, but in this generation we were unusual, and we were very committed. We would go and leaflet factory bulletins. The

branch and the household were almost inseparable to be honest. People
would hang out there and there would always be someone sleeping on
the floor.[87]

Dynamic, at times militant activity not only empowered YS men as
political agents working for local and international change, but informed
their willingness to push against social boundaries constraining their
capacity for social and sexual mobility and pleasure. The men's narratives exuded a self-determination that testified to the self-assertion
they acquired during these years. It was in their work lives where IS
politics most immediately affected their identities as workers. The higher
spending power of working-class youth, which the Albermarle Committee
noted beneath the emerging youth culture, continued towards the end
of the decade to facilitate the bourgeoning young socialist scene. Bob
was one of many working-class youths benefiting from the growing
demand for unskilled and semi-skilled workers in an economic trend
that was accompanied by falling contributions made to parents.[88] In
1968 he worked casually as a painter and decorator; working at the
weekend for double pay was sufficient to keep him afloat for the rest
of the week, allowing him leisure time to pursue music and politics:
'I didn't have a regular routine life and I didn't want one. My life was
about politics, not in a messianic way because politics was about friendships and music.'

Women's minimal place in the men's stories reflected the fraternity
enveloping Trotskyist culture and identity. By the mid-1960s Alan
Woodward was one of several Tottenham comrades to have married,
and yet neither his own wife nor the wives or girlfriends of his comrades
featured in his account. On one level, women's background presence
is unsurprising, given the misogynistic experiences some feminists recalled
from Trotskyist groups.[89] This masculine sociability might be seen as
a logical extension of the fraternal bonds 'angry' working-class protagonists had modelled and which many of the men strongly identified
with as adolescents. However, the YS/IS milieu showed no signs of
the 'sex-hostility' characteristic of 'angries' and of male gangs like the
teddy boys. The 59 Society, for example, contained many young women
of secondary school and university age. Women like Joan Feinmann,
Fiona Scott-Batey and Jane Owens were daughters of Tyneside Labour
councillors, whilst others were drawn in through participation in
Tyneside CND. The fluid membership between CND and the YS encouraged a mutual libertarianism in social and sexual values. These radical
youngsters, unsurprisingly, displayed evidence of the changing sexual
behaviour and attitudes post-war sociologists observed most prominently

within the avant-garde youth subcultures. In the early to mid-1960s young women as well as men around the left milieux expressed a growing sense of social and sexual agency that allowed individuals like seventeen-year-old, beatnik Bronwen Davis to head off alone to London for demonstrations.

John Charlton's reflections on the opportunities CND and the 59 Society provided for social and sexual freedom were echoed by female members like Jane (Lu) Bell, who felt stifled by the paternalistic rules of her Newcastle University hall of residence. The extent to which such sentiments were shared by other young CND and YS members signalled how mutually companionable relations between the sexes could exist alongside the fraternal bonds of comradeship. Bob's casual relationships with Hackney women extended to the branch, cementing his belonging because, alongside sex, activism encompassed an intimate area for personal and political exploration. Di Parkin emphasised how friendships with male as well as female members rested on their shared identities as revolutionaries.[90] This personal and political mutuality would also characterise male–female relations at the height of the VSC. However, this is not to deny the contradictory gendered experiences some women experienced inside early socialist milieux, often an extension of those they had faced in relation to radical youth culture. For Di, belonging to the Wimbledon YS on equal terms to men had meant adopting male mannerisms, including heavy beer drinking. She first recalled a sense of contradiction between her femaleness and the masculine worker ethos when:

> I had a working-class boyfriend, a factory worker, and we went to the pub with other mates of his with their girlfriends, and the blokes were at the bar ordering drinks and they said 'Well, you should be over there' [in the lounge]. I did go over there. These girlfriends of theirs were traditionally female . . . They were talking about things that I was absolutely not interested in . . . like, oh I don't know, fashion or knitting. I was really arrogantly despising of where most women stood at this time.

For Di these bouffant-styled women were entirely removed from her revolutionary self; she belonged at the bar with the men. Yet, along with other girls in her milieu, her post-beatnik dress represented her own political feminine aesthetic: black opaque tights, black kohl pencil drawn around the eyes, white lipstick, and black hair worn loosely to the waist. Aware that comrades' 'dolly-bird' girlfriends were not taken intellectually seriously, she 'kind of wanted to be a man'. Yet, in order to first gain their attention, she drew upon a traditional model of feminine sexuality, displaying her 'play-girl figure with big breasts and long legs' to get 'what I wanted from them'.

Bronwen Davis' experience with north London anarchists revealed similar contradictions. From 1969 she moved freely to and from demonstrations in and around the capital, her mobility reminiscent of the 'swinging' woman commentators noted remapping metropolitan social and moral norms. The more liberal parenting facilitating the social and economic agency enjoyed by sixties' youth made possible her adolescent activism: 'I was sort of left to my own devices quite a lot. They didn't disapprove of me going off and things.'[91] Yet, as for counter-cultural women, this freedom was offset by the indignity of a casual male chauvinism labelling her and members' girlfriends 'chicks'. Inside the group, Bronwen performed a maternal role that saw her manning LSE's make-shift medical centre during the October, 1968 VSC demonstration, nurturing doped-out anarchists. However, this is not to deny her agency in relation to these young men. The group's radical composition expressed her particular social antagonism, and supplied a libertarian space in which to escape the confusions of home and school. One year before going up to Oxford as a student, Bronwen accompanied the anarchists as and when she wished, bestowing care upon members that reflected her sympathy for their sorry circumstances: 'They were a really disparate group ... One of them was on the run from the military police. I think he had joined the army at sixteen and decided by the time he was seventeen or eighteen he didn't like it and dropped out, and he was actually on the run.'

YS men's public displays of political identity and comradeship minimised space for the feminine. Alan Woodward insisted he did not intentionally describe women's role in pejorative terms, signalling his respect for one particular comrade's wife: a 'fully fledged politico'. Yet she stood out because of her activity; most were 'little women' who 'tagged along behind this group of very active, very effective men ... shit-hot basically'.[92] For Alan, the ties of comradeship were explicitly masculine, despite his wife's activism. This traditionally working-class male culture seems to have endured partly because it fed off the traditional gender division of labour inside the post-war family, the powerful discourse of motherhood and maternalism perpetuating women's childcare responsibilities. Yet, Alan did emphasise that he took his turn looking after the children to allow his wife to attend YS meetings. Perhaps conscious of the post-feminist context in which he told his story, nevertheless neither he nor the other YS men perceived young women as threats to their male solidarity even if they accepted women's subordinate status in the group. Their fraternity simply denied their culture an emotive, feminine space.

These young men belonged to a political culture where they were caught between shifting, often conflicting models of class and gender identity. On the one hand, sites of agitation such as the factory, docks and coal mines brought them into contact with an older working-class identity which rested on established ideas of masculinity and femininity. Traditionally gendered notions of class fitted easily alongside the fictional representations many had read as adolescents as well as wider social messages underlining women's subordinate status, where femininity continued to be defined through home and family. On the other hand, within their own families, through contact with those of friends, and friendships and romances with women in their circles, these men had been exposed to increasingly complicated notions of masculinity and femininity, including the companionability characterising post-war working- and middle-class marriage. Bob's description of his East End father echoed the model of the 'new' working-class man described by sociologists such as Michael Young, Peter Willmott and Ferdynand Zweig; one who was increasingly domesticated, even feminised in his softer approach to his wife and children. Although Bob's father was a dock worker, immersed in a gender-segregated industry where heavy drinking underscored a dominant masculinity, his role in the household had distinguished him from other men in the neighbourhood:

> My father had a very different role in the household to the majority of men. There were things he wouldn't do. He would never iron but he did cook. He did wash up . . . he took a much closer involvement in childcare. He had a role of working-class fatherhood which would be more typical of today, but this was in the 1950s. It was to do with his politics and to do with his early experiences. My Dad grew up in the really tough times in the East End and his mother . . . I suspect it was some form of post-natal depression . . . He actually effectively became a functioning family.[93]

The gendered contradictions of these men's YS subculture rested on experiences of and exposure to class and gender models that by the mid-1960s were as much in transition as the Left itself.

This chapter has shown how, for a particular cohort of working-class men, their encounters with the far Left coincided with specific experiences of class, family relations, gender and locality in the early to mid-1960s. Their narratives suggest new ways of viewing the gendered contradictions of the early activist milieu: subjectivity and the bonds of comradeship were shaped within a shifting social and political landscape in which to be a young activist woman was replete with uncertainty. The activity of most scholarship boys and girls, however, began in mid-1960s universities, where their exposure to longstanding labour politics occurred in greater dialogue with international New Left movements. In New Left sites working-, lower- and middle-class students became distanced from their home environments as political subjectivity became invested with a militant internationalism. Young English activists saw at first hand, or through television and photographs, the possibilities which the actions of foreign students and workers presented for external change, in ways that would inform their own experiences of grass-roots activity in the anti-war movement, in student strikes, in the factories, docks and in tenants' campaigns. The next chapter pursues the tensions surrounding gender, class, social mores and subjectivity marking the experiences of university students. In the late 1960s the activist network which spawned from the capital and expanded to contacts overseas acquired an internal, psychic shape as much as a tangible cultural form. For young men and women it facilitated freedom of movement across cultures and away from traditional social norms, though some heard in left milieux reassuring echoes of home. Within these metropolitan and provincial enclaves, radical students made connections to childhood structures of feeling around class, and found political roles and theoretical frameworks which they began to relate to the rapid unfolding of late-sixties global politics.

Notes

1 F. Mort, 'Social and Symbolic Fathers and Sons in Postwar Britain', *Journal of British Studies*, 38:3 (1999), p. 378.
2 M. Freedman, 'From "Character-Training" to "Personal Growth": The Early History of Outward Bound 1941–1965', *History of Education*, 40:1 (2011), pp. 21–43; J. Gledhill, 'White Heat, Guide Blue: The Girl Guide Movement in the 1960s', *Contemporary British History* (2013), pp. 68–9.
3 M. Ingham, *Now We Are Thirty: Women of the Breakthrough Generation* (London: Eyre Methuen), p. 85.
4 Jackson and Marsden, *Education and the Working Class*, p. 148.
5 Charlton, *Don't You Hear the H-Bomb's Thunder?*, p. 56.
6 Interview with Sandy Irving.
7 Interview with John Charlton.
8 Interview with Gilda Peterson.
9 Interview with David Carter, Middlesbrough, 1 June, 2009.
10 Interview with Bronwen Davis.
11 See, for example, L. Segal, *Slow Motion: Changing Masculinities, Changing Men* (London: Virago, 1990), pp. 13–14.
12 Interview with John Charlton.
13 J. Osborne, 'They Call It Cricket', in M. Maschler (ed.), *Declaration* (London: Macgibbon & Kee, 1957), p. 61.

14 K. Tynan, 'The Angry Young Movement', *Curtains: Selections from the Drama Criticism and Related Writings* (London: Longmans, 1961), p. 193.
15 Interview with Ian Birchall.
16 H. Young, 'Representation and Reception: An Oral History of Gender in British Children's Story Papers, Comics and Magazines in the 1940s and 1950s' (Unpublished PhD thesis, University of Strathclyde, 2006), p. 169.
17 Interview with Sandy Irving.
18 P. Bailey, 'Jazz at the Spirella: Coming of Age in Coventry in the 1950s', in B. Conekin, F. Mort and C. Waters (eds), *Moments of Modernity: Reconstructing Britain 1945–1964* (London: Rivers Oram Press, 1999), pp. 22–40.
19 Dawson, *Soldier Heroes*, p. 48.
20 Interview with David Carter.
21 Interview with Victor Seidler.
22 Rowbotham, *Woman's Consciousness, Man's World*, p. 44.
23 G. Eley, 'The Family is a Dangerous Place: Memory, Gender, and the Image of the Working-Class', in B. Rosenstone (ed.), *Revisioning History* (Princeton: Princeton University Press, 1993), pp. 15–29.
24 A. McRobbie, *Feminism and Youth Culture* (Basingstoke: Macmillan Education, 1991), p. 17.
25 Rowbotham, *Woman's Consciousness, Man's World*, p. 12.
26 Interview with Bronwen Davis.
27 E. Wilson, *Only Half-Way to Paradise: Women in Postwar Britain, 1945–1968* (London: Virago, 1980), pp. 2–8.
28 Interview with Gilda Peterson.
29 Interview with Di Parkin, Totnes, 27 April, 2009 and Warwick, 23 December, 2012.
30 Eley, 'Distant Lives, Still Lives', p. 20.
31 Rowbotham, *Promise of a Dream*, p. 8.
32 Rowbotham, *Woman's Consciousness, Man's World*, pp. 13–15.
33 F. Parkin, *Middle-Class Radicalism: The Social Bases of the Campaign for Nuclear Disarmament* (Manchester: Manchester University Press, 1968), pp. 160–1.
34 Interview with James Hinton.
35 J. Diski, *The Sixties* (London: Profile Books, 2009), p. 28.
36 Rosen, 'All in the Family', p. 59.
37 J. Nuttall, *Bomb Culture* (London: Paladin, 1970), p. 47
38 Cited in Fraser (ed.), *1968*, p. 35.
39 M. Veldman, *Fantasy, the Bomb and the Greening of Britain: Romantic Protest 1945–1980* (Cambridge: Cambridge University Press, 1994), p. 151.
40 Interview with Max Farrar.
41 Interview with Bronwen Davis.
42 S. Carroll, 'Danger! Official Secret: the Spies for Peace: Discretion and Disclosure in the Committee of 100', *History Workshop Journal*, 69, Spring, 2010, pp. 158–76.

43 Interview with Lee Comer.
44 Ibid.
45 Interview with Victor Seidler.
46 Interview with Chris Ratcliff, Hebden Bridge, 5 June, 2009.
47 Di Parkin, 'Significant Crossroads as a Teenager or Young Adult or How I Became a Revolutionary', in the Di Parkin Archive (hereafter DPA), p. 3.
48 Interview with Gilda Peterson.
49 Ingham, *Now We Are Thirty*, p. 67.
50 E. Connell, 'The Day I Asked: Are We Going To Die at Three O'clock Mum?', *News on Sunday*, 15 November, 1987, p. 1.
51 Interview with Wisty Hoyland.
52 Interview with Steve Jefferys.
53 Interview with Caroline Bond.
54 Interview with Phil Hearse, London, 23 December, 2009.
55 Interview with John Charlton.
56 *Sanity*, September, 1962, p. 3.
57 Cited in Fraser (ed.), *1968*, p. 34.
58 Rowbotham, *Promise of a Dream*, p. 69.
59 Interview with Steve Jefferys.
60 M. Kenny, *The First New Left: British Intellectuals after Stalin* (London: Lawrence and Wishart, 1995), p. 24.
61 Interview with Phil Hearse.
62 Interview with Joan Smith.
63 Interview with Val Graham.
64 Charlton, *Don't You Hear the H-Bomb's Thunder?*, p. 100.
65 Interview with John Charlton.
66 Cited in Fraser (ed.), *1968*, p. 35.
67 Interview with Victor Seidler.
68 P. Cohen, 'Sub-cultural Conflict and Working Class Community', *Working Papers in Cultural Studies*, 2, Spring (1972), University of Birmingham, p. 22.
69 Interview with Bob Light.
70 D. Fowler, *Youth Culture in Modern Britain, c. 1920–c. 1970: From Ivory Tower to Global Movement* (London: Palgrave Macmillan, 2008), p. 131.
71 Interview with Fred Lindop.
72 Rowbotham, *Woman's Consciousness, Man's World*, p. 18.
73 Interview with Bob Light.
74 Interview with Alan Watts, London, 20 March, 2009.
75 Interview with Roger Cox.
76 M. Shaw, '"The Making of a Party?" The International Socialists 1965–1976', in R. Miliband and J. Saville (eds), *The Socialist Register* (London: Merlin Press, 1978), p. 104.
77 Interview with Alan Watts.
78 Ibid.

79 Interview with Roger Cox.

80 Callaghan, *British Trotskyism*, p. 101.

81 Interview with Sarah Cox.

82 Interview with Bob Light.

83 Interview with Alan Watts.

84 Interview with Bob Light.

85 Interview with Alan Woodward, London, 2 January, 2009.

86 W. Thompson and M. Collins, 'The Revolutionary Left and the Permissive Society', in M. Collins (ed.), *The Permissive Society and Its Enemies: Sixties British Culture* (London: Rivers Oram Press, 2007), p. 160.

87 Interview with Bob Light.

88 B. Osgerby, *Youth in Britain since 1945* (Oxford: Blackwell, 1998), pp. 23–6.

89 S. Rowbotham, 'Women's Liberation and the New Politics'; A. Sebestyen, in M. Wandor, *Once a Feminist: Stories of a Generation* (London: Virago, 1990), pp. 138–9.

90 Charlton, *Don't You Hear the H-Bomb's Thunder?*, pp. 102–3; interview with Bob Light; interview with Di Parkin.

91 M. Luckett, 'Travel and Mobility: Femininity and National Identity in Swinging London Films', in J. Ashby and A. Higson (eds), *British Cinema Past and Present* (London: Routledge, 2000), pp. 115–33; interview with Bronwen Davis.

92 Interview with Alan Woodward.

93 Interview with Bob Light.

3

The student movement and
the Vietnam Solidarity Campaign

Young activists' attendance at institutions of higher education coincided with the global upheavals that came to be associated with 1968. Against a background of university expansion and reform, their student experiences to some extent reflected official recognition of the importance university institutions were starting to play in the lives of an expanding minority of working- and middle-class sixties youth as environments for social self-making.[1] Amidst three years of intellectual discovery, the self-searching of adolescence became intensified in 'liberal' institutions where past and present strands of political, social and emotional education elided. Alongside official curricula, radical students studied Marxist and New Left ideas alongside radical discourses of psychology and sociology. New understandings of class relations, trade union and labour politics accompanied revelations about the moral hypocrisy of western leaders, in the midst of intense experiences of cultural ferment and social and sexual experimentation. The expansion of students' inner and outer worlds created heightened sensations of being. In the late sixties it was not simply that they were spectators to dramatic political, social and cultural shifts. Rather, as this chapter explains, student activists often came to see themselves as dynamic social actors, contributing to a rapidly changing outer world. For many, university marked the start of a genuinely rooted belief in imminent revolution and all the political and personal possibilities they imagined such transformations might entail. Depending upon interviewees' histories, the legacy of this utopian moment continued to inform their outlook on the world and remained a powerful influence in the shape of the stories they told about these years.

This third chapter details the particular socio-psychological, political and cultural experiences young men and women underwent within the left milieux at metropolitan and provincial universities across England in the mid- to late 1960s. Set against the backdrop of late-sixties global ferment, it explores how they interacted with and internalised local, national and international politics. The focus of the chapter is the political, social and emotional processes with which they shaped the eclectic activist cultures that emerged around the VSC and attempted to assemble liberated political and social selves.

Memory, selfhood and 1968

In recent years transnational studies of sixties actors have highlighted certain commonalities in the ways in which former activists narrate and assign meaning to their experiences. Scholars have become attentive to the intricate and shifting relationship between memory, place, identity and cultural discourses surrounding 1968, exploring the complex re-workings activists' memories undergo in dialogue with official discourses as they seek to make sense of their activism in the context of their life histories.[2] Such studies offer useful comparative reflections for thinking about the particular accounts which interviewees in this collection told. They raise important questions about how the stories of post-war English youth fit into the wider narrative framework that has emerged around representatives of the 1968 generation.

Interviewees' life stories bore striking resemblance to transnational stories that interweave personal histories with collective representations of 1968. Memories of student activism were often infused with the dreams and sense of transformation scholars associate with 'the social imaginary of 1968'. Throughout their narratives the iconography of 1968 – barricades, bullets, tear-gas and tanks – suggested how trans-national representations of the era had become as firmly embedded in the past and present identities of English activists as those of their foreign counterparts. Political, social and cultural influences from across the international spectrum often seemed to coalesce into a seamless experience of discovery and awakening. Shared images of remembered student selves echoed stories of political astuteness and agency, success narratives that international contemporaries often told. In these English narratives individual memories had been interwoven within a collective framework where the keynote of experience was liberation – the celebra-tory dimension of 1968. Whether interviewees' early left activity occurred at university or elsewhere, the collective identity they shared was the sense of belonging to an international radical collective, aligned with left-wing actors from across the globe. Within this framework inter-viewees saw their activism as having challenged prevailing orthodoxies in ways many still identified with to the present.

Margaret Renn situated the political excitement and personal devel-opment she had undergone throughout twenty years as an IS activist within 1968 specifically: 'It [1968] was incredibly formative and very confidence building. I am not the person I would have been if I had not . . . the world became a much smaller place and your intellectual analysis of the world became a much finer thing.'[3] The year stood out partly because it represented the start of her membership: she joined IS as an eighteen-year-old student at London's Goldsmiths College. Yet the validation she derived from her activism also made 1968 a symbolic marker because of the associations of political and personal liberation the year held in the public memory of the Left: 'I think in '68 it was all very easy . . . the battle lines were very clear for us who were moving leftwards. You were for or against the Vietnam War. You were for or against the Tory government.' Reflecting on the place the organisation had held in her life, she recalled incredulously a former comrade 'who said 1968 wasn't all it was cracked up to be'. For Margaret, 1968 was a time when 'you just opened the door and said yes'. Her reflection applied to her memories of '68 specifically as well as to those of her activism as a whole: 'How can you, even if you no longer agree with it, how can you not see it as an incredibly positive thing?' Margaret's testimony raises important questions about how and why interviewees drew upon collective discourses of 1968, and why this appeared as a particular feature of their university stories.

Following the work of sociologist Maurice Halbwachs, historians and practitioners of memory studies have focused attention on the ways in which individuals engage with collective memories to shape a coherent self. Historians of 1968 have become attentive to the need to understand how individuals draw upon political and cultural representations of the era in an effort to attain 'composure', the sense of psychic ease individuals achieve through composing a version of the self they can comfortably accept. Robert Gildea, for example, has reflected on the way in which French activists gave similar accounts to the narratives often found in literature about the trajectory of events. He found that interviewees were more likely 'to elicit a ready-made discourse' where they did not have to negotiate a painful path through 1968, but where they had a clear conception of their self-identity.[4] In this context it is important to consider the meaning of collective identity as interviewees in this study understood it at the time of their activism and since. Jan Hassmann offers a useful definition: 'Collective identity is a question of identification on the part of individuals involved. It does not exist "as such" but only as it is present in the mind and behaviour of group members and as it is able to animate their thoughts and actions.'[5] Where interviewees became active as university students in the mid- to late 1960s, it may well be that nostalgia for the social freedoms of these years made them more likely to reproduce social and cultural myths that placed emphasis on subjective liberation. Yet, such an explanation can be only partial and is at best inadequate. Experiences that have a strong emotional or sensory impact are more likely to be consolidated into long-term memory.[6] For this student cohort, significant social and emotional rites of passage – leaving home, new friendships, falling in love and contemplating adult life – coincided with social, cultural and political upheavals in a way that was always likely to intensify their impact and make them more memorable with time. As this chapter will show, sensory perception was a prominent feature of interviewees' narratives and revealed much about impressionable moments and their longevity.

The liberated self was a defining marker of the stories individuals told. The plural subject was the key agent behind the emancipatory impulse underlining most representations of 1968 – students, workers, blacks and women are amongst the social groups whose stories dominate the literature. Collective liberation was the hallmark or 'spirit' of social protest movements whose participants sought to overturn authoritarian, elitist power hierarchies in the West and beyond.[7] In her 'collective autobiography' of Turin student activists, Luisa Passerini highlighted the way in which the '68 spirit had shaped an enduring collective subjectivity for her and her respondents. Its longevity, she suggested, derived from the 'vein of '68 acknowledged as a worldwide phenomenon that changed and will change the course of lives'.[8] Passerini's reflections suggest the psychic need with which interviewees in this collection reproduced this plural self. It made sense of the validation they had acquired from university rebellion and from the shape of activist trajectories which evolved from this point.

This collective identity was informed at least partially by contemporary cultural discourses. In the late 1960s, for example, media commentaries of student protests had labelled prominent personalities as dangerous radicals.[9] Sociological and historical interpretations subsequently built upon contemporary portraits, preserving them for posterity and becoming internalised by young activists themselves. One notable example can be seen in the stories of men and women who participated in the student unrest at the LSE in 1966–68 and who went on to be active in left organisations and community projects, sometimes up to the present. John Rose stated: 'It was the first sit-in in Britain and it caused a sensation. The press were down every day and made us all feel terribly important, and to some extent we were quite important.'[10] Laurie Flynn referred to the twenty to thirty books he had read on 1968, and set his narrative against this wider picture: 'People who had come to LSE had come to create a new space, they were New Left radicals. People had come to LSE to ask why we live this way. Why is society like it is? Can we live in a different way?'[11] He interspersed his account with terms often found in the sociological and historical literature, including 'breakage', 'fracture', 'rupture' and 'new ideas'. Drawing upon cultural representations of the era in this way, he revealed the extent to which his current identity remained embedded within celebratory discourses that stressed the national and global achievements of 1968: the political and social renewal he and his contemporaries had made possible. The utopian spirit that had inspired Laurie and other student radicals to challenge LSE officials in a contest over institutional democracy had left a powerful imprint on his early adult sense of self that held implications for how he lived his life to the present. The political songs of his youth had become a metaphor for his memories of student revolt: 'We lived in daily communion with Martin Luther King and the civil rights movement. These were the songs of our lives: Bob Dylan's "How many roads must a man walk through?"'

Even allowing for blows to the Left in the 1980s, the surviving faith LSE radicals continued to show in human agency suggested that such sentiments could not be attributed to nostalgia alone.[12] The New Left concept of people's control retained a vibrant quality in their current self-understanding. LSE Socialist Society and IS member Martin Tompkinson signalled his surviving faith in the agency of his student cohort by drawing upon language he and his comrades had used in pamphlets written during the sit-in. As is typical with former '68 activists, his memories were interlaced with retrospective commentary about the historical legacy of the protests. He clearly viewed the revolt as a significant dimension of wider global events:

> There was a guy married with two kids and always in the library, determined to get a first. He did and in '68, a few weeks later after graduation, I discovered from the other rugby guys that as a result of what had gone on he had decided he could no longer be an agent of the ruling class, and had jacked his job in with a wife and four kids to support. Because of what we were doing people changed, but they changed as a result of the impact of being involved in things when they could see that they themselves can change the world or a small bit of the world around them.[13]

Scholars' attention to former student activists likely reinforced interviewees' sense of belonging to a '68 collective. Before our interview, Chris Ratcliffe had already participated in several projects for the internet and television, and was eager to tell his story, to compare it with others and to hear my interpretation of his account. The weight he attached to his memories owed much to the agency he had found through his central role in the 1968 Essex revolt. This perhaps became more significant with time because the decision to go to university had represented something of a departure in his young working-class life. His participation in memory projects on these events had probably enhanced his understanding of the possibilities he and contemporaries had gained as a result:

> I was trying to develop myself as a person and what did I want out of life, and I remember thinking... there were speeches, people said we don't just have to go out and get a job in a big corporation and that is it; we could spend the rest of our life trying to work for a better world, and I think most of us did or continue to do.[14]

There are, however, important considerations for how to understand the personal stories of self-making woven within these collective narratives. The power of the collective can challenge the oral historian's ability to access and create space for individual voices of experience.[15] Once young activists began entering universities in the mid- to late 1960s they discovered left circles at formative moments of self-making. Only a small number of interviewees described arriving at university with clearly defined left identities. Even then, these identities were re-worked or consolidated as they became politically engaged. The following section explores several stories in detail to show how accounts of student radicalism and left milieux are cut through with individual histories and subjectivities. It will consider how and why, individually and collectively, these shaped students' affinity for activism, so that some carried it above and beyond university.

Arrival at sixties universities

In the mid- to late 1960s New Left spaces performed particular social and psychological roles for insecure undergraduates arriving at unfamiliar metropolitan and provincial centres. For several working-class students, leaving home to go to university was their first experience of spending any prolonged period away from their home towns. Until he went to Sussex University in 1965, Stephen Trafford's youth was centred on the same council estate in the seaside town of Bridlington. His father, a night cleaner on the buses, had been a prisoner of war in Germany, and his reluctance to stray far from home restricted the family's movements beyond occasional visits to relatives in Hull. Although Sussex seemed an exciting distance away, the southern seaside town of

Brighton also felt familiar enough for an adolescent little inclined to travel far: 'Not until I was seventeen or eighteen really did I go anywhere on my own or with my mates of any distance ... We did go hitchhiking on the continent but I think we got stuck outside Calais and decided oh well, we'll just hang about here, so we weren't terribly ambitious.'[16] Other working-class students, keen for a taste of new cultures, deliberately chose universities far away. Gilda chose Birmingham because of its distance from Hartlepool: 'I wanted to go south, you see, and I thought Birmingham was really south. I was quite shocked when I got there to hear people say they had come up to Birmingham. Up from where?'[17] However, once away, some working- and lower middle-class students felt insecure in the company of more confident students from middle- and upper middle-class homes. For some the uncomfortable class dislocations they had felt at grammar or public schools became heightened within institutions where, once again, they found themselves in a social minority. In 1966 Val Graham arrived at Birmingham University to read Russian Studies. Conscious of what her family's working-class roots meant for her future as a young woman, she felt cautious about the possibilities this redbrick institution had to offer her: 'You know to me the most thing, the most thing I probably could do was be a teacher, you know, that was it really ... You didn't do law because it wasn't in your mind to do it and because you knew that you had to have money.'[18] However, Val remained ill-prepared for the inferiority she felt; as an assertive grammar school pupil she had spoken her mind to middle-class pupils and teachers alike. Now in the company of a predominantly middle-class male student body, she felt alive to her social constraints and unacceptability as a working-class girl:

> I felt I was not like one of them, and I remember once my Dad coming to visit me and people sort of making fun of him ... because he was a factory worker, you, you know it was like a joke to them, and he had come all the way to see me.

The perception of social and gendered difference defined Val's early days at Birmingham, but a few months into her first term she joined the Socialist Society and began a relationship with another working-class member. For Val, the Left carried familiar associations of her Labour-supporting family and home town of Chesterfield, and offered possibilities for social belonging. Her story suggests that motivations for joining left organisations were often pragmatic, interwoven with students' journeys to adulthood as they struggled to manage the social and cultural transitions from secondary school to higher education. Once inside left groups, the identity that students like Val found built upon their experiences of home and family and became embedded in close friendships and early sexual relationships with likeminded members who shared similar backgrounds and histories:

> I got involved with a young man in the Socialist Society . . . We did actually come from a very similar background. I mean Kevin was Irish and his father was a factory worker too . . . Kevin came to university and they'd actually moved, and Kevin's father had got a job I think at the Rover factory, right. And I ended up towards the end of my time actually playing hockey not for the university team but for the factory team, yeah. So that's really, you know, quite where I felt at home.

Val's affinity with her boyfriend's working-class roots initially framed her attraction to him and defined the sense of belonging she came to feel within the Society. Once the couple became immersed in the full spectrum of Birmingham's student politics, their identity as an activist couple shaped their experiences within radical circles and defined their relationship: 'I mean of course we were just interested in student politics, you know.'

The social alienation some working-class undergraduates struggled to manage was often more acute at older elite institutions. Dave Lyddon had spent the months before starting at Oxford's Pembroke College experimenting with radical cultures around CND. He remembered the distress of his arrival, as the social alienation he had tasted at public school felt magnified in the company of Oxford's student elite:

> I suppose really I was ideologically floundering around. What am I? What do I stand for? What do I believe in? What the hell am I doing here? Because, although I had been to this funny school and you are used to lots of isolation and intense work, and while there were some people who came from genteel posh backgrounds who had fallen on hard times, in the main there were loads of people from working-class backgrounds like me. Come to Oxford and suddenly there is all the posh . . . you know the toffs . . . It felt really weird and I have to say I actually did feel suicidal on my first night.[19]

His reflections on the class-ridden world of sixties Oxford and its capacity to hone a deviant identity echoed many testimonies of working- and lower middle-class students. Elizabeth Wilson noted how 'we were all crazed with class'. Her impoverished background inculcated a 'sly, bitter cynicism' and refusal to succumb to 'fashionable enthusiasms'.[20] After Sheila Rowbotham's adolescent efforts to jettison her Leeds roots, her early days at St Hilda's prompted an immediate reversal, inculcating resistance against a culture where 'you were presumed thick . . . if you had even a middle-class Northern voice'.[21] Dave's account illustrates that, alongside narratives of international radical communion, journeys into the late-sixties Left also followed narrower paths of inner self-questioning. Behind young men's immersion into the fraternity of the Left, insecurities and unhappiness sometimes also lay hidden so that where they came across causes that energised them these could feel profoundly personal because of the ways in which they cut through their own struggles. In a climate in which ambiguity surrounded male expressions of emotional vulnerability, voicing outrage on behalf of oppressed peoples permitted young men to articulate something of their own inner confusions. Dave's search for identity reached a climax in 1968, when he found a cause to invest himself in. Oxford's racial politics provided a connection back to his dissonance from his father's right-wing views and became a springboard for his student politics:

> Right towards the end of the term, in June, you became aware there had been a sit-down in the Cowley road outside this hairdresser's called Annette's, because they refused to do . . . basically black women's hair, and there had been a sit-down of about forty people . . . somehow [I] became aware of it, as did my mates, and [we] agreed we would do a follow- up at the end of that first afternoon so a whole raft of us sat-down on the pavement, and the police started to move us away and [began] arresting us, and I am sitting there thinking this is the kind of moment of truth. What do I believe in? I believe[d] in this so I got myself arrested.

This 'moment of truth' marked the start of Dave's involvement in several student demonstrations throughout his second year: picketing All Souls College, joining the third VSC march on 27 October, 1968, and becoming embroiled in the activities of Oxford's Revolutionary Socialist Student Federation (RSSF). By the end of his first year he had also changed course from Chemistry to Politics, Philosophy and Economics (PPE), in line with his new-found interests. Without the prospect of preliminary examinations, he had time to immerse himself into student unrest and to develop his understanding of Marxism. His new social circle helped to alleviate the loneliness and alienation he had initially experienced at Oxford. Like Rowbotham, adopting a radical persona alongside other alternative students enabled him to carve out a social space in which he could feel more at ease before elite sets, who came to seem less threatening. Reflecting back on this self-blossoming, Dave saw a direct connection between the start of his activism and the man he saw himself as today. From the moment of conception Marxism became an intrinsically personal, socially enabling aspect of self:

> I was gradually groping towards some kind of politics, and I'd describe myself, probably, in the year '68–69 as a kind of anarcho-Marxist. That's

how I saw myself. That I kind of had a Marxist view without believing in the need for a party . . . and I think, yeah, there were various things going on in my personal life as well, whereas having been to a single-sex school, and you've got to university where there is almost no female students, you know, you find this very difficult to make relationships. But very soon I managed to cut and break through that, and it was kind of no holds barred after that (laughs).

Radical students and Marxist literature

As radical students stood poised on the brink of activism, the utopian tenets of Marx's writings opened their eyes to new possibilities of being. During the early to mid-1960s cheap translated editions of Marx's early writings became increasingly available and were read avidly by students seeking libertarian socialism free from Soviet Communism. Ian Birchall began to explore Marx in the summer of 1962, when he finally saw himself 'as a socialist':

> I had actually read quite a bit of Marx . . . A friend of mine bought me . . . for my twenty-second birthday . . . she wasn't political at all, but she knew I liked this sort of stuff; and she bought me the selected works of Marx and Engels in two volumes. Now, at that time you could get them fantastically cheaper, for about ten shillings and six pence for two volumes of about six hundred pages each, and I remember in the summer, just after I had done my final exams, I was waiting for my degree results, and I just sat down and read my way right the way through these two volumes.[22]

Narratives about students' Marxist reading experiences show how texts aided their search for political and personal meaning on the Left, adding to the idealistic hopes they nurtured for the future. Dave Lyddon encountered Marx in the summer of 1970, when student politics felt increasingly irrelevant to the class struggles gathering momentum. Following the previous autumn's strikes by car workers, coal miners, local government workers, nurses and firemen, Edward Heath's Conservative government had announced its intention to curb accelerating wages and the unions were gearing up for battle. In this context Dave's close friend, an IS member, awakened Dave to the possibilities membership in the organisation might bring: 'IS seemed very open. It had an account of the Soviet Union which made sense to me and it . . . fitted with what I was groping towards.'[23] Against this background, Marx's writings felt revelatory: 'In my third year at university I read all three volumes of Marx's *Kapital*. It was just very, very profound. It is kind of opening you up to seeing the world in a very different way

and this is at the same time as I am also discovering anti-psychiatry,
R. D. Laing and all that, and so I am getting into a kind of blowing
my mind [sic].' Ian Birchall too discovered in Marx 'all sorts of illu-
minations' because, like Dave, he read them alongside IS writings;
together they helped him to criticise Labour and New Left politics and
to locate his political heartbeat:

> I remember reading the thesis on Feuerbach and suddenly realising
> that . . . the subjective and objective were interlinked, probably in a very
> philosophically naive way, but certainly all sorts of illuminations hap-
> pened together with reading things like *International Socialism*, which
> was having debates on reform and revolution . . . I read *Tribune* avidly
> and yet at the same time I had this sort of dilemma that really this stuff
> in *Tribune*, you know, emotionally I was with it. I knew what they were
> saying, but intellectually it was really a bit shallow. At the same time I
> was also reading *New Left Review* and a lot of that seemed to me to be
> rather pretentious, and rather removed from what was really going on
> in the world, and it was [so] really when I heard some of the people from
> *International Socialism*.[24]

However much Marx's writings moved radical students towards
left enclaves or facilitated collective political thoughts, radical reading
experiences were highly individual; within the texts each student heard
subtly different tenets to make sense of their own histories, and they
carried these personal messages into the Left. James Hinton and
Richard Kuper were close friends in Cambridge University's Labour
Club during the early 1960s. Independently, they each located similar
possibilities in Marx's writings to develop romantic constructs about
the working class. For James, like Dave, Marx presented political solutions to ease his social and psychic discomfort. Read in conjunction
with Dostoyevsky's cautionary and socially critical novel, *Crime and
Punishment*, his writings offered possibilities for coming to terms with
his upper middle-class background:

> I wanted to find a way of finding the ordinary or the working class, and
> that was all to do with hang-ups about this relatively posh privileged
> background . . . Between school and university I hitchhiked to the South
> of France and I took with me Dostoyevsky's *Crime and Punishment*
> and G. D. H. Cole's Everyman translation of *Das Kapital* [Vol. 1] in two
> little volumes. I read these two books side by side and I became a
> Marxist.[25]

South African-born Richard brought a very different history to
Marx's writings. In 1960 he went to Cambridge from the University
of Johannesburg. Although his parents were atheists, he had been raised

in a culturally Jewish environment, and as a teenager had joined a Zionist youth movement because of the solutions it seemed to offer his divided nation. He left South Africa carrying stories of England as a land of freedom and tolerance, but Cambridge's old class customs and *in loco parentis* rules presented a disappointing reality: 'I didn't know what had hit me when I got to Cambridge. We still had the old rules. You had to be in your room by twelve at night. You couldn't have women in your room . . . You had to wear gowns after dark. It was a bizarre environment from someone who up to the age of nineteen in South Africa drove around when I wanted to.'[26] Only the Labour Club offered a place to meet English socialist students.

Despite his specific circumstances, Richard's reading of Marx's early manuscripts echoed wider student stories of the texts' popular appeal; their concept of socialist freedom suggested tangible ways in which radical students could marry the utopian tenets of Marx's writings with their particular political and social situations. Marx presented to Richard the possibility of a world radically removed from either of those he had hitherto experienced. Above all, the writings presented a new political language to amalgamate the socialist Zionism he had embraced in his native South Africa with the alternative Cambridge life hidden inside the Labour Club. The manuscripts assumed further meaning because he read them in 1964, when he first heard Tony Cliff speak. The Soviet corruptions of Marx's early socialist freedoms became even more apparent after he heard Cliff's reflections on post-war Russia, and he abandoned the Labour Party in favour of IS: 'Tony Cliff came and spoke at the Labour Club and answered all my problems, which was how could you be a Marxist when Russia was doing such terrible things, so it was a revelation and I embraced that kind of Marxism which I saw as a liberatory-anarchist Marxism.' Richard's reading experience illuminates how students' individual histories allowed different possibilities of seeing through Marx. Approaching England's class politics from his South African context perhaps made him more susceptible to a romantic construct of English socialism. The tiny libertarian Trotskyist group, with its cohort of young apprentices, allowed Richard to project his romantic reading of the working class onto its politics:

> there [was] the feeling that this group somehow or other was the embodiment of the possibilities of the new society . . . in IS you met generally young trade unionists who were kind of thoughtful, self-educated in that period, almost overwhelmingly, but you kind of felt, yes, there was all this wasted talent and it was there, and together we could do something.

Reverence for education was palpable amongst young activists; exciting intellectual trends taking place in the 1960s came firmly within the purview of this higher-educated cohort. Students' openness to new political, sociological and cultural ideas fed into social and political experience to inform new ways of looking at social relationships and movements developing around them.

Radical students and the far Left

Chance meetings between students and older Marxists shaped already developing tenets of socialist thought and identity and encouraged many to break from the Labour Party and to move towards IS, *The Week* or (from 1968) the IMG. By the late 1960s these groups had begun to displace the Labour Party as left organisations of choice for students frustrated by Harold Wilson's Labour government. The same speakers who in the previous chapter impressed YS apprentices made an impact on university students who, since early adolescence, had been edging their way towards a place on the Left where they could make sense of Cold War politics, personal experiences and feelings.

In 1961 Fred Lindop was active in the Oxford Labour Club when he had his first real encounter with Marxism. He was previously a '"Bevanite" in the old sense of being a leftist Labour bloke', and his meeting with IS speakers occurred at a moment of transition:

> My first real encounter with Marxism, as opposed to, say, simply reading Christopher Hill's work, was listening to a number of then prominent members of the International Socialists or then the Socialist Review Group as it was called, in particular Alistair MacIntyre, who was a fellow at Nuffield, and then of course people like Michael Kidron who were invited up ... MacIntyre was amusing and exciting, but Kidron had an all-embracing view of the world and an ability to connect things up, and I guess he was the most intellectual person developing me into a sort of Marxist.[27]

Ian Birchall was a Labour Club member alongside Fred who, like other former IS members, remembered his decision to join the organisation as the realisation of an authentic self. Between 1958 and 1961, he moved through and out of the Labour Left. Reflecting back on important markers of this leftward journey, he remembered supporting South Bank building workers in the 1958 strike led by SLL militant Brian Bean, his 'hero worship' of Dennis Potter and Ken Coates, and a night on the 1961 Aldermaston march when he and fellow students sat in a tent with Paul Foot until three o'clock in the morning 'arguing about the relationship between capitalism and war'.[28] These experiences consolidated his earlier discomfort with his middle-class conservative upbringing; by 1962, after a year studying in France, Ian had become 'identifiably socialist'. By the time he heard Kidron speak on the permanent arms economy in the autumn term, he had adopted a more radical position:

> I spent a year in France, which was very interesting because it was the very end of the Algerian War, and although I was in a small village, I was picking up a lot of things around this, and it was a completely different sort of politics because politics in England was voting. Politics in France was blowing people up.

The language of International Socialism spoke powerfully to Ian's exposure to a harsher left politics, offering him an intellectual framework and moral stance that sat more easily with his experiences of imperialist oppression. The group's militant street politics provided his closest taste of the 'real' independence politics he had seen in France. Although the intellectual clarity of IS ideas appealed to Ian, so too did the masculine street militancy that reproduced a tangible image of the revolutionary man he had conjured in Potter and Coates:

> I had never heard anyone before who actually understood how the whole thing, how the whole world system fitted together. I mean the people involved around us were involved in, you know, we were out on the streets, and I was with people from the Oxford International Socialists in the week of the Cuba crisis, and we tried to stage a march, and it was the first time I actually got to a police cordon, pushing and shoving at the police, so it wasn't just an intellectual thing, and that, again, very much impressed me, you know, these were the same people who also had a very rigorous intellectual understanding, but they were also out there in the middle of a punch-up.

Radical students found speakers associated with the IMG no less impressive. Unusually, Phil Hearse had joined *The Week* group whilst still in the sixth form at Ealing grammar school. Although aware that the organisation had only about thirty-five members nationally, he was shocked to find only one other member at York University in 1968 and set about recruiting. He remembered how the branch's profile rose when 'Ernest Mandel came to our university. We had the main lecture theatre. We probably squeezed a thousand people into that.'[29] David Carter illustrated the influence glamorous spokesmen could exercise over undergraduates struggling to choose between far-left groups. In 1969 he arrived at York much less convinced than Phil about his dedication to the IMG. He spent his first term grappling with whether to follow through his adolescent dabble in the Isle of Man's 'hippiedom' or to pursue his attraction to the serious politicos he met around campus: 'I was quite enjoying mixing with both and I wasn't antagonistic to either, but I made a conscious decision that if I'm going to achieve anything I have to become a revolutionary.' David was drawn to the Fourth International's Third World politics, and the impressive showmanship of members like Phil helped him to choose his revolutionary route, and in December, 1970 he joined the Spartacus League, the IMG's youth section.

The intimate left landscape students entered in the mid- to late 1960s, with dual ties to the labour movement and academia, exposed them to a diverse range of Old and New Left speakers. The LSE Socialist Society exemplified the fluid connections and intellectual dynamic that came to characterise the VSC network. It also illustrated the different possibilities for subjectivity students found in university left spaces. During 1964–65 the Society was founded by a small nucleus of IS and Solidarity (anarchist) students out of the smaller Marxist Society, a counterpart to the much larger Labour Club. It represented an intellectual and activist powerhouse filled with sharp minds and personalities. The regular Society meetings and seminars, often led by IS speakers Cliff, Kidron, Palmer and Nigel Harris, provided a lively forum for debating and learning about the new Marxist politics, a supplement to the conservative syllabi still prevailing at the School. LSE postgraduate Richard Kuper found sociology 'an intellectual backwater . . . very untheoretical even at an apologistic level'. Even more 'appalling' was that 'it had nothing to say about why there was a war in Vietnam or about class conflict'.[30] Nigel Coward disliked his BSc Economics course, devoted to free market economics and lacking any 'decent Marxists' on the syllabus. However, around the refectory, in 1966, he 'fell in' with the Marxist Society: 'They made more sense than the course . . . There used to be passionate discussions over a lunchtime cheese roll . . . You had a bigger role in that than you did in one of the normal seminar groups.'[31]

The Society's open political culture attracted a wide range of faces, from leading IS and IMG members to trade unionists, building and dock workers and activists around the VSC. David Widgery was a medical student at the University of London who regularly turned up at the Society. He liked its sardonic guide to lectures similar to the one Berkeley students had created during the Free Speech Movement and was one of many members attending Ralph Miliband's popular public lectures (impressed by Miliband's ability to provide a good exposition of Lenin). On any day Cliff and Paul Foot could be sharing the company of Edward Thompson, along with striking building workers from the Barbican dispute.[32] In the late sixties Thompson's socialist human-ism left a resounding impression on many students encountering his work through their degree studies and left circles. *The Making of the English Working Class* (1963) offered a new way of understanding class as an active process communicated through relationships, culture and social being besides political institutions. His new approach came when left students were discovering the transforming potential of human agency in their university protests and in international movements for self-determination. John Rose explained: 'The *Making of the English Working Class* was a must-read book and we all read it, and it played an important part in our formation because the book itself is a testi-mony to the power of the working class.'[33]

Joan Smith had already joined the IS by the time she went to the LSE in 1964 after 'bumping' into members through her Kenton YS branch. She had already begun to articulate a more radical politics and the Marxist Society seemed an obvious society to join, and the familiar-ity of members' backgrounds helped her to settle into university life: 'There was a small Marxist group of twenty-odd because there was a trade union studies group at the LSE and they were the workers who had gone there instead of going to Ruskin. Again, it was a very familiar and easy group to be in from my background.'[34] With the group's transition to the Socialist Society following Labour's 1964 election vic-tory, Joan was appointed secretary, responsible for organising lectures by Marxist historians Thompson, Eric Hobsbawm and Isaac Deutscher. As members of the original core, she and others brought a more the-oretical take on Marxism than the younger wave of radical students arriving in 1965; their militant politics was informed by the sit-in they orchestrated the following year. Yet the two cohorts readily co-existed and the Society's journal, *Agitator*, shows that during the years of unrest, 1966–68, daily meetings included seminars on topics ranging from the Russian Revolution to Antonio Gramsci, alongside meetings on campaigns from the Barbican strike, Rhodesia and apartheid to the Vietnam War and student power. The *Agitator* testified to the intel-lectual identity the Socialist Society, IS and the literature circulating in these gave to young, predominantly male members whose enthusiasm for action was fundamental to their self-conception as Marxists. When the Society published an article on Marx's 'Theses of Feuerbach' in March, 1966, they quickly sold out.[35] Its open, democratic impulse provided an experimental space for men like Steve Jefferys to hone the activist identity he brought from home: 'I went to the LSE to do eco-nomic history and to change the world. That is what I wanted, to change the world, and opportunities then arrived which enabled me to insert myself in that process.'[36] In contrast, students like Martin Shaw were still in the process of moving away from Labour; in 1965 he joined the Society at a moment of growing disillusionment with the Labour government after hearing his local MP, Transport Minister Steven Swindler, defending what Martin and other students thought was an immigration policy that 'countenanced racism'.[37] Whilst he continued to attend Labour Society meetings and be involved in the left-wing Catholic circle around the magazine *Slant*, the stimulating debates he heard in the Socialist Society made the libertarian Marxism he encountered there increasingly attractive:

> It [the Socialist Society] wasn't adopting any particular position. It seemed to be very open and a milieu in which it was possible to explore different arguments, and decisions would be made on the basis of arguments and evidence, so for me I suppose Marxism was a framework within which my basic commitment could be explored and offered a more scientific sophisticated framework for carrying that forward.

For less seasoned politicos like Martin, the Society's intensive programme of debates and activity also supplied a theoretical and activist education to enhance his self-confidence in the company of articulate, older students who had made the transition to Marxism earlier. Its open intellectual ethos extended to the friendly social atmosphere that appealed to newcomers accustomed to their own youth spaces. That he felt at ease with male members from a range of national and social backgrounds perhaps made Martin more conscious of the subjective transformation he was undergoing alongside them:

> I think we were aware we were making a political journey. One moment which stands out in my mind was when I wrote an article for the Socialist Society journal, the *Agitator*, called the 'Remaking of Socialist Politics' in a duplicated form. I remember him [Laurie Flynn] saying very sagely as he took it off the duplicator, 'Perhaps more the remaking of Martin Shaw by socialist politics', which I thought was very good actually, so incidentally it was a sort of development of my identity, but for me it wasn't like a conversion; it didn't feel like a rupture.[38]

Moments of self-awareness could feel profoundly revelatory as well as heightening bonds of comradeship which members sensed growing between them. The clarity of Martin's memory signalled the moment's significance as a staging-post in his political and intellectual life; inside the Society he was reframing his Christian morality within a humanistic Marxism and re-evaluating the sort of political actions he thought appropriate to achieving change. He rejected his pacifism for the militant politics Steve Jefferys and younger Society members championed during the sit-in, the campaigns over Rhodesia and the Vietnam War.[39]

The VSC network

Students discovered revolutionary groups as young adults engaging critically with new cultures, ideas and struggles, and as post-war subjects looking to situate themselves politically, socially and emotionally. Consequently, at the time and since, these meetings felt profoundly revelatory. As they played sometimes central roles in protests against university authorities, they came to feel themselves actively pushing apart old boundaries constraining social and psychological freedoms. Interviewees told of the excitement characterising these years, creating a picture of students moving collectively across a fluid left landscape, whilst experiencing individual subjective change.

Gilda Peterson's story of activism at Birmingham University exemplified this fluidity. Her account confirmed the open character of the network as it emerged around the VSC; its connection to the personnel, ideas and revolutionary organisations of the English student movement; and the interconnections between protesters at different universities. She joined IS after the Warwick files affair of February, 1970. The scandal, which was leaked to the media and to students' unions, sparked off a pattern of imitations at universities throughout the country, including Birmingham. Through information from the Warwick files two Birmingham sociology students discovered their university had been funding the segregated medical school in Rhodesia's University College.[40] They approached Gilda with their findings; she was a sociology student who had actively participated in Birmingham's 1968 sit-in, and together they began raising money to send a Rhodesian student back to his home country to report on conditions for black medical students. One of the medical students Gilda met on the campaign was a member of Birmingham's IS branch and encouraged her to attend.

Gilda's testimony illustrated how the network's heterogeneous politics coloured the subjectivity she and other young activists developed inside it. The very openness of the landscape translated to her memories; temporality itself assumed a fluid quality as experiences over three years merged together, evoking the freedom with which she moved between radical circles and absorbed intellectual currents, unconstrained by organisational hierarchies or cliques:

> We sort of flirted around with things. I wasn't conscious of there being
> a group. Actually, I think it started with Stuart [Hall]; he lectured us.

> We had the *NLR* [*New Left Review*] about and, well, the whole CCC.
> I suppose [I] was conscious of that, but it wasn't organised; it was all
> part, a bit like the reading of everything else ... There was all sorts of
> discussions going on in all sorts of areas, and all sorts of points of views,
> but there wasn't a driving organisation, it was just lots of excitement
> about.[41]

Shifts from topic to topic; from the sit-in and discoveries made in
discussion groups to impressions of the left scene, denoted the intoxicating impact of intellectual and political ferment, whilst her sensuous,
playful language ('flirted') suggested the specific social and sexual mobility the network offered her as a young woman. The plethora of left
groups on campus enabled Gilda to experiment without commitment;
she was peripherally involved in the RSSF, aware of the 'red bases'
connected to the IMG, and friendly with a few Maoists, unaware of
IS until 1969. Memories of the CCC reinforced the intoxicating feel of
Gilda's student years; ideas merged into one another so that she found
it difficult to make overall sense of their meaning either at the time or
since:

> I thought intellectually it was incredibly sort of buzzy about trying to
> systematise, and maybe Chomsky was on to something, and we could
> find out how to systematise thinking in a way that wasn't just cause and
> effect, and we kind of drew more from literature and sociological notions
> as well. Anyway I can't remember why I said all that, so I did all that
> and then ... I took off to France for a while and lived in a little bedsit.
> I just got off the boat in '68 and didn't get involved in the French
> events ... It was easy. I just got off the boat.

On the one hand, Gilda's fragmented descriptions suggested the
intense relationship between the intellectual and social excitement she
experienced. Her expanding body of ideas fed her freedom as a female
social body away from the confines of her northern working-class home.
On the other hand, the ruptures told of her uncertainty about the future;
her search for social place, and feelings about the new ideas she was
discovering and individuals she was meeting. She was caught in a
psychic struggle between the familiar world of home and the diverse
landscape of university and beyond. The latter promised freedom in
new experiences, but its removal from the blue-collar world of Hartlepool
created difficulties for conceiving student politics as a medium for
realising social change; IS class politics offered to bridge this gap. In
1970 the Birmingham branch was active around the Longbridge car
factory, and the industrial site reminded Gilda of Hartlepool's manual
working life:

When I first went over to Birmingham I remember thinking in Hartlepool most people worked in the steel works or the docks . . . I said to people, well, where are the works? . . . I quite liked Longbridge because [this was where] a lot of people . . . worked, and you could see it clearly and I think that was important, but also, intellectually, I think I was looking for something with a bit more sense of, well, how do you change the world? I knew all this philosophical stuff wasn't going to do it, and I knew the students weren't going to be the leaders in changing society, and so I think I was intellectually trying to look for something that could get to grips a bit more with Marxism.

The themes of fluidity and mobility characterising radical student stories suggested the instability of students' emerging ideas, beliefs and values. As the accounts of Dave Lyddon, Ian Birchall and Gilda Peterson highlighted, these young men and women sought new ways of seeing and being in the world that would allow them to negotiate a new relationship to their surrounding communities as well as to national and international societies. Memories of the self, the local and the international merged into one seamless experience in ways that reflected the relentless yet thrilling world of activity and debate they entered.

The sense of fluidity between local and global often felt heightened because of the political interchange between English and foreign students taking place at many universities. In the late 1960s Warwick's History Department ran a student exchange programme with three American universities: Ann Arbor, Berkeley and Wisconsin. The latter two accepted six Warwick students for one term and in return sent two students to Warwick for one year.[42] In the mid-1960s Ann Arbor and Berkeley were at the forefront of teach-ins against the Vietnam War that, by 1967, had spread rapidly across university campuses, and although their time in America allowed Warwick students to participate briefly in the movement, the influence of American students on Warwick's left scene was disproportionately greater because student activism in America had begun earlier and was more extensive than in England, and American students were present on campus for longer. Not only did the political and cultural exchange shape an eclectic protest culture, but for student activists the experience of developing as social and political beings was heightened because of the increasingly dialogic relationship between political and personal life.

Anna Davin showed how, once internalised, student politics could take on an innately fluid quality, spilling over into everyday life and influencing how she conducted herself as a young woman. She went to Warwick in 1966 as a twenty-six-year-old married history undergraduate and mother of three young children. Her husband was a Communist

Party member and the couple's social and political life already encompassed the New Left circle that had grown around the *New Left Review* and which, in the mid- to late 1960s, was extending to the network around the VSC. At Warwick her political activity began when she joined the Socialist Society. The fluid left parameters she found included the nexus between the History Department and the student Left. Edward Thompson was the most prominent of several Marxist faculty members, many of them young lecturers such as IS members James Hinton and philosophy lecturer Peter Binns, who ran the Society's *Kapital* reading group, and the Society was heavily populated by history undergraduates, along with several of Thompson's graduate students. Anna was one of several independent members in the Society along with Solidarity students and others from Communist Party backgrounds.[43]

Anna's recollections about the influence of American students in the Society focused on the membership of notable American women who, back home, had been activists inside the New Left student movement, Students for a Democratic Society (SDS). She explained how these female students heightened the fluid nature of Warwick's left scene through New Left ideas they introduced to Society members: internal participatory democracy, neighbourhood organising and, crucially for Anna and other Warwick women, early Women's Liberation literature that, by 1968, had started to circulate through America's civil rights and anti-war movements. Through their engagement with Warwick socialist students, SDS women played a vital role in expanding the permissible boundaries for ideas and forms of organising within the Society. By the time Anna and other Society women began, in 1969, to meet as a women's group, initially with and then to the exclusion of men, the fluid boundaries between national left cultures and provincial and metropolitan activism allowed for the dialectic movement of ideas and activities between these two arenas.[44] The SDS idea of neighbourhood organising took root outside the Coventry campus when Socialist Society women began meeting with women from the local council estate, Hillfields. Former SDS member Barbara Winslow was studying for her MA in Social History at Warwick when she joined IS:

> What was really so interesting, especially for us middle-class women, is we wanted to meet in Hillfields, where the workers were. These working-class women, they wanted to meet at the University. They wanted to date college boys. We were all in our blue jeans; these women came dressed up. And it was a real lesson in terms of class and expectations and so forth. They thought why would we want to meet in this ugly industrial council estate when we could meet at the university and get away from it all?[45]

The cross-over of class cultures which comes out in this account highlights the personal contacts facilitating social and cultural exchange between the two groups of women, adding to sensations of mobility for female students who found themselves temporarily transported out of their middle-class environment into a world where class delineated social difference regardless of the commonality of gender. In the midst of debates about the social oppression uniting women, new social and cultural encounters that took young women beyond student bodies opened their eyes to the nuanced range of factors shaping women's lives. Warwick undergraduate Jane Storr remembered her own influential experience of socialising with Asian women from a family in Coventry's Swan Lane. Teaching English to the mother and daughter, she observed with shock the social restrictions they faced, yet also learned about the cultural complexities defying any simple explanations about female oppression and its relation to male domination:

> I just found it absolutely fascinating and I learned all about, I found out about exploitation, began to understand . . . I mean, and all of the gender thing because it also made me think about how these cultures aren't fixed because it's like sometimes I'd go and I was definitely a woman and I was in the back room with the women and I only taught the women, and then there'd be an event and I'd be invited into the room with all the men, so it was like, because they spoke more English than the women, so all those things I was beginning to get a glimpse of.[46]

The fluid left politics Anna encountered at Warwick was rooted above all in its capacity to defy interior and external parameters. Her developing socialist selfhood coincided with important personal changes as a young woman at a turning-point on the Left, when women were starting to articulate a 'new' language of left politics embedded in the emotional core. On the one hand, the construction of Anna's story, privileging the personal and the sexual alongside the political, suggested the legacy of Women's Liberation in her self-composition. Nikolas Rose argues that 'language makes only certain ways of being human describable, and in so doing makes only certain ways of being human possible'.[47] His reflections on the role of language as 'one of the keys to our assembly as psychological beings' are highly pertinent in the case of Women's Liberation, because, as will be shown in Chapter 4, the transforming potential of the new politics was rooted in changes to ways of communicating Marxism that would enable women to speak and to be heard. It is possible to see how the language of Women's Liberation enabled Anna to open up what Rose terms a 'psy-shaped space' in which to reconstruct her student self through the language of inner feeling.

Anna's account provides an unusually lucid consideration of the careful stages through which radical politics came to shape subjectivity and everyday experience for female students. As for many interviewees, activism seeped into the most intimate aspects of life because of how wholeheartedly she threw herself into socialist student circles. At Warwick she quickly came to relish an intellectual life independent from her husband and sought the same completeness of experience from her politics. As they came to conceive of themselves as political beings, intensive, constant discussions strengthened the social bonds between Anna and her comrades, whereupon casual sexual encounters became a way of cementing this closeness. In this sexual-political nexus, American students were again influential because they tended to be more independent, often further on in their studies, working to support themselves financially and consequently exhibiting less-cautious sexual behaviour.[48]

Anna's story reveals how intimate relations between student activists became an integral if unconscious site of activism. The open shape of university left circles may explain the intensity with which students came to invest themselves in activity. Alongside wider political, social and cultural changes students witnessed in British and overseas societies, agency derived from within the milieu itself; the libertarian culture fed into sexual as well as political and social relations, shaping men and women's behaviour and subjectivity. Radical cultural codes permitted young women, already conditioned to expect lives of equality denied to their mothers, to push further against the social boundaries governing their freedom in contrast to women's wider social situation. The shifts in traditional attitudes, discernible throughout the 1960s and enacted in the 'permissive' legislative reforms at the end of the decade, occurred only gradually. Although the laws allowed for the possibility of expanding personal freedoms by encoding the primacy of individual 'consent', liberalisation of behaviour was by no means directly proportional.[49] In any case, the benefits of the reforms came to be felt only in the 1970s, too late for this university cohort, who socially, culturally and politically seemed poised between old and new worlds, straining for more liberal spaces but at times emotionally constrained by the customs, values and models of their fifties and early-sixties childhood and adolescence.

Social surveys indicated the overall conservatism characterising the attitudes and behaviour of sixties youth so that, in spite of the increasingly sexualised public culture, private sexual practice remained cautious. Marriage as an institution retained its popularity amongst the young; the figures for first-time marriage peaked at 357,000 in 1971 (compared to 307,000 in 1931), and the age of first-time marriage fell significantly from 26.8 for men and 24.6 for women in 1951 to 24.6 for men and 22.6 for women in 1971.[50] Geoffrey Gorer's 1969 survey, *Sex and Marriage in England Today*, revealed that a quarter of married men and nearly two-thirds of women were virgins upon marriage.[51] Viewed against this cautious picture, the cultural codes and social practices of the activist scene offered young women and men much greater scope for social and sexual experimentation than was possible or permissible in mainstream society. As will be explored further in Chapter 5, commitment to realising social agency outside the dominant patterns of capitalism encouraged the experimentation of political communication and self-expression. Anna Paczuska confirmed the social possibilities the activist landscape permitted to adventurous, bright young women like her: 'There was a way, if you were quite energetic and evidently a bit bright and up for life and challenge, you could get away with it.'[52]

Female narratives of personal and political mobility assumed an integral part of increasingly felt social independence on the part of young sixties women for whom steadily expanding economic and educational opportunities began to be discerned in challenges to cultural norms. The post-war scholarship girl invariably entered higher education carrying the cultural assumption that she shared intellectual equality with scholarship boys. She entered the activist terrain thinking similarly. Men's numerical dominance necessarily made mutuality a characteristic of social and political interaction, continuing accelerated patterns of post-war mixing. For independent-minded students like Joan Smith, the male membership dominating LSE's Marxist Society failed to raise any questions concerning her own status as a woman. She had already earned members' respect for her intellectual prowess, and the radical men were keen to introduce her to renowned Marxist graduates: 'I was fine. I was already in the IS ... in fact they kept saying to me, "You should be in contact with Chris Harman, Richard Kuper", and I was going, mmm, not sure, not sure.'[53] In a culture where intellect and experience on the Left counted as markers of status, Joan's position in the Society was assured. Yet other members also remembered that her down-to-earth countenance meant she was well-liked and ready to put newcomers at ease. As one of few active women, her attraction to male members, including her soon-to-be boyfriend, Steve Jefferys, again illustrates the role that sexual desire sometimes played in drawing young adults into radical left circles: 'She was then kind of the pleasant face, and she was a big recruiter. She looked very attractive, which pulled people in, but she was also normal, had a working-class background, no fancy airs, and she probably signed half of the one hundred members with her personal charms and her influence.'[54] Margaret Renn explained how naive adventurism informed her own early relations with male comrades: 'The first people who got me involved with politics were all young men because that is what you wanted . . . to be with young men, you know, in a way because I was sixteen or seventeen and on the lookout, and they were all very exciting . . . I had absolutely no idea what I was doing, but made it up as I went along.'[55]

Yet contradictions for female activists abounded. Just as Di Parkin's experience in the YS suggested, a female student could remain in tune with her feminine sexuality whilst being alongside men as beer-drinking comrades and potential sexual partners in accordance with her own desires. Notions of comradeship could be seemingly divested of gender, supplanted instead by intellectual and emotional connections concerning class, politics and cultural tastes. Radical politics presented young women with clearly drawn-out social codes. At Oxford, Bronwen Davis joined in with anything that meant 'getting up on the street and direct action'. Explaining her readiness to throw herself into student politics, she suggested how the legacy of moral values absorbed in early adolescence fed into radical codes shaping the assertive actions of young womanhood: 'It was clear what was right. You just got on and did something.'[56] Margaret Renn readily got up in the student's union and spoke in front of an overwhelmingly male audience, because 'that is what you did'.[57] She and other women revealed how flirtations with male comrades added to the fun to be enjoyed as a student activist without necessarily undermining their sense of inclusion in activities. Sexual dalliances with male comrades, initiated on their own terms, could in fact consummate young women's sense of belonging. Gilda Peterson reflected on her sense of place in the Birmingham IS group: 'I didn't feel there was a big oppressive male scene. I felt reasonably equal and I had already had some relationships.'[58] Instead, in the class politics and factory activism of IS she found a new identity and gained a set of political skills, from chairing meetings and organising demonstrations to leafleting factory gates and selling the weekly paper. At a time when she was reaching out for new directions in her life, transitory sexual relations with comrades was a way of drawing herself deeper into IS culture: 'I suppose it was a way of getting fully involved in the scene and being more central, and sort of jumping for it all with two feet.' Such conduct may be seen as an extension of the free social and sexual mixing already discernible in the early sixties avant-garde, where women's sexual agency had begun to shape a new female morality. By the late sixties young female students were at the forefront of more liberal sexual attitudes and patterns of behaviour that saw them voicing demands for more easily available contraceptive advice, adding to the pressures for reforming the abortion law. Women's testimonies in this collection echo stories and contemporary survey evidence that show the assertiveness socially mobile and highly educated young women were exercising in their attitudes towards contraception and their rights to sexual pleasure.[59] For these radical women, pre-marital sexual activity was an unquestioned feature of long-term or serially monogamous heterosexual relationships; they showed initiative in gaining information about and access to contraception, or occasionally abortions, and willingly entered into and initiated casual sexual relations in an intense, experimental culture informing relations between the sexes. Jane Storr exemplified the self-determination women displayed in relation to their bodies and personal lives as well as their political struggles:

> At seventeen, eighteen, to go to the doctor behind my mother's back and get the contraceptive pill, was so liberating. It was the most amazing liberation, to take that. You know, I want to have sex, I want to enjoy sex, and I don't want to get pregnant and I can do this, and I don't have to ask anybody's permission, and it was, you know, in that context of the times, that was such a liberating thing to do . . . and so, you know, I think all those things were sort of informing how I sort of, how I saw the world.[60]

However, such accounts need to be read alongside female testimonies that accord psychic conflict preceding Women's Liberation as the price of radical social behaviour. Sheila Rowbotham notably recounted the difficulties of being an autonomous woman on the male left: cut out of discussions and at a loss to know how to manage her own desires in relation to men's submerged, but discernible vulnerabilities. Lee Comer told of her IS boyfriend's confusing behaviour, his charm offset by moments when she was 'just the moll, you know, the beautiful girl that you had in the background'.[61] When, in 1968, the couple argued over the Prague Spring, his refusal to consider her family's experiences left her hurt and angry. Unwillingness to acknowledge her 'much more emotional, human, woman's angle' stung, especially, perhaps, because emotional investment that went into couple relations could feel heightened when feelings ran high over global and local struggles. That an emotional, experiential perspective held validity as a political framework would be a key tenet of the Women's Liberation politics women like Lee soon embraced.

Despite the agency many young women exercised in defying moral norms, they were not immune from heartaches and conflict over how to relate to the radical young men in their circles. Like Rowbotham, they often felt confused by contradictory behaviour hiding young men's anxieties following failed relationships and their own confusions over sixties masculinity. Even within the libertarian activist climate, female students remained under pressure from social authorities and wider culture to follow predominant social trends, and in the early to mid-1960s those who met boyfriends at universities were likely to be married and sometimes young mothers by the end of the decade. Wisty Hoyland met her husband through CND at London University in 1962–63, and by 1967–69, when he was involved in the VSC, the couple had two young children. She echoed the conflicting voices many 1970s feminists recalled from their time in the late-sixties Left:

> I mean I arrived at university, at London University with fairly passion-ate feelings about all these things, about justice, etcetera . . . but then there was also this conflict because there was this sort of feeling that, you know, when I was sort of exposed to men at university, this feeling that somehow you weren't sort of looked upon as an equal. You were looked upon . . . I remember one guy saying, oh well we judge women in terms of their fuckability, so it's like we'll give them a certain number out of ten . . . It was very confusing because in a way we'd also, because of our age group I suppose, a lot of us had thought in terms of oh we'll get married, you know, even though I had this quite articulate background.[62]

The contradictions young women discerned between the public and private behaviour of some left men carried a host of social, cultural and emotional explanations. It is beyond the scope of this chapter to explore this topic in detail, though it has illustrated some of the confusions young men faced over how to manage difficult emotions surrounding class, family, friendships and heterosexual relations. In the late sixties, alongside everyday thoughts about studies and domestic arrangements, these anxieties became interwoven with experiences in political struggles and groups. The latter carried their own normative standards for masculine self-determination, leadership and the com-petitive spirit prevalent in other areas of male life, including the grammar and public schools.

Alongside the thrills and everyday business of activism, radical male students were also preoccupied by issues governing the self, about how to be in the world of university and society more generally.

Stephen Trafford remembered becoming active in protest politics at Sussex University in the context of a painful break-up with his first girlfriend. The couple had met in the sixth form in Bridlington, she was a year younger than him, and Stephen's first year at Sussex had been shaped around his efforts to maintain the relationship over a distance.

His reflections illuminate the insecurity that could also afflict male students over how to relate to self-assertive young women, how to manage the feelings accompanying intense relationships, as well as young men's reluctance to share these feelings with male friends:

> I, you know, was I think very much in love, you know, in a very kind of naive way and I wanted to maintain the relationship . . . She was very confident, and more confident than I was, and I think in that sense I think she was more dominant in the relationship, which was something very exciting and different for me . . . so I was kind of finding my way through it rather than this relationship is better than the other ones I've had. It took me a while to get the message but I did get the message. It was with great sadness but yeah, okay. You know it's not going to work. But on we go . . . you know I didn't discuss it intensively with anyone. I just dealt with it myself and . . . and got on.[63]

Ultimately, tension arose within and sometimes between male and female students because the activist landscape around the VSC was predicated upon competitive masculine social and sexual codes that women, and sometimes men too, had to negotiate to gain recognition. Chapter 2 highlighted the way in which male socialist selfhood invariably rested on shared bonds of militant street politics, intellectual competition and comradeship. In the late sixties, division between activist men and women often occurred in the discursive arena of politics where men held a physical and psychological monopoly, thriving off the intellectual intensity and rhetorical competition of meetings. Whilst less articulate or socially confident male undergraduates sometimes felt intimidated in the company of more experienced activists, repeated references from women suggested that even the most intellectually assured and politically active scholarship girl could find it hard to make herself heard on the same terms as her male peers. In the LSE Socialist Society Wenda Clenaghen remembered that, as a woman, 'you did have to push your way in and sometimes you couldn't push your way in'.[64] Yet, moving freely between open left circles alongside men, it was hard for female students to distinguish this mobility as set apart from authorial male voices, especially when they emanated from respected friends. Wenda explained the contradictions she faced as a female Society member:

> The guys were quite respectful; we were clever women, but quite often they had strings of girlfriends . . . Some of the more famous ones, let's say, of course, it would be like having groupies around them, and of course some of them took advantage of that, but on the whole they were a pretty decent bunch.

Anna Paczuska was an IS member at Durham University. Her perception of social difference between men and women remained unresolved, submerged beneath layers of consciousness of herself as an immigrant never quite fitting in: 'I think I thought student life ... wasn't about men, but women who were students and men who were students; they did things together, much more together, but I did sense that feeling that you didn't ... that there was something quite unresolved there, but I must admit I found university quite socially uncomfortable.'[65] Her sense of difference showed that before activist women became truly conscious of themselves as gendered beings, socially apart from male comrades, other registers of selfhood defined activist experience. Anna's predominant recollection of the group focused on leading IS men, but she accorded greater emphasis to its social and intellectual exclusivity, never quite able to connect the two: 'I saw it as rather an exclusive intellectual group, you know, it seemed to me as if they saw anybody likely [to be interested in their politics, then] they would ask them to join, but it was a laying on of hands, a privilege conferred.' Men too voiced feelings of marginality and insecurity around core groups on the student Left. When initially exposed to Socialist Society members' activist agenda, Martin Shaw 'was quite a shy young person' and 'felt a bit of an outsider to this sort of milieu, which was still quite new to me'.[66] David Carter found IMG students at York 'quite frightening people actually ... they were quite intimidating and scary'.[67] For the most part, however, young men found a measure of social belonging from a radical culture that connected fluidly to a plethora of old and new masculine cultures, whether in the working world of the labour Left, or late-sixties youth cultures of rock 'n' roll and the underground. All these offered a range of possibilities for male selfhood that denied young left women space to make sense of themselves and their femininity in their own cultural and emotional terms.

The metropolitan activist scene

Interviewees' emphasis on the permeable shape of the university left reflected the growing activist scene. By the late 1960s increased far-left activity responded to a host of national and international issues. The decline of the British economy provided the domestic background against which the Left expressed bitter disillusionment with the Labour government: public spending cuts, wages restraint forced by the Prices and Incomes Board, immigration and race, the Industrial Relations Bill of 1969 and the difficulties of Rhodesia all occasioned the Left's frustrations with Labour.[68] After initial hopes that the Wilson government might live up to its promises to reinvigorate British society through real social reforms, the betrayal was deeply felt, especially by students from long-standing Labour families. Wenda Clenaghen remembered: 'The Socialist Society got bigger and bigger, but I still didn't want to leave the Labour Party at that point because I had put quite a lot into it . . . but at the point at which Labour took away the passports of the African Asians I left . . . and joined the International Socialists in 1968.'[69]

But it was activity against the Vietnam War and the prominence the VSC came to acquire on the Left that facilitated the dynamic relationship between activist groups in the provinces, focused around universities, and the metropolitan centre. From the mid-1960s IS and IMG expanded steadily in alignment with the VSC, and from 1967 the Campaign operated as the main organisation for an activist network in which the student movement supplied mobile bodies for demonstrations and protest activities, or to man picket lines as required.

The position of the LSE's Socialist Society, at the nexus of the metropolitan network, illustrates the social and political dynamics around the activist heartland. Throughout 1967–68 LSE's reputation for radicalism accentuated the ties between the Society and growing radical enclaves in north and east London. The Society's reputation as a libertarian site quickly made it a haven of activist sociability; an open door policy guaranteed lively discussion, parties, and foot soldiers for demonstrations. The fluid boundaries between the Society's core membership, affiliated largely to IS, and a counter-cultural milieu where students were concerned essentially with cultural and lifestyle experimentation provided for a wide array of political contacts, including radical theatre, art and information groups: CAST, Agitprop Information, Agitprop Street Players and Poster Workshop; members serviced campaigns with alternative, imaginative propaganda, drawing upon political and cultural traditions from Russian agitprop, the San Franciscan Mime Troup theatre and rock n' roll to the Parisian Atelier Populaire and surrealist ideas circulating in the art schools.[70] These cultural activists co-existed with Society members and a core of young apprentices Paul Foot had recruited from the YS when he was a reporter for Glasgow's *Daily Record*: Frank Campbell, a building worker, and Ross Pritchard, a print worker who had represented young printers on the strike committee of the 1959 Glaswegian apprentices' strike. Ties between students and apprentices rested on the shared sociability of youth culture, Friday-night drinking sessions and intellectual exchange. Steve Jefferys remembered: 'These were days when we would all be drinking down in the Three Tuns and people used to come down to see us.' The apprentices were attracted by the Society's dissident ethos,

promise of direct action, support for their dispute with Myton's construction company and female students. In turn, socialist students were
drawn to the energy and intellectual capacity of apprentices who were
well read in Marx and economics as well as general politics, who represented a working-class tradition of activism in the labour movement
and whose presence complemented the mature Trade Union Studies
students in the Society. Steve Jefferys admired the apprentices because
they possessed 'fifteen years of experience outside the movement' in a
trade union tradition he and others saw as the key to revolutionary
change.

The porous boundaries surrounding the Society facilitated the dia-
chronic participation sociologists have emphasised in relation to new
social movements; individuals became involved through their pre-
existing links, but their very participation also forged 'new social
bonds'.[71] Steve Jefferys illustrated this process:

> The network forming is partly by definition by others, partly by self-
> definition and selection of areas of work; and simply the fact of working
> together, drinking together, sleeping together creates a bonding over
> probably what was by any accounting ... what must have been an unusual
> example of student activity. The links were also there with the Committee
> of 100. In 1967 the Colonels in Greece staged a coup and seized military
> power, and at that time we were using anarchist printers who I had
> contact with through the Committee of 100. People were still around
> doing stuff, and these anarchist printers suggested to us that what we
> should do was to occupy the Greek Embassy. We called together a number
> of Greek students and about 25–30 of us went in this big furniture van
> and occupied the Greek Embassy.[72]

His narrative shows how political and cultural influences from the
English and overseas Left were transferred to a new activist stage
through individuals' political and personal lives, to inform their identities and actions. Within this network, changes which young individuals
felt at work around them, in their social circles, globally and internally
contributed to sensual perceptions of social and physical movement,
and interpellated new subjectivities.[73]

International subjectivity

Many of the most politically active students, often members of far-left
groups, were at the forefront of university protests.[74] They established
connections with student activists at other institutions across the country, and were often involved in efforts to orchestrate these into means

for wielding student power. In June 1968 the RSSF was the most con-
certed attempt to set up a national revolutionary student organisation
modelled on the West German *Sozialistische Deutsche Studentbund*,
and this also functioned as an umbrella for socialist students, incorporating IS, IMG, the *New Left Review* circle, Maoists and libertarians.[75]
At the forefront of the underground media servicing the network, the
newspaper *Black Dwarf* kept a predominantly student readership abreast
of the latest developments in the occupations. From the first LSE sit-in,
in March, 1967, Wenda Clenaghen remembered being always on the
move: 'We used to travel the whole country agitating'.[76] Within these
same circles law student Sarah Perrigo 'was involved quite heavily in
the student movement in the RSSF, and Richard [Kuper] and I went
speaking at universities across Britain at one stage . . . talking about
sit-ins, and I certainly remember going to Birmingham and Leicester'.[77]
At Birmingham Val Graham and her IMG comrades 'were a bit like
revolutionary tourists. We all used to look for the next sit-in at the
next university and all hop into a car.'[78] Yet only a small proportion
of students who participated in campus unrest were also involved in
the network around the VSC.

Interviewees' perceptions of movement are perhaps more revealing
than actual instances of mobility. Not only did physical movement,
street politics and grass-roots campaigning give meaning to activism in
the sense of 'doing', but they also aroused powerful interior understandings of the political and social agency resulting from activity. Within
the VSC network 'activism' assumed subjective meaning as a sensation
of inner being. Various factors contributed to this subjectivity.

As student protests became a familiar sight on campuses across the
country, and the VSC mobilisations attracted ever larger numbers, underground news media may have contributed to activists' self-perceptions
of agency as much as to expressions of alarm from government officials
and media spokesmen. In June, 1968 the headline for the first issue
of *Black Dwarf* allied the actions of English radicals to all Western
European activists resisting capitalist and imperialist oppression. The
slogan 'We shall fight. We shall win. Paris, London, Rome, Berlin' was
intended to be a defiant message of opposition to ruling authorities as
well as one of collective solidarity for activists themselves. Interviewees'
testimonies suggest the newspaper's editors and producers were at least
partially successful in their aim to 'act as a voice' for radicalised youth;
Black Dwarf symbolised the radical representations against which young
activists modelled themselves.[79] Despite the minority of members composing the network, the liberation struggles to which young activists
committed themselves had powerful psychological effects, expanding

their mental horizons and enlarging the psychic space available for social mobility.

Thinking about how 'activist' terminology shaped subjectivity means considering, as Rose argues, what that language did for young radicals, 'what components of thinking and acting' it connected up to and what it enabled them 'to dream into existence, to do to themselves and to others'.[80] A pertinent example concerns the internationalism prevailing throughout the VSC network since its earliest beginnings and embedded within activists from their earliest memories of political awakening. Solidarities with international movements for civil rights, national liberation and social and personal freedoms were as much internal feelings as they were forms of interpersonal communication across national borders. For serious left-thinking students, iconic revolutionary figures from international conflicts were not mere cultural icons, but models of social justice and humanitarianism.

There is no doubting that the revolutionary 'myth' of 'Che' and Vietnamese Communist leader Ho Chi Minh involved an idolisation that could at times blind young activists to the harsh realities of their methods. In March, 1969, twenty-six-year-old youth worker and mother Sue Crockford accompanied Camden VSC members to London's Abbey Road to meet Madame Nguyen Thi Binh. The Foreign Minister of the Provisional Revolutionary Government of the Republic of South Vietnam was in Britain during the Paris Peace talks, underway since October, 1968. Sue recalled delegates' enthusiasm for the gritty details of guerrilla struggles: 'Someone not long before had said something like, "how did you get involved with the Vietcong? Do you know how many people Ho Chi Minh has killed?"'[81] VSC posters glorified Vietnamese guerrilla fighters taking on the technological supremacy of the United States and winning. The prevalence of masculine tropes within VSC ephemera may be seen partly as an expression of the militant codes carrying over from the YS/IS culture. Rowbotham mocked the 'naked genitals' of 'street-fighting man – the cult of Che, the paraphernalia of helmets, the militancy that could shout the loudest'.[82] In volunteering to take up the guerrilla mantle of the NLF, some young men drew upon romantic constructions of the 1930s International Brigades, expressing the street-fighting masculinity visible in the first two VSC marches. Mike Martin had first become active at the age of twenty when he set up a Peace in Vietnam Committee in Hull with Labour Party member Tony Topham. By 1967 he was a full-time assistant for the VSC, surviving off the small savings he had made in labouring jobs and ready to fight for the cause: 'If somebody had said we'll send an army of volunteers to Vietnam to help the Liberation Front I'd have put my hand up.'[83] Reverence for liberation icons also spoke of an engagement and empathy with peasant struggles that gave the concept of 'internationalism' an implicitly felt dimension. There was no doubting the conviction motivating the sentiment to fight overseas; young activists believed deeply in the righteousness of the NLF claim for self-determination. Camden VSC member Stephen Merrett recalled how 'I wept tears of joy the day the Americans withdrew from Vietnam in 1973'.[84] Dedication to the NLF cause ultimately cost him his job when, in 1969, the Ministry of Technology discovered he had been publishing material exposing British complicity in the war.

Nor was international solidarity confined exclusively to men. The defiant heroism of the NLF was typically portrayed with images of male and female freedom fighters, symbols of people power pitted against anonymous technological might. In a 1970 special issue of the Women's Liberation Workshop journal *Shrew*, Anna Davin reported a meeting between members of the Workshop and Ma-Thi-Chu, executive member of the NLF, in which she devoted attention to Vietnamese women's guerrilla role in the armed forces.[85] Sue Crockford's memories of Madame Binh told of her deep respect and reverence for the revolutionary woman, based largely on their shared identities as mothers:

> She had this bun, one of these ageless faces . . . I can remember talking to her and how it started; Barney was only three months, six months, just a babe in arms, and she was really sweet to him. I didn't know enough about her, and I said, 'Have you got kids?', and of course she did, but she didn't know where they were, and I just thought, oh, how could you do this? I mean you are so passionate and committed, and you have given up being with your kids, and you don't know where they are. I was just devastated.[86]

Young activists' alertness to overseas protest represented a logical continuation of growing up in the Cold War, where the perils of nuclear annihilation had expanded the immediacy of the childhood landscape. Where youngsters had been even marginally engaged with CND, the possibilities for envisioning alignments with Third World nations increased. Participation in CND spoke of an inherently moral, emotionally felt outrage, which carried on into activists' responses against South African apartheid, American military action in Vietnam and struggles for democracy within their universities. New mass visual mediums of communication, notably television and film, heightened the urgency of this moral impulse. Jane Storr explained how for her, as a sixth-former, 'the images on the television would be presenting you with a sense of injustice all over the world . . . at the time you thought how can people

not want to change this because we can't close our eyes to it?'[87] Vietnam
was the first televised war and the medium raised the profile of the
conflict.[88] The power of the visual image to evoke emotion and arouse
empathy for the victims of American bombing helped to sharpen the
divisions between left-thinking students and an outmoded, authoritarian
government cloaked in the mantle of the Left. Confronted with the
horror of napalm, bombing, mass graves and executions, young activists contemplated their own government's policy of moral support for
American military action and felt an urgent need to stand up and take
action. Sandy Irving remembered 'coming home from school and seeing
pictures on the news at six o'clock about what had been happening
in Vietnam, and it was just so terrible; I couldn't wait to get to university and go on the big anti-war demonstrations'.[89]

As a symbol of wider political and generational discontent, Vietnam
swelled the ranks of left-wing students seeking radical solutions. In
1967 Joan Smith and her Socialist Society comrades threw their support
behind the VSC, hosting the Campaign's photographic exhibition to
raise support for the International War Crimes Tribunal.[90] The Society's
responsiveness to VSC's solidarity message reflected the explosive impact
of the war in compounding members' frustrations with Labour: 'America
was the new colonialism and it was just so brutal and, of course, it
was the first time television showed you what was going on, and so
I suppose that was the biggest thing then. We didn't think Marxism
was wrong because every day it was being confirmed that, yeah, this
is how people behave, how the ruling class behaves when it's threatened.'[91] At a time when left students were sharpening their Marxism
in relation to the Cold War and post-colonial world, parallel struggles
against injustice confirmed their own place within wider political and
societal structures. Drawing links between international, national and
local struggles enabled them to situate their own fight against their
universities in a larger framework and to see themselves allied to activists overseas. At the LSE Laurie Flynn explained, 'We wanted radical
socialism in the West in solidarity with the civil rights struggle and
anti-colonial struggles.'[92]

Empathy with foreign liberation struggles also derived from real-life
social relationships students formed at their universities and through
travels abroad. The anti-apartheid campaign was a notable example.
Friendships with South African students made the issue immediately
personal and emotional. In 1966 Socialist Society members compiled
a report opposing the appointment of Dr Walter Adams, previously
principal at University College, Rhodesia, as the new director of their
'multi-racial' college.[93] This and their demonstration outside Rhodesia

House resulted partly from their membership in a cosmopolitan student body which fed into the School's anti-colonial tradition. Richard Kuper was one of several Jewish South African students, including the President of the Students' Union, David Adelstein, alive to the oppressive apartheid system upheld by Ian Smith's all-white government. South African refugees like David Lazaar and Basker Vashee were also Socialist Society members. The latter was a Rhodesian Asian economics student, imprisoned for a year before the Smith regime expelled him for efforts to uphold human rights at Rhodesia's University College of Salisbury. Together they informed Society comrades of the brutal realities surrounding the regime and the dangers it posed to its opponents. Steve Jefferys heard first-hand testimony of the brutalities which apartheid inflicted when, as a boy, he came into contact with a network of South African refugees living nearby in London's Highgate area. In 1963–66 north London had become a base for several hundred South African exiles and a centre for anti-apartheid activities linked to the ANC and the South African Communist Party (SACP).[94] By the time he came to the LSE, stories of the ANC's radical agenda had already sensitised him to the brutal oppression black South Africans faced, enlarging the possibilities the Committee of 100 had shown for directly challenging oppression: 'The kind of political agenda that became totally acceptable was hearing people supporting the limited initial campaign blowing up electric pylons and the very limited stuff the ANC started at that time, which involved responding with huge demonstrations.'[95] In 1966 exiled SACP member Ronnie Kasrils enrolled at the LSE and began recruiting students to act as couriers between London and South Africa. Several volunteers were drawn from Socialist Society circles, where students witnessed Kasrils' persuasive contribution to debates on South Africa and the Six Day War. John Rose was one member who became friendly with him; the young Jewish student admired Kasrils as a 'highly trained professional revolutionary' and a comrade helping him to test IS arguments.[96]

The VSO programme provided another channel fostering an internationalist perspective, one rooted in life-changing experiences and relationships. In the late 1960s South Africa was a common destination. In 1965 Wenda Clenaghen went to the LSE just months after completing VSO in Nigeria, where she 'got a very good idea about Nigeria and the dominance of the whites'.[97] Stories of personal transformation show how first-hand exposure to apartheid radically sensitised young individuals to oppression; many returned unable to settle back into their old lives, compelled to invest themselves into campaigns for justice and equality. Love affairs as well as close friendships brought the struggle painfully home. Prue Chamberlayne's relationship with a South African medical student aroused a deep attachment towards the country's politics. After two years in Zambia, in December, 1967 she returned to rural Gloucestershire, further apart from her parents' narrow middle-class expectations and the cultural narrowness of English class politics:

> I'd gone to find out about African culture as an alternative to European culture, and, and I'd found myself in this virtual South Africa, you know. I had one friend, the artist guy was very torn about whether, should he train in, he had all sorts of invitations and scholarships all over the world. You know, would that destroy his Africanness if he took them up, so we discussed that endlessly . . . we had lots and lots and lots of discussions about what was happening to African politics and [what] was African socialism.[98]

In this 'African frame' Prue's love for her boyfriend became interwoven with her hopes for his country; the couple dreamed of a future together in East Africa. Through personal relationships, then, political and personal life became intertwined so that young activists' internationalism often imbued the anticipation, determination, hope and anger they felt on behalf of close friends and lovers.

Before women began to call for new ways of conceiving politics, the eclectic protest culture around the VSC had already begun to open up a psychic space for young activists to envisage new forms of being in the world. At the height of the May '68 protests 'the subjective in struggle' assumed a privileged position as part of an international New Left politics embraced by a generation of young activists.[99] This language suffused the activist culture around the VSC because the sight of French students and striking workers fed into the global imaginary of '68 which individuals absorbed from witnessing at first-hand or receiving news of the events from media sources. The French demonstrations made a profound impact on many radical students at a time when they were being drawn into militant action in their own universities and contemplating their place in the world. Chris Ratcliffe watched the events in the students' television room at the height of the Essex protests, when the need to be more than a long-distant observer prompted him into action: 'We said if we don't go we shall just regret it and so we hitchhiked; we had to go through Belgium and we helped to build the barricades, and breathed in the CS gas, and just took in the spectacle, and that as much as anything had an amazing effect on me.'[100] Chris's account was suffused with images of barricades, posters and graffiti, CS gas, rows of *Compagnies Répulicaines de Sécurité* anti-riot police, red flags adorning the Odéon and book stalls of political literature lining the boulevard St Germain. Although he spoke little French, the power of the 'spectacle' generated a visual process of cognition and created a powerful sense of connection with French students in a way that coloured his dreams of utopian socialist change: 'I had seen the possibilities. I had seen that it was just possible for a whole country to just take control and rise up and help each other, and the poetry of the streets and all the graffiti and everything, and, you know, in your wildest dreams you could not have imagined it.'

Political and social contacts between young activists and members of the English labour movement brought a local dimension to a network being mapped out externally and internally on a global and local scale. Many individuals found struggles inside factories, the docks and local communities to be just as informative as international liberation struggles in shaping an understanding of what it meant to be a Marxist and activist. Some felt the discovery of local poverty brought them nearer to working-class struggles and created a more tangible role to improve people's everyday lives. By 1969, following the disappointments of May '68, the VSC began to diminish as a site of activity and some young activists began to turn their attention to subjective struggles closer to home. As they embarked upon lives beyond university, a new language of liberation politics confronted them with new possibilities for social and political selfhood but also raised profound challenges for the type of relationships they wished to experience. At the end of the decade the contradictions and confusions young activists had first discerned inside families, at school and in neighbourhoods bubbled to the surface as questions about who they were as women and men and social and sexual subjects became enmeshed with new understandings about what it meant to be political and on the Left. Questions that for many years had remained unspoken or at the level of the unconscious began to be given voice by small communities of young women as part of wider discussions which New Left activists were starting to have about the future of the radical Left. It is to this we now turn.

Notes

1 P. Marris, *The Experience of Higher Education* (London: Routledge, 1964), p. 3.
2 J. Mark, A. von der Goltz and A. Warring, 'Reflections', in R. Gildea, J. Mark and A. Warring (eds), *Europe's 1968: Voices of Revolt* (Oxford: Oxford University Press, 2013), pp. 284–93; Cornils and Waters (eds), *Memories of 1968*; A. von der Goltz (ed.), *'Talkin' 'bout my Generation': Conflicts of Generation Building and Europe's '1968'* (Göttingen: Wallstein,

    2011); A. Hajek, *Negotiating Memories of Protest in Western Europe: The Case of Italy* (London: Palgrave Macmillan, 2013).
 3 Interview with Margaret Renn and Anna Paczuska, London, 4 January, 2010.
 4 R. Gildea, 'The Long March of Oral History: Around 1968 in France', *Oral History*, 38, Spring (2010), p. 71.
 5 Cited in W. Mausbach, 'America's Vietnam in Germany – Germany in America's Vietnam: On the Relocation of Spaces and the Appropriation of History', B. Davis, W. Mausbach, M. Klimke, and C. MacDougall. (eds), *Changing the World, Changing Oneself: Political Protest and Collective Identities in West Germany and the US in the 1960s and 1970s* (Oxford: Berghahn Books, 2010), p. 42.
 6 Thomson, *Moving Stories*, p. 298.
 7 G-R. Horn, *The Spirit of '68: Rebellion in Western Europe and North America, 1956–1976* (Oxford: Oxford University Press, 2008) pp. 1–2.
 8 Passerini, *Autobiography of a Generation*, p. 60.
 9 N. Thomas, 'Protests against the Vietnam War in 1960s Britain: The Relationship Between Protesters and the Press', *Contemporary British History*, 22:3 (2007), p. 341.
10 Interview with John Rose, London, 30 October, 2008.
11 Interview with Laurie Flynn.
12 T. Book and L. Flynn, 'Celebration of the Life of Basker Vashee and of the 40th Anniversary of the LSE student sit-in', April, 2007, pp. 1–3 [consulted at www.lse.ac.uk/collections/alumniRelations/reunionsAndEvents/2007/0420.htm (11 May 2008)].
13 Interview with Martin Tompkinson, London, 6 November, 2008.
14 Interview with Chris Ratcliffe.
15 A. Green, 'Individual Remembering and "Collective Memory": Theoretical Presuppositions and Contemporary Debates', *Oral History*, 32, Autumn (2004), p. 42.
16 Interview with Stephen Trafford, London, 8 July, 2013.
17 Interview with Gilda Peterson.
18 Interview with Val Graham.
19 Interview with Dave Lyddon.
20 E. Wilson, *Mirror Writing: An Autobiography* (London: Virago, 1982), p. 49.
21 Rowbotham, *Promise of a Dream*, p. 44.
22 Interview with Ian Birchall.
23 Interview with Dave Lyddon.
24 Interview with Ian Birchall.
25 Interview with James Hinton.
26 Interview with Richard Kuper, London, 31 March, 2009.
27 Interview with Fred Lindop.
28 Interview with Ian Birchall.
29 Interview with Phil Hearse.
30 Cited in Fraser (ed.), *1968*, p. 97.

31 Interview with Nigel Coward, London, 7 April, 2009.
32 Ronald Fraser interview with respondent C896/18, April 1984, interview 1 – side 2, p. 1, Ronald Fraser Interviews: '1968 A Student Generation in Revolt', British Library Sound Archive.
33 Interview with John Rose.
34 Interview with Joan Smith.
35 Ibid.
36 Interview with Steve Jefferys.
37 Interview with Martin Shaw.
38 Interview with Martin Shaw; M. Shaw, 'The Making of Socialist Politics', *Agitator*, Vol. 3, No. 2, October, 1967, pp. 8–10.
39 M. Shaw, 'Violence and Demonstrations', *Agitator*, Vol. 4, No. 1, October, 1968, p. 9.
40 Thomas, 'The Student Movement in Britain', p. 77; *Campus*, No. 64, 6 March, 1970, p. 1.
41 Interview with Gilda Peterson.
42 *Campus*, No. 51, 24 October, 1969, p. 6.
43 Ronald Fraser interview with respondent C890/0, p. 28, Ronald Fraser Interviews: '1968 A Student Generation in Revolt', British Library.
44 Ibid.
45 Kate Weigand interview with Barbara Winslow, Williamstown, Massachusetts, 3–4 May, 2004, Voices of Feminism Oral History Project, Sophia Smith Collection, 2004, [consulted at www.smith.edu/libraries/libs/ssc/vof/transcripts/Winslow.pdf (24 October, 2009)], p. 22.
46 Interview with Jane Storr.
47 Rose, 'Assembling the Modern Self', p. 238.
48 Ronald Fraser interview with respondent, C890/0, p. 49.
49 J. Weeks, *Sex, Politics and Society: The Regulation of Sexuality since 1800* (London: Longman, 1989), p. 252.
50 J. Lewis, *Women in Britain since 1945* (Oxford: Blackwell Publishing, 1992); p. 44.
51 G. Gorer, *Sex and Marriage in England Today* (London: Thomas Nelson, 1971), p. 30.
52 Interview with Anna Paczuska.
53 Interview with Joan Smith.
54 Interview with Steve Jefferys.
55 Interview with Margaret Renn.
56 Interview with Bronwen Davis.
57 Interview with Margaret Renn.
58 Interview with Gilda Peterson.
59 N. Dunn, *'Talking to Women'* (London: Pan Books, 1965), p. 9; C. Dyhouse, *Girl Trouble: Panic and Progress in the History of Young Women* (London: Zed Books, 2013), p. 167; H. Cook, *The Long Sexual Revolution: English Women, Sex and Contraception, 1800–1975* (Oxford: Oxford University Press, 2004), p. 288.

60 Interview with Jane Storr.
61 Rowbotham, *Promise of a Dream*, pp. 158–60; interview with Lee Comer.
62 Interview with Wisty Hoyland.
63 Interview with Stephen Trafford, London, 8 July, 2013.
64 Interview with Wenda Clenaghen.
65 Interview with Anna Paczuska.
66 Interview with Martin Shaw.
67 Interview with David Carter.
68 C. Ponting, *Breach of Promise: Labour in Power, 1964–1970* (London: Hamish Hamilton, 1990).
69 Interview with Wenda Clenaghen.
70 S. Wilson, 'The Poster Workshop' [consulted at www.posterworkshop.co.uk/aboutus.html (3 November, 2010)].
71 M. Diani, 'Networks and Participation', in D. A. Snow, S. A. Soule and H. Kriesi (eds), *The Blackwell Companion to Social Movements* (Oxford: Blackwell, 2007), p. 339.
72 Interview with Steve Jefferys.
73 J. Tanner, 'Motions and Emotions', in M. Klimke and J. Scharloth (eds), *1968 in Europe. A History of Protest and Activism, 1956–77* (Basingstoke: Palgrave Macmillan, 2008), p. 77.
74 N. Thomas, 'Challenging Myths of the 1960s', *Twentieth Century British History*, 13:3 (2002), pp. 283–4.
75 'The Revolutionary Socialist Student Federation', in D. Widgery (ed.), *The Left in Britain 1956–68* (Harmondsworth: Penguin, 1976), pp. 339–40.
76 Interview with Wenda Clenaghen.
77 Interview with Sarah Perrigo, Leeds, 4 June, 2009.
78 Interview with Val Graham.
79 *Black Dwarf*, 1 June, Vol. 1, No. 1 (1968), p. 1; Ali, *Street Fighting Years*, p. 200.
80 Rose, 'Assembling the Modern Self', p. 239.
81 Interview with Sue Crockford, London, 30 September, 2009.
82 Rowbotham, *Women's Consciousness, Man's World*, p. 24.
83 Interview with Mike Martin, Warwick, 15 June, 2010.
84 Interview with Stephen Merrett, Wells, 16 December, 2009.
85 A. Davin, 'Women in Vietnam', *Shrew*, Special double issue, 1970, pp. 5–8.
86 Interview with Sue Crockford.
87 Interview with Jane Storr.
88 D. Caute, *Sixty-Eight: The Year of the Barricades* (London: Hamilton, 1988), p. 3.
89 Interview with Sandy Irving.
90 'Vietnam War Exhibition', VSC flyer for the photographic exhibition and a talk on the International War Crimes Tribunal by David Robinson, 22 February–1 March, 1967, Private papers of David Robinson.
91 Interview with Joan Smith.

92 Interview with Laurie Flynn.
93 'LSE's New Director: A Report on Walter Adams', Modern Records Centre, Warwick University (hereafter MRC), Papers of Steve Jefferys: International Socialists, MSS. 244, Box 6.
94 R. Kasrils, 'Introduction', in K. Keables (ed.), *London Recruits: The Secret War against Apartheid* (London: Merlin, 2012), p. 6.
95 Interview with Steve Jefferys.
96 J. Rose, 'Memories of Ronnie Kasril at LSE', in K. Keables (ed.), *London Recruits: The Secret War against Apartheid* (London: Merlin, 2012), p. 43.
97 Interview with Wenda Clenaghen.
98 Interview with Prue Chamberlayne, London, 8 May, 2009.
99 S. Rowbotham, *The Past is Before Us: Feminism in Action since the 1960s* (London: Pandora, 1989), p. 246.
100 Interview with Chris Ratcliffe.

4

New Left politics and
Women's Liberation

At the end of the decade the activist scene around the VSC began to
re-shape. In April 1969 the collapse of a National Left Convention ended
hopes of unifying the Left, whilst a fatal rupture in the *Black Dwarf*'s
editorial board mirrored the wider disintegration of the Campaign.[1]
The next decade saw the continuing growth of the far Left, IS and
IMG, one the one hand, and the 'non-aligned' Left collectives, on the
other hand. During the 1970s members within these divergent milieux
committed themselves to different visions for grass-roots socialist agitation. Whilst Trotskyists concerned themselves with building revolutionary organisations oriented towards the industrial working-class,
the 'non-aligned' Left came to be characterised by loose communities
of socialists, feminists, gay liberation activists, anarchists and squatters
whose libertarian 'do-it-yourself' politics was already alive in the community politics of the early sixties.

Within the English scene, as with other western movements, the period
1969–71 heralded a transition when the 'new politics' began to transform cultural, social and emotional life inside the extra-parliamentary
Left. The 'new politics' was Sheila Rowbotham's term for Women's
Liberation as distinct from the alienating culture she had encountered
around Trotskyist groups in the VSC.[2] Yet, in 1968 the emotive tenets
and psychological hallmarks of her new politics echoed elsewhere in
the extra-parliamentary Left: in voices young activists expressed in
diaries, inside their heads or occasionally in printed writings. Visions
of socialist revolution began to be expressed that demanded release
from 'inner and outer bondages', asserting the need to transform internal
perception, being and personal relations as much as external structural
change. Calls for attention to the ways in which capitalism penetrated
the head as well as the social body drew upon emotional experiences
and intellectual impulses from the US New Left and E. P. Thompson's
socialist humanism as well as older utopian impulses of late-nineteenth-
century New Life socialists.

This chapter examines the meaning and impact of the 'new politics' as a new political language on the Left. It shows how the arrival of Women's Liberation coincided with political, social and psychic shifts in the activist terrain as female and male activists alike, dissatisfied with far-left tactics, embraced a 'new' pre-figurative politics to politicise the everyday. This 'new politics' sought to challenge the isolating, atomising effects of life under capitalist society by transforming social relations within local, grass-roots public and private spheres. It emerged at a point of political and personal transition as young activists, poised on the brink of adult life, began to leave university, to undertake employment and began formative relationships and, in some cases, family life; in all such milestones, commitment to grass-roots activism shaped their experiences. The chapter focuses on a north London VSC branch in Camden Town which, in the autumn of 1969, re-formed to become a New Left collective, the CMPP. The political culture of this collective provides an early example of the 'new politics' in practice. In CMPP, members' personal problems and needs were seen as integral to the political life of the group. Activism in the local community was understood to derive from analysing one's own personal sense of oppression. CMPP embodied socialist ideas that found expression in the Women's Liberation politics which was beginning to spread throughout 1969. Through analysing the personal roots of oppression, individuals in a collective could learn how to relate to each other in new ways, discovering in each other a collective strength and consciousness in relation to capitalist society. The chapter shows how, at the end of 1968, American women in CMPP took this discourse of personal politics into the Tufnell Park Women's Liberation group, one of the first four groups to compose the LWLW when it began in mid-1969. Prior to joining, almost all members had been involved in 'non-aligned' left circles, notably in Camden VSC, alongside male comrades, friends, lovers and husbands. Many American members had also been active in New Left movements in the United States and the beginnings of the women's movement there. For these women and men, attraction and commitment to realising a 'new politics' was mutually shared and the social and emotional impact was mutually felt.

Focus on this metropolitan New Left group complements recent efforts by historians to examine how the 'globality' of 1968 operated not only in national cultural contexts, but also in localities and at the level of individual subjectivities. Timothy Brown has raised the spectre of the macro- and micro-1968, arguing the importance of understanding 'alternative cognitive maps' which local actors created as the means by which to imagine themselves in communities transformed by a new type of grass-roots politics.[3] Drawing upon this framework the chapter addresses how New Left ideas which English and American activists introduced into CMPP transmuted into a specific New Left culture in Camden Town.

The story of CMPP and the Tufnell Park Women's Liberation group presents an intimate account of young activist life at a breaking political moment. Members' testimonies suggest the arrival of Women's Liberation was more nuanced than the few secondary accounts allow for. Portraits of women confined solely to the margins of radical movements, typing minutes and subject to male misogyny exclude the women and men whose stories do not fit this narrative.[4] They also overlook the importance of understanding these women's and men's experiences on the Left in the overall context of the post-war society in which they had been conditioned as gendered beings. The chapter tells a relational story of the early days of Women's Liberation to consider the political and personal challenges it presented to CMPP's own 'New Left' politics, to members' sense of self and to the intimate familial ties binding them to the collective.

The Camden Movement for People's Power

CMPP and its 'new politics' arose out of personal interchange around the VSC which facilitated the international transfer of ideas. The Camden VSC emerged out of the north-west London ad hoc committee, which had been formed to organise the anti-Vietnam War demonstration of 27 October, 1968. However, its political origins extended to Old Left Communist Parties in which core members had spent formative years. Geoff Richman, the group's main theoretician and a socially critical and creative medical student who wrote poetry and read Mayakovsky, joined the Hampstead YCL in 1953. Upon entry he found himself inwardly transformed as a revolutionary and, unable to 'rest content with any ordinary sort of existence', embraced it as 'a complete life system' that shaped his thinking about humanity, marriage, family and occupation.[5] A general practitioner in Kilburn, he became frustrated with the National Health Service and, echoing wider critical voices in the late 1960s, saw modern life as responsible for the isolation and alienation of the individual that came from the division between public and private life. Alongside a host of medical sociologists and psychologists, he was convinced that most patients' illnesses were socially induced. Secretary of the Socialist Medical Association (SMA), Richman and his wife, Marie, built up an extensive network of contacts ranging from London Communists to East German SMA representatives who attended dinner parties the couple hosted at their Cricklewood home. In 1966, a decade after the exodus of young Communist intellectuals from the Party, the Richmans broke with the Communist Party of Great Britain and became involved with a Maoist opposition inside it; the Party expelled them after they refused to recant Geoff's arguments that the Party was failing to address real issues in society. Out of their involvement with the Maoists, in 1967 the Richmans developed the Friday Group; here they met an American couple, Henry and Sheli Wortis, who provided the link to the VSC and the New Left ideas the couples began to develop.[6]

Despite the different national contexts in which they had initially engaged on the Left, the Richman and Wortis couples found in each other kindred political spirits. Henry Wortis was a medical researcher at London's Mill Hill, the National Science Institute, whilst Sheli had trained as an experimental psychologist. Henry's work had brought the couple to London from San Francisco, California in 1965 as the anti-war movement was starting to take shape. Both were 'red-diaper babies' with shared family backgrounds of Communist and trade union activity and had come of political age during the dangerous McCarthy years.[7] As a medical student in the Mid-West at the University of Wisconsin, Henry had adopted a public stance as a Communist when to do so demanded conviction in the face of potential ruin. Sheli came from a Jewish Communist family, but her left upbringing had been culturally tempered by hootenannies and socialist summer camp activities. When the couple first came to London from New York, in 1965, they gravitated to people of Communist Party backgrounds, engaging the Richmans in the increasingly disturbing issue of the Vietnam War and introducing them to a community of young Americans in London who were active against it. Many were graduate students, a significant number attending the LSE, or wives and girlfriends who had accompanied husbands and boyfriends to the UK. The Americans had come to Britain drawn by the cheaper cost of living, and often propelled by a desire to avoid the draft.[8]

In 1967 Henry and Sheli joined the Stop-It Committee (Americans in Britain for U.S. withdrawal from Vietnam), a London group of around 350 members supporting American draft resisters, running study groups and performing publicity actions for the organisation. Stop-It's loose organisational structure replicated the participatory democracy of student movements in the United States. It also embraced an agitprop protest style that testified to members' efforts to inject a radical flavour into what many saw as England's staid demonstrations.[9] Within this forum the couple met activists who would gravitate into the Camden Vietnam Solidarity Campaign (CVSC) when the Stop-It Committee decided to disband in November, 1968. They included film editor Ellen Adams and her biochemist husband, Richard Hammerschlagg, along with LSE postgraduate David Slaney, who, like many Socialist Society activists, briefly joined IS and participated in the national VSC committee.

The Old Left rituals of soap boxes, megaphones and newspaper selling and the formulaic rhetoric dominating meetings stood in sharp contrast to the cultural innovation and fun characterising Stop-It's New Left milieu. The young Americans' alienation from the VSC's Old Left imprint resonated with the sentiments of Geoff Richman and other CVSC activists disillusioned with the increasingly factional anti-war movement. Geoffrey Crossick was a history postgraduate at London's Birkbeck College who had worked alongside Geoff Richman on the VSC national committee and, along with Henry, Sheli and other CVSC members, led calls at the February, 1969 National Conference to reorient VSC around individual membership rooted in a series of local branches.[10] The Friday Group provided a model for the CVSC branch in which members sought to realise their vision for localised activism. In the Friday Group the Richman and the Wortis couples had already begun to 'consider the problems of being a revolutionary in a non-revolutionary situation' and to amalgamate the new revolutionary politics both couples envisaged.[11] Geoffrey Crossick recalled that by the time he met Geoff Richman in VSC, the socialist doctor was articulating 'a different vision of politics on the Left', looking to 'Gramsci's idea that had a critical component of rethinking what political movements and what political oppression were all about'.[12]

The New Left ideas Henry and Sheli injected into the Friday Group derived from their activism in the San Francisco Bay area of California. In 1967 the couple had participated in a series of small political groups initiated by New Left activist James O'Connor. In 1964 O'Connor had played a formative role in shifting the discursive and activist landscape of the American New Left onto the agency of the poor and the marginal when the New Left journal *Studies on the Left* published his article on community unions, his model for future working-class organisation and struggle.[13] His political imprint was transposed to CVSC, adding its weight to the eclectic international discourses shaping members' vision for the local community as a site for a New Left identity.

Beyond the Richman and Wortis couples, the Camden core included artistic-minded Sue Crockford and Tony Wickert, a couple influential in shaping the collective's creative culture. Tony was an Australian actor at the BBC when, in late 1968, he first encountered CVSC. He was one of the film and television workers attending the political meetings at Tony Garnett's house in Kensington Square, where he encountered the Trotskyist brandishing of Gerry Healy. He was seeking to recruit left-wing media workers, and Healy's 'heated and intimidating' personality did little to entice Tony, who lacked grass-roots political experience and wondered 'was this, what politics was like?'[14] In September, 1968 he and Sue found a politics 'more our style' when, attending their first anti-war meeting in Hampstead High Street, they became 'enthralled' by the Richman and Wortis couples and their humanitarian and culturally oriented socialism.

Sue Crockford was a film student attending Hornsey College of Art when she joined CVSC. Her own political consciousness had been shaped in the early sixties when she was an undergraduate at Leeds University, horrified by images of American segregation which she saw on New York news reels. Equally shocking had been photographs of the March, 1960 Sharpville massacre which her friend's father had smuggled out of South Africa: 'I'd been brought up with police living across the road and the idea that police were shooting unarmed people was so horrific.'[15] She joined the university's anti-apartheid campaign, where a dangerous encounter with two white South African students brought the stakes of the cause closer to home:

> I was putting up the exhibition. Two white South African engineering students threatened me, threatened to break my arms, and I was absolutely petrified, but I can remember having two thoughts in my mind. One was petrified, thinking I've got to think of a different route home, and the other was this is nothing. I'm in a country where I'm just threatened with my arms being broken. I'm not going to be shot. And I think it was . . . it was the connection that I gradually pieced together that our country was complicit.

For Sue, as a young woman with a passion for social justice, politics was always implicitly personal, imbued with the empathy she felt for the individuals underlying the campaigns: 'I couldn't not put myself in someone else's shoes . . . I always wanted to know the motives behind why people did things.' Her attachment to art and literature shaped her connection to people's stories; in the case of Vietnam, the graphic televised images of wounded civilians meant that the issue never became bigger than these individuals.

Around the CVSC, core members were drawn into the group via word of mouth through London's American anti-war community, left circles around the LSE and artists and scientists active against the war; all brought valuable international contacts for the collective to draw upon. The young members shared common characteristics: many were newly married or just starting families, professionals in science and education, artistic, and all passionately opposed to the war. Many had histories of political activity in other national contexts and were attracted by CMPP's attempts to carve out a participatory socialism and to explore moral and political issues around the war in ways that drew wider parallels with their own experiences in a capitalist society.

Matthew and Anita Merryweather joined CVSC after returning from Los Angeles, where they had been active in the anti-war movement at the University of California, Los Angeles. Matthew was South African, on the Left, and, like other white South African émigrés in north London, had participated on the edges of the anti-apartheid struggle before coming to England. The couple were part of the scientific left circle around CVSC; Anita knew Henry Wortis through her work at Mill Hill prior to moving to Los Angeles.[16] Stephen and Alicia Merrett joined CVSC after Alicia moved to London, in July, 1967. He was an economics researcher at the Ministry of Technology and Alicia was a librarian at the LSE. She had left her home country of Argentina, where she had participated in student demonstrations at the University of Buenos Aires. The couple had met during Stephen's work-related travels through India and Latin America.[17] Upon returning to London, Stephen was initially involved in the May Day Manifesto project, launched in May, 1967, but both made political contacts through the LSE's scientific circles, including Medical Aid for Vietnam.[18]

From their origins in the north-west London ad hoc committee, the aim of CVSC members was to work locally to raise understanding about the Vietnam War. The initial motivation behind this community focus derived from the vision members held for the national VSC movement. Discussions following the 27 October demonstration had led to consensus that, in order for the national movement to evolve, it had to realise its potential for mobilising consciousness about the war. The CVSC modelled its collective on Geoff Richman's understanding of the NLF 'People's War'. Like anti-war activists around the globe, CVSC members were inspired by the example the Vietcong presented 'of people running their own lives, their own country, their own war against oppression'. To win 'the people to revolutionary views', members sought to initiate 'direct dialogue with local people' to raise understanding about British complicity in the conflict.[19]

New Left 'personal politics' for Camden Town

Geoff Richman's vision of 'New Left' politics represented an amalgam of radical voices responding to the affluence, consumerism and popular culture which critics believed had shaped an impoverished mass society. Since the late 1950s, laments ranging from Richard Hoggart's *The Uses of Literacy* (1957) to Raymond Williams' *Communications* (1962) found similar tenets in the Marcusian strands of thought critiquing the 'repressive tolerance' of post-industrial Western Europe and the United States, where consumer society could be seen diverting human energy away from fulfilling real social, civil and sexual needs and into the false illusion of consumption. CMPP members saw themselves amongst many social groups – students, teachers, apprentices, clerks, doctors, technicians and white- collar workers and skilled manual workers – alienated from the dehumanising impulses of bourgeois society. They argued that 'beyond work the major patterns of our lives are fixed for us. We are free to act only in isolation, individually, to teachers, bosses, T.V., landlords, housework, children, racism, ill health, loneliness.'[20] They saw the solution in civic power, community control and collective will.

The group's New Left critique took on visual dynamic in its street-theatre play, *The Hole in the Wall*, which was written and first performed in 1970 from its stall in Camden's Queen Crescent market, where, every Saturday morning, members tried to engage stallholders and passers-by in discussion on issues ranging from Vietnam to alienation and social concerns affecting the local community. Following the critical tradition of the literary critic F. R. Leavis and his post-war disciples, *The Hole in the Wall* spoke of the stultifying effects of television as but one of the modern mass-communicative mediums damaging community bonds and civic engagement.[21] The play depicted the monotonous routine of two separate households centred on the nightly television programme, to dramatise the damaging role of consumer technology on social relations.

In accordance with New Left thinking, the economic struggle over the distribution of wealth was, for CMPP, 'subsidiary in importance to the conflict over culture, social values and social control'.[22] The *raison d'être* of CMPP – community – saw a continuation of the New Left socialist humanism amalgamated with Third World revolutionary discourse, perpetuating the preoccupation of radicals and intellectuals whose search for an organic community harked back to poets and theologians from T. S. Eliot and C. S. Lewis to the impulses of D. H. Lawrence which Cambridge radicals had injected into post-war cultural criticism.[23] Geoff Richman understood that for people to counter their isolation and powerlessness, they had to come together through a variety of relationships. Due to the absence of a revolutionary movement capable of replicating Fidel Castro's revolutionary vocation, the creation of a collective was the first step in winning people to revolutionary views. Before the slogan of the WLM, 'The personal is political', penetrated the English Left, Richman's vision for a New Left collective drew upon C. Wright Mills' idea of personal politics as elaborated in *The Sociological Imagination* and evoked by Tom Hayden, author of *The Port Huron Statement*, in the pre-figurative politics of the American New Left movement, SDS. In SDS the purpose of pre-figurative politics had been 'to create and sustain within the live practice of the movement relationships and political forms that "prefigured" and embodied the desired society'.[24] In CMPP, members' personal problems and needs were seen as integral to the collective life, fusing 'the personal and the political, the public and the private'.[25] The implication was that all aspects of activists' lives acquired a political dimension, the private individual dissolved; within the collective people were 'bound together by their identification with the group, and no longer with themselves as individuals'. This was an all-encompassing vision that placed a premium on members' commitment to a new life and ways of being.

CMPP and the VSC network

Important for all CMPP members was the desire to foster a spirit of fun through subversion, a core tenet of the youthful play-power contesting the 'repressive tolerance' of post-industrial society. In CVSC, members' artistic talents and organising skills were facilitated by the 'do-it-yourself', collaborative ethos prevailing across the metropolitan network. Camden Town was home to radical cultural and community groups servicing the activist scene: Poster Workshop, CAST, Agitprop and the Camden Community Workshop, the latter one of several community organising projects like the Notting Hill People's Association which emerged in the wake of CND and the May Day Manifesto.[26] The group's eclectic culture testified to members' shared interests in international politics and reflected the range of north London's international and local contacts at its disposal. Tony Wickert and Sue Crockford became regular visitors to Poster Workshop on the Camden Road soon after it opened in the summer of 1968. It was modelled on the Parisian Atelier Populaire, set up in the Ecole des Beaux Arts in May, 1968, and volunteers, young and old, brought an array of left histories, artistic and practical skills into the airless basement where they created silkscreen posters for the political groups and campaigns springing up in the capital.

Relations between the Angry Arts Society and CMPP symbolised the latter's place at the nexus of the global and local perimeters in the network and the intimate ties guiding projects inside it. The Society emerged out of the Angry Arts Week Stop-It held during the summer of 1967, when Ellen Adams and Richard Hammerschlagg revitalised film showings to pay off a debt Stop-It had incurred from the week's activities.[27] By the autumn of 1968 the couple had become distributors for Newsreel films, a New York group founded by SDS activist Norm Fruchter and radical film director Robert Kramer. Like Agitprop and Poster Workshop, Angry Arts performed a vital servicing function for the activist network, communicating political ideas, news of recent projects and American protest forms to groups and campaigns across the country. CVSC members facilitated this cultural interchange; after collaborating with the making of the VSC film *End of a Tactic?*, Ellen began attending CVSC meetings and participating in activities.[28] At the end of 1969 Angry Arts became closely integrated into CVSC as the collective embarked on its transition from a local VSC group. CMPP members aided Sue and Tony in the organising of Newsreel films. In the voluntary spirit of the network, Sue put herself forward after Ellen and Richard announced their intention to leave London, motivated by a tendency to 'assume personal responsibility for any silence in a room' and by the affective ties binding members together, so that she remembered 'acts of kindness just used to happen'.[29] Whereas activists had previously viewed political films as passive consumers, CMPP members reorganised the Society to stimulate post-film discussions. In these forums the aim was to encourage maximum participation by challenging the Old Left style of formal meetings. Watching films together, sharing discussion, soup and coffee in small groups away from the regimentation of rows echoed the participatory democracy of the O'Connor groups and testified to the international New Left culture informing CMPP's philosophy that 'only by being socialist in your behaviour can you presume to be socialist in your ideals'.[30]

Members' subjective responses to CMPP's cultural life tell much about their experiences inside the group. Individuals' memories focused heavily on CMPP's shared cultural agenda to highlight symbols of belonging as well as tension, their stories providing insight into this New Left milieu at an important moment of political and personal change. CMPP's creative activities echoed the 'expressive politics' of SDS activists who embraced participatory democracy. The idea was that individual participation in a political struggle would bring fulfilment, create a sense of community and radicalise participants. Hence the Berkeley Free Speech Movement slogan, 'The issue is not the issue'.[31] Activities took on important personal and political focus inside the collective, where they offered to reveal how members related to each other.

The personal and the political in CMPP

Understanding how individuals engaged in the activities of CMPP raises questions about gendered group dynamics and how friendships and loving relationships shaped experiences of the new politics. How, for example, did the challenges of pre-figurative politics become intertwined with the new politics of Women's Liberation? Starting with the premise that power in the collective lay with the core, the spectre of influential personalities, subtly gendered power relations and members' conflicting feelings becomes apparent. Initial challenges confronting the collective concerned the working practice of participatory democracy and how to resolve divisions between articulate and less confident members. These are significant because of the emphasis traditionally placed on contradictions between the participatory democracy of New Left movements and the marginalised role women played inside these anti-hierarchical yet patriarchal organisations.[32] Core members established CMPP in reaction against the VSC's Old Left militancy. Consequently, it must be considered how far they were able to realise more equitable social relations and to dissolve divisions between personal and political life. It is notable that as early as March, 1969 new CVSC member Carole Sturdy felt compelled to speak out on behalf of young individuals like her who had joined without any prior experience of activity in a political group. Although she underlined the 'informal, truly democratic nature of the meetings', she also noted how she and others felt 'too politically naive to participate much in discussions, looking instead to the old campaigners for leadership'.[33] At a meeting on 12 March Sturdy and others accused 'the so-called "top-table"' of running the group as 'an intellectual elite'. On the one hand, that they felt willing and able to share these insecurities testifies to the New Left culture of subjectivity in which young individuals were clearly learning to understand their feelings as valid matters for political discussion. One the other hand, the incident implies that from an early stage individual belonging in CMPP was predicated on members' position in the collective.

Despite CMPP's emphasis on participatory democracy, an internal contradiction lay at the heart of the collective, allowing intellectually articulate voices to dominate. Core members Geoff Richman, Geoffrey Crossick and Henry and Sheli Wortis were preoccupied by the need to avoid Old Left-style issue politics, and this created problems for group relations and subjective belonging; every activity had to be scrutinised for what it revealed about members' social behaviour and relationships. What this meant in practice was that prior to meetings the inner core met to discuss ways in which to ensure group activities adhered to its new politics. Geoffrey Crossick reflected how:

> I, Geoff, Henry and Sheli would say, well, we've got to take this back. We've got to get people thinking about this, this and this, and it was something that there is a problem about; this identity. There's too much just activity going on and what's the direction, and so on? . . . If we felt that activity was what built identity, surely we would just trust the activity . . . but we didn't trust that because we could end up just being an activist group, a single-issue group, which we had immense hostility for.[34]

CMPP's power and sense of identity as a collective derived from a consensus of what it was not – a political party – rather than what it was. This insecurity created a set of expectations about how members should invest themselves inside the group, which Geoff Richman outlined in 'On Strategy'. In his view, the denial of a separation between daily life and politics anticipated members subordinating their private lives to the group, based on the need to engage in constant activity from which collective identity would develop. Attention to social detail included a list of twenty questions designed to scrutinise members' social behaviour during meetings. These included: 'Does everyone speak at a meeting, or only one or two people? If someone remains quiet does anyone try to find out why? If a person is inactive do they feel guilty or inadequate, rejected or under moral pressure?'[35] Viewed against these questions, Sturdy's comments show how concern to encourage a participatory, egalitarian culture could inadvertently lead to the controlling behaviours core members sought to avoid. However, these contradictions did not translate to a straightforward model of authoritarian relationships. In CMPP, social status, relationships and emotional belonging rested on a complex fusion of radical and traditional social values and attitudes that found their most overt expression in members' mixed responses to Women's Liberation.

In the first instance the capacity of core members to exercise an influential presence and to shape a challenging intellectual ethos owed much to the way in which CMPP members' sense of place related to age and political experience. Rita Vaudrey was nineteen and a first-year undergraduate at Cambridge when, in the autumn of 1968, she became involved with CVSC through her boyfriend, Geoffrey Crossick. Although, like him, she came from a working-class, Labour-supporting family, before Vietnam she had never been active politically, so that it was Geoff's commitment to the Campaign that led to her presence on the October demonstration: 'He was proud of that, the Vietnam movement, and what was going on . . . I wasn't too keen on the demonstrations because of the prospect of violence.'[36] Rita met the core CVSC members as 'political allies' and 'friends' her boyfriend had recently made at a time of heightening discord in the movement, and she understood them as 'kindred spirits' who supported his hopes for its future direction. Initially only present at CVSC activities on weekends, she was one of its youngest members. Rita's insecurity amidst the collective derived partly from her inclination towards shyness and lack of social and intellectual confidence tied to her youth: 'It was quite judgemental and so I wouldn't put on the line what I thought . . . but then I was younger than them, not by much, but those years between twenty and twenty-two are when you are developing your confidence and ideas.' In contrast, Henry and Sheli Wortis articulated a political and social self-confidence that derived at least partly from the fact that, along with the Richmans, they were in their early thirties, as compared to most members a decade younger. Unlike other core members, the Wortis couple also had a history of American pre-figurative activism behind them and experiential faith in its participatory practices and potential to shape personal and social change.

Sheli Wortis was an influential member of the Camden core and her role denies any simple explanation of male domination that might account for Carol Sturdy's protest. Characterising herself and her husband as 'the social head of the group', Sheli saw herself as a core member on the same terms as her male comrades: 'Whatever we decided to do was fully consensus politics even though there was leadership. I mean Geoff [Richman] clearly dominated in terms of his intellect. People looked up to him, and I think they looked up to Henry too, but there were other people in the group who were strong and convincing, and we could have discussions without people feeling intimidated by others in the group.' Although her reference to the two leading intellectual men implies an absent female presence, her emphasis on how she felt fully part of decision-making processes confirmed other interviewees' memories about her role in relation to her husband. To observers, the couple's commitment to personal and political mutuality seemed to showcase the potential for personal and political life to successfully co-exist. Amidst the wider network, Henry's libertarian and egalitarian attitudes provided a refreshing outlook on personal and political relations between young men and women.

In December, 1967, following a meeting of the East London VSC, Sheila Rowbotham had listened with astonishment as the 'good-looking' Stop-It comrade driving her home calmly explained that the brusque manner with which opinionated Trotskyist men had cut her out of the discussion carried with it a political name: male chauvinism.[37] Sue

Crockford similarly recalled the deep impact Henry and Sheli had made on her at a time when she was negotiating the sensitivities concerning Women's Liberation and male feeling: 'They just took it for granted that you were radical, and what was good; they had a good working marriage . . . I couldn't take for granted that your sexual relationship was also your political relationship. They did.'[38] The political framework of Sheli's relationship with her husband provided her with an intellectual role alongside but independent from him. Integrating the meaning of personal politics into their marriage as well as their political lives, the couple's egalitarian relationship seemed to embody the very relationships that from the early 1970s socialist feminists were seeking with men.

Sheli's decision as a prominent core member who enjoyed good relations with CMPP men to establish the Tufnell Park Women's Liberation group was far removed from the critique of male supremacy and sexism which, from 1967, characterised American women's revolt against male comrades, and which from 1969 also began to define the 'fraught' 'collective urgency' of English female activists elsewhere in the network.[39] Her early involvement in the Tufnell Park group was an organic extension of the mutual personal politics she and her husband had invested in CMPP, conceived to complement and not to oppose the collective. Henry fully supported the argument that 'women needed a political space away from men', to be 'women identified . . . to develop ideas and to develop as people', and it seems that once this started to take shape in practice, he was happy to see it develop as a complement to and not in competition to the weekly core meetings.[40]

In the June, 1969 *Red Camden* bulletin Sheli detailed the attempts of women and men, active around Tufnell Park and CVSC, to set up 'A People's Crèche' in north-west London. Her ideas show her understanding of Women's Liberation as a logical extension of the group's core identity developing around 'community control'. According to Sheli, the adults using the crèche met together in a private home for about seven hours on the weekend; they read and compared 'bourgeois and socialist manuals on child rearing and child development' while others supervised the children. The intention was to provide a place 'for parents to do collective political work near their children, but not always administering to them'.[41] They proposed setting up crèches at future conferences, and children sleeping at these on some evenings to allow their parents to go off to meetings together. For Sheli there was an explicit connection between this practical parental need and CVSC's politics: 'We want them off the streets, playing together, and having the sort of collective life of their own which would reinforce the ideas

we have about socialisation and development rather than the ideas of
competitiveness, hostility, racism, religion and aggressiveness which
they learn through school and the mass media.'

The principles of the crèche drew upon the West German Action
Council for the Liberation of Women. At the Frankfurt SDS Conference
in September, 1968, Helke Sanders had directed a strident criticism to
SDS men, condemning their complicity in the capitalist system by perpetuating a sexual division of labour in their private lives. In response
to men's refusal to correct the situation, women employed the device
of setting up *Kinderläden*, Kinder-Shops or Day Care Centres, mainly
around universities, as centres for children and their mothers.[42] However,
unlike the SDS model, the crèche Sheli envisaged was informed by her
understanding of CMPP as embedded in her and her comrades' everyday family lives. Sheli was one of a number of interviewees for whom
the leitmotif of family denoted the affective solidarity prevailing throughout the collective. One of the principal sources of pleasure she and her
husband derived from CMPP was the space the group provided for
incorporating members' own nuclear family life into their activism:
'People were wonderful with other people's children ... We were all
really aware that this was something different from other left groups.'[43]
Henry's and Sheli's two young daughters attended the group's weekend
and outdoor activities; their close attachment to the Richmans' children
and to adult members reflected social bonds that replicated older
kinship ties as well as members' efforts to cultivate more respectful,
equal relations.

Family and friendship in CMPP

Memories of CMPP showed the symbolic significance the family held
in members' understandings of the group. Yet, in their various narrative
shapes and cultural symbols, these were also replete with tensions. They
suggested an uneasy presence of traditional and radical social values,
bonds and emotions shaping subjectivity and complicating women's
and men's feelings about Women's Liberation. In CMPP the arrival of
Women's Liberation confused traditionally gendered social roles and
kinship ties and provoked torn loyalties between members and the
collective.

The dominant presence of familial tropes suggested a network of
intimate ties binding members to CMPP's political project and to each
other as comrades and family members. Portrayals of CMPP as a community where personal and political lives came together in a joyful and
supportive manner drew upon nostalgic representations of working-class

communities with their extended kinship ties. Queen's Crescent market and Hampstead Heath, for example, represented two collective sites of remembrance which members' saw embodying the spirit of self-determination, support and trust they had envisaged for the group and Camden Town at a point of transition in traditional working-class London communities. In 1969–71 CMPP members were amongst an array of metropolitan grass-roots activists protesting against the urban redevelopment schemes displacing old communities and exacerbating the homeless crisis.[44] For Sue Crockford, Queen's Crescent market was an emblem of the mythic community CMPP envisaged. She understood it as one of the few 'egalitarian places' allowing for 'normal human transactions regardless of class', and illustrated this with her story of Bill the stallholder:

> [CMPP] were at the top on the left and down on the bottom on the right was Bill, who ran the fruit and veg stall, and so after we finished off I'd go down with Barney in the pushchair and buy my fruit and veg, and the January after we started . . . I think it had snowed. It was bloody horrible weather anyway, and Bill suddenly said 'You're from the Vietnam stall aren't you?' I said 'Yes'. He said, 'We took a bet. We only thought you'd last a couple of months but you've been here six months. You've earned the right to tell me about Vietnam' (Laughs). It was the weirdest, really one of the loveliest conversations because I used to go down and buy my fruit and veg without talking about Vietnam, because I thought this is oppressive. I'm not going to buy cabbages and say oh by the way, but he asked me, we had proved, and we had a lovely conversation and I used to go back there afterwards and get my fruit and veg from Bill.[45]

Sue's remembered landscape cast CMPP as the desired socialist community she and other members had envisaged. At one level the symbols of remembrance drew upon the narrative members had represented to others and to themselves as a group of people who genuinely enjoyed political activity together. Geoffrey Crossick indicated how the collective style of CMPP's activities, predicated on the belief that politics had to be 'enjoyable and fulfilling, not a moral duty', informed this nostalgic spirit of community: 'It was the collective style activity, the construction of a story of ourselves that made all these decisions together.'[46] Story-telling and imaginative forms of representation were vital tools for how members shaped a shared image of CMPP as an embodiment of the new political and social relations. This extended to how members depicted themselves in their bulletins. Reporting on the Liberation Tour of June, 1969, a series of street-theatre performances demonstrating British complicity in the Vietnam War, Geoff Richman noted how

'People take to our happiness; they are not antagonised, as by the usual demonstration'.[47]

Familial tropes, channelled through collective sites of remembrance, also signalled members' sense of place in what had become a psychic landscape. Sally Alexander has argued that 'memory, a way of thinking as figurative as it is literal, fuses the imaginative world with everyday life, dramatizes and recreates the past as it is retrieved'.[48] For Sue, CMPP denoted a surrogate family that was interwoven with her joyful memories of early motherhood. She depicted her son, for example, as 'born into' CMPP; 'the adopted little babe'.[49] The egalitarian relations she associated with the market were also interwoven with the participatory ethos she had found in CMPP's activities as opportunities for artistic exploration and political and self-development: 'I think you could hesitate, you could admit you didn't know something, you didn't have a ten point plan. You changed your mind; if things didn't work you found a better way to do things; and because we were constantly doing plays and demos you were constantly being creative.' In this respect, she saw CMPP standing out from other left groups, where mundane administrative tasks were often relegated to women. In CMPP, she explained, activities were equally shared: 'We all did it. I really think that was different. We all did it. I mean in terms of cyclostyling and the designing and things it was whoever was good or who could or was free.'

Rita Vaudrey's narrative, mediated through the market and the Heath, told a similar story of friendship, love and kinship ties, but in her account these collective sites also assumed conflicting connotations of authoritarian family relations. Her memories of CMPP were interwoven with those of her developing relationship with Geoffrey Crossick and what membership had meant for them as a couple as well as for her as a shy young woman. Her testimony signalled subjective tensions within CMPP's pre-figurative politics. These took vivid focus in:

> a wonderful photograph of Geoff and me at Queen's Crescent market and Geoff is sitting typing on the market stall, and it is obviously a cold day, and I am sitting next to him, quite the girlfriend, you know, sitting by, looking over his shoulder as he is typing, and the whole world is going past us and we are not connecting in any way . . . And I am all wrapped up because we would be going to see Spurs in the afternoon . . . We had Saturdays together. We wanted it.[50]

The scene Rita depicted was redolent with feeling: the unspoken companionship between the couple signifying the intimacy between them; her thick layers of clothing suggestive of the cocoon their private world promised, away from the collective. This private world represented a haven away from the life of the market and the need to connect with the people in it. Her commentary accompanying the scene denoted the tension she felt during the two years the couple spent together amidst the collective, torn between her loyalty to Geoff, his attachment to CMPP as well as her own affection for members within it: 'In between . . . there were other things. I mean we were cultivating a relationship as well, and doing other things together, and going off at weekends together and so, actually I don't know how we did it in a way, in the midst of all of that.' Her story told of the collective's capacity to envelop young members at a point in life when they were hungry for personal and political transformation. The parental role models Geoff and Marie Richman assumed in some interviewees' memories symbolised the conflicting emotions surrounding this leading couple and the survival of traditional patriarchal relations which their roles denoted. Positively, the couple's familial roles enhanced Rita's ties to the collective, bonds that were interwoven with her love for Geoff and desire to support his commitment to the group. On the weekends when she visited, the Richmans frequently enveloped her into their large Kilburn home, welcoming her into the collective: 'Actually I suppose that was one of the first attractions, that it was kids and a family.'

Rita's introduction into the Richmans' cultured middle-class circle coincided with a recent taste of freedom from her Liverpool upbringing, so that their household and political circle were simultaneously imbibed with the familiar associations of home alongside the excitement of otherness: 'Actually it was Geoff and Marie I was drawn to initially . . . they were quite cultured people anyway, and there were lots of conversations around arts, and it was a nice milieu, and it was a middle-class milieu which I was unused to, and liked that sort of easy, you know, eating, drinking and talking which didn't happen in my house or my life really.' Besides this engendering of feelings of belonging, Rita soon came to appreciate that community and family ties carried their own pressures to conform. CMPP's parental figures presented unwelcome challenges to her newly found independence: 'I was really enjoying a room of my own, being by myself, thinking what I wanted to think and not joining anybody else's party.'

The family motifs were not exclusive to women's stories. Geoffrey Crossick also drew upon parental tropes to depict the divisions of loyalty which CMPP created between self and collective. As a paternal role model, Geoff Richman was 'inspiring', and his wife was nurturing – 'Marie would cook for lots of us. That's how I got to know them. They would feed me, an impoverished PhD student, before national

VSC meetings.'[51] Yet Geoff Richman's expectations for members' exclusive loyalty to the group also challenged Geoffrey's filial loyalty to his own parents and family customs. On Friday evenings 'my parents would expect me to go to them because in Jewish families you go home on Friday evenings, and then I think there was this [Gramsci] reading group; so there was this real sense that my loyalties were being torn.' During 1970 his life began to move away from the core: he had begun to build an academic career for himself, his relationship with Rita was developing, he knew CMPP was not central to her life and part of him was beginning to tire of the repetitive activities. Pressure from the Richmans for the young couple to cancel a hitchhiking holiday to participate in the Liberation Tour confirmed Geoffrey's doubts about how far he was prepared to meet his friends' expectations: 'I remember thinking I am living this, it matters to me, but is it really going to deliver anything and do I want to make the total commitment, and the answer is no.' In 1971 the couple's withdrawal from CMPP coincided with its fragmentation as other core members began to move away. In mid-1970 Henry and Sheli returned to Boston, where they continued their anti-war activism; Sue increasingly focused on Women's Liberation and set up a collective childcare centre, One, Two, Three, whilst Tony Wickert developed Angry Arts. For Geoffrey and Rita, the end of their relationship with CMPP was a conscious decision to follow wider postwar patterns to build a secure private life based around romantic love and shared aspirations for home, career and family. Their accounts signify the challenges CMPP's pre-figurative politics presented for young, upwardly mobile adults who continued to see themselves as private domestic citizens as well as political beings. Of additional significance is the threat the new politics posed to Rita's freedom as a modern woman. Her experience points to the masculine subtext of CMPP's new politics, illuminating barely discernible divisions between the women and their male partners that informed the arrival of Women's Liberation.

Gender roles, relations and CMPP

Outwardly, CMPP's kinship ties and women's full inclusion in its political and social life seem far removed from stories of female marginality or 'casual' male chauvinism through which other female activists entered the early WLM. CMPP's New Left politics was designed to privilege space for the subjective every-day of the personal; its small group meetings, where every voice was to be heard, would find continuity in the intimate political and emotional space characterising the Tufnell Park consciousness-raising group. Despite Marcus Collins' claim that late-sixties radical enclaves represented a powerful challenge to mutuality, the narratives of CMPP men and women present evidence to the contrary.[52] Inside the collective, emotional belonging was interwoven with relationships based on understandings of comradeship and post-war constructions of romantic and sexual love and paternal and maternal models. That many interviewees from the Tufnell Park group highlighted the intellectual character of the group and the politically attuned minds not only of Sheli but of other American women, Ellen Adams, Caroline Roth, Sue O'Sullivan and Karen Slaney, highlighted that these women came to Women's Liberation with a background of rigorous political engagement alongside and not in deference to men. Sue O'Sullivan recalled that in political discussions with her school and college friends the women dominated as much as the men.[53] Rita Vaudrey remembered the awe in which she held CMPP and Tufnell Park women: 'The women were pretty intellectually strong in that group. They had a role.'[54] Yet, underlying feeling within the familial tropes spoke of the women's struggles as wives, mothers and young women negotiating contradictory social and emotional codes; the disjuncture they felt in relation to men outside the group assumed a much more subtle subjective shape within the egalitarian culture of the collective.

In CMPP the traditional model of gender relations never entirely dissipated, so that, beneath members' affective bonds, women's and men's subjective states rested upon invisible but fractured gender divisions. The social constraints Rita came to resent derived from an implicitly masculine authority; Geoff Richman's understanding of the new politics drew upon a traditional model of gender roles that posited equality based on difference. His and Marie's expectation for members' total commitment drew upon their own family model, where not only were their children's lives integrated into the collective, but their own leading positions echoed the traditional roles each fulfilled in their marriage. At CMPP's core the social shape of the Richmans' family life was on public display. As the leading intellectual, Geoff Richman exuded an authoritative presence and fulfilled a traditionally dominant role. Geoffrey Crossick saw the weekly reading group as part of his attempt 'to impose an intellectualism on the group' which he believed necessary to its success.[55] Within his marriage, too, Geoff Richman was the main breadwinner. Marie had been a full-time housewife from early in the marriage, when she gave up work as a costume maker for the Royal Opera House. Although she exerted an equally influential presence within the core, she did so through a traditionally female role that supported men and women's separate spheres and encouraged women to defer to male intellectual authority. On one occasion, Rita remembered, 'there was a camping group and I was asked [by Marie] to do the catering for it. I was twenty, you know, and I had never fed anyone in my life.'[56] Interviewees recalled how Marie regularly typed up her husband's notes, deferred to his opinion and could be quick to defend him if she sensed other members criticising him. Through her domestic role she carved out her own influence within the collective. Cooking meals for members was one way of cultivating the close relations she and her husband sought to foster.

The Richmans' traditionally gendered roles instilled a powerful social dynamic into CMPP and a gendered paradox. At one level, the group's mode of organising – building collective enjoyment, trust, openness and self-development through creative activities – implied a subjective politics to anticipate Women's Liberation by rejecting the individualistic, egocentric behaviours that had prevailed in the VSC. Yet the very demands its new politics made upon members to 'interact freely, openly, frankly', to achieve equality without difference, rested on an understanding of equality for men and women that imbued a discursively masculine model of social authority. It failed to account for the individual loyalties and different modes of relating which each core couple had developed, and denied the possibility for emotional frivolity or 'persistent personal weakness'. This was a political vision that embodied emotional and behavioural codes reminiscent of the self-restraint still championed in the male boarding and grammar schools, and held up as models in English professional life. Geoff Richman's notion, for example, that 'kindness' could 'be patronising' and that constructive criticism was part of a larger exploratory process suggested that within the collective the possibility for social equality depended upon members conforming to a model of social behaviour that allowed little space for insecurity, inhibition or the expression of emotional vulnerability.[57] Tellingly, Carol Sturdy's protest was never followed up in any subsequent bulletins.

Despite Sheli's prominent role in CMPP, Rita and Sue's experiences confirmed how women's and men's subjective positions were complicated not only by their status in the core but also by their relationships with each other as post-war gendered subjects. Sue reflected, for example:

There were three main couples: Sheli and Henry, Geoff and Marie, and me and Tony, and I would deliberately never sit next to Tony . . . the power and synergy of some couples where the whole is greater than the sum of its parts can be a great force for good, and can be a negative influence on other people, can make them feel slightly adolescent, smaller, not joined up yet . . . and Tony used to see it almost as a sign of disloyalty, and it wasn't meant like that at all . . . I was trying to be loyal to all the other people in the group.[58]

Sue showed that internal fractures between the men and women were not simply a matter of torn loyalties between the individual, the couple and the collective, but involved an invisible gulf felt most often by women, for whom their sense of difference related to their marginalised societal role. She illustrated how, despite the intimate ethos and fun that often prevailed, women like her sometimes felt ill at ease alongside articulate male comrades:

> There was a couple there, I shan't name names, but who would be dis-
> cussing the next project or whatever it was, and they would start to say
> 'we should probably . . .' and they would have deliberate pauses, and I
> would think the confidence to talk when you haven't thought it all out,
> to have a pause and to know people would listen. I would be spewing
> it out so fast I would have to repeat it, because nobody would hear it,
> and I thought that's confidence, and it was mostly the men.

Sue's awe of the men's self-confidence suggested the gendered social conditioning of post-war higher-educated youth and the complex ways in which it translated into subjectivity inside late-sixties New Left milieux. Throughout 1968–69 her thoughts echoed in women's voices across the wider activist terrain as, collectively, they began to articulate a social and emotional gulf from the militant politics surrounding the VSC. The previous chapter showed how even the most intellectually assured and politically active woman could find it hard to make herself heard on the same terms as her male peers. In CMPP, too, women continued to feel a sense of themselves as not just marginally separate from, but inclined to want to defer to CMPP men; this seemed to find expression most commonly within the discursive arena of the collective.

When asked about her involvement in CMPP, Anita Merryweather repeatedly emphasised how 'very unclued up about theory' she was. She explained, 'I think there was a hidden agenda which was the-oretical which perhaps I wasn't part of.'[59] Nor was this feeling simply an outcome of her absence from the core. Her relationship with her husband and their role as a couple in the group enabled her to feel included even after their baby's arrival restricted her time, because Matthew 'continued to go to meetings and so on'. The implication was that through her husband she retained a place in CMPP, but because of her inability to access the group's meetings and discussions this was a secondary status. As she struggled to remember her time in CMPP, it was notable that she failed to recall or deliberately omitted to tell how both she and her husband began to withdraw from the group after their child's birth. Having recently purchased a new house in Tufnell Park's Dalmeny Road, the couple chose to spend more time together away from the collective. Their absence attracted criticism from the Richmans, who argued that the couple had responsibilities to the group.[60] This omission was one of many areas where Anita seemed reluctant to discuss or even mention her husband's role in relation to her activism. In this instance her difficulty in remembering her time in CMPP seemed directly related to him; the discursive confidence individuals needed to participate in the collective made it a political arena for her husband which she never felt fully able to access: 'I was eight years younger than my husband and he was much more sophisticated I suppose, much more well-read. He brought a lot.'[61]

Geoff Richman's emphasis on members' equal and full participation encouraged the intellectual ethos that young women found uncomfortable. Rita felt the pressures to conform most acutely in small meetings:

> I remember one evening everybody brought along poetry they found interesting or inspiring, and I found that very difficult because . . . people challenged you for your ideas so you couldn't just sort of say something and not back it up if you like . . . I was a literature student. In my head I had a vast array of poetry I could have chosen and would have chosen if I had been in, if you like, an unthreatening environment.

Within this discursive setting the masculine authority shaping sixties social codes acquired a psychological shape in the assertive voice of activist men. Underlying Geoff Richman's new politics, and echoed in the articulate voices of leading male members, the implicit assumption was that they had the right to speak, to be heard and to direct individuals' political actions. Such authority rested on the belief not only that they had something important to say, but, as female interviewees observed, that women around them would want to listen. The subtle social gulf that could lie between these higher-educated men and women was rooted in a post-war culture which not only restricted female social freedom but psychologically constrained even self-assertive young women. It was not that these left-thinking women did not have as much to say as their male contemporaries, or even that they never managed to contribute fully to discussions. Rather, their ease to communicate ideas could falter on the inward uncertainty that their opinions carried equal weight. Sue O'Sullivan noted how, when in the company of an all-male group, the certainty with which men spoke could be hard to equal. She remembered 'feeling that, oh my god, they are just going to talk and talk and talk'.[62]

The Tufnell Park Women's Liberation group

What complicated young women's connection to CMPP and made it difficult to identify any immediate need for Women's Liberation were the feelings of respect, warmth and love they held for their male comrades, who mostly supported them in their new politics. Rita Vaudrey immediately countered her claim that CMPP was 'a threatening environment', saying of male members, 'I always liked them'.[63] The arrival of Women's Liberation had a mixed reception; the psychic fractures that emerged in the milieu reflected its challenge to women and men's sense of political and social selfhood as it had been shaped by the collective's mutual ethos.

It is difficult to identify the founding moment of the Tufnell Park Women's Liberation group. Sheli Wortis was unable to remember when she and Karen Slaney first started the meetings. Most Tufnell Park members dated their entry to 1969 and the first issues of *Shrew* confirm that by the autumn of that year they held regular Tuesday evening meetings at the Slaneys' Camden house, 31 Dartmouth Park Hill. For CMPP women who joined the group, Sheli was formative in communicating emerging ideas of Women's Liberation. She and her husband allayed Sue's fears about whether or not to attend: 'When the women's movement came along I resisted for the first three months because Tony said, along with others, this is going to divide the Left, and I talked more with them [Sheli and Henry] and then I thought I'm just going to go.'[64]

As a member of San Francisco's O'Connor group, Sheli had joined one of the first Women's Liberation groups set up by the activist Mary Lou Greenberg. By the time she set out her ideas for the north-west London crèche, she was drawing directly from Sander, arguing for an all-female collective to aid Camden women to make connections between their isolated lives as women and capitalist oppression. She and Henry had been alerted to Sander's paper and the development of the West German women's movement by SDS leader Rudi Dutschke and his wife, Gretchen. The couple had come to London to seek refuge after the attempted assassination on Dutschke in April, 1968, and with the aid of the VSC network they lived near to the CMPP milieu, in Golders Green.[65]

The all-female collective Sheli envisaged derived from her understanding that in political matters affecting them as women, women felt most comfortable talking to other women. Her statement echoed sentiments marking two generations of women's movement campaigning that had seen middle-class feminists consciously urging women's claims to female

representation. However, set against CMPP's mutual politics, her desire
for a separate female group implied recognition of a deficiency in its
New Left vision. The chauvinism and marginalisation she had experienced in Californian's anti-war scene was absent in the closely knit
collective. Yet, intruding upon her place in the core, she discerned a
contradiction between her intellectual and social validation alongside
CMPP men, with her egalitarian marriage, and her sense of place as a
woman in late-sixties English society. She explained her decision to
establish the Tufnell Park group:

> I personally felt the effects of sexism in many ways: professionally, I was
> trained as an experimental psychologist, and I didn't feel there was a
> place for women who had children. My entrance into the women's move-
> ment was really as a young mother . . . I wanted to form a group around
> the politics of being a woman who wanted to be active either profession-
> ally or in work or in society, who also had children in a society in which
> women as mothers were not really valued and so that is how that came
> to be, and it was just never as much a priority in CMPP to talk about
> that.

Sheli's identity as a mother constrained her internal life as a female
activist, removed from her relationship with her husband or the wider
collective, despite her attachment to both. Nor was this sense of separation unique to Sheli. She soon found common parlance with women
who came into Tufnell Park through either CMPP or the wider milieu
of anti-war activists living around north-west London, many of whom,
like Nan Fromer, Sue O'Sullivan, Ellen Hammerschlagg, Karen Slaney
and Caroline Roth, were also American. What initially drew women
to the Tufnell Park meetings and made them return was identification
with at least some of the contradictions they saw in their lives as women
only after having children. It was no coincidence that over half of the
women were young mothers. Many had also received a university education and were in relationships with highly intellectual, active left men.
Most highlighted Tufnell Park's significance as having awoken perceptions and submerged feelings that for Sheli had risen to the surface
much earlier. Nan Fromer, pregnant at the time of her first meeting,
recalled:

> Late in 1969, a woman I barely knew invited me to a woman's meeting
> in Tufnell Park. 'They call themselves revolutionary socialists', she said.
> . . . If it did not provide me with instant sanity, it did provide assurance
> that I need no longer consider myself a candidate for the 'farm', since so
> many of the women arrayed in that small sitting room, despite their
> surface differences, seemed to share what for so long I had believed to
> be my own idiosyncratic suffering.[66]

Before they attended their first meeting, women from outside CMPP often found it difficult to conceive a connection with a women's political group. In 1968 Sue O'Sullivan first heard about Women's Liberation as a new mother whilst visiting friends in New York's Lower East Side: 'They were in SDS . . . and were talking about Women's Liberation, and I can remember thinking, oh this is vaguely interesting, but what the hell does it have to do with my life?'[67] Many women recalled how it was husbands and male friends around the anti-war scene who alerted them to the group and encouraged them to attend. To these New Left men, Women's Liberation represented a logical extension of the more general liberation struggles framing their activism, and they were keen to support it.

In the winter of 1969 John Cowley encouraged his wife, Sue O'Sullivan, to attend an early Tufnell Park meeting. One of several couples situated on the edge of CMPP, they had recently returned from New York, where John had been involved with the New Left scene around the New York School for Social Research, teaching graduate students, many of them SDS members, and editing issues of *Studies on the Left*. John knew David Slaney from the LSE and, knowing his wife's unhappiness at the time, when he heard about the Tufnell Park group, persuaded her to attend. Yet, Sue was initially doubtful about Women's Liberation. Like other young activist women, hers had been a largely external, global political focus; she had looked outwardly from a radical land-scape that presented plentiful opportunities for female mobility. The physical and emotional demands of carrying, delivering and raising a child recast her and other women's sights to the everyday domestic world and local community. Their own internal condition came more overtly to the fore as their identities as mothers raised new questions, doubts and possibilities about their lives to come. Sue felt 'not entirely clear about what I was going to be doing except having a baby, and that was already clear, in a shocking sort of way . . . there was going to be conflicts and contradictions in my life from thereon in.'

Mica Nava heard about the Tufnell Park group directly from David Slaney in the summer of 1969. Along with her Mexican husband, she too was situated on the edge of the VSC network; in Camden's Netherall Gardens they lived alongside activists and underground participants, Israeli, South African and Latin American radical émigrés. Mica's story of joining the women's group told of an inner conflict between middle-class maternal identity and her search for an intellectual and political life she envied her husband:

> Not only was I looking after two kids, I was working. I taught English as a foreign language and so I didn't get to go to Hornsey, you know.

Pepé was out there doing the political thing . . . I was always aware of
the politics . . . I remember having a big meeting in '68 after the massacre
in Mexico and so I was looking for a place and not really finding it,
okay, so looking for the Left and feeling I didn't really belong.[68]

Mica was caught between motherhood and politics, and her restlessness
signifies the appeal Women's Liberation held for left-thinking young
mothers within the CMPP milieu. The new politics offered a means of
reconciling competing maternal and intellectual selves, and a way of
making sense of the contradictions surrounding sixties womanhood.

Sue and Mica's accounts of joining the Tufnell Park group echo many
personal and secondary histories of Women's Liberation, emphasising
the instant revelation, transformation or homecoming the women found
in discussions. Concluding her story, Mica reflected: 'I suppose what
happened with the women's group . . . this is where I belonged, and
although in a way I had been building up to it, there was this huge
transformation because here, yes, this made sense.' Sue similarly recalled:
'I had never experienced this sort of feeling before. It was as much a
feeling as an intellectual sort of amazement and challenge and so on,
but it was as much a feeling, a gut feeling that this was something [that
was] going to transform my life.'[69] The close resonance between these
women's accounts and the official histories might raise questions about
how far they consciously or unconsciously drew upon publicly available
narratives to construct their own stories. In oral history work with
Australian feminists, Julie Stephens has argued that cultural scripts are
most likely to emerge when questions follow a chronological template.
In her view, questions about a respondent's first experience with feminism often prompt them to recount 'a "conversion-like" experience'.[70]
Although Mica and Sue's accounts were framed by the life-history
interview, even allowing for the influence of cultural scripts, when
listened to and read in the overall context of their histories, they
expressed consciously reflective, individual feelings. Sue adopted the
dual role of narrator and interpreter when she considered the pitfalls
of retelling experiences she had first recounted in the 1980s: 'If you've
put your mind to recalling the past, it becomes almost like "the past"
rather than what you . . . I am struggling to think because sometimes I
feel like I am paraphrasing what I have written, like, fifteen, twenty
years ago, but I don't think there is any reason to doubt that my feelings were overwhelmingly, just staggeringly wow, this is just it.'[71] Yet
the sense of enlightenment they and other women have often expressed
masks more subtly felt emotions that contemporary and secondary
accounts of the movement's beginnings often overlook.

The introduction of the Tufnell Park Women's Liberation group marked the start of a long and uneven process of political and personal change for members and their male partners. Women's turn of focus occurred at a point of transition in the collective, as CMPP struggled to move from anti-war to community-based politics. As Tufnell Park members began to address the personal dimension embedded in the new politics, and to start 'changing the way we lived', they continued a political and personal process CMPP members had initiated in their pre-figurative politics.[72] The emotional challenges Women's Liberation initially raised became interwoven with tensions arising from the Richmans' efforts to reorient the group and encourage members to invest themselves in the collective. The family tropes embedded in interviewees' memories, and their traditionally gendered connotations, signalled political, social and psychological continuities following the arrival of Women's Liberation. Close attention to Sue and Mica's testimonies revealed hesitations and uncertainties alongside revelation, hinting at forthcoming political and psychological contradictions they would face in the early years. Although 'instantly captivated', Sue acknowledged she had also felt 'frightened, I think probably, like what did this mean?'[73] Mica had found her 'place to operate in', but she stressed that the experience was 'sometimes quite difficult and extremely disruptive to our personal lives, and extremely consuming in terms of what we thought about all week, and how we changed'.[74] This mixture of feelings signified the complex emotional picture following the group's arrival; in and around CMPP, women and men faced challenging questions about what it now meant to be political and how they might reconcile competing discourses with their own lives and subjectivities.

Finding new ways of being: Tufnell Park and CMPP

There was considerable continuity between CMPP's politics and the Tufnell Park group, from the membership of the surrounding network to ideas both groups shared. Most CMPP women attending Women's Liberation meetings did so out of curiosity, and not animosity with male comrades. They felt no immediate desire to end their involvement with the collective; the structural and emotional fissures that culminated in CMPP's demise emerged gradually; when, by the end of 1970, members finally moved on to other projects, Women's Liberation had only exacerbated this turn. By the end of 1969 the growth and co-ordination of a national Women's Liberation Movement, orchestrated by the LWLW, led to women in and around CMPP becoming increasingly absorbed in Workshop activities. Sheli reflected, 'I don't think the women wanted to, you know, constrict their activities in CMPP. They wanted to be part of the wider women's movement.'[75] Sue Crockford agreed that 'some of us started to do other things. There were natural growth patterns ... and that was because you couldn't do it all.'[76]

In many ways the co-operation between men and women in the north-west London crèche typified the relative ease with which CMPP and Tufnell Park co-existed for the short period up to Tufnell Park's division in April 1970. By this time pressure to accommodate an expanding membership prompted the decision to divide the group across three north London regions: Islington, Tufnell Park and Belsize Park Swiss Cottage.[77] Within CMPP the general consensus of support for Women's Liberation derived from the group's pre-figurative politics. Geoffrey Crossick reflected: 'Given that an awful lot of that politics was how people lived their lives and their relationships ... CMPP was supportive of the women's movement. You couldn't *not* be supportive of it.'[78] On the periphery of the collective, Rita Vaudrey observed the relative ease with which women established the group alongside CMPP: 'Henry was very pro and my Geoff was never a problem, and he was quite happy with it, and on the whole it wasn't a problem and most people tried to be aware of course [that] it was women's difficulties.'[79]

As an early advocate of Women's Liberation, and an actively involved father, Henry Wortis played an important role in setting up the crèche with parents from the Workshop. With their female partners, men in this milieu fostered a mutually supportive environment for both sexes to balance activism with family life. Affective political and personal ties between them facilitated women's ability to unleash their energies into the early WLM. When, over the weekend from 27 February to 1 March, 1970, Tufnell Park women helped to organise and attended the first Women's Liberation conference at Oxford's Ruskin College, Henry Wortis and David Slaney assisted John Cowley in setting up the first crèche of its kind, run by men, to support the conference.

Along with Liberation Film members Sue Crockford and Ellen Hammerschlagg, Tony Wickert made a film of the conference to commemorate the occasion. He intended *A Woman's Place* to be an ongoing project exploring the movement's development. At the time there were few women with technical training or film expertise, and for Sue the fact that there were always 'thoughtful men around to help to make the project successful' exemplified the understanding and support her male comrades showed her and fellow women.[80] Tony's decision to assist this event derived from his earlier involvement in the making of the eight-minute film, *Woman, Are You Satisfied With Your Life?*, produced in the spring of 1969 by Tufnell Park members.

Made from still photographs, the film had raised questions about the socialising influences on women, including advertising, education and popular imagery and, in line with the group's socialism, it suggested links between women's oppression and capitalist society.

The film projects exemplified the symbiotic relationship between CMPP and the Tufnell Park Women's Liberation group; women active in both groups transferred into the latter political ideas and modes of organising. Sheli recalled: 'The things I learned from CMPP I would pass on in terms of ways of interacting and establishing involvement of the people, you know, organising, I could bring that into the women's group to help other people to develop, so in my mind they were very supportive of my own political development.'[81] Tufnell Park's small consciousness-raising practice drew upon CMPP's pre-figurative politics. In an article on the small Women's Liberation group, 'Organising Ourselves', alongside overseas articles such as 'Small Group: Big Job' by Arleen Sunshine and Judy Gerard and 'The Small Group Process' by Pamela Allen of Sudsofloppen, the second Tufnell Park group acknowledged the 'helpful ideas on the small group' that came from Geoff Richman's 'On Strategy'.[82]

The 'small group process' central to Women's Liberation rested largely on the 'universally acknowledged' acceptance that it created 'a secure, accepting, positive place' for women to engage in political meetings where 'inarticulacy, shyness' and 'the habit of depending on a man' had previously inhibited them in large meetings. These were New Left tenets also embedded in CMPP. Both saw the small group not just as 'a model for political work', but as a 'microcosm of a future good society', a community where members' decisions would 'arise directly from the experience of its members' to combat the isolation capitalist society imposed on individuals.[83] In an October, 1969 transcript from a recorded meeting amongst Tufnell Park members CMPP women disagreed with proposals for traditional mass mediums of communication which they and their male comrades eschewed as alienating. Advocating small group discussions as a more effective method of communication, they also expressed concern for members to participate 'in the right way'.[84] However, the distinction between the two forums was evident in the caution Tufnell Park members advised women to exercise to avoid sharp criticism and conflict. In contrast, Geoff Richman's concern to foster total participation meant that he did not shrink from potentially forceful engagement between members, arguing that 'the method of criticism, like that of questioning', was 'to discover the contradictions between an individual's stated views and his/her actual behaviour'. This distinction underlined the gendered subtext of political participation in the collective. CMPP women understood the mass meeting as especially detrimental to their hopes of reaching women because, like the authoritative education process they had undergone, mass communication denied the possibility for political and social interaction; hence their 'opposition to the notion of "the expert" telling us about his subject'. Both CMPP and the Tufnell Park group emphasised that liberation could come only with 'real trust', but whereas CMPP's small group called for a social model of self-assertion and self-improvement with which few of the young women felt comfortable, in the small consciousness-raising group freedom to criticise remained secondary to 'the freedom of the group to sustain the trust of its members'.

Yet Tufnell Park also raised questions of loyalty for CMPP members. The arrival of Women's Liberation represented an uncomfortable intrusion for Geoff and Marie Richman, who, individually and as a couple, saw the new politics as threatening. Geoff dismissed Women's Liberation as a distraction from the total commitment he envisaged from members. In his view, a Women's Liberation group could only ever remain 'a social interest group', a subsidiary to the collective, an argument not altogether removed from that of far-left men who saw it as a 'diversion' from workers' struggles. He explained his opinion accordingly:

> To take an example of a woman, who may be concerned with her work, a women's liberation group, her neighbourhood and the children, school . . . if she maintains a revolutionary position, and fails to give primary consideration to the needs of the revolutionary collective . . . then not only will the collective be disrupted, but her behaviour in the social interest groups will be inadequate.[85]

Women's Liberation challenged Geoff's understanding of equality between the sexes, especially the traditional division of labour within his own marriage. Rita Vaudrey remembered that as some CMPP women started becoming more assertive, he was asked to explain his attitude: 'He didn't see it as the main issue. Women were equal anyway. "We are all equal here, we are all equal", so therefore it wasn't an issue.'[86] The main departure between Geoff and Tufnell Park women rested in the latter's aims not merely to critique the nuclear family structure, but their desire to explore alternatives that, whilst not intended to 'abolish' the family, included a commitment to eliminating the sexual division of labour.

Marie Richman found this critique and feminist arguments exposing the 'myth of motherhood' personally threatening, because they undermined the domestic identity she had developed as an activist, wife and mother. The Tufnell Park group threatened to dismantle the political life she and her husband had cultivated over several years in Camden. In July, 1970 she underlined her political and emotional distance from Women's Liberation in an account of the film showing of Mai Zetterling's *The Girls*. The event was hosted by about thirty members of the LWLW, including Tufnell Park members. After some members of the mixed audience resisted the women's suggestion that they break into small groups to discuss the film's ideas about women, Marie intervened to facilitate discussion. However, she emphasised that her action was motivated not because she was a member of Women's Liberation, 'but because I *am* a member of CMPP, a political group working locally in Camden, who have been consciously seeking new methods of communicating with people for over a year now'.[87] Her loyalty clearly lay with the collective that was interwoven into her and her husband's family life. She had attended the event along with two CMPP men and, like them, she expressed how she too felt 'despair and frustration at the way the meeting was going and the inexperience of the WLM in this situation'.

Marie's hostility to Women's Liberation strained the affective ties between herself and Sheli, intertwined as these were within the collective the two couples had created. For Sheli:

> It was awkward. I mean Marie who was intelligent, really wonderful and responsible for carrying out a lot of activities in CMPP, she very much took a back seat to Geoff's ideological arguments, and in fact she typed all of his writings . . . I was well beyond that in my thinking, but I also felt that it gave her such satisfaction, that she felt so much part of a team with him that I didn't really want to challenge her.[88]

Other CMPP women also decided not to join the Tufnell Park group. Alicia Merrett remained ambivalent towards Women's Liberation, though she was otherwise committed to pre-figurative politics; she and her husband eagerly joined the collective household at Bramshill Gardens with Ellen Hammerschlagg, Sue Crockford and Tony Wickert. At a time when the early Women's Liberation groups were struggling to find ways of drawing in more members, Alicia's apprehension reveals some of the misperceptions and internal fears precluding involvement.[89] Unknowingly, she shared much in common with Tufnell Park members: she was committed to improving women's role in society; in Bramshill Gardens she was waging her own struggle against the sexual division of labour, putting pressure on her husband to cook. As a mother she was also interested in progressive education, reading A. S. Neill's writing on the experimental school, Summerhill, which echoed in the movement's early support for collective childcare. Yet her reluctance to join rested on her sense of social and intellectual inferiority in relation to Tufnell Park members, a feeling that extended from her marginalisation in CMPP. As for many female interviewees, her identity as a mother did not detract from the meaning she found in being active; she interpreted her community politics primarily through her interests as a mother, but believed this removed from the anti-maternal attitude she associated with Tufnell Park. Asked about her own encounter with the group, she replied:

> I think they were much more high-powered in their outlook than I was at the time. You know I seemed to work on my own more. I am a joiner in some things, but not in others, but it is funny, I never felt any strong compulsion to join that group, but I was never specially invited to join it. I had my point of view, you know.[90]

Alicia's belief that an invitation was necessary to join the Tufnell Park group ran contrary to the ethos of this early consciousness-raising group, which placed emphasis on its openness to newcomers. Her reluctance to concede that major changes could be made to the roles of men and women seemed to derive from the domestic identity she maintained and, like Marie, sought to protect: 'I was kind of into the thing that people should have more of a say but I wasn't convinced that you could change the male and female ways that much.' The myth, since perpetuated, that Women's Liberation condemned the experience of motherhood, had real roots for Alicia and Marie, for whom Tufnell Park represented a threat to their identities as homemakers and activists.

Around CMPP and the Tufnell Park group questions of political loyalty and commitment cut across domestic modes of female selfhood as well as close relationships, challenging personal loyalties and tempering the release women found in the new politics. Sue Crockford's account of her early days in the women's group presented a host of contradictions, torn between loyalty to her partner and their mutual politics, her newly found attachment to the Tufnell Park women and the sense of self she found in Women's Liberation. In 'Organising Ourselves' the second Tufnell Park group warned about the 'uneasiness that comes with a shift in loyalties from one's husband or lover, maybe, to the group'.[91] It recognised the powerful emotional ties women had to straddle after joining, but it failed to articulate the dual loyalties previously political women strained when their personal relationships and political selves were also deeply embedded in their left groups. The public and the private, the personal and the political existed in relentless tension throughout Sue 's narrative, and spoke of torn loyalties between her partner, CMPP politics and the newly found collective identity in the Women's Liberation group. In Tufnell Park she discovered an affective connection with women she had never known in any previous relationship; her entry seemed to mark an inner rupture with a political self that had been rooted in an intellectual and social world profoundly shaped by men: 'I would always have said I learned far more from blokes up to my thirties than I had done from women.'[92] Sue came to Women's Liberation from a political group that had already stressed the relevance of direct experience and social relations, and her testimony showed how the new politics recast her earlier understanding of personal pre-figurative politics away from CMPP. The 'homecoming' she experienced related to the legitimate political space the women's group provided for the expression of emotional interiority:

> When the women's movement came along all other kinds of things were put on the table to discuss that hadn't been up for discussion; they had not been deliberately not up for discussion, they had just not been part of the plateau of conversations . . . You were more relaxed because you were with your own sex, that's for sure, so if you said something daft they are more likely to giggle . . . I think that it wasn't so much sex in CMPP, it was the intellectual rigour; so you wouldn't have been daft because you had things to get through; so some of the things that might have been worrying you, you would have censored as not being important enough.

Women's Liberation reshaped her conception of public and private within the framework of political and personal life, but demands to realign inner and outer life created tensions between her and her partner, who felt threatened by the capacity of the new politics to penetrate private life in a manner CMPP had never done. Asked how, if at all, she had incorporated CMPP's concept of personal politics into her life, she responded: 'I suppose to some extent it didn't cross my mind not to . . . I assumed I was in a relationship that was equal. I think I got a shock the first time I got an inkling . . . that he didn't really respect the women's movement. I assumed he would.' Sue's 'shock' registered her awakening to the political departure of Women's Liberation. Despite the collective political and social life she and Tony Wickert shared as a CMPP couple, clear demarcations remained between political and personal, public and private life. At Bramshill Gardens, they shared the social and political life of the floating commune, but retained their own private life as a couple in the next-door house. For Sue, this arrangement had given them the best of both worlds because 'we went home to be private and they had a communal house next door, and we liked that'.

Tony's insecurity over the intrusive capacity of Women's Liberation cast into doubt Sue's initial enthusiasm for a personal politics where no areas of life were denied political space. Her self-questioning became evident through her contradictory reflections on the distinctions between the personal politics of CMPP and Women's Liberation. Acknowledging Rita's insecurity, for example, Sue defended the intellectual rigour of CMPP and the need for clear distinctions between political issues in relation to personal life: 'It wouldn't have been appropriate, there wouldn't have been space to say, oh, I am feeling a bit left out . . . We were there for a reason, Vietnam, that was above our lives.' With these thoughts she deferred to the very sentiments she and other women had reacted against within Women's Liberation, where direct experience had a relevant bearing on every aspect of political and social life. She echoed the sentiments of her partner, who had believed 'personal life should be completely private; you shouldn't talk about it with anyone else'.

Sue's reflections revealed how her entry into Tufnell Park posited her not only between her women's group and her partner, but between two concepts of New Left politics that, in their own separate ways, had each defined her anew. Keen to affirm the honour with which she upheld intimate subjects, she expressed the internal dislocations Women's Liberation had created for her when it recast understandings of public and private life on the Left: 'I didn't lie. I said, yes, we discuss things, but there is a level of honour . . . I wouldn't discuss everything . . . I've always had this split that you can go so far in your relationship with a group but actually you have a loyalty in your relationship.' In emphasising the distinctions Women's Liberation had taught members between the personal and the social, Sue showed how she had reconciled her loyalty to CMPP, to her partner and to Women's Liberation; in her mind she had created space for a hidden private world that was better kept out of the public arena for group discussion: 'What the women's movement did was, you could put all of your issues on the table and learn that this little bunch was absolutely primarily yours, oh this bunch is political and finances and so on, and yours to deal with and what it did, it helped instead of saying, god all of these problems or issues, you learned which of these were for society to do something about' [and which were not]. This internally negotiated position contrasted with the release other women found in the early consciousness-raising groups, which provided therapeutic forums where no private issues were out of bounds.

The political and personal challenges Tufnell Park presented for CMPP members marked the beginning of larger political and psychic demands Women's Liberation made on them and the wider north London 'non-aligned' Left. From the early 1970s these young activists embarked on 'the long and difficult task' of transforming their daily lives and relations in accordance with the new politics. The threat Marie Richman and Alicia Merrett had perceived to their identities as mothers, homemakers and socialist women represented only the start of internal dislocations that ran across the milieu, crossing class background, political experience, education and social and gendered roles. It was a politics rooted in the personal lives of members, and tensions and conflicts were often deeply personal, emotional occurrences, especially in the early days when women and men were feeling their way in efforts to change their personal lives. For the women especially, commitment to the Tufnell Park group and to the new politics demanded several layers of realignment, emphasising, as it did, awareness of one's own life as the first major step for the realisation of women's oppression in society. Releasing themselves from 'inner and outer bondages' necessitated a left politics that would allow legitimate space for emotional interiority to inform the everyday.

As a mutually envisioned project, the new politics of Women's Liberation meant men as well as women learning new ways of being political and social subjects. Above all, the new politics called for young 'non-aligned' activists to live their politics, to make real changes in their individual lives and social relations in ways far beyond anything CMPP had conceived. It implied activists carrying their politics into their internal selves in order to consciously rework post-war social models. The next chapter turns to the stories of young men and women on the north London New Left who, in the first half of the 1970s, took up this new socialist challenge.

Notes

1 R. Williams, 'A Convention of the Left', *Black Dwarf*, Vol. 13, No. 10, 27 January, 1969, p. 8; Ali, *Street Fighting Years*, pp. 329–30.
2 Rowbotham, 'Women's Liberation and the New Politics', p. 5.
3 T. S. Brown, '"1968" East and West: Divided Germany as a Case Study in Transnational History', *American Historical Review*, 114:1 (2009), p. 70.
4 Eley, *Forging Democracy*, pp. 366–9; Marwick, *The Sixties*, pp. 688–90; E. Setch, 'The Women's Liberation Movement in Britain, 1969–1979: Organisation, Creativity and Debate' (Unpublished PhD thesis, University of London, Royal Holloway, July, 2000), p. 20.

5 Interview between Geoff Richman and Margaret Dickinson in M. Dickinson (ed.), *Rogue Reels: Oppositional Film in Britain, 1945–90* (London: British Film Institute, 1999), p. 225.

6 Ibid.

7 See J. Kaplan and L. Shapiro (eds), *Red Diapers: Growing Up in the Communist Left* (Chicago: University of Illinois Press, 1998).

8 Skype interview with Henry and Sheli Wortis, 1 September, 2009.

9 R. Hurwitt, 'Stop It Gets Started', *Peace News*, 29 December, 1967, p. 3, in Private papers of David Robinson.

10 R. Guiton, E. Guiton, H. Wortis, S. Wortis, G. Crossick, G. Richman and M. Richman, 'Proposals for Discussion by the National VSC Council', 1969, pp. 13–14, Hull University Archives, DYO/12/87.

11 Geoff Richman, 'On Strategy', p. 11, Private papers of Geoff Richman (hereafter GRA).

12 Interview with Geoffrey Crossick, London, 21 April, 2009.

13 Anthony Ashbolt, 'The American New Left and Community Unions', *Illawarra Unity*, 8:1 (2008), pp. 37–42.

14 Correspondence from Tony Wickert to the author, 21 April, 2009, p. 1.

15 Interview with Sue Crockford, London, 30 September, 2010.

16 Interview with Anita Merryweather, London, 10 October, 2009.

17 V. Samuel (ed.), *Darling Alicia: The Love Letters of Alicia Kaner and Stephen Merrett* (Leicester: Matador, 2009).

18 Interview with Stephen and Alicia Merrett, Wells, 16 December, 2009.

19 Richman, 'On Strategy', pp. 6–11, GRA.

20 Geoff Richman, 'Camden Movement for People's Power', p. 3, GRA.

21 R. Hewison, *Too Much: Art and Society in the Sixties, 1960–75* (London: Methuen, 1986), p. 11

22 Richman, 'On Strategy', p. 3.

23 Wilson, *Only Halfway to Paradise*, pp. 134–5.

24 W. Breines, *Community and Organization in the New Left, 1962–1968: The Great Refusal* (New York: Praeger, 1982), p. 6.

25 Richman, 'On Strategy', p. 14.

26 J. Cowley, 'The Politics of Community Organising', in J. Cowley, A. Kaye, M. Mayo and M. Thompson (eds), *Community or Class Struggle?* (London: Stage 1, 1977), pp. 222–42.

27 R. Boston, 'Out of the Way: Angry enough about Vietnam?', *New Society*, 6 July, 1967, p. 22.

28 Interview between Ellen Adams and Margaret Dickinson, in Dickinson (ed.), *Rogue Reels*, p. 228.

29 Interview with Sue Crockford.

30 S. Crockford, 'Article written for the *Morning Star*', 24 June, 1970, in CMPP pamphlet accompanying the Angry Arts film week-end, 3 July, 1970, p. 2, GRA.

31 G. J. DeGroot, '"Left, Left, Left!" The Vietnam Day Committee, 1965–66', in G. J. DeGroot (ed.), *Student Protest: The Sixties and After* (Essex: Longman, 1998), p. 90.

32 See, for example, S. Evans, *Personal Politics: The Roots of Women's Liberation in the Civil Rights Movement and the New Left* (New York: Vintage Books, 1979).
33 C. Sturdy, 'Viewpoint on … Camden VSC Meetings, *Red Camden*, Vol. 1, No. 4 (1969), p. 3.
34 Interview with Geoffrey Crossick, London, 23 June, 2009.
35 Geoff Richman, 'From a Group to a Movement', p. 5, GRA.
36 Interview with Rita Vaudrey, London, 2 September, 2010.
37 Rowbotham, *Promise of a Dream*, p. 161.
38 Interview with Sue Crockford.
39 Rowbotham, 'The Beginnings of Women's Liberation in Britain', p. 34.
40 Skype interview with Henry and Sheli Wortis.
41 Sheli Wortis, 'A People's Crèche', *Red Camden*, Vol. 1, No. 9, June, 1969, p. 4.
42 Authors' Collective (ed.), *Storefront Day Care Centres: The Radical Berlin Experiment* (English translation by Catherine Lord and Renée Neu Watkins, London, 1973, of orig. edn, Cologne, 1970).
43 Skype interview with Henry and Sheli Wortis.
44 G. Crossick, 'The Greater London Development Plan', *Red Camden*, Vol. 1, No. 12, 19 September, 1969, pp. 9–10.
45 Interview with Sue Crockford.
46 Interview with Geoffrey Crossick.
47 G. Richman, 'Liberation Tour', *Red Camden*, Vol. 1, No. 7 (1969), p. 2.
48 Alexander, 'Memory Talk', pp. 236–7.
49 Interview with Sue Crockford.
50 Interview with Rita Vaudrey.
51 Interview with Geoffrey Crossick.
52 M. Collins, *Modern Love: An Intimate History of Men and Women in Britain, 1900–2000* (London: Atlantic 2003), pp. 175–6.
53 S. O'Sullivan, 'My Old Man Said Follow the Vanguard', in S. Maitland (ed.), *Very Heaven: Looking Back at the 1960s* (London: Virago, 1988), p. 121.
54 Interview with Rita Vaudrey.
55 Interview with Geoffrey Crossick, London, 21 April, 2009.
56 Interview with Rita Vaudrey.
57 Richman, 'From a Group to a Movement', p. 6.
58 Interview with Sue Crockford.
59 Interview with Anita Merryweather.
60 Interview with Geoff Crossick.
61 Interview with Anita Merryweather.
62 Interview with Sue O'Sullivan, London, 19 January, 2010.
63 Interview with Rita Vaudrey.
64 Interview with Sue Crockford.
65 Skype interview with Henry and Sheli Wortis.
66 Nan Fromer, Draft transcript for the 1978 *Spare Rib* article, p. 1, Private papers of Mica Nava (hereafter MNA).

67 Interview with Sue O'Sullivan.
68 Interview with Mica Nava.
69 Interview with Sue O'Sullivan.
70 J. Stephens, 'Our Remembered Selves: Oral History and Feminist Memory', *Oral History*, 38, Spring (2010), p. 84.
71 Interview with Sue O'Sullivan.
72 'Nine Years Together: A History of a Women's Liberation Group', *Spare Rib*, 69, April, 1978, p. 43.
73 Interview with Sue O'Sullivan.
74 Interview with Mica Nava.
75 Skype interview with Sheli and Henry Wortis.
76 Interview with Sue Crockford.
77 *Shrew*, April 1970, p. 5.
78 Interview with Geoffrey Crossick.
79 Interview with Rita Vaudrey.
80 Interview with Sue Crockford.
81 Skype interview with Sheli and Henry Wortis.
82 Tufnell Park Women's Liberation Group, 'Organising Ourselves', an article published in *Shrew*, March, 1971, p. 4, The Women's Library, London Metropolitan University, Papers of Sheila Rowbotham, 7SHR/B/1 Box 4.
83 Richman, 'On Strategy', p. 3.
84 'The Discussion', *Shrew*, No. 6, October, 1969, p. 3.
85 Richman, 'Activities', p. 3, GRA.
86 Interview with Rita Vaudrey.
87 R. Guiton, 'The Girls', CMPP pamphlet, July, 1970, p. 6, GCA.
88 Skype interview with Henry and Sheli Wortis.
89 'The Discussion', *Shrew*, No. 6, October, 1969, pp. 1–4; 'The Politics of the Campaign', *Shrew*, October, 1970, p. 3.
90 Interview with Alicia Merrett.
91 Tufnell Park Women's Liberation Group, 'Organising Ourselves', p. 105.
92 Interview with Sue Crockford.

5

Adulthood and activism in the 1970s

Against the background of late-sixties debates over sexuality and the changing social and sexual practices of the young, Women's Liberation thrust questions of women's and men's roles and relations into the forefront of activist life. In the spring of 1969 Sheila Rowbotham's pamphlet, *Women's Liberation and the New Politics*, argued that 'profound social transformation' required revolutionary change in the way human beings related to one another.[1] Couched in a discourse of subjectivity and affect, it championed political practices 'directed specifically towards transforming people's perception and comprehension of themselves in the world' alongside efforts to realise more equitable material conditions. The desire for activists to pay attention to how they lived, felt, saw and communicated with one another derived not only from insensitivities young activist women had faced from male comrades in meetings and during activities, but also from the confusion with which young activists sometimes comprehended each other as women and men. The new politics raised profound questions about the social and emotional models that had shaped male and female English life since the mid-century, and called for nothing less than the radical transformation of the social and emotional landscape. The liberation politics of the late 1960s and early 1970s represented a revolutionary departure away from the self-restraining tenets and public/private divisions which young activists saw continuing to shape post-war life. As the reward for the new socialist life, individuals would realise a liberated, authentic selfhood by reshaping themselves as political, social and sexual subjects unrestrained by a capitalist ethics of competition, ownership and exploitation. In the meantime, however, as the story of CMPP illustrated, attempts to foster collective practices meant for young activists negotiating the opposing cultural codes of two social worlds: their activist milieu as well as the post-war society with which they continued to engage as parents, husbands, wives, workers and citizens.

In June, 1970 the start of the Heath Conservative government heralded a more militant national climate as rising economic instability, unemployment and trade union power made domestic struggles a more immediate focus than at the height of VSC activism. Whilst international conflicts such as the Chilean military coup of September 1973 and the Portuguese Revolution retained young activists' attention, from the first half of the 1970s, on both the 'non-aligned' Left and the Trotskyist far Left, the question of how as citizens and activists they were to live in and yet challenge state and society became a pressing concern. This and the following chapter address the complex relationship between early 1970s society, and the social patterns and emotional condition of activists embarking on adult life. Amidst increasing stratification amongst the extra-parliamentary milieux, the personal politics of the WLM came to be felt at different levels of the political world. 'Non-aligned' men and women, actively embracing the new politics, explored 'the internal experience – inside the home, inside the head, inside the bed – as well as the external, verifiable experience'.[2] This attention to external and internal meanings of politics realigned conceptions of personal and political, public and private in ways that sought to radically reshape how they lived and felt as social citizens and as private internal beings. Without eschewing the identity politics of feminism or gay liberation, Trotskyist men and women continued to see personal life as the exclusive concern of the private citizen. The two chapters argue that in both 'non-aligned' and far-left cultures conceptions of personal, political, public and private often existed in fluid and competing states, because immersion within the activist world created multiple identities that women and men struggled to reconcile. The first half of this chapter continues to follow the stories of women and men in the 'non-aligned' left milieu around the Tufnell Park and Belsize Lane Women's Liberation groups. Later sections consider the collective living experiments of young activists from other parts of north, west and east London.

Motherhood, subjectivity and the new politics in Tufnell Park

Central to the 'new politics' of Women's Liberation were subjectivity and love; these discourses offered women and men new models for selfhood and social and sexual relations. The possibility of redefining these models away from capitalist modes of production meant for women, firstly, understanding how the social and economic means of control were translated into the way they thought, felt and related every day. The small consciousness-raising groups that characterised the early WLM underlined the political and psychological importance socialist feminists attached to subjectivity and affect when it came to redefining politics. Narrating the female self in small, self-supporting groups offered women the possibility of realising an assertive, authentic and liberated self as they learned to see previously private feelings of depression, isolation and unhappiness in social terms of female oppression. Instead of a left politics that was situated externally to members' personal lives, defined through effect, structural theory, paper sales and mass-demonstration tactics, Women's Liberation called on women to understand their experiential relationship to society, and to men, women and children, in psychological as well as social terms of attachment and dependency. The small consciousness-raising group was to be the starting-point for the creation of a new, self-assertive, self-developed woman that in time would also lead to the creation of a new man.[3] Since female self-confidence was vital to internal and external change, women in the early movement argued that it was often necessary to exclude men from meetings because of the inhibition their presence often aroused. Whilst in the early 1970s this was still considered to be a temporary measure, it privileged the small group as a new site for liberated female selfhood and held up honest, intimate and loving relations between women as new models for the collective life that was to develop out of the movement.

This revised concept of revolution involved a commitment for members to change the way they lived and how they saw themselves as political agents. After the initial, sometimes hesitant steps of joining the group, women in the Tufnell Park milieu embarked on collective and individual efforts to incorporate the new politics into their personal lives and political activities. Yet, as they sought to make sense of the personal turmoil, confusion or curiosity which each brought to the group, not only did they raise familiar contradictions about their social situation as women, but they also met unanticipated psychic challenges from within themselves and between each other. The women's testimonies reveal how individual and collective experience within the milieu was profoundly shaped by the internal imprint each brought from their upbringing and their relationship to society and to the activist scene in which many had come of age. Alongside objections from some male partners that they should take a greater share of childcare and domestic tasks, the women struggled to reconcile desire for liberation with ingrained patterns of thinking, feeling and acting. When considered alongside men's accounts, their experiences suggest the possibilities for expanding our understanding of the new liberation politics as a new mode for political and social selfhood and relations.

Remembering and speaking honestly about how they had felt within their first Women's Liberation groups, several women voiced emotions they had at the time felt unable to share, for fear of hurting other members. Their fragility showed the unstable psychological roots on which their early understandings of liberation rested. Commitment to the small group and to the movement as a whole raised questions about every aspect of the women's identities, challenging and reframing loyalties, concepts of love and relationships. Whilst some Tufnell Park and Belsize Lane members discovered real possibilities for replacing male authority with a new female subjectivity, for others, realigning concepts of personal and political proved unrealisable and sometimes painful.

The greatest subjective challenges the women faced in the early years of meeting concerned their experiences of motherhood. In the winter of 1970 Tufnell Park members read and talked about a paper psychologist Sheli Wortis had written on maternal attachment. Based on her own preliminary study of mother–infant interaction, Sheli critiqued child psychologist John Bowlby's influential attachment theory, published by Penguin in his 1953 best-seller, *Child Care and the Growth of Love*, which argued that children separated from their mothers were likely to suffer permanent emotional trauma.[4] In the 1960s Bowlby remained an authoritative voice on normative child development amongst medical professionals and childcare experts, including teachers; not least, his ideas continued to hold sway over mothers themselves, who saw their constant presence as vital to ensuring their child's normal psychological development.[5] However, by the end of the decade Sheli was one of several psychologists questioning the concept of 'maternal deprivation' as misguided; she also represented one of the first feminist voices criticising the oppressive effects Bowlby's ideas had on women themselves. Sheli demonstrated the way in which the attachment theories had been interwoven into western societies to bolster ideological arguments for confining women to the home. She challenged social scientists and child psychologists to study infants' responses to their fathers, and men in general, to determine what effect paternal or masculine interaction had on child behaviour. Finally, she highlighted the importance of an overall stable and stimulating environment for children, whether provided by the mother, father or several people.[6] In February, 1970 Sheli presented her ideas to the first Women's Liberation Conference, where they soon became interwoven into the more general discussions of the movement criticising the social isolation afflicting women confined to child-rearing at home. They also set the tone for the movement's commitment to a radical transformation that placed collective childcare practices and more equitable, loving relations between men, women and children at its heart.[7] For Mica Nava, Sheli's critique provided 'the single most significant and liberating experience of the early movement'.[8]

Having first read Bowlby's work as a sixteen-year-old at Bedales School, by the time she became a mother in her mid-twenties, she too had internalised the discourse of maternal deprivation; when it came to caring for her children, her youthful rebelliousness was no match for the authoritative pronouncements of childcare experts. Like many other women of her age, she 'accepted without question', albeit with 'increasing disquiet and resentment', the notion that the care of the children was primarily her responsibility and felt 'wracked with guilt about the harm' she could do to her children by her absence.

Sheli's critique resonated because it touched upon the internal division Mica felt between herself as 'natural' 'earth mother' and radical. Delighting in the experiences of pregnancy, breast-feeding and raising her children, in the late 1960s Mica was also searching for a space that might accommodate her maternal identity with her intellectual and radical instincts, together with her relatively privileged, middle-class background. In 1969, when she arrived at the Tufnell Park group, this internal tension had been heightened, following the '68 upheavals:

> I was always aware of the politics . . . I remember having a big meeting in '68 after the massacre in Mexico and so I was looking for a place and not really finding it, okay, so looking for the Left and feeling I didn't really belong. I thought it was just too phoney to be part of the revolutionary Left when I could drive and I had the kids in the house, you know that didn't feel appropriate.[9]

Once she was inside the Tufnell Park group, conflicting opinions between members exacerbated the psychic tension Mica felt between political and private life and between collective and individual subjectivity, as criticisms from other women cut across these. When Sheli used the term 'bourgeois solutions' to refer to the au pairs she, Mica and other members employed, she struck at the core of Mica's unease over her middle-class status and desire for political life. She thought, 'what, am I supposed to give up my bourgeois solutions and have collective households?' Mica felt torn between Sheli's ideas and her own instincts about how to reconcile middle-class mothering with the new socialism. She felt Sheli's comments acutely because of how strongly she admired her as a professional woman and radical.

Within the narrative of each Tufnell Park and Belsize Lane interviewee was the trope of the divided female and activist self. The mystifying conflicts young activist women had felt whilst trying to negotiate contradictory images of womanhood became replicated in new forms within the early consciousness-raising groups. Members entered the Tufnell Park group struggling to reconcile popular discourses of contented motherhood with real sensations of frustration and loneliness. For these women, desires for identities beyond maternal life remained a private struggle of the self, an extension of the conflict between duty and self-fulfilment common to many post-war women. Yet, for them as pioneers of a new politics that offered hope of an authentic, liberated woman-hood, the lived practice of self-transformation proved sometimes equally confusing and frustrating; attempts to discuss feelings openly and honestly added further layers of internal division as the women grappled to manage torn loyalties between the group identity and their own feelings, at odds with women they felt otherwise bound to as socialist sisters. Privileging the political primacy of experience and subjectivity, the early days of Women's Liberation saw Tufnell Park members arriving emotionally fragile, and vulnerable to reading each other's stories as personal criticisms. Reflecting back on those tense early days in the late 1970s, Mica explained the 'complex and unpredictable process' by which political discussion was 'profoundly affected by the personal'. She saw discussions about the 'myth of motherhood' directed at her personally. In *Red Camden* CMPP and Tufnell Park member Caroline Roth had characterised Tufnell Park members as still 'victims of the myth of motherhood', describing the rewards of having children and loving them as mere 'token payments'.[10] Played out within the small group, and in articles printed in *Shrew*, such arguments extended the critiques Sheli had voiced about Bowlby's attachment theory. They criticised discourses of motherhood which provided ideological justification for withdrawing women from the labour market and containing them within the domestic sphere; by perpetuating the myth that through having children women proved their legitimacy as 'real women', members saw such discourses as maintaining women's service to men and children to support capitalist enterprise. Instead of providing woman with a rewarding experience, it was argued, too often motherhood isolated her so that 'her helpless child' became 'her jail'.[11] Intellectually, Mica conceded the rationale of members' arguments. But whilst 'very ready completely to restructure the process of childcare', she 'could not bear to concede that all I'd been through, that the sometimes rich and sensual feelings of pregnancy and babies were mere illusion, that I was a victim of a myth perpetuated by capitalism.' The debates disappointed her hopes of marrying the political with the emotional and of reconciling individual and collective desires surrounding Women's Liberation.

Sue O'Sullivan's account of this sensitive moment shows the divisions between how the women felt at the level of interiority and the outward presentations of self they performed to the group and to others. She felt in 'emotional, psychic conflict' with Mica because listening to her passionate tales of motherhood confirmed Sue's fears that she was a failure as a mother: 'I can remember feeling that she had the moral high ground; that that's what everybody would want, you know, and somehow I had failed.' Following adolescent years in which she had 'loved kids' and been told 'you'll be such a good mother', for Sue the birth of her first child had been traumatic and disappointing, and she struggled to manage the ambivalence she felt about mothering:

> I think my sense of not belonging was especially after D was born was that I was a failure as a mother and I really was miserable some of the time and everybody else would talk about their frustrations with mother-hood but then they would always end it. They would always either start the discussion or end what they were saying by, 'of course, I absolutely adore my children. I wouldn't be without them', and I sometimes didn't feel like saying that. I sometimes felt like saying why did I do this?[12]

For Sue, Mica seemed to be the very embodiment of idealised mother-hood she and other sixties women saw represented in child-rearing manuals, popular newspapers, women's magazines, and which Sue had held since her college years when she performed the role of 'dorm mom'. Her own conflicting reading of the affair suggested the deeply indi-vidual, sometimes isolated place from which it was possible for women to be situated inside the new collective; this complex picture of feminist subjectivity challenges familiar narratives of the early days of Women's Liberation which depict a burgeoning female community as a site for instantaneous self-blossoming. This is not to question the very real self-growth and subjective change that some feminists who joined the early groups recall. Nor is it to doubt the intimate bonds that quickly developed between Tufnell Park members through the consciousness-raising practice. The interior conflict Mica and Sue experienced arose precisely because of the emotional attachment they felt to the women in the group and because of the investment they sought to make in constructing a new feminist community.

Subjectivity in the Tufnell Park Women's Liberation groups

Sue's accounts about the two Tufnell Park Women's Liberation groups illuminate how women in this milieu invested different components of self within their small female collectives as private individuals and as collective subjects. After the division of the first Tufnell Park group in April, 1970, she joined the reformed second group. The following month she recorded in *Shrew* her feelings of 'solidarity' with women in the first group, at odds with sensations of herself as an outsider in the second.[13] The affective ties of solidarity Sue found with members in the first group were interwoven within sensations of optimism which she and other women held in the wider Women's Liberation politics then emerging. In 'Rambling Notes', she wrote: 'I at times could falter over WL intellectually but emotionally I knew it was right . . . The hope behind everything we did was that the women we reached would begin to question their roles in all sorts of ways.' Her sense of political and affective belonging derived from her self-understanding as an agent in a wider female socialist cause even if, at times, she felt individually removed from her small group. For Sue the 'very, very important' relationships she formed in the first Tufnell Park group were 'primarily contained for me within the project of the small group and whatever activities and however else we situated ourselves within the movement'.[14]

The women's stories illuminate the psychic dislocation that arose from trying to situate themselves individually and collectively within the group and the growing movement. They show that during the political transition, between the demise of the VSC and the ascendancy of Women's Liberation, the internal divisions that had plagued many women around the male-dominated VSC continued to prevail in new forms as they sought to realign themselves as political and social beings. These self-divisions derived from the psychic landscape of post-war girlhood. Opening up oneself to being vulnerable in front of the female collective was at odds with the upbringing of a number of women, the institutional culture of post-war education and the manly, competitive left culture where young activists performed identities as militants and Marxist theoreticians. This was in spite of close female friendships many had enjoyed at school and university. The women's difficulty was learning how to articulate with confidence opinions that derived from experience, and to trust that such arguments held political validity. Many had long invested themselves in the hetero-couple and comradely relationships with men that characterised late-sixties activist culture, and the process of learning how to relate to members of their own sex through this new, intimate practice was filled with uncertainty as well as excitement and self-realisation. The socially and culturally specific shape of the women's subjectivity that emerged in consciousness-raising and in general group discussions was noticeable in the Tufnell Park group because of the considerable number of American members. Sue O'Sullivan reflected on the cultural distinctions she observed between herself, other American women and English members who, against the Americans' sometimes 'brash' confidence, seemed to her to be 'all so quietly spoken and reticent'.

Anita Merryweather was one of these quieter English members. She came from a 'very repressed English family' and remained 'in many ways very conventional'.[15] However, this did not prevent her from relating closely to the members. She expressed delight at the thought that she had participated in the early movement:

> It was a very positive, supportive environment and we were very much feeling our way . . . I mean I think the whole 'personal is political' is a cliché now, but I think it really did mean something, it did help you to see that the family life is socially constructed . . . I think I am a very conventional person in many ways and yes, I had seen 'politics' as one thing and 'personal' as something else, and it was the first time and it was exciting.

Anita's joyful reflections echoed the very real testimonies of feminist agency that cut across narratives of hesitancy and doubt. They suggested how, individually and collectively, the women internalised the egalitarian ethos to shape a sense of themselves as political pioneers; this understanding had been strengthened over time as the movement's historical legacy had developed. For Anita, this collective identity had been sufficiently empowering to transcend the intellectual insecurity she felt in relation to her husband. Yet, she too revealed how, inside the group, individual and collective subjectivity could be conflicting and problematic, creating discomposure for members. Anita felt intellectually apart from Tufnell Park women, just as she had from CMPP men:

> I do remember really enjoying it, although *again* I do remember that some people had a really quite academic agenda. There was a whole kind of psycho-analytic sort of school of writing and so on, which I think had quite a strong influence, which I could never really access . . . I think when we split and we became much more local groups, and we had small children, it was more around the sort of lived local experience. It was great.

The distinction Anita made between the academic agenda of the first Tufnell Park group and the community focus of the second is notable because it signalled how affective attachment to Women's Liberation was for her removed from an intellectual site of politics which she associated with male authority, where she felt inhibited and liable to become deferential. The discussions and activities of the first Tufnell Park group do not corroborate her memories that the first group was overtly more theoretical than the second. Throughout 1969, members of the first group interviewed women at the February Ideal Home

Exhibition, attended the equal pay rally in Trafalgar Square on 18 May and handed out leaflets at the photographic exhibition on women held in April at the Indoor Coventry Arena.[16] Both the first and second groups were keenly discussing issues surrounding motherhood and childcare, which found practical application in the childcare groups each attempted to set up: the crèche in the first Tufnell Park group and the playschool and baby-sitting rota in the second.[17] Throughout her interview, Anita struggled to remember details of her experiences in CMPP and the Tufnell Park groups; her narrative was disjointed, and it may well have been that she confused her time in the second group with her involvement in the Wittington Community Centre that began in 1972, two years after she joined the second Tufnell Park group. The distinctions she made are significant because they reveal how she felt most at ease in discussions or activities that rested upon her identity and experience as a mother.

For many Tufnell Park members, the WLM signified a new female authority on the Left that brought a new psychic power within their milieu. Mica transferred this collective agency into the home, where she felt a sense of power in her marriage and family life: 'It was a passion for the political moment. I think . . . the men couldn't cope, but I don't sort of blame them and the women, we discovered something and we were so strong.'[18] The domestic setting of meetings symbolised this agency. Women's Liberation literally entered members' homes on a weekly basis, giving new meaning to the 1920s site of female emancipation: the room. For generations of women growing up in early twentieth-century England, yearning for a room of one's own had signified desire to retreat from the anxiety of an uncertain female future.[19] However, for Mica the meeting room expressed the opposite, an assertive engagement with the body politic and the promise of the long-deferred change in the female self. Despite her hidden anxieties over early debates, Women's Liberation had given her prominent intellectual status in her small group, and agency in the growing movement.

However, there were exceptions, where the Tufnell Park collective accorded more closely to the 'transitional space' the room had previously performed. Ann Hunt and Judith Milner were members who felt a 'shared connection' through their working-class backgrounds, 'a belief in activism' and their dislocation from the VSC and the Tufnell Park group.[20] The Tufnell Park meeting place, Anita Merryweather's living room, assumed an important position in their stories and told much about their sense of place on the group's edges. The women's personal associations with the house made it likely to be memorable. Judith and her husband were lodging in the upstairs rooms of Anita and Mark's house when the group started, and Ann and her husband had briefly lodged in the same house in 1968. Both women associated the house with their struggles for identity during their separate times there and with their disappointment with the group, unable to attain that 'grounding of self' most women found in the movement. In their stories, the room assumed a place for momentary escape or desire rather than a site for new subjectivities and political engagement.[21] Ann's social insecurities in the company of university-educated members prevented her from accessing the personal, exploratory space other women enjoyed: 'They were very well spoken, most of them. I felt stupid really and I felt patronised slightly too.'[22] Disappointed by the group's failure to meet her hopes for personal transformation, for Ann, Tufnell Park became a site that provoked but never realised her private desires: 'I wanted to support them and to be part of the group . . . I wanted things to change at home. I hoped that . . . I could learn from them . . . The reality was that there was mainly theoretical discussions at the meetings. I do not remember discussing my personal problems very much.' Judith held a more ambiguous relationship with the group; unlike her friend, she felt no desire to be absorbed by it. Rather, she took pleasure from the legitimacy the group offered for private time and space away from being a wife and mother. She performed the same compliant outsider role she had performed in the VSC: 'I didn't welcome a group identity and was always struggling to maintain individuality, but certainly in the early women's group . . . there was a great feeling of struggling out of a net.'[23] Yet at times for Judith too, the collective assumed an uncomfortable presence; membership forced her to confront long-held insecurities about how she judged herself in relation to her own sex: 'I lagged behind with a lot of different things that women did, but it raises the point that in a mixed group of people I didn't think that way but in a women's group I did.'

The women's memories showcase the simultaneously unsettling and empowering presence the new female authority raised within these political sites. Not only did the new politics demand a much more emotional, personal investment from the women as political beings, one that could provide freedom from previously submissive roles, but it also raised searching questions about internal identity and social roles that prompted members to reflect on how they saw themselves in relation to other women. In this respect the personal became political, but also public and often comparative, as the feminist conscience encouraged supportive collective practices alongside critical scrutiny over how far members were each striving for change.

Collective childcare in Tufnell Park

From the women's early discussions in the first Tufnell Park group, liberation was understood to mean challenging 'historically considered limits and "natural states"' constraining women's and men's lives.[24] Discursively, this meant understanding the social and economic roots of the family as an oppressive institution tied to the capitalist system. In everyday life it meant women and men formulating practical alternatives to the social practices surrounding the post-war nuclear family. Inside the Tufnell Park and Belsize Lane groups women learned together what it meant to be political as affective beings. But the ambition to translate the new politics to the personal, previously private site of home called upon husbands and male partners to engage in a joint process of realigning traditional roles.

Alternative childcare, where men would take a more equal part in caring for children, was a logical first step following the debates on maternal attachment and the glorification of motherhood. Projects such as the first Tufnell Park crèche and the second Tufnell Park play group were designed to respond to these debates by providing alternative units of socialisation for children outside the nuclear family where several adults, men and women, could be involved in 'helping children grow'. However, activists participating in the radical Berlin-inspired crèche soon discovered the difficulties of attempting to transplant political ideas directly from one national context to another. Sue Cowley (née O'Sullivan) reflected on the problems in *Shrew*: 'The German experience was not totally relevant, here we were in England with no "movement" to base ourselves on, no storefront to provide a public and permanent place for the crèche and not much idea of what could hold us together besides the kids.'[25] The English state was not the West German Federal Republic. Whereas political education in the Storefront Day Care Centres expressed defiant anti-authoritarianism, far more central to Tufnell Park was the emphasis on nurturing; the desire to develop 'feelings of mutual commitment, solidarity and trust' amongst adults and children alike.[26]

Such ambitions represented an extension of the liberationist discourse of love underlining the new politics; like socialist feminists writing early in the century, in the early 1970s feminists like Rowbotham continued to place faith in the revolutionary capacity of love to bring about subjective and social transformation.[27] However, this was to be love released from the mid-century social framework that stressed its connection to self-realisation and matrimonial union. As Claire Langhamer has illustrated, following the Second World War conjugal understandings of romantic love became interwoven into the modern project of selfhood and into the reconstruction plan that saw 'happy nuclear families' as the solution to the upheavals of war and the anxiety of the nuclear age.[28] Young sixties activists had come of age within a landscape in which this specific discourse of love had coloured the everyday. Tied to prevailing concepts of 'normality', images of 'ordinary' men and women finding existential meaning through loving marriages and happy family life pervaded the mass commercial culture they and other young people had looked to as social and emotional models. Aware of the investment individuals increasingly made in the pursuit of a spouse, Lee Comer critiqued the idea of romantic, monogamous love as 'an effective and useful form of social control', but one which too often led to self-division and emotional fragmentation as the promised rewards failed to materialise.[29] For Lee and other feminists, love and affection did indeed hold a self-transforming capacity, but only when freed from the restrictions of marriage and the nuclear family. Renewing their capacity to love as human beings was for these feminists integral to the task of realising liberated selves. Extolling the virtues of Bolshevik Alexandra Kollontai's writing on 'Communism and the Family', Rowbotham questioned whether, following the example of social revolution enacted in 1920s Soviet Russia, English socialist men and women might begin 'to disentangle the criss-crossed skeins of our unrealised selves'.[30] As we will see, as the network of 'non-aligned' milieus spawned throughout the capital, this feminist discourse became embedded into activists' constructions and understandings of political, social and sexual relations. The hope was that women and men, free to choose the circumstances in which they fostered and invested their love, might overcome the divisions between the public world of labour, power and economy, and private emotional life. However, in the early days of the new politics these were utopian hopes. It seems that Tufnell Park women experienced similar difficulties to their West German counterparts when it came to men's tendencies to want to 'co-opt' the new childcare projects to fit their own political agenda, and their inclination to run the proceedings.[31]

Activists' commitment to egalitarian relationships arose out of their new roles as parents amidst a milieu in which memories of their own childhood relations remained influential. Lacking personal models on which to draw, women and men adapted alternative social and political practices they read and heard about to their own lives as activists, citizens and parents. A pamphlet for the Children's Community Centre, the parent-controlled, collective nursery at 123 Dartmouth Park Hill, Highgate New Town, explained the founders' belief in the transforming potential of Women's Liberation: 'We do not want to reproduce the social relationships present in society at large ... We believe that it is possible to rear . . . people who can work together (at school they call it "cheating"), who support and care for each other and who are sensitive to each others' [sic] needs'.[32] For Sue Crockford, this faith reflected her own childhood experiences of relationships and hopes as a first-time mother:

> When you have a kid you suddenly realise there is nothing more important. This first couple of years are crucial . . . so we absolutely believed in alternative childcare . . . My parents loved each other, for which I am amazingly glad, but they didn't have what I would call an intelligent, creative, thoughtful, loving relationship . . . So there we all are trying to make relationships with no models at all.[33]

Her participation in the Children's Community Centre also responded to her needs as a politically active mother living in densely populated, predominantly working-class north London, where a child of three often had to wait at least a year for a nursery place.[34] Aiming to meet the childcare needs of New Town's poor, working-class families, the Centre expressed members' ambitions to transcend class as well as gender hierarchies as part of a 'consciousness-raising process' for all concerned.[35] But hopes of recruiting local volunteers were disappointed; New Town's full-time working parents were able to give little if any time to running the nursery. Dialogue with the neighbourhood was uneasy, as many older residents, disturbed by the changing topography and social composition of the district, argued that in providing childcare places for squatters, families on social security, unsupported mothers and middle-class families, the Centre was further destabilising the neighbourhood at a time of redevelopment when the Council refused to spend money on repairs for older houses.

In the initial years of Women's Liberation the alternative projects of Tufnell Park activists supplemented private childcare arrangements the couples continued to make. Before 1972 and the wider growth of New Left communities, the milieu represented a transitional radical cohort, poised between mainstream post-war models and a new collective life. Tufnell Park and Belsize Lane members often took turns sharing childcare, to allow individuals the space for activity and self that Judith Milner valued. In 1970 women and men around the second Tufnell Park group set up a baby-sitting rota as an immediate, short-term solution to women's isolation, out of recognition that a full-scale playgroup would take time to create.[36] Sheli's critical reference to the use of au pairs was no doubt made in full awareness that, in the absence of effective alternatives, as professional working parents and activists, she and her husband saw no choice but to employ middle-class practices.

New Left politics under scrutiny

How far these men and women had, by mid-1970, already begun to incorporate co-operative principles into their daily lives could be seen in their weekly Sunday gatherings on Parliament Hill Fields. The gatherings had expanded from the original CMPP core to members and their families from the second Tufnell Park and Belsize Lane groups. Mica Nava highlighted their purpose, for men and women alike. For the men, she noted, 'this was an opportunity for them not only to play v.b.[volley ball] but also to watch the way in which we related to each other (among ourselves?), to get to know the other women and to meet other men in the same position as themselves'.[37] The 'most significant feature of the picnics in the long-term', though, she saw as helping to provide support and reassurance for the women as principal agents of the new politics. They enabled them to 'establish connections with each others' [*sic*] children, men and friends so that our relation to each other was broadened and no longer confined to the context of meeting and the movement'.

Implicit within Mica's narrative was the political and emotional upheaval these women and men were facing as activists, parents and loving partners. Her reflections raise the question of how far the new social and domestic practices evolved out of a mutual arrangement between couples or whether the impetus came mainly from the women, supported by their small groups. The fact that the men liked to come to these picnics, Mica inferred, reflected their healing purpose for private couples, as well as the male collective: 'Over the years those most involved with us had felt quite threatened by their exclusion from our meetings and activities.' That they had not, by 1971, progressed as far as many of the women would have liked was evident from observing the children's interaction with their parents. The gatherings put the men on trial: 'They had to demonstrate the quality of their relationship with the children. Often they only demonstrated their ineffectiveness. Many of the children were very young and still quite dependent; it was sometimes difficult for some of the women to play for any length of time without the kids demanding their attention.' For Mica, such an incident represented 'an almost shameful demonstration of our inability to progress beyond the stage of consciousness-raising'. The importance she attached to displaying transformed domestic practice echoed Judith's sentiments about the capacity of the new female authority to evoke woman's inner self-critic and to hold herself up for comparison. Mica's account illustrated the internal pressures that existed, for female activists especially, to publicly demonstrate personal change, and the frequent disjuncture between 'inner and outer' life that was supposed to dissolve through the new politics. The scrutiny Mica exercised amidst the company of Women's Liberation members, their men and children, reveals the insecurity the new politics aroused within women whose psychic lives were still embedded within the maternal ideology they had eschewed. Their dilemma was 'not only to recognise our own complicity in tolerating what was suddenly so patently intolerable, but also how to distinguish between what of our old lives had to be jettisoned and what was worth keeping'.

Mica's narrative draws attention to the psychic tension hanging uncomfortably between the sexes during this transitional period. In public and private, women struggled to manage their own as well as their partners' uncertainty as to the changes being demanded of them. Tension over domestic responsibilities showed continuing constraints that had been a feature of mid-century middle-class living, as both sexes faced the challenge of suddenly rejecting '29 years of social moulding'. Wisty Hoyland was not unsympathetic to the plight of her husband when she detailed the 'crisis situation' that had arisen in their relationship: '[He] spent a large part of his time at political meetings or discussions with friends, or writing in his study . . . I demanded that he take an equal share in looking after the kids . . . At first he refused to agree to this until I found something to do as productive, idealistic and useful to society as his work was – this response, of course, carried with it the assumption that my work was menial, meaningless, and totally useless to anyone.'[38] Through involvement in the second Tufnell Park group she had acquired 'a hypercritical awareness of my own oppression' that made her sensitive to the challenges of 'giving up privileges'.

Ann Hunt felt frustrated that, outside meetings, the group offered no practical support for how to achieve a greater division of domestic labour. Being able to call upon other members to baby-sit did not help to change the basic problem: 'David was often out at meetings in the evenings and I was then needed to look after our children.'[39] In March, 1971 Wisty made her struggle with her husband public and political when she consulted her Tufnell Park group for advice and support. Members called an emergency meeting which all the men were asked to attend, not as 'a personal vendetta' but as an opportunity for honesty and resolution. However, attempts to 'get down to basics' failed to transpire, for several reasons. Neither sex opened up to the other because only the women shared the secure familiarity from their ongoing meeting. Individuals felt 'nervous', 'shy' or simply uncomfortable. Where earlier efforts to incorporate men into meetings had seen them voicing disproportionately loud opinions, by 1971 women had redefined the criteria for political conduct in the small group. Men had no experience of consciousness-raising and no political or social model upon which to draw to open up the sort of personal dialogue the Tufnell Park women hoped for. In this new, intimate setting issues that had come out in Tufnell Park meetings failed to materialise as tasks for political action.[40]

The new activist woman and the new man

The emergency meeting pointed to personal and collective fissures discernible in the Tufnell Park milieu by the early 1970s. The new politics widened pre-existing tensions in already fragile couple relationships, but private struggles also signified wider social and psychological fractures on the 'non-aligned' male Left as Women's Liberation began to challenge the political masculinity men had internalised since their early days around the VSC. When read against men's meetings, appearing from the summer and autumn of 1972, the men's silence suggested internal dislocations that would inform the new masculine politics of the second half of the 1970s. Grappling to comprehend and access the affective, subjective discourse of the new politics, men in the early groups sought to develop new narratives of masculinity through which to express hidden feelings surrounding Women's Liberation and to explore their uncertainty about what it meant to be a man at this historical juncture. The men's search for a new subjectivity through the language of consciousness-raising responded to feminist critiques of men's emotional restraint when it came to relating to women, children and other men. Drawing upon feminist discourses of love and emotional honesty, they sought to transform male homo-social relations to allow for closer, loving ties they saw feminists model.[41]

Yet, in the early 1970s men's uncertainty about how to understand and respond to the emerging feminist language remained a largely private concern. It is difficult to access any real, honest account of their feelings during these years. Few contemporary personal sources are available to show a picture untainted by the retrospective reflections that colour men's oral history testimonies and memoirs, and not least the writings that date from the heyday of the late 1970s men's movement. Guilt, regret, lessons of late '70s identity politics, therapy and the self-transformation that comes over time informed many men's desire to assemble psychologically and politically comfortable stories that claimed their swift support for Women's Liberation. However, it is possible to discern something of the dislocation characterising early feelings and responses. Mike Reid remembered his surprise when his wife, Tina, joined the second Tufnell Park group:

> I think it was a steep learning curve kind of thing. I know that I was hostile to the notion that women had any need to meet separately from men even though it was perfectly obvious that, you know, we lived in a patriarchal society, and probably even at the time would have, but then suddenly I thought, oh of course, yes that has to be done, you know, and I kind of, and I know that I went from being resentful to supportive.[42]

Mike's years of communal living and involvement in men's politics coloured his memories of this sensitive moment when his commitment to Women's Liberation was not as forthcoming as he would have subsequently liked. He attempted to explain the speed with which he came to terms with it by invoking a psychological, gendered narrative that stressed his emotional maturation as a man reaching his mid-twenties:

> I went from something that affected my personal life, and I think . . . even knowing that Tina was at home I would still stop at the pub on the way home and not rush to get home to look after the kids, 'cos I was trying to do my bit, but I'd certainly, I wouldn't have thought twice about that, but at that point Tina had become resentful of that and I would have thought, oh I can't do that, and oh yes that's right, of course. Grow up Michael. I don't know, so it's all, you know in your twenties you're still learning stuff aren't you? And then, you know, at some point have become a man who supports Women's Liberation.

Before 'non-aligned' men began meeting together in men's groups, the personal implications of Women's Liberation was a topic that could be heard in day-to-day conversations they shared as friends in each other's homes or the pub, sometimes 'within ear-shot' of the wives or female partners they might be discussing. Although pro-feminist men later critiqued their emotional illiteracy, John Hoyland's diary entries for 1972 mention several meetings with male friends in which they intimately discussed difficult feelings related to sexual and emotional relationships. Stephen Trafford remembered going 'around the houses' with male comrades about the complications of the new politics. These shared intimacies were not, he insisted, simply occasions for complaining, but reflections for resolution: 'We would talk about it, but not simply to moan and groan but to you know, what d'you think about that? She's saying this but, you know, I don't know. What would you do?'[43] At a time when female friendships were taking on new emotional and political meaning, comradeship offered these men emotional support and possibilities for making political and personal sense of Women's Liberation.

The new politics aroused profound questions about male subjectivity. John Hoyland's 1972–76 diary, read together with his oral history testimony and his unpublished, late 1970s novel, 'The Iguana Woman', reveals the emotional challenges of trying to achieve composure as a 'New Left' man. Removed from his comrades and the adrenalin-fuelled days of the VSC, John experienced the monotony which women had long argued characterised days spent alone with young children, and felt his agency diminished. In March, 1975 he noted that nearly a whole month spent looking after 'sick kids' had left him feeling 'profoundly depressed'.[44] He described his 'frustration & isolation' 'cut off from the left' and his 'need' to feel connected with 'old boys' from the trade union movement, NUM representatives and dock workers' leaders who signified the traditional 'legitimate' masculinity he worried he failed to live up to with his political writing alone.

John's feelings spoke of a larger displacement of male political authority in the wake of the VSC's demise. Through his protagonist, Steve, he illustrated further how constraints on his activity led him to question his legitimacy as a male activist:

> Jenny's liberation as a woman was nearing its completion. This, he thought, was on the whole splendid and right-on. But the trouble was he didn't feel any more that he was achieving very much for himself. His own fulfilment, which he had always envisaged as something rather more grand than learning to cook, didn't seem to be taking place. Sometimes, in fact, he even felt a sense of panic that he wasn't what you might call a proper *man* anymore.[45]

Conceding the new politics as a real presence in his personal life meant John also re-learning a new manner of being political as a 'non-aligned' left man. The Iguana Woman symbolised the discursive and psychic presence of the new politics in his life. She is a myth his protagonist conjures in response to the movement, embodying feminists in his milieu; 'what he had heard called the Anima – the supposedly perfect female counterpart of his male self'. This crisis of male identity derived from John's understanding of active masculinity embedded within the street militancy around the VSC and in a Communist father who had been active in the labour movement and who was killed fighting fascism. Although he relished active involvement with his children, and approved of Women's Liberation, the personal politics presented him with a new role far removed from the street politics upon which he had fashioned himself as a young activist. The waning of the VSC occurred inversely in relation to the ascendancy of the WLM; unable to connect with the far Left, John felt at a loss for a sphere of activity that only appeared with the community activism and collective lifestyle politics after 1972, though, as his diary entry above reveals, even this never provided a secure left identity as he understood it. Speaking on behalf of 'non-aligned' comrades, John reflected:

> All of us [who were 'non-aligned'] understood Marxist theory and there was no question about it. You worked through a revolutionary organisa-tion. You couldn't really pretend to be a proper revolutionary if you weren't in anything . . . The fact that we couldn't connect with any one of the organisations was something which on the one hand we defended as being honest but on the other hand felt like a real lack.[46]

The social and emotional transitions accompanying early adult life coincided with ruptures on the activist Left that, at times thrilling, could also be unnerving for men and women carving out new social and cultural practices. David Widgery referred to the 'under life' of the new personal politics. Where class politics above ground was familiar and fathomable, Women's Liberation represented an unknown, unpredict-able, even frightening force that was often difficult for a male activist to comprehend.[47]

Maternal and paternal subjectivity and the new politics

The experiences of Sue O'Sullivan and John Cowley illustrate how realigning gender roles also brought unanticipated contradictions for maternal and paternal subjectivity. Of all the couples in the second Tufnell Park group, outwardly John and Sue provided the nearest live model of mutual personal politics. Since adolescence, John had sup-ported female emancipation and alternatives to a nuclear family model that had seen his father removed from domestic life even after return-ing from war service in Palestine: 'I had a very strong commitment to trying to find another way of living with women other than the way my mother and sister [had lived], and I was strongly committed to that and so I liked all that engagement of getting involved in the cooking and cleaning.'[48]

As a keen new father, John welcomed the ideas Sue brought home from the Tufnell Park group, and the couple arranged to share domestic and childcare responsibilities as needs arose. One day John saw his wife 'giving the kids fish fingers . . . I remembered my mother's cooking and I took over the cooking, at first it was just at the weekends and then it was all the cooking'. In contrast to Wisty Hoyland and Ann Hunt, Sue remembered the ease with which she and John discussed Women's

Liberation; the couple soon adapted their lifestyle to allow each other time for politics and parenthood:

> Once it was discussed, it was like 'yeah, that seems right. Yeah, yeah, let's do that', and when we were around the house together he would have three hours and I would have three hours, and one of us would disappear and go and read or whatever ... I think probably of all the fathers in our group he was certainly the one who lived up to the ideal of what you wanted a male partner to do ... in terms of sharing and equality.[49]

John's commitment to active fatherhood was facilitated by the supportive Women's Liberation network that by the early 1970s had begun to evolve in north London. By 1970 CMPP had successfully established the much-planned 'people's centre', the 'Hole in the Wall', in Kentish Town, which was intended to provide alternative political space for Camden activists as well as a social facility for the local community.[50] John was one of several men and women around the centre helping to run a local crèche. His role in running the Camden Community Workshop also helped him to get to know neighbours and children in the Stratford Villas area and to set up childcare arrangements with local mothers on a weekly rota. The Cowley's home became a collective base for childcare, community organising, the LWLW and weekly *Capital* reading groups in a manner that exemplified the interpersonal web of CMPP and Women's Liberation members.

However, beneath the collective arrangements, the couple's egalitarian roles sat uneasily with inner selves that were embedded in post-war discourses. The maternal guilt Sue struggled with in her Women's Liberation groups was compounded in the site of motherhood: 'I think I felt in the first period ... , I think I felt pleased and grateful ... you know, oh isn't it good to be in a relationship where ... but I think, you know, through no fault of his own, his enthusiasm for dedicating himself to those kids and getting a lot of pleasure out of it made me feel guilty.'[51] Her husband's commitment to his children and the apparent ease with which he managed their needs magnified the critical internal voice that echoed maternal discourses confirming her inadequacy as a woman.

Yet John also struggled to reconcile commitment to Women's Liberation with internalised images of fatherhood. The lived reality of the new politics saw him acting as an individual private agent, striving to maintain separate boundaries between his roles as a father, community activist and full-time lecturer; his paternal guilt signalled the emotional vulnerability 'non-aligned' left men also faced as fathers, as the new politics added to the weight of representations against which to measure themselves as post-war men.

> I called it walking on two legs. It is a phrase that comes out of the Chinese Cultural Revolution, you know, trying to modernise society and maintain some strong traditional practices like they did in villages . . . I used to call [walking on two legs] my having a job and trying to be critical in my work, and a union activist, and on the university senate and council, everything and doing all these things here . . . I felt my kids were in the middle of it.[52]

Paradoxically, the couple's difficulties echoed the very constraints Tufnell Park and Belsize Lane members sought to liberate individuals from. In their group discussions and in *Shrew*, members championed collective living as a logical solution to the isolation of the nuclear family. In May, 1971, in a hand-sketched diagram, Belsize Lane members Carol de Jong and Sally Frazer illustrated the emotional and practical support mothers might gain from pushing 'down a few walls and fences'.[53] Sue Crockford and Nan Fromer drew upon CMPP's 'do-it-yourself' spirit to encourage women to change their own housing arrangements: 'If you leave it all to Them: the big boys, the government, the councils, the businessmen, when will your needs ever be the priority?' Nan hoped that the Belsize women's group, 'with our kids and our men, would embark on this experiment together'.[54] Yet most members made only concessions to collective living, recognising, as Nan acknowledged, that in these transitional political years 'the old responses and resistances' to lifestyle and self-change persisted. Having 'the positive conviction that a communal environment might make less intensity and more variety in human relationships' was 'one thing'; living it out was 'quite another'.

The new collective life

Beyond the Tufnell Park milieu, however, other 'non-aligned' men and women more readily embraced collective living as part of the 'avalanche of new ideas' guiding social and subjective transformation.[55] By the early 1970s the rapid growth of the WLM saw loose assortments of left libertarians mushrooming across relatively poor, working-class provincial and metropolitan areas; in north, east and south London the post-war urban redevelopment schemes made run-down Victorian terrace housing empty and available for squatters; across districts in the boroughs of Islington and Hackney, and in Brixton in Lambeth, a host of interconnecting radical communities arose, a heterogeneous rainbow of 'non-aligned' left women and men, variously styling themselves socialists, feminists, squatters, anarchists, gay liberationists, radical psychologists and, by 1972, anti-sexist men. Committed to subjective struggle through collective action, they took further a liberationist politics that combined the New Left, 'do-it-yourself' tenets of CND and CMPP with developing feminist discourses of Women's Liberation. Within this open radical network, politics and dreaming went hand in hand; collective action was about working for revolutionary change from the point of one's own oppression, belief in the potential of individual agency to liberate the self was central to the new collective life that young activists began to embrace. Alongside the time and effort activists devoted to advancing local working-class labour, tenants', anti-racist, women's and homosexual struggles, the new politics placed the emotions, sex, the self and gender relations at the centre of young life. Previously, stories of subjectivity from inside this landscape have been weighted towards feminist politics and the contested relations of 1970s sisterhood; minimal attention has been given to the relational male–female stories accompanying the political and gendered power shifts of the first half of the decade. The reasons for this are contentious; the greater visibility of feminist memoirs belies ongoing feelings of ownership, loyalty and guilt on the part of 'non-aligned' women and men when it comes to remembering 1970s sexual politics. This section explores a selection of men's and women's stories to show the complex extremes of emotional and social experience in this period as young activists tried to negotiate old and new moral codes, values and attitudes and to make sense of the new possibilities liberationist politics offered for selfhood. It focuses on the collective household as a new public and personal site for remapping political life and subjectivity.

Although an overall commitment to the new politics informed the decision to live collectively, in the early 1970s men and women also had their own pragmatic reasons for entering into collective arrangements. Common to the early residents of Laurieston Hall were hopes to 'Make a good place for the children,' 'Live on a lot less money,' 'Share Resources,' 'Pool our skills' and 'Be more creative.'[56] Individuals hoped to spread alternative institutions already established in urban centres, such as health food shops, community centres and free schools. But others had less ambitious dreams: Maureen, a young wife and mother of four hoped the collective house might simply be a place for some peace and quiet.

For many young activists setting up collective houses at the start of the decade, the logic of pooling resources and sharing domestic responsibilities represented an extension of the shared living space they had experienced as students or young people working in large cities. In an era of rising rents, shared living made economic as well as political sense, and for those middle-class radicals embarking upon professional jobs or with inheritance funds, run-down working-class districts offered affordable, relatively spacious Victorian and Edwardian terrace-housing for purchase, ideal for letting out rooms and making collectives. For activists who turned squats into collectives, the motivation was often similarly pragmatic. From the late 1960s, the growth of the squatting movement fed into the discourses of anti-authoritarianism, individual agency and community control suffusing 'non-aligned' left action campaigns. Throughout the 1970s alternative newspapers were filled with accounts of activists' struggles against local council officials, offering practical and legal advice to working-class families, many of them evicted tenants, for whom they argued squatting offered a solution to the housing shortage and 'unfair' rents.[57] However, for 'non-aligned' radicals too, squatting facilitated full-time activist lifestyles, supported by social security payments and readily available part-time employment. Chris Ratcliffe's story of metropolitan collective living typified many interviewees' experiences at the start of the decade. In 1970, 'feeling pretty down', recently split from his girlfriend and unsure what to do following graduation, he headed to the capital from Essex, when a friend invited him to join a group living in a Stamford Hill flat, round the corner from Stoke Newington.[58] The collective offered Chris cheap rented accommodation, sociability, a place for studying Marxist literature and connections to the various demonstrations and radical activities developing in and around the north-east district; he joined the squatting campaign housing working-class families in Stepney's Arbour Square. At the start of 1972 he and his flat mates were evicted and began squatting in Hackney's Downs Park Road. The sudden growth of squatting in the neighbourhood accompanied the popularity of experimental lifestyles spreading across the 'non-aligned' Left, and Chris felt inspired. As with his memories of student activism, recollections of the speed and enthusiasm with which he took up collective living spoke of its enabling role for assembling a new identity. No longer a student radical, Chris found the new politics resolved his uncertainty about his place in the world; collective living gave him a sense of belonging and purpose as a radical pioneer building a new urban movement:

> We decided to go squatting in Downs Park Road and at the same time some other friends were also thinking about squatting and they ended up squatting nearby, and then all of a sudden the whole thing multiplied, just mushroomed, and within, it seemed like two or three months there was about twenty or thirty squats all just in the same area of Hackney . . .

We were creating it and obviously there were disagreements but we tried hard to resolve them and we used to have meetings and things. I can't believe we did it. There were so many things.

At the height of growing ferment on the wider left, the shared investment of collective living created strong ties of comradeship between young activists. Matt Cook has recently shown the 'formative' experience Brixton's squatting communities provided 1970s gay activists, heralding new political and sexual identities through the collective cultures and companionship that derived from these distinctive living spaces.[59] The intensity of community, trade union, international and Women's Liberation struggles often became mirrored in the relationships developing within households themselves. Emphasis on collective living as a route to new kinship ties created powerful emotional expectations around the collective house. By the early 1970s, discourses of love running through the counter-culture and informing feminist hopes for new intimacies between women became focused on relationships between household members. Reflecting on the early utopian hopes guiding the nervous Laurieston residents, Mike Reid noted, 'we clung to the notion that, out of all this, we would emerge saner, healthier, more loving'.[60] In 1971 Victor Seidler joined a group of friends establishing a collective house in Stoke Newington, inspired by collective living experiences in Boston's alternative districts, Cameron Avenue and Prospect Street:

> [It was] the idea that we were creating something. We weren't sure what it was but we were sharing a space and I remember we got this cardboard table which was a kind of biodegradable cone or something, but I remember this was one of the first things we constructed, this round cardboard table that we ate around ... And there were quite intense meetings around the notion of issues of various conflicts. And a certain kind of practice of equal relationships, or wanting them to be an equal relationship and how you negotiate differences between having your own space ... and it was a sense that it was new.[61]

The feminist consciousness-raising practice informed new ways of thinking about the quality of relationships between household members, raising searching questions about difference and equality concerning people's roles and sense of place within the collective. This was most visible in the weekly meetings commonplace in collective houses, where members were encouraged to express openly and honestly feelings and ideas pertaining to the running of the house, its ethos and dynamics. For Victor, the agency he found in the Boston commune derived from his discovery that he was 'very good in groups', enjoying the exploration of feelings and insights members brought to household meetings.

His collective identity, shaped around the house, was embedded in the new political practices that went on inside it, complemented by the men's consciousness-raising group he joined at Massachusetts Institute of Technology. The very real sensations of subjective transformation he underwent as a commune member were interwoven with sensations of release that came from a political culture beginning to integrate radical discourses of psychotherapy with Women's Liberation to create a politics around 'truth telling'. Before he encountered the growth movement in Britain, the ability to speak openly about his feelings and to make connections between comrades' thoughts, feelings and family histories brought new insights into his hidden past. The self-realisation felt 'liberating. It felt like wow this is who I was':

> It was certainly an opening and a, a sense of how these personal, very intimate feelings, which you'd assumed to be private, were in fact shared in one way or another, but they also mediated through the particular family histories people had . . . I mean it made you less individualised in some ways, but in another sense it deepened your sense of individuality, your sense of self and selfhood.

Belief in the actualising potential of new kinship ties outside the nuclear family derived not only from family histories individuals carried with them into the Left, from the influence of the anti-psychiatry writings of David Cooper and R. D. Laing and from feminist critiques of the nuclear family, but also at least partly from activists' pre-existing generational ties, a conception of themselves as members of a new, more loving generation. In the late 1960s protest slogans such as 'Make Love Not War' and song lyrics such as the Beatles' 'All You Need Is Love' had proclaimed these youngsters' loving capacities, whilst testimonies of comradely and sexual ties arising from sit-ins and demonstrations suggested such love in practice, enhancing their collective self-belief as loving subjects. By the 1970s, young activists were drawing upon this generational identity to think about how to live out new collective relationships in practice. As feminists often argued, capitalism had corrupted men's and women's capacity to love; breaking economic ties between social relationships, reproduction, sexuality and the upbringing of children would free this emotional capacity. Yet, at the level of interiority, 'non-aligned' women and men also considered their own sense of self in relation to these discourses. Feminist memoirs, personal letters and the self-writing regularly appearing in the WLM newsletters, journals and magazines reflected the new political emphasis on subjectivity, affect and self-reflection that encouraged women to engage in the individual as well as collective practice of self-reflection. From the appearance of the early men's news sheets to private undisclosed diaries or hastily scribbled notes, men too reflected on their own thoughts and feelings in response to new understandings of love and relationships concentrated around the collective house. In February, 1975 a weekend of dancing, lovemaking, music and friendship prompted John Hoyland to reflect on the emotional and psychological 'strength' he derived from 'belonging to a generation full of so much love, so much to give, so much generosity'.[62] This abundance of love had, he felt, not only been life enhancing but, for him, life saving: 'I for one have been rescued – I think so anyway from a life of unhappiness by the immense love and caring of my friends.' The closely knit radical community had equipped him with valuable emotional resources for self-realisation based on the capacity 'to love' and to 'give – myself' as an activist supporting working-class struggles, as well as a comrade, husband, lover and father. John described the overall experience as 'amazing', though he noted that at times the intensity of the love he had felt over the weekend had been 'too much' so that 'I got a bit sad about it at one point'. He worried for his generation that they might find themselves 'historically irrelevant, all our love come to nothing', but reassured himself that his own self-transformation denied that possibility.

However, the optimism and idealism surrounding some 'non-aligned' narratives accompanied more psychologically complex and emotionally troubled stories of everyday life and subjectivity. Men's and women's stories of these years present an intensely felt, often conflicting picture of striving for self-change; they reveal that the collective household could be variously a place of emotional refuge, a new site for selfhood, yet also an emotionally confusing landscape, a hindrance as well as a resource for self-liberation. Feminists have spoken about personal and political conflicts they confronted inside 1970s collective houses. On the one hand, many remember the support collective living gave them as new, unconfident mothers or socially insecure young women; on the other hand, they also admit the reverse side of the new co-operative practices, the pain that could arise when sexual desire traversed bonds of sisterhood. Collective households did indeed provide economic and emotional refuge for many young mothers in the milieu. Lynne Segal has stressed how the practical help and ties of friendship she received as a collective householder enabled her to feel a more capable mother, even if she now questions how selfless she may at times have been.[63] The loving bonds she remembered from collective life shored up a fragile sense of self that came from her upbringing inside an unhappy Australian nuclear family. As a collective being, she saw more possibilities for self-expression than she had ever experienced as a lone individual in her early twenties; the constant presence of other young radicals confirmed her existence so that she felt secure in the political path she was pursuing:

> Yes, I think I very much liked to wear a badge as it were. I liked to see myself as a socialist and feminist and anti-racist, and all those things. Yes, that's [what] I was and am ... I think that I also had this very strong sense of the individual being a fragile unit. You know I always had a very strong sense of that and yeah, so I didn't see being politically engaged as being at odds with expressing yourself. It seemed to create a place and spaces where you could express who you were and people would pay more attention to you.[64]

Other women took comfort from the assistance collective house-holders gave them in raising their young children, especially during emotionally vulnerable periods, though not all households were as organised as Lynne's. In 1970 Jo Robinson was a new single mother needing a place to stay after leaving the maternity hospital. Comrades from Poster Workshop directed her to Grosvenor Avenue, a large, mixed collective house in Islington. With no allocated rooms, residents slept where they could; the house also lacked any rotas for domestic chores, and the chaotic arrangements caused her milk to dry up so that she was unable to breast-feed as she had wished. Yet, when she had nowhere else to turn, Jo remembered the members' kindness in rescuing her: 'I'd got nothing organised, nothing together for the baby, and they took me in and looked after me. I remember being given a mug of tea and the mug was filthy, but I didn't want to offend them and so I just took it, thankful really.'[65]

As young activists strove to realise more relaxed, nurturing, less hierarchical and authoritarian relations, both women and men remembered the enriching experience of raising children in the company of adults all committed to being more loving. In 1973 Jane Storr and Max Farrar set up a collective household in Leeds with another couple from the Leeds Libertarians. Jane explained how the supportive structures and members' shared goals had complemented a culture in which the children were an everyday part of their political work: 'It was never about putting them in a nursery or putting them somewhere else where you then had to think I'm doing my political business. They were the political business as much as everything else we were doing and that felt absolutely right.'[66] 'Non-aligned' men too recalled emotionally rich opportunities for fatherhood that contrasted with distant and awkward relationships with their own fathers. Despite recording the messy and time-consuming tasks of childcare, John Hoyland regularly noted his overwhelming feelings of love that came from caring for his children. They were his 'brightest reason for living'.[67] Tony Wickert described how, in the communal house at Bramshill Gardens, the children were the 'epicentre' of their lives. As a regular member of the One, Two, Three nursery, he delighted in the extra time he was able to spend with his young son, whilst also enjoying the opportunity to watch the growth of the other young child in the house. He remembered 'what an essential event' her birth was for members: 'It inspired me to make a film . . . about the wisdom that comes out of baby-talk . . . she used to do wonderful goo-goo sounds, you know, and there was a wonderful cadence to them and I thought, oh she's really trying to say something.'[68]

Underlying the philosophy of 'sharing the caring', collective childcare was also designed to dissolve the bonds of ownership which activists saw in nuclear parent–child relations. Those who had yet to have children of their own took pleasure from being able share in the lives of children growing up in their households. Elizabeth Mansfield described the 'big influence' a collective house in Colchester, Essex had on her as a radical actress beginning to reflect on her own isolated upbringing and hopes as a future mother: 'It was my first access to kids. I, I was now meeting kids as an adult in a way that I had intimate access to them because of this open house, and I thought this was marvellous, older people, younger people, so, so yeah, but my parents were from a different time and a different era, and I didn't judge them harshly for that, but I, I was looking for a new way.'[69] Other activists whose own mothers and fathers had been equally engaged parents adapted these models to their new structures. James Swinson was one of several 'non-aligned' young men supporting feminist single mothers in 1970s collective households, first in Brixton and later in north London. His own father provided a 'fantastic role model' for the emotionally open masculinity he and his male comrades were striving for; James found that he easily adopted the role of surrogate father:

> A certain kind of masculinity actually deprived men of a proper relationship with their children and wanting to be, positively wanting to be involved in bringing up children and so on . . . I mean there was a sense of collectivity in . . . I mean I used to take people's kids to school; I used to ride and look after them, run crèches. I always liked children. I had no problem with that. I liked being responsible for children.[70]

Yet commitment to these new gendered roles was sometimes insufficient to protect young activists from the confusing and complicated emotions that arose from new kinship patterns. Men and women recorded their surprise and uncertainty about how to handle attachments arising between themselves and the children. These unanticipated ties could be sources of tension over gendered roles women and men were seeking to change. In a 1978 *Spare Rib* article, women from a Leeds collective house reflected back on how altruistic motives to support parents entangled them in traditionally nurturing roles, 'a duty of care' towards the children, compromising their independence.[71] Conversely, aims to dissolve nuclear ties between parents and children and to reshape parental love belied the powerful feelings of ownership parents continued to feel towards their own biological children. For men like James Swinson, feminists' sometimes defensive claims upon their children created problems for how to negotiate the more equal and supportive roles he hoped to see developing. Continuing claims upon long-held identities and traditional relational patterns solidified emotional barriers between the sexes, which the new collective structures were supposed to break down:

> There was that double-edged thing where there would be senses that people [single mothers] would moan, you know, and moan about the fact that how disadvantaged they were or penniless or child . . . For sure, it was really difficult. But also, almost the moment you offered them, or you would start to play with the child they were kind of really protective and defensive . . . it gave them their identity in totality, both the negative side of that and the positive side of that, so it was always complicated about how people were reluctant to let go and what people wanted to let go of in those roles.[72]

Men too found it difficult to extricate themselves from the private and individual relationships they had cultivated with their children in early nuclear settings. In the same *Spare Rib* article, women critically noted the solitary relationships fathers continued to maintain with their children in spite of collective structures; one showed his 'commitment to doing his share of childcare' whilst 'isolating himself and his child at the same time'.[73] The prevailing exclusivity of father–child ties represented a source of tension between the sexes over men's reluctance to change. The women criticised the men's individualised behaviour that perpetuated a culture of 'possessiveness' in which they typically focused attention exclusively on women or children in turn.[74] Mike Reid confirmed the difficulty of reframing intense father–child bonds. In the early days at Laurieston Hall he missed the private intimacy of family time spent with his wife and two children: 'I often would say, "Look, I really would like just, why don't we have breakfast up here with just our kids? I'd like us to be a family sometimes". I remember saying that to Tina . . . I'm sure I expressed it as a feeling sometimes, because it was just that would be a feeling of loss for what we had

before.'[75] Yet these individual longings cut across the firm commitment
he made to the collective childcare Laurieston members negotiated.
Adults shared the everyday, 'generally pleasant times with children':
cooking their meals, collecting them from school, reading stories, and
playtime. Responsibilities such as the cleaning of children's rooms, dress-
ing and putting them to bed, and attending to them at night, remained
'mainly the domain of parents or lovers'.[76] However, Mike recalled many
occasions when he went over and above these minimum arrangements;
his efforts in this and other areas became part of the self-performance
he enacted as a core Laurieston founder. Recalling some of the disputes
that arose, he vigorously denied members' accusations that Laurieston
Hall didn't 'have communal childcare': 'C would tell anyone who
listened how crap we were at communal childcare because it meant we
didn't, but I remember washing her child's, children's nappies and I'm
damn sure she never did any of mine, you know.' Such conflicts denoted
the tense business of men and women negotiating an unstable sexual
landscape. Claims and counter-claims about how they each enacted or
subverted the new collective arrangements signified insecurities and high
expectations shaping residents' attitudes and behaviours towards these.
Mike noted, for example, how his commitment to collective childcare
represented the men's typically 'frantically over-achieving' efforts in this
area. The implication was that such behaviour represented conscious
efforts men were making to actively demonstrate their support for
Women's Liberation, even if they saw such work to be at the cost of
Laurieston as a political project; in 1973 and 1974 Laurieston women
made the long journey south to attend Women's Liberation conferences
in London and Bristol. Mike recalled his concerns about their going:
'You know four women going away for two days, it was losing a week's
work sort of thing... I'd probably say well you've obviously got to
go, but we should be aware that we're really making a bigger effort.'[77]

Divisions between the sexes also reflected men and women's differing
experiences of their previous roles and responsibilities. Mike explained
another reason for Laurieston men's enthusiasm towards childcare:
'For most of the men, childcare was "time off work". Whereas, for the
women, work (e.g. on the people centre/kids project/garden) was time
when a nagging nervousness about the kids rarely left them.'[78] Some
women expressed profound disillusionment when collective households
provided alternative contexts for old anxieties and domestic burdens.
Wisty Hoyland explained, 'I just used to hate it from day one really,
and I just wanted to leave, to go away and to live on my own.'[79] The
regularly changing membership inside her Tufnell Park home made it
difficult to implement any firm rota for household management and

she never felt able to articulate her dissatisfaction to other members so that 'I ended up doing everything . . . It was either a case of that, of watching the place fall apart or . . . I would feel I had to do it in order to maintain a beautiful place to live in.' Disappointment at the failure of collective life could be exacerbated when the blossoming of other householders enhanced members' own sense of isolation. In autumn 1972, Maureen chose to leave Laurieston in pursuit of the 'peace and silence' she had failed to find there.[80] For her as an anxious mother with a new-born child, the collective arrangements had proved unable to ease her insecurities. Preoccupied over the welfare of her baby, she felt detached from the activities and bonds she observed residents forming. In a note, she explained to members her decision to leave: 'I saw everyone else beginning a new life, learning new crafts, making projects, climbing mountains – all things I wanted to do. Instead of endless breast-feeding, nappies. Carrying, calming and rocking M, pacing the bedroom with him at night. I began to feel I didn't have any right to say anything at meetings, because I didn't share the work.'

As 'non-aligned' activists attempted to live out ever more radical social and sexual transformations, claims for individuality and collectivity became increasingly complex and sometimes contested. Despite the political currency of truth-telling, men and women's individual subjectivities sometimes remained submerged beneath the roles and identities they performed in the company of householders or inside small political groups. Mike Reid based the different protagonists of his Laurieston memoir on the multiple identities he had adopted there. 'Len the leftist', for example, represented Mike 'the Marxist, you know, pointing out that all our subculture stuff is middle-class waste of time'. 'Len' embodied the serious, politically 'hard-line' side of Mike's personality, 'the political visionary', 'the founder', 'the person' who 'was always writing position papers', and who felt 'betrayed' when majority rule contravened his own opinion. This was the persona he still found it hardest to 'forgive': 'I know that I've upset people and I know that people have felt tyrannised by me or brow-beaten certainly.'[81]

Libertarianism could encourage activists to adopt extreme behaviours and identities, polarities that reflected the radical positions they supported across their politics. James Swinson explained the confusion of negotiating male identity in this 'complicated terrain': 'I had about five different identities at the time, you know, where you would situate yourself.'[82] Art student, revolutionary, intellectual, surrogate father and comrade, he and other young activists moved across multiple sites of 'non-aligned' politics whilst also trying to situate themselves as individuals in mainstream social settings. The contradictions of libertarian male life made it even harder to make sense of who he was. The soft masculinity James performed in his household contrasted with the 'hard-edged' masculinity he performed as a revolutionary 'on the front line', 'like going to leaflet at Ford's' at five o'clock in the morning in a 'nasty harsh industrial environment'. Whilst he managed the divisions, partly, he reflected, because of his move into radical psychotherapy in the late 1970s, other men and women experienced a loss of individuality, which felt threatening.

Losing sense of oneself as an individual often meant the loss of agency. The alternative moral codes arising in some 'non-aligned' circles created insecurities within activists over who and what they were. Alison Fell reflected how 'ideology was just everywhere, you know, what was the right thing to do and the right way to go on'.[83] In the early 1970s she lived in one of the more extreme collective households owned by her husband in the Holloway Road; collective identity extended to common spaces and possessions in a way that made it difficult for individuals to find any privacy. The extremes of everyday life were only accentuated soon after, when, following the break-up of her marriage, she turned to squatting on the Caledonian Road in a bid to stave off homelessness for herself and her young son. The pressures of keeping up with the pace of full-time activism were coupled with the intellectual demands of adopting individual positions on the extensive range of micro and macro politics pervading these circles:

> I mean there was just one thing after another, there was always something to respond to as well as trying to do everything for the movement, you know, work out what we were doing, what were our positions, and how did feminism fit in, what did we think of the Black Panthers and, but you always had to know what you thought about everything, and have it all worked out. It was completely exhausting.

Eventually, the psychic 'strain' of suppressing her internal 'day-dreamer' evoked a crisis; in 1973 she had a break-down, which she would later describe in her novel *Every Move You Make*. 'The tyranny of structureless' pervading Islington libertarianism threatened to dissolve individual freedom under the weight of constantly shifting cultural codes and political discourses, which could impose their own models for social and emotional control. Subjectivity became further fractured where these compounded self-restraining models which activists had internalised from childhood: 'If you were good at suppressing emotions as I was, and had been brought up to, you sort of got on with it in a fog . . . just sort of carrying on, carrying on, getting more and more like this terrible revolutionary sort of workhorse, grim, you know ideologue.' Collective spaces thus brought sometimes unwelcome echoes of the past to create uncomfortable continuities in subjectivity. Alison's flatmate, Michèle Roberts, drew a parallel between relinquishing her individuality and the obedience of Catholic girlhood. Her reflections bear the imprint of the late-1970s feminist turn to psychoanalysis framing many of the narratives from this milieu. Yet, their historically specific shape makes them no less valuable for understanding the subjectivities this political culture shaped. The women's reflections suggest how individuals' emotional vulnerability to extreme new orthodoxies depended upon their own social and emotional histories, starting in the post-war family. They complicate the linear post-war narrative of modern selfhood, suggesting how the psychic imprint of self-restraint continued to haunt internal lives even as individuals expressed freer external modes of being.

By the mid-1970s a host of political writings increasingly formalised what at the start of the decade had emerged as pragmatic, experimental practices to present activists with alternative discourses for shaping the self. The new politics made powerful claims upon individuals' internal lives, as well as shaping their behaviour. Nowhere were psychic tensions more evident than in the area of heterosexual relationships. Understanding how and why discourses and practices of free love emerged in the 'non-aligned' landscape frames wider questions of post-war sexual agency for sixties higher-educated youth and illustrates the importance of sexual expression, freed from reproduction, as a new mode of social and political selfhood. The sexual libertarianism that came to prevail amidst some quarters of this milieu represented longer-term changes in sexual mores and practices already underway amongst this generation, a move towards the late-modern landscape in which individual autonomy and sexual pleasure became tied to the goal of self-actualisation.[84] Chapter 3 has already shown how, at the height of the student movement, radical culture opened up a new 'political-sexual space' linked to subjectivity. We have seen that for young women as well as men this radical climate legitimised sexual agency as an extension of the wider social mobility permitted to women. However, women's revolt at the end of the decade revealed the limitations of this 'sexual liberation'; they argued that permissive culture affirmed young men's masculinity and made women sexual objects.

By the early 1970s, feminist critiques of monogamy represented radical women's search for sexual self-actualisation within a new egalitarian framework of heterosexual relations that promised women true autonomy. Such discourses were not new; in the early twentieth century, New Life socialist Edward Carpenter had gained a following amongst socialist feminists excited by the possibilities which his ideas offered them for sexual pleasure, personal exploration and emancipation.[85] However, in the early 1970s feminists' stress upon realising desire and liberating love suffused a social and political landscape in which discourses of self-actualisation had become widespread and expectations of female freedom had advanced substantially, alongside expectations for enjoyment and self-fulfilment. Sociological surveys revealed notable shifts in wider sexual attitudes and behaviour, especially amongst the young. In a seven-year follow-up to his 1964 study, *The Sexual Behaviour of Young People*, Michael Schofield recorded, 'one of the biggest and most welcome changes' in the attitudes of the original cohort was 'the diminishing influence of the double standard of sexual morality' that sanctioned premarital sexual intercourse for men but not for women. He also noted the loosening ties between premarital intercourse and love. Despite a wider cultural climate that continued to exalt 'sexual attitudes in the name of love', a large number (58 per cent) of young people refused to accept this moral principle, 'prepared to satisfy their sexual desires without pretending that it is part of a loving relationship'.[86]

However, 'non-aligned' women and men were willing to expand the social and sexual boundaries much further than most young people in early 1970s England. In February, 1972 Michelene Wandor illustrated how the pursuit of pleasure had become a political marker for social and subjective change. Drawing upon Marcuse's argument of pleasure as a source for resisting monopoly capitalism's 'reality principle', she saw 'the erotic quality of sexuality' as the driving force towards liberation.[87] By the end of the decade, clusters of writings had emerged in the underground press, in radical pamphlets and newsletters by socialist feminists and anti-sexist men, that suggested the spread of sexual experimentation tied to the new politics in practice. Whilst a substantial body of such literature set forth the utopian political hopes embedded in experimental heterosexual relations, a minority of these sources hinted at the contested feelings activists were seeking to resolve in consciousness-raising and radical psychotherapy groups from the second half of the decade.[88] However, we have little clear picture of how 'non-aligned' men and women were internalising radical sexual discourses, nor of how activists' early experiences of non-monogamous relationships were informed by their individual histories. The testimonies revealed how, in this period, heterosexual relations became a testing ground for the radical subjectivity 'non-aligned' men and women hoped to achieve; quality of sexual life became a measure of self-change. Yet the interior conflicts that resulted signalled the difficulties activists faced in subverting post-war social and emotional models, of relinquishing themselves from enduring discourses of 'goodness' tied to self-discipline and self-restraint. In the wake of shifting power dynamics between the sexes, sexual libertarianism added to the wealth of confusions about what it meant to be a new woman and a new man.

Activists' conceptions of themselves as collective loving subjects held important implications for their sexual conduct. The open heterosexual relationships that emerged in the early days of some collective households became another way of expressing intimate bonds members fostered with one another. Desire for revolutionary change and feelings of closeness towards other activists became bound up with physical desire in a context where members were looking to dissolve the boundaries between public and private life. Together with music, drug taking dance, and collective action, sex became another way of relating as a collective subject. It drew upon the New Left practice of the body as an expression of political agency recently taken up by the WLM, and could occur in dialogue with these other practices. Explaining the open sexual relationships of his Boston commune, Victor Seidler recalled the capacity of music to arouse desire in an intimately experimental ethos: 'Music was, was really important, because I think Larry used to play the guitar and kind of song and music thing, and then there were relationships between . . . and what that felt like as you were getting closer, so I think you were living very closely when you . . . you were feeling loving and sexually engaging.'[89]

Tellingly, men were more likely to see the act of sex as an expression of love and collectivity, at the time and since. Stephen Trafford confirmed how the 'political intensity' of collective life coloured how he and other Red Ladder members began to relate sexually to each other as comrades: 'It's about relationships with people that you know and have some feeling for and it's part of wanting to be close to them and share with them, whether it's their pain or whether it's their pleasure.'[90] Like Victor, Mike Reid suggested how collective belonging enhanced his capacity for love; he defined subtle distinctions in his loving feelings towards Laurieston members, men and women. But alongside new possibilities for love, he also showed how new forms of relationships between men and women existed precariously alongside traditional monogamy and marriage. He privileged the love he felt towards his wife above the 'funny kind' of love he felt towards his other main sexual partner. The apparently spontaneous growth of 'partner-swapping' accompanied Laurieston residents' early excitement at the start of their collective experiment and, for Mike, at least, had not been intended to dissolve 'the nuclear couple'.[91] The arrangements had felt comfortable in a revolutionary context. But, in a post-script letter to his lover, he implied how, from the early 1970s, the new collective life had begun to reshape his emotional language to assuage anxieties over how to preserve the sacredness of his marital relationship: 'At first, I didn't *love you* and I wasn't *in love* either. I was much too scared of both. It seemed to me that *loving you* would be being unfaithful to T in a way that *just fucking* wasn't. But *making love* with you, besides being great, was also *being communal.* Plus I *fancied you.*' Defining the physical act of 'making love' as a new expression of socialist relations provided a way for Mike to negotiate the confusing, yet different feelings of affection and desire he felt towards his wife and his lover.

In a milieu in which meanings of friendship had also taken on new political and emotional significance, sex between male and female comrades became a way of sharing and enhancing closeness. Lee Comer criticised the way in which mid-century society had amalgamated 'attraction', 'warmth' and 'affection' under the generic rubric of 'love' 'so that sex is legitimized'.[92] She and other activists saw important distinctions between different kinds of love, which had implications for how they conducted relationships. We have seen already the emotional investment that from the mid-1960s young activists made in their intimate network of friendships, and which either complemented or in some cases supplanted traditional kinship ties. John Hoyland's diaries show the frequency of casual sexual encounters with female friends and acquaintances. They also portray the impact of Women's Liberation politics, feminist friends and lovers in changing his understandings of heterosexual relationships and his sense of sexual selfhood. In 1972 he expressed an anxious preoccupation with the question of power, his feelings as a man and the currency of the feminist labels of 'sexism' and 'chauvinism' in the milieu. He noted the confusing dilemmas these terms created, for example, for his loyalty to male and female friends. In a situation where a couple he was close to had recently separated, he expressed 'the pressures' he felt 'on both sides. My own struggle against sexism made M my ally – yet N is the older friend etc'. After starting to 'collude' with his older male friend, 'finally, quite late' he acted on 'what I'd known all along, namely that it was insensitive to carry on "as normal" when M was miserable'.[93] Conversations and sexual encounters with feminist friends helped him to negotiate the confusion and guilt he felt as a heterosexual man in relation to these loaded terms. In September he noted the transformation he had undergone since learning to understand sexism as 'undifferentiated sexual desire – the desire merely for those aspects of women that make them women – principally their bodies'. He regretted that 'for fifteen years sexism has lain like a black curse in my mind, producing recklessness, dissatisfaction, self-derision, pain and, always, failure'. Now, he understood the meaning of sex as an expression of 'companionship'. Supporting Sheila Rowbotham's 'point about sexual love becoming the repository of tenderness, fantasy etc', he too considered its 'regenerative' potential, and in April, 1973 expressed his gratitude to female friends who, as lovers, had been 'so good to me', 'fucked me so warmly, so generously'. His comments suggest the power shift that had taken place between men and women as sexual as well as political subjects, and its potential for creating new gendered subjectivities. For John, Women's Liberation had given these women a sexual agency and power over him so that through their 'kindness' and 'warmth' as friends and lovers they had lessened his 'fear and apprehension' of women. He reflected with gratitude on his self-development and self-fulfilment owing to these 'precious people . . . My eyes are so much more wide open.' However, throughout the first half of the decade John remained anxiously watchful for signs of sexism in his conduct with women.

'Non-aligned' men remained conscious of their power as sexual agents in relation to women, and sometimes knowingly exploited anti-monogamy discourses to fulfil their desires. From 1972 to 1973 Chris Rawlence was one of several Red Ladder members openly engaging in heterosexual relationships with fellow members or with other activists. Like other 'non-aligned' men seeking to make sense of conflicting feelings around sexual politics, he had joined a men's group in the late 1970s. Echoing the self-atonement that had resonated through much of men's group politics, Chris's oral history interview became a repository of the guilt he had struggled to reconcile in relation to Women's Liberation.

> So there's this furnace of ideas and lived life that we were going through day-by-day, and if you're trying to think about where I was at in all of that, emotionally, 'cos that's what matters at the end of the day . . . I suppose . . . <long pause> there still wasn't any sense when I wouldn't try and fulfil my desires, put it like that. And yet the whole balancing act of the centre of those years, in a way, was finding a way of reconciling desire with something more socially workable than what the selfish pursuit of desire results in.[94]

Perhaps still seeking the composure that a confessional narrative offered, Chris explained how the political emphasis on legitimating desire had provided a self-justifying discourse to continue openly acting upon his sexual passions. Whereas, as a young man in the late sixties the 'risk' 'of being found out' had been 'an inner driving force' for his promiscuity, the new political landscape had simply provided an alternative context for pursuing his desires. Implicit within this confessional, self-critical account was the validation of feminists' accusation that all too often the obduracy of male power had made women the greatest emotional casualties of the so-called sexual freedom; according to this narrative, men had subverted the new politics to satisfy their own desires, just as men's groups had tried to hijack the agenda of the WLM.

There is no doubting the pain and emotional conflict that often followed when intimate boundaries of commitment dissolved between loving couples. Men's narratives reveal that they as much as women suffered as they attempted to contain feelings of jealousy, betrayal, anger and desire. The self-writings of John Hoyland and Mike Reid illustrate the confusion these feelings created for their efforts to make sense of themselves as New Left men, and the loneliness especially which they felt in their jealousy. In September, 1972, mulling over 'jealousy that was not simply jealousy, not simply inadequacy and insecurity, not simply lack of faith in my own physical powers', John wondered despondently whether he could 'ever overcome the patterns of self-consciousness and self-hatred that have burnt themselves into my brain'.[95] Even following the emergence of men's groups, their internal struggles remained individual, private dilemmas of the self which involved powerful moments of self-denigration. Yet, it is notable that female pain lingers more visibly and enduringly in accounts of radical sexual experimentation, highlighting the diminished agency many women clearly felt in this area of collective life. Where women continued to hold distressing memories of this experience, they were more likely to hold men accountable for driving this sexual agenda. Jane Storr explained the conflict that removing boundaries of commitment created for her as a socialist feminist and as a post-war woman in love: 'It was very difficult for me and women in that situation because you, you're feeling just about the anger and jealous and distress of it was at odds with what you felt was the critique that you sort of, well, you know, you thought did you really agree with the critique or not.'[96] Sexual politics posed powerful dilemmas for activists between head and heart, fracturing collective and individual identities. Where all-consuming activism led individuals to feel a demise of agency, this held implications for how they acted as heterosexual subjects. At the height of her activism prior to her break-down, Alison Fell experienced the closing down of individual personal space. Within this remembered framework, intimate heterosexual relations became reduced to sexual activity so that she saw her actions as a female agent in terms of 'who you got into bed with'.[97] Yet, like Jane and other women, Alison too remembered how the removal of social structures traditionally guiding sexual behaviour

reduced her possibility for making even this choice freely: 'The thing
is that it was like a free for all. I mean anyone could suddenly decide
to, that they'd like to go to bed with you regardless of who you were
with.'

How 'non-aligned' activists acted as sexual and emotional individuals was often determined by their early experiences of heterosexual
relationships. Stephen Trafford suggested how distress at the sudden
ending of his first sexual relationship heightened his willingness to
engage in open relations with female comrades:

> I'd had a very intense passionate relationship when I was a teenager and
> felt very hurt at the rejection and hadn't really committed to a relationship
> in that sort of way since that time, and then I'm involved in relationships
> that are on and off, casual, and then I'm into a political sphere where
> the on-off casual nature is actually inherent in the theories of liberation
> that, that are afoot, and so I'm on a trajectory that is leading me. I'm
> not . . . as it were directing it. It's a bit like stumbling on, but isn't that
> what we all do.[98]

Trying to make respective sense of disordered feelings and actions, his
narrative presented an emotionally vulnerable young man swept along
by the cultural power of the milieu. Explaining his behaviour in this
way not only felt more comfortable, but also denoted the very real loss
of individual agency Stephen had felt in an emotional web of competing relationships that had felt 'too complicated for me to handle'.

With this collective sexual setting, then, went the emotional difficulties of managing the pain, confusion and jealousy which compromised
the self-liberation it was meant to realise. This chapter has shown how,
in some of the more socially and sexually experimental collectives,
extreme transformations in the everyday encouraged new understandings of social and sexual norms which presented men and women with
an array of alternative possibilities for fashioning themselves as political, gendered and sexual subjects. Yet, within the intensity of the
'non-aligned' landscape, the task of realigning the self was beset with
emotional and political challenges. Men and women's stories of young
adult life in this milieu show the distinctive gendered shape of memory
and experience that testified to the enduring impact of the new sexual
politics on subjectivities and heterosexual relations. The narratives complicate understandings of how shifting discourses of modern selfhood,
gender and politics were played out at the level of interiority; in a
radical culture where revolution went hand in hand with self-expression,
new moral, social and subjective codes could create alternative barriers
to individual agency and emotional honesty for men and women. From

the early 1970s, 'non-aligned' activists tried to negotiate these codes and to make sense of themselves as internal individuals as well as collective political beings committed to living out more egalitarian, loving relations. But alongside new kinship ties and intimate communities, turbulent, private emotional currents underscored the subjective difficulties of breaking from the past. In their capacity as workers, mothers, fathers, lovers and comrades, men and women found that the psychic imprint of post-war moral and social structures remained harder to relinquish than they had initially anticipated.

Notes

1 Rowbotham, 'Women's Liberation and the New Politics', p. 30.
2 M. Wandor, 'The Small Group', in M. Wandor (ed.), *The Body Politic: Writings from the Women's Liberation Movement in Britain 1969–1972* (London: Stage 1, 1972), p. 114.
3 Rowbotham, 'Women's Liberation and the New Politics', p. 15.
4 M. Nava, 'Rough Notes for the Belsize Lane, *Spare Rib* article', c. 1977, p. 3, MNA.
5 A. Davis, *Modern Motherhood, Women and Family in England, c. 1945–2000* (Manchester: Manchester University Press, 2012), p. 122.
6 R. P. Wortis, 'Attachment Behaviour Reconsidered', Draft copy of a paper for the conference of Biopsychology of Development, New York, 20 November, c. 1969–1970, pp. 3–4, MNA.
7 Rowbotham, *The Past is Before Us*, p. 105.
8 Nava, 'Rough Notes', p. 3.
9 Interview with Mica Nava.
10 C. Roth, 'Women's Liberation', *Red Camden*, Vol. 2, No. 1 (1970), p. 12.
11 *Shrew*, October, 1970, p. 1.
12 Interview with Sue O'Sullivan.
13 S. Cowley, 'Rambling Notes', *Shrew*, May, 1970, p. 3.
14 Interview with Sue O'Sullivan.
15 Interview with Anita Merryweather.
16 M. Nava, 'A history of the first Tufnell Park group', c. 1977, pp. 1–3, MNA.
17 'Playgroup', *Shrew*, May, 1970, p. 4.
18 Interview with Mica Nava.
19 S. Alexander, 'Room of One's Own: 1920s Feminist Utopia', *Women: A Cultural Review*, 11:3 (2000), pp. 273–87.
20 Correspondence from Ann Hunt to the author, 31 January, 2010, p. 4.
21 L. Segal 'Who Do You Think You Are? Feminist Memoir Writing', *New Formations*, 67, Summer (2009), p. 127.
22 Correspondence from Ann Hunt to the author, p. 4.
23 Interview with Judith Milner.

24 E. Adams, 'Family', *Shrew*, Vol. 3, No. 2 (1970), p. 5.

25 S. Cowley, 'The Tufnell Park Crèche', *Shrew*, Summer, 1969, p. 3.

26 'More than Minding', *Shrew*, Vol. 3, No. 2 (1971), p. 6.

27 S. Brooke, *Sexual Politics. Sexuality, Family Planning and the British Left, from the 1880s to the Present Day* (Oxford: Oxford University Press, 2011), p. 86.

28 Langhamer, *The English in Love*, pp. 24–6.

29 L. Comer, *Wedlocked Women* (Leeds: Feminist Books, 1974), p. 220.

30 S. Rowbotham, 'Communism and the Family', *INK*, 25, 7 January, (1972), p. 19.

31 Cowley, 'The Tufnell Park Crèche'.

32 'Children's Community Centre: our experiences of collective child care', a pamphlet written by members involved in running the project, c. 1972, Private archive of Sue Crockford, p. 7.

33 Interview with Sue Crockford.

34 'More than Minding', p. 6.

35 'Children's Community Centre', p. 3.

36 Cowley, 'Rambling Notes', p. 3.

37 M. Nava, 'Volley Ball and Picnics', Rough notes for the *Spare Rib* article, c. 1977, p. 1, MNA.

38 'Charity begins at home', *Shrew*, Vol. 3, No. 2 (1971), p. 4.

39 Correspondence from Ann Hunt to the author, 31 December, 2009, p. 6.

40 'Meeting the Men', *Shrew*, Vol. 3, No. 2 (1971), p. 5.

41 John Hoyland, 'The Women's Movement', hand-written notes in Private papers of John Hoyland (hereafter JHA); 'Islington Men's Group', Private papers of Andrew Tolson. For details of the beginnings of the men's movement, see J. Rowan, 'Achilles Heel and the Anti-Sexist Men's Movement, *Psychotherapy and Politics International*, 3:1 (2004), pp. 58–71; Segal, *Slow Motion*, pp. 280–3, and A. Tolson, *The Limits of Masculinity* (London: Routledge, 1977), pp. 135–9.

42 Interview with Mike Reid, Sheffield, 12 July, 2013.

43 Interview with Stephen Trafford.

44 The diary of John Hoyland, 28 March, 1975, p. 57, JHA.

45 John Hoyland, 'The Iguana Woman' (Unpublished novel, c. 1977), Part Two, p. 10, JHA.

46 Interview with John Hoyland.

47 Interview between Ronald Fraser and respondent C896/18, 9 October, 1984, p. 12, Ronald Fraser Interviews: 1968 A Student Generation in Revolt, British Library Sound Archive.

48 Interview with John Cowley.

49 Interview with Sue O'Sullivan.

50 'The Hole in the Wall', a CMPP leaflet about the community centre, GCA.

51 Interview with Sue O'Sullivan.

52 Interview with John Cowley.

53 *Shrew*, Vol. 3, No. 4, May 1971, pp. 6–7.

54 N. Fromer, 'Rough notes for the Belsize Lane *Spare Rib* article', 1977, p. 2, MNA.

55 M. Roberts, *Paper Houses: A Memoir of the '70s and Beyond* (London: Virago, 2007), p. 45.

56 M. Reid, 'Mix Café: Laurieston Hall, 1972–77', Unpublished account, 2008, p. 10.

57 See, *Islington Gutter Press*, 1, 1972; *Kite, Community Newspaper of West Kentish Town and Gospel Oak*, 3 August, 1972; Ned Gate, *North Kensington Area Paper*, 3 March/April, 1973; *Brixton's Own Boss*, 3, May, 1971.

58 Interview with Chris Ratcliffe.

59 M. Cook, '"Gay Times": Identity, Locality, Memory, and the Briton Squats in 1970's London', *Twentieth Century British History*, 24:1 (2013), pp. 90–3.

60 Reid, 'Mix Café', p. 21.

61 Interview with Victor Seidler.

62 The diary of John Hoyland, 16 February, 1975, p. 39.

63 Segal, *Making Trouble*, p. 83.

64 Interview with Lynne Segal, London, 30 January, 2010.

65 Interview with Jo Robinson, London, 18 January, 2010.

66 Interview with Jane Storr.

67 The diary of John Hoyland, 27 April, 1975, p. 62.

68 Skype interview with Tony Wickert, 31 May, 2010.

69 Interview with Elizabeth Mansfield, London, 8 July, 2013.

70 Interview with James Swinson.

71 M. Rowe, 'Changing Childcare', *Spare Rib*, January, 66 (1978), p. 14.

72 Interview with James Swinson.

73 Rowe, 'Changing Childcare', p. 18.

74 Ibid.

75 Interview with Mike Reid.

76 Reid, 'Mix Café, p. 82.

77 Interview with Mike Reid.

78 Ibid.

79 Interview with Wisty Hoyland.

80 Reid, 'Mix Café', p. 33.

81 Interview with Mike Reid.

82 Interview with James Swinson.

83 Interview with Alison Fell, London, 8 June, 2010.

84 Anthony Giddens, *The Transformation of Intimacy: Sexuality, Love and Eroticism in Modern Societies* (Cambridge: Polity Press, 1992); Jeffrey Weeks, *The World We Have Won* (London: Routledge, 2007), p. 137.

85 S. Rowbotham, *Edward Carpenter: A Life of Liberty and Love* (London: Verso, 2008), p. 327.

86 M. Schofield, *The Sexual Behaviour of Young Adults* (London: Allen Lane, 1973), p. 194. See also Gorer, *Sex and Marriage*.

87 M. Wandor, 'Exploding the Myth', *INK*, 2, 21 February, 1972, p. 12.

88 See, for example, Wandor, 'Exploding the Myth', p. 1; B. Campbell, 'Sexuality and Submission', *Red Rag*, 5, 1974; 'Exploitation in Bed – Ideas towards a Workshop', n.d., c. 1975; 'The Fourway Workshop on Sexual Identity and Sexual Politics', 1975; Report on the workshop 'From Our Sexuality to Sexual Politics', 1974; 'The Politics of Sexuality', Red Collective Pamphlet, 1978. All MNA.

89 Interview with Victor Seidler.

90 Interview with Stephen Trafford.

91 Reid, 'Mix Café', p. 22.

92 Comer, *Wedlocked Women*, p. 220.

93 The diary of John Hoyland, 26 June 1972, p. 3.

94 Interview with Chris Rawlence.

95 The diary of John Hoyland, 28 September, 1972, p. 6.

96 Interview with Jane Storr.

97 Interview with Alison Fell.

98 Interview with Stephen Trafford.

6

Trotskyism and the revolutionary self

Trotskyist men and women faced greater continuation of political culture between student and adult life than did their counterparts on the 'non-aligned' Left. In IS and the IMG the upsurge of union militancy and industrial strife that flourished during 1969–72 confirmed the leadership in its ambitions for building the revolutionary party. Politics focused on external sites of struggle, and the masculine militant culture that had characterised the VSC continued to prevail. However, activists remained emotional, gendered subjects, and political pressures to demarcate inner and outer life created their own demands for men and women to compartmentalise conflicting identities in public and private sites. Adult life and the ascendancy of a new women's movement created a host of subtle differences between the ways in which women and men invested themselves as activists and social subjects. In the early 1970s adulthood on the far Left also meant learning new ways of being.

The oral narratives of Trotskyist adulthood provide the historian with valuable access to the 'small' private self of men and women who dedicated young lives to far Left organisations. Alan Johnson has noted the difficulty of opening up the subjective experience of Trotskyist members 'to understanding in their own terms'. Too often, personal pressures, especially the tension between political activism and 'domestic life', 'remain a private struggle conducted by the individual'.[1] After 1969 sociability in the IS and IMG built upon the youth subcultures that had permeated the left network in the mid- to late 1960s. But the organisations' discomfort with the identity politics of the WLM and Gay Liberation Front (GLF) testified to the way in which the inner self was often subordinated to the struggles and activities of the moment. The oral testimonies militated against this culture and, equipping activists with a route through which to channel the personal, they reveal how, for Trotskyist men and women, the markers of early adulthood – social relationships, work and parenthood – were equally subsumed

by the politics of the milieu. It is to these themes that this chapter now
turns, starting with the transition from student activity.

Entry into adulthood and activism

Young activists immersed themselves into the two far-left organisations following graduation, to cement identities they had developed as
adolescents or students. Despite the disappointments following the
exhilaration of 1968, they retained their belief that revolutionary change
was only a matter of time. Channelling members into new campaigns,
the leadership's consolidating efforts gave cause for hope. In November,
1968 the IS initiated democratic centralism, reflecting Tony Cliff's aim
of creating an open revolutionary organisation. The ambition to build
a new workers' party meant attention to the question of workers' control
and industrial struggle at home. However, Cliff continued to foresee a
role for students who had contributed to the membership's expansion
at the end of the decade; told to put down their books and go to the
factory gates, many did just that, though often the reorientation coincided with graduation and the need to consider a future beyond student
politics.[2] Young activists, already drawn into the leadership's orbit, had
little hesitation about contributing to the next phase of the organisation's development. In north London students who had joined IS through
the LSE Socialist Society remained nearby its main centres of activity,
sharing houses close to Tottenham, Islington and Hornsey branches.
Total immersion into activism was a logical end-point to the politics
they had pursued, whether since adolescence or university. John Rose
explained his motivation to move to west London, around Greenford
IS. He and LSE comrade Alan Balfour had been sent by Cliff to agitate
in engineering factories dominating the area: 'All I wanted to be, quite
simply, was a professional revolutionary. That's all I wanted to be.'[3]
Steve Jefferys' ambition to become a professional agitator was tied to
his family's history of trade union activism:

> My father had been secretary of Dunlop's Trade Steward Committee,
> which was quite unusual for an unskilled worker. When I saw my life
> I suppose it was acceptable, one of the things you could do within my
> family, and their history was to work in a factory, and so when I saw
> myself as being an agitator, as soon as I left LSE I got a job in Lucas
> CAV in London in 1968 and learned there from the Shop Stewards who
> were both Communist Party and IS Shop Stewards, about the stakes.[4]

Laurie Flynn's Scottish socialist heritage similarly informed the activist
trajectory he envisaged: 'I was going to be a trade unionist . . . I had
received an education to help people who didn't have one.'[5]

IMG students were equally determined to continue their activities and saw the organisation as a means of realising revolutionary roles. From 1970 the IMG leadership also began to reassert the primacy of the working-class and looked to build up the organisation. However, the membership retained its student orientation, offering graduates a reassuring continuation of culture and social networks. Phil Hearse graduated from York University in 1970; after three years of intensive activity, he had no desire for the distractions of a profession or the responsibilities of a full-time job: 'I had the idea that I wanted to be a professional revolutionary; it was really the only thing I was interested in.'[6] Like many young graduates, he benefited from the ready availability of part-time teaching following the expansion of further education colleges in the wake of the Robbins Report. The accessibility of early 1970s social security further enabled young activists with no desire for the material or monetary trappings to which university graduates traditionally aspired to retain basic standards of living whilst agitating full time. In some cases the leadership directed promising young graduates towards specific regions of the country. In 1973 David Carter was sent by the IMG 'to colonise Newcastle'.[7] Following news of a staff suspension in a teacher-training college, he and a small male cohort moved from York to respond to the conflict. Renting a house together, the men quickly immersed themselves 'in one form of agitation or another . . . selling newspapers on Northumberland Street in Newcastle or going off to one infernal conference or demonstration [after another] so it was like a full-time job but without the pay'. The IMG's student orientation gave the young men links with Newcastle University's student politics and a base for sociability. Supported financially by dole money, they continued earlier patterns of activity alongside the partying that had marked their student days:

> Well you would get up fairly late really but not too late, and if there were newspapers to sell we would often get up early and go and sell them, and then probably go down the university and sell there, and there was often a meeting or debate that would be going on in which we would try to intervene . . . We went to various student discos. That was a good night out either a Friday or Saturday night because one of our mates was president of the student union.

Not all young activists wished to become full-time revolutionaries. IS member Wenda Clenaghen wanted to be 'a rank and filist working in the community'. Teaching four days a week at Hackney's Woodberry Down Comprehensive School left her with 'the energy to run around after work', plus one full day for the print shop recently set up in

Paxton Road, round the corner from the Tottenham Hotspur football ground. In April, 1970, to Martin Shaw's 'shock', Cliff asked him to go to St Helen's and establish an IS branch following the strike by glass workers at Pilkington's factories. However, Martin turned him down, content with his doctoral studies and friendships inside Angel Islington's libertarian branch:

> I wanted to have a base that wasn't entirely tied into the organisation . . . Most people, like us, were in their early twenties. We had been around the scene for three or four years and so [were] experienced enough to organise things, but it was a young group, and so it was a good social network, and we all . . . had our a counter-cultural take on IS. There was always a sense we regarded ourselves as part of the wider milieu.[8]

However, even where young activists continued to enjoy the headiness of their student days, from the early 1970s the upsurge of industrial struggle, the organisations' reorientation, and members' new roles inside these brought new political and subjective challenges as they worked to prove themselves as committed members. Dedication to the organisation and immersion into militant labour politics placed various demands on young activists pursuing this life into adulthood. The male-dominated, hard physical environment of the factory, docks and mines called upon activists to subordinate the self to a working-class industrial world in which activist culture was imbued with a discourse of industrial efficiency carrying connotations of speed, agility and productivity. Interviewees who had been active inside this world narrated themselves in terms of action and political skill, showing how the external art of politics engaged internal psychic life as activists learned to think of themselves as mediated through the culture of the organisation. Rapid absorption from student activist to full-time politico entailed an immense learning curve, set against the 'glorious summer' of 1972, when a wave of factory occupations, national strikes by builders, dock workers and miners saw the number of strike days rise from less than five million in 1968 to 23.9 million in 1972.[9] Activists' effectiveness within the organisation became interwoven with the momentum of its internal life and external politics. The politico whose life revolved around the union politics of the factory floor judged him or herself in relation to members' abilities to keep pace with the speed of national and regional events.

Dave Lyddon's account of his sudden transition from student to full-time IS organiser testified to the pressures of the new activist landscape. Time and motion were central to the subjectivity he shaped inside it. Released from Oxford's rigid rules and conservative expectations into the organisation's all-consuming revolutionary culture, he felt

himself transformed. In October, 1971, twenty-three year-old Dave
became editor for the new rank-and-file paper, *Car Worker*, based in
Oxford' car manufacturing centre of Cowley. Initially this saw little
change to his student lifestyle; sharing cheap housing with IS comrades,
he maintained a subsistence standard of living on the dole, nourished
intellectually by Marx's *Das Kapital* and 'having scenes with other
female comrades, as one did'.[10] At the beginning of 1972 the start of
the miners' strike 'rudely interrupted' the idyll. The organisation's rapid
response set him on a new trajectory into the heartland of industrial
militancy and organisational politics:

> So I get this phone call from the centre saying can people go down to
> London to help out. We need people to man the phones . . . from early
> January until November I'm basically living in London but am registered
> on the dole in Oxford . . . I would be staying with one woman or another
> but found myself being drawn into the heart of the so-called industrial
> side of IS because I had proved myself to be fairly competent by then.

Dave's account of this period represented a patchwork of anecdotes
interwoven with detailed knowledge of the summer's events. He repeatedly
emphasised the multiple layers of learning – social, intellectual and
organisational – he underwent, and the experience he remembered was
his struggle to make sense of a working-class upsurge that suggested
the imminence of revolution:

> I mean it's a phenomenal learning experience, and we've got people from
> all over, from all different industries and parts of the country, so you
> are kind of soaking this stuff up . . . going down to building-site picket
> lines in London. There were factory occupations . . . there was Stanmore
> Engineering where you had a black convenor going into the factory, . . . and
> another one we went to there was an occupation at Dennis that made
> fire engines and ambulances in Guildford, so you are going around, you
> know, you are kind of absorbing.

Dave's self-making as an activist depended upon his ability to keep
pace with the speed of events moving around him, his present tense
narration evoking the tension and energy of his everyday. Implicit was
the threat which the uncertainty of events posed to the order which
the organisation had imposed upon his life following the class displacement of adolescence. His experience of inner transformation was more
tentative and emotionally complex than the self-image he conveyed.
Inwardly his wealth of emotions sat uneasily with the appearance of
efficiency which activists were concerned to uphold in front of comrades
and worker militants. Amidst the upsurge, his individual agency seemed

vulnerable; he struggled to cope with the increasing demands the organisation placed on him and felt insecure in relation to older comrades on the
executive and national committee: 'I'm feeling, I'm not really sure that
I have enough depth, that I know enough to be able to feel comfortable?'

Dave's account showed how political and personal relations around
the organisation informed the subjectivity of young male activists striving
to live up to its goals. Although they were in awe of experienced male
comrades, such relations also contributed to the security that life in IS
created. In the early 1970s the national organisation was dominated
by older male members and, in a week at the centre attending meetings,
demonstrations and travelling to sites of struggle, Dave spent most of
his time in the company of IS men. Bonds between male comrades
rested on rules of activity, which provided a tangible guide for conduct:

> What was happening, I would turn up. You would have lunch together
> in Tina's Caff, god, boiled chicken ... you would have your meals in
> there, and if you were working late you would go off and have a curry
> with someone like Steve ... and we went off for a curry or to a Turkish
> place, or whatever, and so I kind of related to the people ... based at
> the centre.

In contrast, sexual and emotional life was more complex and chaotic.
As Dave worked to keep up with the increasing pace of campaigns, he
lost control of relationships he had been trying to maintain with female
comrades in London and Oxford: 'One of them jumped bed[s] ... and
got involved with this working-class comrade, and the other one, and
so I had to pay kind of exclusive attention to the other one when that
kind of meandered on.'

Place and motion framed the stories of other men who similarly
devoted themselves to their organisations to find new adult identities
and social belonging. In 1969, IS member Mike McGrath differed from
most of his middle-class contemporaries still attending university. Since
the mid-1960s, he had chosen to be a brick layer on London building
sites; the strikes of the period provided a militant environment in which
to engage in the brick layers' union and to agitate for IS: 'I was in the
buildings, a brick layer, already in IS, branch secretary in the local
branch, and so obviously I want to engage in the union, so branch
secretary of the union, a big branch of the brick layer's union ... But,
most importantly, I went on the Joint Sites Committee. Joint Sites
Committee ran a lot of big disputes in London, including the Barbican
dispute.'[11] By the winter of 1969, however, the outsourcing of labour
and apathy amongst the workforce were making his position as shop
steward untenable. Mike struck lucky when a sympathetic Communist

employee at the British Library secured him a job cataloguing in the Egyptian Antiquities department, and he adapted his activism accordingly, throwing himself into the union and assembling an IS branch inside the museum. Mike's story confirmed Melanie Tebbutt's argument about the importance places play in how individuals construct accounts of their personal lives and identities.[12] His narrative of these years showed how his sense of self as an activist rested on memories of movement across core metropolitan sites, mapping his life for the forthcoming decade. Crossing work, home and leisure, the experience of full-time activism was bounded by place and relationships within specific sites. His activities at the British Museum, around Great Russell Street, remained memorable because of the skills he had acquired opposing the president of the union, 'the key right-winger', in the 'office for Population and Census Statistics, just down the road'.[13] Further east, Mike's attachment to IS was interwoven with ties to comrades in his Stoke Newington branch and household in nearby Manor Road.

No less than in the 'non-aligned' milieu, for young Trotskyists, politics informed the everyday, entering the household through members' day-to-day discussions, the materiality of the house, its posters, journals and leaflets, and through friendships and romantic relationships members forged through shared hopes, ideas and activities. Personal life became public by virtue of meetings and a culture of sociability based around local public houses. Mike's description of friendships the householders made with young Stoke Newington workers illustrated how activist subjectivity was grounded in the working-class areas in which members lived, socialised and agitated:

> We started drinking in the Rose and Crown . . . a lovely pub in Stoke Newington. And mixed heavily with the locals, of which there was a big interesting group of working-class lads who sort of branched out in various ways, you know, and were running small businesses, and Bob was a good welder and he lived with us, and he joined IS. So we were all in the same group, you know, it was . . . a big branch doing lots of things. We were all drinking fairly heavily, just tremendously exciting times.

Memories of movement across these local sites also confirmed the adrenalin on which young activists lived at the height of industrial upsurge. The sheer pace of day-to-day activity was often frenetic; interviewees remembered life as a seamless movement from one site of activity to the next. Mike reflected incredulously:

> One was always in such a rush, you know, you were delivering papers or doing a demo or giving them some leaflets on this, that and the other,

or talking about a particular thing that was going to happen. I think my life . . . was pretty bound up with IS, the trade union, work, the BM, the British Museum, and my relationship. I don't think . . . one was always so busy I think. Never ate a meal, really for six days . . . You know you'd go straight from work to an early evening meeting, a pint and a sausage . . . I mean it was insane.

In 1973 the physical and psychological pressures of sustaining this exhausting schedule took their toll and Mike suffered a break-down. However, as for others, the energy he invested in his activities reflected a powerful combination of hope for the possibility of change, and pleasure derived from 'the absolute sense of belonging' it brought him.

At a time when young activists saw Britain's workers holding the government to ransom, they derived agency from simple signs of political success, the steady growth of branches they were building or the thrill of recruiting a worker. What heightened the satisfaction to be gained from these small successes was the sense of speed with which industrial struggles and their own lives seemed to be moving along in tandem.

Branch life and recruitment strategy

Parallel to the constant momentum of activity, organisational selfhood incorporated the methodical, routine patterns of branch life. Interviewees' attention to the daily minutiae of branch activity conveyed the markers against which they assessed themselves as effective activists. In a careful exposition on branch culture, organising speakers, building the contact list and composing and distributing leaflets, Sandy Irving illustrated the methodical dedication shaping activist selfhood. His account of the public meeting, framed around Newcastle's Bridge Hotel, was not simply a lament for a lost radical culture but suggested how the steady rhythms of branch life provided a set of guidelines for ordering the self. His identity as a Newcastle member was grounded in the routines and political events situated in the hotel and nearby sites. He vividly remembered, for example, how he and his friend 'walked down Percy Street right down to the Bridge Hotel where, you know, a lot of the activities and the meetings are going to take place'.[14] This was the place where Sandy's trajectory as an IS activist began and where 'on a Thursday night' the regular sight of 'people walking, passing through selling *Socialist Worker . . . Workers Press, Militant*, the *Morning Star*' taught him the discipline and dedication that made effective grass-roots activists. For Sandy, the mundane, the repetitive and the ordinary were central to activist selfhood, along with loyalty to the organisation that had kept committed branch members like him active: 'The idea that you regularly go out once a week to a meeting is something that many people [now] would feel too demanding of their time . . . It never occurred to me . . . it didn't seem onerous going out at least once a week to a political meeting, and then there was this great ready-made place where the meetings took place.' The eagerness and diligence with which he had performed routine branch tasks conveyed a self-discipline and pride of belonging that went hand in hand with the discourse of efficiency and productivity permeating Trotskyist culture. Such discourse had created a set of expectations which members applied to themselves and others alike, and which held implications for the kinds of comradely relationships they formed.

Sandy's testimony expressed the economy of feeling that could surround the politics of comradeship. He ranked attachment to the organisation's politics above the relationships members might develop within it: 'I've always thought you should go to meetings because you want to go, and whether you like people or don't like people is a secondary question.' However, in their branches and during the course of campaigning, young activists often formed strong bonds with senior members, contacts and workers they tried to recruit. The language with which men in particular described such relationships revealed much about the organisational culture shaping their emotional lives. Senior members who had stood out for admiration by young branch members were those most likely to exhibit the consistency, loyalty and reliability understood as necessary for the smooth running of effective branches. Sandy had looked up to leading Newcastle member Dave Peers, who had invited him to the Bridge Hotel following Sandy's arrival in the city as an undergraduate and nurtured him in the ways of the branch. He had admired Dave because he:

> Was very practical and wanted to get on with running the organisation. I used to go out with him in his car going round meeting some of these guys he was trying to sign up. I admired him because he was organised, focused, whereas a lot of the other members of the branch I thought were dilettantes because at meetings they liked . . . shooting their mouth off, but when it came to selling *Socialist Worker* they did bugger all.

Often, senior branch members or leading national members introduced young activists to militant workers, important 'contacts' inside local factories or the docks. These men presented models of working-class militant masculinity to respect and emulate, and young members looked up to them for the dedication and skill they displayed in union struggles and strikes. Sandy 'really admired' workers whom Dave Peers introduced him to from Newcastle's CA Parsons factory. They had led a strike at the factory shortly after Sandy had joined IS and he attended some of their committees. What impressed him was the way in which 'these people were putting a lot on the line, their marriage, their job prospects, their health, and they were very talented people, very smart people. You could see their skill at taking on management and beating them.' Young men like Sandy were additionally struck by workers' humanity in the face of everyday economic and social hardships. Working closely alongside such workers, they learned to see the individual complexity behind class as a marker of social and political experience. This was especially the case for middle-class activists whose meeting with workers was often their first exposure to the daily grind of industrial labour and the economic motivation frequently inspiring union activity. As Sabby Sagall testified, this could result in pragmatic as well as more idealistic views of the working class. In the early 1970s Sabby was agitating around Ford's Dagenham factory, where successive walkouts made it a notorious site of the unrest spreading throughout the car industry and other industrial sectors. Visiting contacts, shop stewards and workers, he began to see 'a whole new dimension' of class and humanity 'opening up':

> They were ground down by these conditions of work, you know, and I mean low pay compared to what I was used to, my family and my families' friends . . . so I could see people at the lower end of things, and yet they, you know, they had this fantastic ability to organise in their defence, you know, and the best of them also had this wider universal image of, you know, that they weren't just fighting for their own family, they were fighting for all the workers in the factory beyond that.[15]

Young activists particularly enjoyed meeting and were most likely to be romantic about worker-intellectuals. During the 1972 miners' strike John Charlton drove three Yorkshire miners to a strike meeting near Wolverhampton. He vividly remembered his surprise when one of the young miners asked him a question:

> I was driving down the motorway and Jim says, 'Eh, John. Could I ask thee a question?' 'Yes Jim.' He says, 'I'm trying to understand the second chapter in Karl Marx's *Kapital*, volume two.' He says, I think, 'I have got through volume one' . . . I almost went off the road. I almost crashed the car. I asked him to explain what the problem was and we had a discussion about it. I don't know. I probably hadn't read it myself . . . I mean this man, Jim Deacon, was not someone who was active in the union even.[16]

For activists like John, who had benefited from the post-war expansion of higher education, such men's self-education felt humbling, yet it also fed romantic constructions about the revolutionary possibilities even non-unionised workers offered.

Chance encounters with worker-intellectuals could break up the tedium of weekly branch duties of paper sales or leafleting factories, pubs and working men's clubs. Sandy showed how the meetings could also temper the uncomfortable feelings these unpopular but necessary tasks sometimes aroused. He recalled an engineering worker stopping him on his rounds selling *Socialist Worker* at Heston's working men's club. The man wanted to discuss the Dostoyevsky novel he was reading: 'Clearly he had no one else to talk to it about it in his circle and saw me as a young lad passing by.'[17] The meeting represented a 'once in a blue moon' pleasure during sales rounds that Sandy 'hated because you only ever sold a few and you felt a fool'. His admission suggested that, beneath external displays of discipline and duty, young activist men held in check more complicated feelings which the experience of activity sometimes aroused.

In the course of protracted workers' struggles, the loyalty and affection activists developed towards worker-intellectuals informed the fraternal bonds binding them to the organisation. Yet these ties could exist uneasily with more uncomfortable feelings that complicated how they understood workers as emotionally vulnerable men. During the 1972 miners' strike Sandy toured working-men's clubs in Ashington, Cumbria selling copies of *Socialist Worker*. He expressed conflict between the need to relate to workers as potential recruits and his desire to be accepted as a fellow man and comrade:

> At what point do you reveal this more political task? There were one or two people I got to know in Ashington with whom I remained long-term friends, but I think it was very difficult because at what point do your personal preferences to move on and mix with people socially erode whatever obligation you feel to these people you have picked up with?

Admiration for worker-intellectuals suggested the dignity of labour which nineteenth-century middle-class radicals had projected onto the working class.[18] Yet social relations that took activists beyond political sites of struggle and into workers' homes could also unmask a social realism fuelling a grittier sort of dignity. Sabby became 'close friends' with an Irish dock worker who had joined IS following their intervention in the London dock strike in 1967. He recalled his shock when, on one of his visits to the family's home, he witnessed his friend, drunk, having 'a go at one of his kids'.[19] The incident complicated Sabby's admiration for the dock worker as a militant masculine model and he tried to offset his disapproval by understanding 'it in the context of the hardship, not just the economic hardship but kind of emotional and psychological difficulty of providing for his family of five, you know, it was hard. Life was hard.' In 1972 a visit to coal miner Jim Deacon's home dissolved some of John Charlton's idealised reverence towards workers and prompted him to temper his approach to recruitment:

> He was a young man who read books. He had three children and lived in a colliery house just west of Barnsley. I would go to the house and there was a young working-class wife. 'Would you like bacon and egg?' You know it was like that. It was an insight really into the world, into a workers' world. It was actually a bit of a ... I don't like the word humbling actually, because it is a bit ... it isn't quite the right word, but it made you think and it made you cautious in ramming ideas down people's throats.[20]

Another meeting with a miner from Bentley, near Doncaster, provided a stark lesson about the sometimes prejudicial world of the working-class man, cautioning John against the dangers of idealising such men as political agents, and providing a mirror with which to scrutinise his own behaviour as a husband:

> I was on a regular visit to this guy and it's kind of 'Mary will make your tea. What would you like? Mary, a cup of tea. Two cups of tea, Mary. Do you take sugar?' You felt bad. You've got a lot of children around. You felt this guy actually was really indulging. He was enjoying the company of intellectuals ... in particular of my companion who happened to be an attractive middle-class young woman.

At a time when IS women were struggling to get the messages of Women's Liberation heard and taken seriously by leading men, including John, the miner alerted him to sexism in a way female members had been unable to, because he (the miner) embodied a militant masculinity John sought to emulate: 'You know you might be a bit more articulate about how you deal with these matters at home, but basically you were just like they were.'

Integral to the political skills young activists had rapidly to acquire was the challenge of learning how to initiate and build relations with workers they were trying to recruit. This applied particularly to the cohort of IS student recruits who became caught up in the process of education and organisation known as the 'turn to the class'. After 1969–70 IS began systematic efforts to work around industry and the trade unions, which meant turning the mainly student and middle-class membership into a force capable of exerting influence amongst the industrial working-class. A break-down of membership showed that even by Easter 1972, IS had only 26 per cent manual workers and 31 per cent white-collar workers. In September, 1970 a recruitment campaign began in earnest, aimed at bringing in five hundred new members over three months.[21] Members engaged in intensive work around the factories, equipped with new propaganda, notably Cliff's book on the 'employers' offensive' of productivity deals, which had been compiled from contact with industrial workers up and down the country and in which members held faith for its ability to make an impact. The tasks of recruitment, intervening in struggles, winning workers' faith in IS politics, and the challenge of persuading new recruits to stay, placed a series of political and social pressures on members. Where new activists had no family history or prior experience of working with the labour movement, the need to acquire a working knowledge of its traditions and practices compounded pressures to earn workers' trust, a task often made more difficult by the entrenched Communist Party influence in industrial sectors of the trade union movement.

The goal of recruiting workers cut to the heart of members' IS identity and self-image as activists building a revolutionary party. Members made inroads into factories and other industrial sites through building relationships with contacts inside factories. John Rose showed how uncomfortable the industrial environment and its shop floor politics could be for the middle-class graduate. The sheer physicality of the men he sought to recruit symbolised the social gulf he felt from them and the difficulties of living up to them as idealised masculine models. In the early 1970s John established contact with engineering militant IS member Ian Morris. Proving himself to Ian as a serious activist inside the factory became a means to fulfil this masculine image he saw embodied in Ian's physical strength and political foresight: 'Ian was very important for me because he was an older worker, completely without any bullshit, a hard, tough welder, skilled engineering worker, very suspicious of the Communist Party.'[22]

Male activists devised a variety of techniques to help them overcome the nerves recruiting aroused. Diligent attention to shop floor politics, day-to-day social and workplace patterns and factory organisation offered protection against hostility or humiliation from workers and shop stewards who disliked the men's politics or saw them as a threat to their authority with workers. Nigel Coward suggested how activists' discipline and eagerness to prove themselves saw them quickly building up detailed knowledge of their particular recruiting ground. In the early 1970s he was assigned responsibility for recruiting from several London power stations. Although brief experience as a salesman gave

him confidence about his ability to 'get on with people', the element
of risk remained: 'I had to pretend I was an electrician with me donkey
jacket and go in with fifty copies of something the bosses didn't want
on their premises.'[23] His detailed description of practices he employed
illustrated the careful planning behind his subtle performance as a
recruiter; his ability to merge into the background and to identify
potential recruits depended upon knowing how to map the power station, its spaces, rhythms and hierarchies.

> You couldn't go in at the same time as everybody else . . . a shift change
> is the best time but you generally head for the canteen and ask for
> the chippies' spark. They are the carpenters. The spark works alongside
> them, they are the ones you want to get close to. Provided there is a
> chippies' spark, and it makes sense, the chances are you're in, so that
> was quite fun.

Recruiting entailed a series of methodical steps that invariably began
with the organisation's newspaper or pamphlet that activists carried
in their hands. This had to be followed up with a carefully managed
conversation drawing upon detailed knowledge of workers' leisure
practices and social institutions. John Charlton illustrated a typical
conversation between an activist and a potential recruit: '"Have you
seen it before, the paper? Oh where've you seen it? Which lodge are
you in? . . . I've been to your club you know? I've been to the academy
club. I was there a couple of Saturdays ago. You had good entertainment
on that night . . . a comedian". "Oh yes, he was very funny wasn't he?"
I mean this is the way you do it really.'[24] Successful recruiting meant
activists reading workers' behaviours and understanding the symbolic
meaning they denoted. Nigel Coward showed that where young men
mastered these conversational and psychological skills, encounters with
workers became enjoyable, and important to the self-confidence they
developed as committed members: 'If it's done genuinely it can be
enjoyable and worthwhile, and it's always instructive because it's a
different kind of knowledge from your own experience so I quite liked
it, though every time you went up to someone you took a breath because
they might've had a bad day.'[25]

Worker activists from outside

The ultimate test in the industrial landscape came for the minority of
activists who joined the assembly line. Motivation to take up a factory
job often derived from a combination of political commitment and
economic expediency. In November, 1972, Dave Lyddon began night

shifts at Cowley's Morris factory; he felt mounting pressure as an industrial organiser and, against advice from the IS leadership, decided he needed first-hand experience as a car worker. The reality of surviving on the dole had taken its toll and the factory offered a short-term solution at a time when industrial manual work paid a good hourly and weekly wage. By the end of the 1970s an average manual worker could expect to earn up to £40 a week more than a public sector employee. At Cowley's Morris plant the flat hourly rate for men over twenty was £1.05 per hour for 'A' grade work (all machine operators in the full bonus scheme), and £1.0125 for 'B' grade work (those on 90 per cent work). There were also additional rates for overtime and night-shift premiums.[26]

Yet the shift to full-time assembly work entailed another social and cultural transition. Whereas everyday needs had previously been subsumed by the ever-changing demands of political struggle, the assembly line carried a steadier, predictable rhythm that brought Dave back to the physical body: 'Everyday life when you are working can be very mundane . . . when you are effectively full time it takes over your life, but when you're on night shift there are certain elements of survival, getting enough sleep, getting something to eat.'[27] The monotony of assembly work and the endurance of adapting to night work created a distance between self and politics as the reality of workers' lives awakened him to the limitations of industrial militancy. Just as personal encounters with worker-intellectuals could temper activists' hopes for such men, the daily grind of the assembly line was a stark reminder of distinctions between the moderate mass of workers and industrial militants aiding activists to make inroads inside unions:

> The only thing, all you are doing is tempering people. You are not trying to build a wet blanket. You are thinking, well, actually, the world, we have our bright ideas, but actually most of the time people aren't concerned. They are concerned about the bloody football results.

In addition to the militant world of the organisation and the sometimes emotionally intense world of the home, the factory represented a new social and political landscape that exacerbated divisions between the public activist and private internal man and presented problems for composure. At the IS centre Dave had begun to feel increasingly comfortable as a well-known member, surrounded by comrades from similar working- or lower middle-class university backgrounds. However, to survive in the plant he had to temper his militancy and disguise his background, which heightened his sense of social dislocation as a 'de-classed' militant, and added to the strains of managing a complex emotional life, as the pressure of night work created problems for his relationship with his girlfriend. However, like the organisation, the factory too provided a self-contained world from which to avoid the uncomfortable feelings that loving relationships could arouse.

> You're permanently tired, and I was only on nights until about September the next year, September '73, partly because I felt my relationship with D was suffering so I applied to go on days, but of course by the time I got them it had ended, and then you think, well, perhaps I should have stayed on nights. I don't know, because you can hide away from certain things, and you, because you've got an excuse (laughs) . . . Then of course I'm dealing with the fact that I'm not . . . I'm a militant who comes from a working-class background, in a working-class occupation, but actually I'm de-classed, so I don't feel like I actually fit.

Life on the factory floor also created a broader space for identifying with the mass of workers through the 'healthy contempt' they displayed towards management. In this respect, belonging came from a shared culture of hostility where Dave renewed the 'instinctive class feeling' of his Oxbridge days. The class solidarity which activists only fleetingly found as outside political agents came within closer reach on the assembly line through sharing workers' physical discomforts and social humiliations. In *The Assembly Line* French Maoist Robert Linhart conveyed how the 'gradual anaesthesia' of the Choisy Citroën factory hindered his student dreams of insurrection.[28] Tasting at first hand the monotony of workers' lives, he came to respect the factory's social and political equilibrium, the indecency of raising workers' hopes and stealing precious breaks for political meetings. Steve Jefferys described his experience in the Glasgow Chrysler plant in similar terms: 'Initially I had social relations in a kind of non-political way because that is what you did. You found solidarity in the work experience.' However, unlike Linhart, on the line Dave and Steve consciously managed the psychological challenges that monotonous work presented by using opportunities to develop as intellectual and militant actors. At Cowley, Dave would be 'spot-welding a screen on and it would take you about a minute, and you release the jig from the car and so I would read, and I learned to read a page a minute, yeah and you kept it in your mind'. At Chrysler, Steve not merely survived but thrived as an agitator who displayed his politics for all to see. Building contacts inside the factory, he transcended the physical grind of Dave's experience and continued to live out his self-image of agitator:

> Within the factory I began operating as an activist, talking to people, and asking if they were interested in *Socialist Worker*. Eventually I had

a newspaper round of about forty people . . . Very opportunistically I said we needed to have a union member and there was no contest. I got elected, so I became the AEU steward for the whole building . . . I also got put onto the Engineering Union Workers' Committee, which meant once a week I was allowed to go for a two-hour meeting to meet the engineering senior stewards from all the other buildings, and so very rapidly they got to know me throughout the whole building. They used to call me big Stevie.[29]

Worker activists from inside

The minority of men who joined IS as apprentices found even greater continuum between factory and organisational life, moving fluidly between the shop floor and branch life. Whereas the organisation discouraged middle-class activists from going into factories as outside agitators, they recognised the valuable information factory workers could bring to their new recruitment strategy.[30] Consequently, worker-activists performed the Trotskyist politico unlike any other member, maintaining a constant level of agitation that saw them arguing and persuading, leafleting and selling papers, organising stoppages and strikes even whilst they worked their tools. The ability to live out this militant identity, held up for admiration within the organisation, and, even if vilified, alive inside the factory, infused workers like Alan Watts and Roger Cox with a political agency and self-confidence that came from witnessing small but progressive shifts in their workplaces. At the MK Electric factory where Alan Watts worked in the early 1970s, the Amalgamated Union of Engineering Workers held a strong position that gave him a ready base for militancy. The active life of the trade union workshop created a high level of political interest that facilitated equally high paper sales. Moving swiftly around the factory, distributing literature and making himself a familiar face amongst the two hundred workers, he took 'great delight' in working out their politics and negotiating to win their solidarity: 'I remember this one guy once said to me "the trouble with you is that you make people think about things they don't want to think about".'[31]

Worker activists saw themselves actively informing the dialogic relationship between the organisation and blue-collar workers. Roger Cox derived agency as a militant pushing for workers' control, but his ultimate loyalty remained to workers in his various workplaces, Acton's Lucas CAV factory where he was a diesel engine tester, a nuts-and-bolts factory and Paddington station. His identity as a worker was integral to his self-image as an activist: 'What drives you is that you always have to do the best for the people you are trying to represent . . . One of the things in the working-class movement is that you have your say, especially if there is an attempt to actually make things better for them, to give them a lead.' Roger's collective identity as a member of a broad labour movement informed his sense of duty towards workers as a member of an enlightened revolutionary organisation. He saw himself as responsible for initiating resistance amongst workers against state bureaucrats, and injecting workers with the best values of liberal toleration he had received from his IS education. Using an old parable of his father's, he signalled the kinship ties informing his workplace activism:

> You have got to line the working class in one line and get them to spit [at the people on the other side], and there is so many of us, you get them to spit at them and they will drown them. The problem is instead of spitting at them they will start arguing amongst themselves and spit at each other. It was a bit crude but my role was to stop workers spitting at each other and get them to fight at one common enemy.[32]

The social divisions that could feature in the factory on account of class, race or nationality failed to translate into the organisation where workers and graduates derived collective belonging from IS politics and an interpersonal network binding them as comrades. Alan Watts viewed leading IS men with awe and often felt intellectually insecure in their presence: 'In my head all these people were up on a pedestal because they were so good at speaking in front of meetings.'[33] Nevertheless, the organisation provided a socially pacifying role, directing his militant class consciousness away from middle-class graduates towards 'a common set of ideas': 'You know that everyone around you is singing from the same hymn sheet, if you like.'

Open identification with IS politics inside factories brought clear social dangers as worker-activists risked antagonising supervisors and workers alike. Alan knew only too well the precarious position he occupied as a militant; frequently appointed as shop steward, he had a confrontational style with management that resulted in his repeated dismissal from tool rooms, from Enfield's Auto Light factory to Southgate's Standard Telephone and Cables factory. Selling *Socialist Worker* throughout the factories also brought its own set of difficulties at a time when the paper openly supported the IRA and opposed immigration control. Roger came face to face with these difficulties at CAV: 'It was an absolute nightmare let me tell you. Every time you sold it they would go, "what's that then, what is it this time? I suppose you're supporting the Irish".'[34] However, when it came to recruitment, their experience in this physically challenging, morally black-and-white world lent them resilient insight into how to approach workers and negotiate prejudice. To survive and thrive as militants, they had to be audacious, able to read and negotiate awkward social situations. Alan and Roger used the class solidarity uniting workers in their common suspicion of outsiders in a bid to earn their trust and respect. In this they benefited from IS opposition to the trade union bureaucracy Tony Cliff saw as a threat to growing shop-floor militancy.[35] Worker-activists were able to fulfil active roles as trade unionists because, although encouraged by the organisation to do so, the servicing role they saw IS performing strengthened their agency to speak for workers. According to Roger, 'if anything went wrong you could point to the fault of the trade union leadership, it's them, look'.[36] As agitators negotiating the organisation's ambitions with workers' interests, their stance as trade unionists equipped them with a get-out clause to guarantee the loyalty of men on their shop floor.

However, some worker-activists were far less willing to moderate their political loyalties or temper their activities to blend into their workplaces. Bob Light illustrated how family history and local identity combined with audacity and the capacity for violent resistance to shape his particular experience in Newham Royal London docks. At the end of 1969 he reluctantly made the decision to sign up as a dock worker, won over by the economic and political advantages the work offered: 'I didn't fancy working there. I knew my Dad was crippled by his experience and I didn't like the clothes they wore. But I knew politically it could be useful ... The money was £36 a week ... so I thought I could do it for three weeks and buy a couple of suits, and it was principally for political reasons.'[37] Unlike Alan and Roger, Bob's Communist Party background and his parents' egalitarian relationship automatically set him apart from most workers. Yet his refusal to conform to the cultural norms of dockland masculinity also made the task of recruiting more challenging: 'The first time I went to work I had these boots and I put my hair under a collar, but I wore a class purple jumper and there was a brutal honesty, and I didn't have that measure of acceptance partly because I wanted it on my terms.' Whilst activists approaching workers as outsiders risked losing face if they failed to recruit, as a new dock worker and open dissident, Bob risked physical violence from antagonistic workers. In the rough landscape of the docks his first step in establishing himself as an IS recruiter was to demonstrate his physical manliness. To survive as an activist he had first to survive the combative initiation rites where established workers tested new recruits for physical and mental weakness. This was no easy task:

I did have quite a tough time. I would go to work and you didn't know where you'd be working and there would be people you didn't know. There would be some people who would ostracise you . . . my Dad told me what I had to do. He said the first person who insults you to your face you've got to hit them and once you've done that people know you won't be messed with. You're waiting for it to happen. It did and this big dog of a man came at me, and I smacked him around and he smacked me around, and people knew you weren't to be trifled with.

At the height of the VSC demonstrations, Bob was one young man for whom the physically combative culture of street marching had appealed to traditional images of working-class manliness. However, the 'scale of violence' in the docks was exceptional, exacerbated by its twenty-four-hour drinking culture. His ability to establish a foothold as an IS representative resulted from his willingness to fight men challenging him, the protection he gained from his father's name and the political defiance he had shown in April, 1968 contesting dock workers' support for Enoch Powell. One year later he was remembered 'as Jimmy Light's boy' by 'a small slither of guys' who had been 'disgusted by the strike, who were confused and didn't know what to do'. The respect he earned by 'saying the right things' enabled him and Fred Lindop to establish a core of contacts amongst these men who 'were beneath the dissident shop stewards' and provided inside information about the politics in the yard.

As for Alan and Roger, Bob's familiarity with his workplace enabled him to map its politics, culture and the social spaces connecting these. He also knew which dissident dock workers to draw into the IS 'orbit'. Unrest in the London docks had been rising since the introduction of new working practices, including containerisation. Resentment against Transport and General Workers' Union leader Jack Dash's handling of the 1969 strike had left its mark on some Communist-affiliated dock workers and Bob identified a core of these men as potential recruits. By 1971, discontent over the introduction of the Industrial Relations Act added to the militant atmosphere in which he was canvassing for IS. Bob used his knowledge and sense of place to manoeuvre within Newham's tight political web:

The Left had places they went. They tended to huddle so there were tonnes of cafes and seven twenty-four hour pubs. People would be drinking all night with a wife and family at home. There was a cafe called the Kremlin run by a guy who was himself a leftie, and me and Fred used to go round there and sell the paper . . . We used to produce 5,000 bulletins and hand them out at the dock gates and go round all the canteens. I used to spend all my break on Thursday handing out the leaflets in the canteens and we built up a small force-field.

Intimate knowledge of Newham's 'dockology' – the language, images, ideas, stories and humour of dock workers – was crucial to Bob's success in winning over recruits, a deliberate and carefully considered process enacted over several months.[38] His close involvement in events leading to the imprisonment of three dock workers at Pentonville in June, 1972 offered the ideal moment in which to win over Mickey Fenn, Communist Party member and leading representative of the unofficial National Port Shop Stewards union, whose support offered to win over a larger circle of recruits. Bob distinctly recalled their pivotal conversations during the illegal picket of Chobham Farm container depot on Hackney Marshes. His account highlights the interplay of intimacy and a more hardened masculine sociability framing the growing respect between the older and the younger man. It illustrates that although recruiting was for young worker-activists no less politically and socially demanding, it also created strong emotional attachments through homo-social, comradely relations between younger and older workers. Where such relationships came out of unanticipated working-class victories they had the capacity to strengthen the political agency workers derived from their activism:

> Mickey Fenn was always on the picket line but he was always standoffish ... We found ourselves sitting during the winter of 1971, sitting during long boring hours on two planks of wood held together by bricks with nothing to do but talk about politics, and I made sure my picketing rota was the same as Mickey's so I just bashed his fucking ear-holes for about four months. We would talk about whatever, even the politics of gender ... We became friends. I remember the moment he gave me his phone number and he did it through [his wife] Pauline. He said 'Pauline has been asking if you want to come over for something to eat.' It was the break-through moment. Me and Mickey were very close friends and all the guys on the picket line were now buying *Socialist Worker*.

Trotskyist women

For women as much as men, validation as a far-left activist derived from the mobility, efficiency, intellectual debate and action that revolved around daily organising and class struggles. Drawing upon these terms to describe the thrill of meeting workers, branch activity and demonstrations, the militant labour culture shaping Trotskyist membership defined a normative standard of political agency for women as well as men. In the public spaces members occupied from the meeting room, the pub, the factory forecourt and the picket line, women exercised key organising skills just like men and felt affirmed as revolutionary beings.

Far-left organisations provided women with the same security and identity to ease the uncertainty following graduation. In 1971, Bronwen Davis received as a 'horrible shock' the news she had received third-class honours.[39] The disappointing result ended her plans to undertake an MSc in Development and Economics in Delhi; continued membership in the Oxford IS branch gave her – unemployed and squatting – an immediate purpose: 'In a way joining IS solved a lot of problems because you didn't have to think too much about an individual solution because you had a line and a paper to sell.' At a time when other left women were campaigning against the gender differentials oppressing women, for Bronwen, membership within the IS network cloaked any distinctive female identity: 'I am not sure we did get treated very differently as far as possible. You know you were expected to get up and sell the paper and do everything men would do.' Other women confirmed the ready-made network of friendships and acquaintances the organisations created; members who provided beds, food and emotional support, and the constant of branch meetings and activity to offset existential anxieties. In 1969 Gilda Peterson abandoned several attempts to complete an MA at Birmingham and moved to London, where IS branch life provided a structure for life and self: 'I'd looked at trying to get into Tavistock to do therapy and you had to pay for your own therapy and God knows what. I felt outfaced by all of that financially and intellectually really . . . but I got a job and I got back into IS straight away in London, and joined Camden IS.'[40]

Several women testified to powerful sensations of transformation they underwent as IS and IMG members; their experiences complicate feminist accounts of the alienating masculine culture that made these uncomfortable spaces for women. Sheila Hemingway's story was striking for the unusual class dimension of her experience as well as the narrative framework of self-liberation she employed to tell it. In 1969, like several of the women in this book, she was the mother of two small children. However, unlike them, she had left school at fourteen to follow her mother into the tailoring industry before marrying and having her first child three years later. Her introduction to the Leeds IS branch came through her husband, who one evening asked her to accompany him to a meeting at the local Trades Council hall. Sheila's vivid memory of her anxieties and careful preparation preceding the meeting denoted the way in which her insecurities and cultural expectations as a working-class housewife shaped the sense of revelation she found:

I was a bit reluctant to go. I said, 'I don't know anything about politics. I'd feel such a fool', and he [Sheila's husband] said, 'no, no', and I got

dressed up 'cos I never went out you see and when you go out you get
dressed up, so I got all dressed up ... I put on my best dress. I did my
hair, put a bit of make-up on and went toddling along and walked into
this room in the middle of Leeds in the old Trades Council building, and
it was a bit of a dump actually, and I walked in and there was this room
full of people that were all in jeans, men women, fairly equal, yeah.[41]

She described her sense of self-discovery at the meeting in strikingly
similar terms to women who joined the Tufnell Park Women's Liberation
group; the occasion gave Sheila new insight into herself as an autonomous woman, beyond the roles of wife and mother:

At the end of the meeting I just sat there and this woman came up to
me and said, 'Hello, who are you?' ... I said, 'Oh I'm Brian's wife.' She
said, 'No, you're not. What's your name?' And I thought this woman's
mad so I said, 'My name's Sheila.' She said, 'Well there you go, you're
not Brian's wife, you're Sheila.' Well I thought that was really strange,
but it took me a while to get it into my head what she was on about
and then it clicked. I thought, oh, she's right, you know ... It made me
feel really good once I realised ... I felt I was an individual. I had always
thought of myself as Brian's wife.

In contrast to middle-class feminists narrating stories of self-
transformation, as a far-left and northern working-class woman Sheila
represented herself in something of a cultural vacuum. Yet she told her
story with ease. Penny Summerfield offers possible insight into why this
was: 'Women come to oral history interviews with experience of a range
of confessional occasions from which they are likely to select a model
that seems most appropriate.'[42] In modern western culture women have
been especially encouraged to release private experiences into the
public domain for common consumption through popular literature
and the media. Indeed, Sheila readily gave what became a confessional
account, reassessing her social and sexual conduct in the light of her
current values and status as a single woman, grandmother and ex-party
member. But the dramatic, emotive nature of Sheila's introduction to
IS made it likely to be memorable; it held significance as the start of her
life as an independent woman and IS activist. The organisation opened
up a new social and cultural world: 'Friday night at the Fenton pub,
Saturday night at Victoria pub and Sunday night at Brickie's.' From
the first nervous occasion when she asked a question at a meeting to
selling the papers and becoming branch treasurer, Sheila developed in
self-confidence and 'felt a sense of freedom', moving out of her 'husband's shadow'. The discovery that her experiences as a working-class
woman and mother held political value to the organisation proved

crucial to Sheila's developing autonomy and sense of validation. In 1974 Paul Foot asked her to write a series of articles for *Socialist Worker*. Free to select topics interesting to her, she discovered her voice and wrote on subjects connected to her own experiences; for example, as a mother reflecting on child murderer Mary Bell. She remembered the day when she first saw her words in print: 'It were unbelievable. But actually, I don't know whether it did make an impact because once you started doing it, it was like you were expected to do it ... It was part of being IS, part of being a comrade and you just did it. Yeah, I was just another comrade.'

Women in the Tufnell Park milieu rejected left groups in the VSC for their formulaic, belittling culture that denied affective internal life. However, Sheila's narrative signifies the autonomous space the far Left provided women as political, publicly situated beings; through external activity came internal renewal and camaraderie. They derived the same exhilaration and authentic emotion that arose from the spontaneity, creativity and adrenalin of sustained activity. In 1974, IS member Di Parkin wrote of an 'exhausting' week, 'fly posting till 3am', 'rushing about', but she felt fulfilled, inspired and secure in her agency: 'my eyes shine, succeeding at one thing gives you the zest to get into another, so I'm organising a Women's Group in the branch as well as doing hospital and anti-racist work.'[43] The organisations put women in touch with a wider world, from local and national class struggles to international liberation and Third World conflicts, and judged them like the men for their organising, writing and speaking skills. Consequently, women lived out identities as revolutionaries within the same fraternal spaces inhabited by male comrades and defined themselves through the prevailing discourse of efficiency, productivity and mobility.

Joan Smith's story of IS activism in early 1970s Glasgow illustrated the way in which women too internalised and narrated themselves as organisational subjects. In Chapter 3 we saw Joan earning credibility as an activist and intellectual in LSE's Socialist Society. From 1971, she continued this role as a PhD student in the all-male, predominantly blue-collar Glasgow IS branch. In the early 1970s the Scottish branches remained small and geographically removed from the London centre; average membership figures rarely surpassed ten.[44] Within her closely knit branch Joan attained prominent status as chief organiser and speaker. Any deference members showed to her as a woman occurred only after meetings, when the men selected a pub:

People would say 'Joan, are you coming for a drink now after the meeting', and I would say 'no I don't think so'. They would say 'okay', and

I didn't know they were going to the Tenant's bar up the road because it was better beer, and this was the bar that had the sign above it 'no women or dogs allowed'. If I said I was going they would go to the other pub underneath, *The Chancellor*, and nobody ever said anything. They would just hover by the door to find out where I wanted to go. It was fine and they were just nice.[45]

Any sense of difference Joan might have felt whilst organising on issues from Ireland to the Upper Clyde yard work-in of June 1971 dissolved under the weight of branch responsibilities. In a setting of constant activity, even the challenge of feeding scores of hungry activists elided into the political realm; domestic arrangements fell to Joan not because she was a woman, but as principal branch organiser. She approached the task with the same artful efficiency she applied to all activities, allowing male comrades few opportunities to evade their share of domestic work: 'I would say to the butcher I think I need twenty chops . . . I just threw it all in the slow cooker . . . They could scrub baked potatoes. It was a ten-minute job. It was as much as I would do.' When it came to managing the day-to-day business of branch life, organisational selfhood allowed little space for gender demarcation. However, there were exceptions to this experience.

IS women and the Women's Liberation movement

The personal politics of Women's Liberation seemed to challenge the essence of far-left selfhood. As revolutionaries, Trotskyist women derived agency from a politics that privileged the masculine world of industrial work, far removed from the subjective consciousness raising of the small groups. However, as word of the new women's movement began to spread, IS and IMG women actively supported Women's Liberation, albeit imparting their own political line. The shared enthusiasm with which they attended the first Women's Liberation conference reflected the broad, inclusive nature of the early movement and the initial excitement women shared for incorporating the personal alongside the previously class angle of the political. Yet women inhabited their corporeal and psychological selves in complex dimensions, and for some activists it took time to work out their relationship to an emerging politics that touched their core identity unlike any other. This uncertainty reflected the complexity with which women inhabited political and personal spaces inside and around their organisations, and the contradictions they lived out as activists equal to but different from male comrades.

In both their organisations and the WLM, many women found a collectivity that was not always compatible with either one. The women

who founded the North London IS Women's Group in 1970 exemplified the way in which, as IS members and women, they invested different components of self in different political sites. The group emerged
at the Ruskin conference of 27 February to 1 March, 1970 as a discussion forum for about twenty women from the North London branches.
Attending the conference independently from the organisation, Anna
Paczuska was astonished to see so many familiar faces. She arranged
to have a Tannoy announcement for IS women to meet in the lobby,
and between thirty and forty members responded.[46] The spontaneous
meeting exemplified the interpersonal female network that grew rapidly
after the conference. Anna shared the excitement of women elsewhere
on the revolutionary Left, embracing the intimacy of the small groups;
away from mixed IS branches, the North London group offered members legitimate political space to begin to work from the personal,
from direct experience and feeling, in a manner disapproved of by the
organisation:

> There was a connection that the IS politics didn't always have. I didn't
> have to talk about the theory with women. I didn't have to read a book
> on what Lenin said on it and what Marx said on it. We did read a lot
> about what Marx said on it and what Lenin said on it because that was
> kind of a weapon in our debate with the male comrades, but it felt kind
> of close to home . . . the theory began to make sense because you were
> starting with you.

Yet, having come to left activism through IS, her loyalty to the organisation remained steadfast. She derived agency as a woman from the
new politics, but political agency from IS; and it was out of enthusiasm
for Women's Liberation, not antagonism as a woman to the organisation, that she sought to carry it into the branches. To Anna, having
discovered the mutual joys of IS membership in the upsurge of 1968,
it seemed logical that male comrades would want to share Women's
Liberation as an extension of the liberation politics they had embraced
as students. She told them: 'This is exciting. You've gotta listen. This
is great. You've gotta listen.'
    Finding their political voice as women so soon after finding their
voice as IS activists, women like Anna and Margaret Renn found it
hard to see their involvement in the growing movement as a threat.
After all, the organisation had given them space as young women to
be autonomous and daring. Margaret recalled: 'We were absolutely
pulsing with confidence. And in a way we had no idea that we were . . . I
mean we obviously knew we were being challenging, but in a way we
couldn't see what the problem was. I mean we had sort of been kept

quiet without knowing it because we were young and not involved and these things happened very quickly on top of the other.' Genuinely surprised at the 'scornful and unhelpful remarks' with which male comrades greeted the new politics as 'frivolous' and 'diversionary', initially female members adopted a defensive stance by 'trying to "sell" Women's Liberation' to the organisation, arguing that support for the movement would increase membership.[47] IS women worked alongside Women's Liberation members, supporting the Women's National Co-ordinating Committee. By December, 1970, a dozen women's groups were being run by IS women or in conjunction with IS branches, encompassing non-IS and Women's Liberation members. But, by 1971, the organisation's continuing opposition provoked female defiance after a resolution attempting to discuss Women's Liberation was defeated by the Easter conference. Anna signalled the North London group's refusal to continue pacifying male comrades, by proclaiming Women's Liberation 'an important principle that must be recognised by any organisation that calls itself revolutionary and socialist . . . irrespective of whether it increases our membership or not'. Southampton member Kathleen Ennis confirmed that IS women could not 'hope to make things easier for ourselves within the group without a tough fight'. However, though IS women continued to support the WLM, by early 1972 Anna's endorsement of personal politics had fallen on deaf ears as women's organising was increasingly brought in line with the IS industrial strategy; female members criticised the movement's failure to 'get through to ordinary women', and the thirty-two women's factions prioritised activity around 'working women', arguing that they offered 'more developed' politics and 'greater value' to IS than housewives.[48]

IS men's response to Women's Liberation needs to be read against a culture that privileged class struggle and fostered an underworld of private emotion beneath the official business of organising, to which personal life and intimate relations were an unwelcome distraction. Women were respected as equal comrades and their desire to organise on behalf of women's activities was tolerated as long as they subscribed to the image of a good IS activist. Sandy Irving epitomised this attitude when he explained: 'The IS might give the impression of being male dominated, but nonetheless you would meet in the course of things a number of very strong women and you just accepted that's how it was. They were good organisers, good speakers, held their own ground.'[49] Male comrades supported women in their endeavours with women's politics where they saw their activities as helping to develop their skills as effective activists and working to extend the organisation's influence.

Anna reflected on her husband's encouragement towards her campaigning efforts:

> I think my husband at the time used to like to say, well, if you are going
> to do the National Abortion Campaign this is how you take it over. This
> is what you do to be a real influence. It was always a very organisational
> bias to the thing. It wasn't how we get abortion or equal pay or whatever.
> It was how can you be the most dominant person in the movement, and
> influence the politics of everybody else around you.[50]

Men found it difficult to understand women's need to work separately,
when the class framework of their activism seemed to provide a unifying cause. Dave Lyddon remembered his bemusement when surveying
the slogans of the first women's conference: 'Women in Labour Keep
Capital in Power. I remember seeing the slogans . . . I was conscious
that something had happened, but I wasn't part of it.'[51] His distrust of
the new women's movement and its meaning for IS expressed a nar-
rowly masculine view of trade union politics that excluded reference
even to the Dagenham Ford women's strike of 1968, although this
gained national press coverage at the time. Dave was unable to recollect
important early campaigns which female comrades organised around
women workers, and his attitude betrayed a genuine sense of bewilder-
ment. This arose from his inability to situate the new politics within
any recent historical frame of labour politics or experience of comradeship: 'I saw the women's movement as a middle-class movement and
I didn't really like it, and I didn't really like the idea of us having a
middle-class kind of IS movement, particularly. I didn't really see what
that achieved, but I had no real experience of women trade unionists
or politics. D'you see what I mean? To know how one handled this,
yeah?'

Men's responses to the early movement saw them negotiating
personal and political experience. The support some showed their female
comrades testified to young men's uneasiness with the traditional gender models their parents had often embodied. Sons, and not simply
daughters, were alive to the emotional undercurrents of their mothers'
lives. Sabby Sagall's 'fascination' with Women's Liberation owed much
to the insights it gave him to better understand his mother's behaviour
in relation to his father:

> To me it was a revelation because my mother, for example, you know,
> had been a sort of willing slave to my father, you know. She thought the
> world of my father . . . She firmly believed her role was in the home,
> looking after the home and being a mother, and I, I felt uneasy about
> this I think, as I was growing up, but really it was listening to the kind

of radical women talking about, you know, liberation, what it meant to them, that really had a big impact on me. It really opened my eyes to the possibilities of women being equals as men.[52]

Some IS women too supported 'women' as a legitimate area for activity only if mediated through class. Wendy Henry epitomised the hostility some women displayed towards Women's Liberation; at the 1971 Skegness Women's Liberation conference she reportedly made IS delegates 'tremble' by reporting that Women's Liberation members spent their time talking about 'sexual hang-ups'.[53] Di Parkin recalled her distaste for the 'navel-gazing' of the consciousness-raising group she briefly attended at the University of Kent, Canterbury in 1972; it sat uncomfortably with her self-image of revolutionary woman exuding autonomy and authority.[54] These feelings of discomfort sometimes came as a surprise to women. In her Leeds women's group Sheila Hemingway 'didn't feel as comfortable' as she thought she would with WLM members. She felt disloyal to the men she enjoyed working alongside and wanted to defend them: 'I used to feel uncomfortable. I used to say not all men are the enemy, and you can't expect men to change overnight, just as you think you've changed overnight or you'd like to think you've changed overnight.'[55]

For some, Women's Liberation marked an overt dislocation between inner psychic and outer political and social life that echoed the conflict of 'non-aligned' activists struggling to realign personal identities and social roles. Gilda Peterson remembered the internal tension which activism in the women's movement aroused over how, as an IS member and a woman, she invested herself in the far Left. In terms of personal oppression, Women's Liberation felt removed from her life; she was 'pretty caught up with IS . . . caught up in this big relationship with my other half'; he was open to women's politics, activism was a shared bond between them.[56] Open to radical psychology and sociology, she sought a 'class politics, but one that would make sense of the personal' to also encompass her interest in social work as a means of empowering families. As a result she took an interest in IS women's discussion groups, and in the mid-1970s participated in women's demonstrations as a socialist feminist in the National Abortion Campaign (NAC). However, she puzzled over how she might practically accommodate class and women's politics to her own female future. Observing the difficulties IS women faced over childcare, she felt uncertain about the possibility of real change: 'There was a kind of sense in your life that maybe you couldn't have it all . . . a conflict in terms of wanting to be active . . . one's identity as a woman, particularly with a family, was something quite complicated and something set aside I suppose in that sense.'

Yet, when she was marching on abortion demonstrations alongside thousands of other women, her doubts about the liberating potential of Women's Liberation temporarily melted. In the interview she chanted out loud the NAC slogan she and demonstrators had shouted through loud hailers: 'Our Bodies, Our Lives, Our Right to Decide'. The emotional power of this all-female demonstration provided a tangible connection between womanhood as a corporeal identity and female political agency, transcending differences on the Left, and uniting Gilda with other feminists. Her experience echoed Sheila Rowbotham's reflections on the emotional components of political consciousness driving the NAC, the way in which it repeatedly brought campaigners into contact with women's personal stories, to shape individual and collective subjectivities.[57]

Women in the IMG

Despite the self-coherence which revolutionary women derived from their organisations, their struggle to comprehend themselves as female subjects sometimes placed them at odds with male comrades. Jacqueline Thompson's story showed how contradictions women had felt inside early subcultures sometimes followed them into the adult milieux. She joined the IMG in late 1970 and rapidly came to think of herself as an extension of the organisation. For Jacqueline, unemployed and with few social ties in London, full-time activism provided a 'total life' cemented by camaraderie in shared houses in Brick Lane and Camden's Tolmers Square: 'I sold all my literature books to give the money to the organisation. I was that devoted.'[58] In the early 1970s the IMG's involvement in controversial struggles such as the Irish Solidarity Campaign enabled Jacqueline to develop covert organisational skills and to fashion a romanticised self-image based on Italy and West Germany's red guerrilla factions. By 1971 the IMG was declaring unconditional support for the IRA against 'British imperialism and its puppets', and, for grass-roots activists like Jacqueline, civil rights demonstrations presented live experiences of police resistance that felt comparable to battles previously seen only overseas.[59] On 30 January, 1972 she and her comrades had a close encounter with mounted police in a 20,000-strong demonstration through the Catholic area of Derry. On a day later known as Bloody Sunday, troops from the British Parachute Regiment opened fire on unarmed demonstrators, killing thirteen marchers fleeing a car park.[60] For the IMG, the event symbolised the brutality of British imperialism, but Jacqueline remembered the romantic shadow colouring the occasion. Following the demonstration, she went into hiding, assuming an ultra-militant mantle complete with party name, Molly Maguire, after the nineteenth-century Irish-American secret terrorist organisation.

As a militant activist not only did Jacqueline feel of equal status with male comrades, but her sense of womanhood seemed to dissolve amidst the intensity of covert activity that subsumed the personal: 'We felt ourselves equal. We didn't dress up, we didn't act sexually overtly . . . in the Irish thing it was incredibly intense and intensive. Going back to how I felt as a woman I don't know. It is hard to say really. I felt just like a man.' She was reluctant to participate in activities concerned specifically with women's oppression because they denied her opportunities for a revolutionary role; women's issues lacked legitimacy as an area of activist politics. Within IMG's total culture the female goodness of post-war girlhood was inverted to shape a new meaning of duty. For Jacqueline, living out the identity of 'good activist' meant suppressing emotions which threatened to undermine her organisational role. This revised concept of 'goodness' represented a psychic continuity with a post-war model of womanhood that had also meant subordinating personal freedoms to the wider culture.

Jacqueline's ambivalence towards women as a legitimate campaign area mirrored the rather inconsistent approach the IMG adopted towards the women's movement during this period. Initially, IMG women were at the forefront of campaigns against women's oppression. In 1969 Leonora Lloyd headed a group supporting the trade union organisation for women's equal pay and equal rights, the National Joint Action Committee for Women's Equal Rights.[61] The IMG recognised the legitimacy of the WLM, and from early 1969 female members in Nottingham set up a Socialist Women's Committee (SW), followed in the summer of 1970 by a group in London, with branches thereafter extending to Oxford, Leicester, Lancaster, Glasgow, Cardiff and Bristol. The organisation also set up a separate women's caucus to deal specifically with women's struggles.[62] The Socialist Women's Committee characterised itself as a 'Women's Liberation Group' and members worked alongside Women's Liberation groups in campaigns such as the London and Oxford Night Cleaners Campaigns and the Fakenham Women's Work-In of March, 1972. This socialist-feminist network enabled women like Hilary Wainwright to mediate autonomously between the IMG and the WLM. In the Oxford IMG she was 'immediately elevated to a kind of leadership position' and she enjoyed the company of 'interesting guys', leading theoreticians such as Tariq Ali, Robin Blackburn and Peter

Gowen.[63] Simultaneously, she played a central role setting up the Women's Action Group, which made links with women from Oxford's working-class housing estate Blackbird Leys. In contrast to Jacqueline, Hilary kept her distance from the organisation, her primary allegiance being to the politics and friendships she found in the WLM. This independence showed the more instrumental membership which it was possible for women to hold inside far-left organisations. It testified to the self-determination educated young women had become accustomed to exercising within late-sixties left spaces, and which they continued to practise as socialist feminists working to advance the movement in the following decade: 'I had a sort of semi-detached relationship to them [the IMG]. My, my base was really the women's movement and then I would sort of play a role in the IMG to try and convince them to be more involved in the women's movement or less instrumental towards the women's movement . . . It was an education, if you like, in a way for me.' Yet the ability to negotiate between the organisation and the movement in this way owed something to the IMG's sympathetic response to the new liberation politics. The organisation also showed early support for gay liberation, with members participating in GLF activities such as the LSE think-ins.[64]

However, 'class solidarity' rather than 'sex solidarity' remained at the forefront of the IMG's approach towards women's oppression.[65] In June, 1971 the Nottingham Socialist Woman Group came into hostile conflict with the majority tendency leadership when the latter took over the *Socialist Woman* journal in an effort to sever the women's links with the WLM and to bring the group in line with its turn towards 'the industrial front'. In response, members of the original editorial board printed a letter in *Socialist Woman* denying any link between the new journal of March, 1971, produced in London using the SW name, and the original committee members.[66] In May, members of the Nottingham SW Committee – Antonia Gorton, Anne Black, Jo O'Brien and Mary Donnelly – found themselves accused of 'direct defiance' against the IMG National Committee and women's caucus meetings; having taken no action to publicly dissociate themselves from the view expressed in the insert, they had shown 'disloyalty to the IMG' and 'utter contempt for the right of the leading bodies of the IMG to direct the work of its members'. After an internal commission was set up to investigate the allegations, the four members were ordered to cease all women's work. In an appeal to the National Committee the women argued that, after a decision taken in their absence, they had already resigned from the Nottingham Women's Liberation Group and had not since then spoken to members in it. They defended their right to continue working in the Nottingham Women's Action Co-ordinating Committee, since it was 'an independent organisation building actions on one of the four main demands of the WLM', publicly supported by the IMG. They also expressed understanding that the IMG's position towards the WLM was that the movement had to be brought to an industrial orientation by giving priority to those demands which the majority believed related to most working women. The women accused the majority leadership, in barring them from internal women's discussions and the Nottingham SW Group, of showing 'an attitude of indifference, tokenism, and tail-endism towards the WLM'; of trying 'to separate' them from their 'sisters' who were 'striving for their liberation'; and of creating 'a factional, witch-hunting atmosphere' in its efforts to man-oeuvre against them to solve its own political issues. They resolutely refused to be 'ghettoised' and to leave the Fourth International, as Nottingham National Committee member B. Simister was urging them to do.[67]

The dispute between the Nottingham SW members and the majority leadership represented fractional divisions Trotskyist women had occasion-ally to confront in the face of outright chauvinism and hostile manoeuvr-ing on the part of the male leadership. It illuminates the political culture informing Jacqueline Thompson's self-understanding of the 'good activ-ist'. She performed a masculine revolutionary model that encompassed suspicion towards the WLM as a competing source of political author-ity. It included an implicit understanding that 'personal' and sexual issues represented distractions from class struggles. After the miners' strike of 1972 the organisation turned towards an overt workerist line. The John Ross tendency that succeeded Pat Jordan and Tariq Ali ini-tiated a sustained campaign to improve the IMG's standing amongst manual workers, calling for a general strike and removing a leadership associated with the VSC and a largely student membership.[68] Although embedded within this revolutionary culture, Jacqueline remained unable to deny her emotional responses towards debates and ideas she heard filtering through from the WLM; unconsciously, her conduct as a woman apart from her androgynous militant self began to be shaped by them:

> I didn't wear make-up because men should take you as you are. I was very anti being a sex object. That was the women's movement . . . I used to love high heels and things but that was a part of me that was quite contradictory . . . It is difficult really. I was difficult. I wanted to be equal in a man's world and I felt I was, but I was chatted up quite a lot because I was attractive and that annoyed me intensely.[69]

Jacqueline testified to the contradictions the movement created for her as a committed revolutionary. Her role in the organisation reflected opportunities the IMG created for women to enact self-assertive images of sociability in a way that had yet to translate fully into early 1970s society. Women's Liberation alerted these women to the reality of the social restrictions constraining them, and in so doing signalled the impossibility of demarcating political and private life. The problem for Jacqueline was how to negotiate these conflicting pictures to compose herself as a political and female social subject. She attempted to reconcile the competing identities of revolutionary and woman by fantasising herself as revolutionary mother: 'There didn't seem to be any difference between being a mum and being a revolutionary, because of course we had read so much about the African movements and so many international movements where women were fighting and having babies.' The vision represented an attempt to bridge an activist landscape that demanded attention to the present and a conservative society that continued to elevate motherhood as the pinnacle of female achievement; denying potential conflict between the two identities, she achieved psychic composure as a revolutionary woman acknowledging the role society and physiology shaped for her future.

Activist as mother

Where activism coincided with motherhood, female life often became problematic. The multiple pressures accompanying each role shaped political subjectivity quite differently than for male comrades. Di Parkin is one of few women to have written on the experience of far-left activism and motherhood. In 1972–73 she began a correspondence with her close friend and IS comrade, Annie Howells, after leaving Canterbury for Oxford. The women had been founding members of the Canterbury IS branch. As young mothers and activists they had cemented their friendship through the shared thrill of activity; getting up at the crack of dawn to sell *Socialist Worker*, printing leaflets on the hand-cranked duplicator bought from a vicar and stored in Di's basement and picketing Dover docks and power stations during the 1972 miners' strike. The letters began as a way of securing the comfort and understanding that would normally have come from a face-to-face conversation, when moments of everyday domestic chaos threatened to overwhelm either one. Over time, they became akin to a series of diary entries. The women confided the daily minutiae of their lives; battles with poverty, the difficulties of single parenthood and the challenges of living as women engaged in the present, working to change tomorrow. In a milieu which allowed little time or space for personal reflection, the intimate letters gave them momentary release from the demands that befell them as activists and mothers and testified to a friendship rooted in their shared identities as revolutionaries, mothers and women. Their lives integrated all these elements to foster a collective way of being that they felt only each other could understand.

Di's letters to Annie illustrate the untidy daily business of integrating the responsibilities of branch life alongside the practicalities of mother-hood. Each intruded rudely on the other, making it impossible for the women to approach domestic dramas of nappy rash and lost bubble bath with the same neat efficiency that Joan Smith applied to the catering challenges of the Glasgow IS. Details of political activity and opinions on current issues were interspersed with tales about the children's development and domestic tasks made harder by surviving on little money. They also illustrate the psychic division the polarising identities could have for female activists. Di felt complete only when immersed in activism. Motherhood threatened to impinge upon her far-left iden-tity and to fracture her sense of self. In December, 1971, following the birth of her second child, Rosa (named after Rosa Luxemburg), she joked to Annie that 'I did a quick check over myself like they feel people for broken bones after accidents. Finding myself able to think about Gramsci and Trotskyist Tendency and the nature of scientific objectivity, I concluded that I still existed.'[70]

Women's struggles to fit organisational life alongside motherhood aroused turbulent, uncomfortable emotions that pervaded their experi-ences of these competing worlds. The weight of guilt was often the most difficult to bear; its powerful, disruptive impact on their emotional lives was evident in its longevity. Women's stories of revolutionary motherhood were sometimes difficult to tell. The distance of time allowed possibilities for regret and shame as well as catharsis and self-healing, and interviewees could be harshly critical of their younger selves. Di shamefully remembered how, in 1972, she left Rosa in her carry cot, parked around the corner from a miner's picket where she was busy fighting with police. Sometimes desperate to immerse herself in activity, she had resented her children as 'my jailers', though she 'knew it was not their fault'.[71] IS member and single mother Prue Chamberlayne explained the insufficient space motherhood had allowed for revolutionary life. The adrenalin which activism aroused made it easy to lose sight of her responsibilities towards her son: 'I would be eking my time out and not going at the appointed time, and I imagine I would find myself so engrossed in what I was doing and think it was so important.' She could only ever inhabit either realm at any one time. Like John Cowley, she wore 'two heads' so that 'the minute I was back home I would be immediately back in that sphere [of motherhood]'.[72]

The women's guilt overrode boundaries they tried to maintain between domestic and revolutionary life. Di recalled: 'just as the day light [*sic*] hours were drilled with paper-sales, with writing, duplicating, and giving out leaflets, they too were drilled with guilt'.[73] Sheila Hemingway felt guilty 'because I used to get baby-sitters in more than I should have'.[74] By the mid-1970s, her self-blossoming inside IS had seen her becoming more self-assertive in her marriage, and when the couple separated the organisation filled the gulf. She reflected with some regret:

> Oh it was my life. I did reflect, especially where the children were con-cerned, and as the children got older and more independent, I got more independent, and I suppose I did have guilty feelings. Well it is like any-thing else, you want to do something with grown-ups because you're lonely and as soon ... I think in a lot of ways I missed out on a lot of things being a member of 'party. I think I missed out on ordinary life. We didn't have a close family.

The contradictions between the masculine far-left culture and inner female life impinged upon the revolutionary mother perhaps more intru-sively than any other female member. Di's letters to Annie show how motherhood opened up an emotional depth of existence that disrupted her early masculine self. Suffusing the correspondence is an implicit understanding of the psychological transformations each woman had undergone since becoming a mother. In 1972 Di told Annie: 'You and I are the only people we meet in the hours of children time who con-firm, who we really are – that we are not party to the small chaos and impossible tension of the domestic hysteria of the under 3-year olds. They are the forces of the wild and irrational, while we are part of the force of revolution.'[75]

The women's letters are striking for the feminist terms they employed, far removed from the class discourse typical of far-left circles, including the IS women's group Di joined. Di's letters echoed the feminist belief in female nurture and self-love that Margaretta Jolly has argued were an important constituent of feminist relationships and values.[76] She extended her maternal role to encompass care for her friend's welfare, her gradual acceptance of motherhood tempering the restless energy she had previously exhibited as an activist: 'You get too agitated my duck and are too thorough and committed. Being a mother and all, one has to cool it quite a lot ... be more of a dilettante (what heresy!).'[77] Di propounded feminist virtues of self-love, telling Annie, 'You are a person of magic and are not to suppress yourself'. The feminist language fram-ing the women's friendship suggests that, outside the immediate web of the WLM, the new feminist code of ethics offered new possibilities for heterosexual far-left women to conceive of female love in terms of relational selfhood. Yet it represented something of a contradiction, departing from Di's sense of herself as a political agent, far removed from the consciousness-raising practice of the small Women's Liberation group. In so far as this self was relational, it involved a feeling of connection with working-class, invariably male militants and their struggles with employers, union bureaucracy and the state. But her sense of femaleness and the inner life she explored in the letters were rooted within a rich emotional world of female friendships that drew upon feminist ethical discourse. The women's friendship confirmed the complex demarcations far-left women negotiated as social, emotional and far-left subjects.

The Trotskyist personal and political

Intimate relationships, particularly, allow the historian to map the far-left world of personal and political. Conducted in and around the organisations, these performed specific social, political and psychic functions. Di and Annie illustrated the emotional support friendships provided revolutionary mothers. In public sites of activity, competitive comradely bonds provided standards for measuring the revolutionary self. Yet such relations could also induce insecurity in activists. In the Greenford engineering factory John Rose's friendships tied into a social life shaped by the business of organising, hosting parties and educational evenings for workers whom it was his task to recruit. But he felt uneasy in their company, preferring to 'sneak back to north London where I used to live and see my old friends'.[78] In Newcastle David Carter's friendships with IMG men informed a subversive revolutionary image of the 'red mole'. In a 'high octane life' mediated through the branch and household, bonds of friendship were rooted in a common hinterland of Trotskyist agitation and factional debate, reinforcing a public school experience that had denied the personal: 'People were quite theoretical, very intense, a bit too intense ... We were men who were Trotskyists ... The idea that we would all open up and talk to each other about each other's personal hang-ups, that just didn't happen.'[79] IS national committee member John Palmer spoke of close male comrades 'with whom I discussed the politics intensely, and the personal feelings came through, but I never sat down with any of them and said I think this is having an effect on me'.[80] The organisations' distance from the new subjective politics saw far-left men struggling to make emotional sense of the messy world of personal life. This was particularly the case for older activists like John who had joined the organisations in the early 1960s. He reflected on comrades' hidden emotions when marriages and relationships broke up: 'Men didn't have the language to talk. I mean you would get to know about it. It wasn't a secret, but there wasn't a language for it.' However, David Widgery showed that male silences were not exclusive to the older far-left generation. He remembered the personal ignorance IS men held towards each other during this period. Even though he had shared adjacent bedrooms to comrades through intense emotional experiences, he never once saw them cry.[81]

The personal did, however, feature in sexual and romantic relationships in the close political world male and female comrades shared. But whereas the organisation presented guidelines for activity and political conduct, personal and emotional life was far less ordered. In an ever-changing political climate male activists like David Carter were able to evade the uncomfortable language of feeling by extending the rules of political engagement to personal relationships. In Newcastle, David extended his peripatetic lifestyle into a secret series of relations with women from his branch. Just as Jacqueline Thompson justified her distance from the women's movement by subscribing to the role of the 'good activist', David evoked the same image to evade complications and tensions surrounding his relationships:

> I knew I wasn't being totally honest but part of being a revolutionary is by definition not being totally honest. It is a subversive activity. You don't reveal everything. That is part of revolutionary politics. Firstly, I didn't see personal relationships as being that important and, secondly, subverting what I felt and keeping my relationships hidden from other people that wasn't very important because revolutionaries did that.[82]

Within this moral framework his own personal conflicts formed an extension of the national power struggles he saw played out at conferences and national meetings where personal attacks were not uncommon.

David's behaviour reflected a continuation of the transitory sexual patterns around the VSC and in the 'non-aligned' milieu. Sex became another way in which personal and political life fused together, dissolving boundaries between public and private life and adding further meaning to activists' sense of socialist selfhood. Women and men who spent all day in the company of comrades, sharing the heightened emotions of struggles, sometimes found political passions spilling over into their sexual lives. Dave Lyddon explained how 'this certain [sexual] fluidity' owed much to 'a very intense life. You are drawn to each other, as much as anything else because you share a similar world view.'[83] In this frenetic context sex could be a way for men and women to express the complex, intense emotions surrounding what felt like real revolutionary moments. These 'obvious one-nighters' could be a way 'to clear the air'. Whereas in 'non-aligned' circles non-monogamous relations could be a way of challenging the possessive individualism entrenched in capitalist society, in the IS and IMG they were an extension of the cultural patterns members had carried through from their student days. Sexual freedom formed a further expression of the social self-determination, visible in the underground and student movement, and facilitated by the greater availability of contraceptives, notably the pill, and the increasing publicisation of sexuality. Roland Muldoon highlighted the importance of the emancipating climate shaping his and others' sexual behaviour when he explained that sex 'was in the air. Everybody did it. It was liberation, everybody was free'.[84] Sex was there to be enjoyed because it could be. Faced with the decision to have sex or not to have sex, Roland questioned, why not?

The social and psychological empowerment of organisational life extended to sexual selfhood to enhance political subjectivity. Women also testified to such experiences, which denied the split some feminists expressed between their feelings as Marxist subjects and sexual objects in relation to men. Jacqueline Thompson explained; if a man on the Left came on to her, she responded as she wished, her revolutionary and sexual subjectivity mutual components of her agency:

> We saw the men in power in the organisation as political figures who were like Lenin and Trotsky. They were the substitutes for political gurus in a sense so we saw them as being political. The fact that they chatted you up didn't sort of seem . . . I don't know how much predatory behaviour there was because as women we saw ourselves also as being as sexual.[85]

Women and men testified to the ways in which romantic relationships acquired an explicitly political edge as comradely, loving and sexual relations fused together to shape new meanings around love and desire. The idea of personal life as a deviation from politics was not exclusive to IMG men. Julia Fairchild explained how, within a personal relationship between two members, 'the parameters were not around relationships, the parameters were around politics', so that love remained subjugated to members' responsibilities to the organisation.[86] The emotions accompanying love were not necessarily absent for activists but, rather, reframed around revolutionary life. Conversely, the discipline that activists showed towards organising sometimes helped to sustain partnerships during turbulent periods. National IS committee member

Richard Kuper reflected upon 'living with someone who was engaged in the struggle and we were just always involved, and I think we just carried on, and if it ever caused any difficulties I think we would regard that as a lack of energy and as a weakness'.[87]

Loving, committed relationships could play an important role in cementing political and emotional union between activist couples. Carole Reagan described herself and her husband, Bernard Reagan, 'growing up' together in left politics, a process that continued when, in 1973, they both took the decision to leave the IS and join the IMG.[88] Dave Lyddon highlighted the importance of an intense relationship with a female comrade in transforming him into an IS politico: 'Obviously if you have a very intense relationship that counts for a lot . . . we had a shared world view and it is one which we felt . . . it is hard to explain how uplifting it can be. It sounds almost . . . you have got a way of understanding of the world.'[89] At a time when oppressed peoples were finding a political voice, intimate mutual discovery between two activists could imbue love with tremendous hope and purpose.

Intimate relationships formed within far-left organisations were, though, a double-edged sword. When they broke down, the organisation was unable to supplant the emotional props they had fulfilled. Anna Paczuska explained the political and emotional dislocation she felt when her marriage to a leading IS member ended: 'I felt displaced, terribly, terribly displaced. I didn't feel the party was a substitute or a comfort in any way. In fact I felt very exposed by being a single person in the organisation without anyone supporting me . . . I think I felt phone calls from male comrades, who saw this as an opportunity to maybe get a look in, rather devastating and distressing.'[90] Her comments illuminate the sort of behaviour that informed the leadership's reluctance to take seriously the issue of women's oppression. As long as personal life remained a deviation from the class struggle, Trotskyist culture did little to challenge the sexually exploitative attitudes and behaviour some older members, especially, continued to display towards their wives at home or towards younger female members.

The revered status of leading men gave them a certain social and sexual cachet they sometimes took advantage of. The heavy drinking culture that accompanied meetings, educational weekends and the annual IS conference at Skegness miners' camp informed the social and sexual conduct of older men unaccustomed to the self-assertion of young female members. John Palmer suggested how, caught between conflicting continuities and change, older men were also consciously pushing the boundaries of permissible social freedom away from their family background and education. In the late sixties the influx of IS students signalled changing sexual and moral norms, presenting new possibilities for self-fulfilment for the older generation:

> Those sixties young women had no precedent . . . so stunningly beautiful and self-confident . . . the fact that they were socially self-confident was a very appealing thing . . . I'm not proud of everything that happened. There was a degree in common with a lot of men, one tended to take advantage. There was perhaps a degree of superficiality I would definitely say, and being slightly prominent in the organisation gave one a certain . . . I don't know, how d'you say? I think, you know, looking back I would say I wouldn't be proud of that.[91]

His narrative points to the complex emotional histories that informed men and women's conduct during this period of self-experimentation and change. We see the mixture of envy and desire with which he traversed shifting models to make sense of himself as a sexual subject in relation to younger members: 'We were all children of our period. I was quite attracted to it [the social self-assertion] and slightly envious certainly in the late adolescent years of those comrades who were much less oppressed, and you have got to think I was educated by the Jesuits and at the age of eighteen, I mean sexual experience came very much later at twenty-one.'

Interviewees' attempts to come to terms with uncomfortable stories from their pasts expressed the undisclosed depths of private emotional life that existed for many activists. At a time when political and personal life had begun, often unintentionally, to co-exist more closely and far-left women were finding comfort in close female friendships, the de facto segregation that had traditionally existed between these areas nevertheless continued. Organisational subjectivity involved conflicting feelings that remained difficult to manage. Just as motherhood unleashed its own set of responsibilities and divided loyalties, fatherhood created pressures for Trotskyist men to straddle the divide between the organisation and the home. Several admitted that the organisation often won out, sometimes with damaging repercussions for marriages and loving relationships. We saw earlier how Yorkshire miners presented John Charlton with an unflattering image of himself as a husband. Alan Watts regretted missing the signs of his wife's post-natal distress: 'I was out going to meetings all the time and my wife was at home looking after the kids, and I guess I was out all the time. She had a hard time after my son was born . . . I was a little boy, looking back now. I know I was thirty but I don't think I had a clue what was going on'.[92]

The challenge of how to manage responsibilities in the organisation and at home became more acute when politics threatened to endanger the latter. In February, 1972, John Palmer was active in the Anti-Internment League and declaring support for the IRA, when the Aldershot bombing at the headquarters of the British Army's 16th Parachute Regiment saw him become the target of police searches. The experience was particularly disturbing because the police searched his baby's cot with the child still in it. His recollection of the event sparked a self-criticism about his frequent absence as a husband and father: 'I think the family suffered. I didn't give the time I would have given otherwise, small things that are often important like being away at weekends at conferences and so forth, which my first wife would tell you about. You know there were three in the marriage and it was rather crowded, except that the third person was an organisation.'[93]

In the early 1970s IS women made demands for the organisation to address the problem of wives left at home minding the children. Yet, even by the second half of the decade the rota system of work sharing that the North London district had set up was by no means nationally operational and arrangements for child-minding were invariably left up to individuals to manage.[94] It was sometimes marginally easier for activist couples to balance home and organisational life because each understood the pressures the other faced. Ian Birchall and his wife extended their organising skills to childcare arrangements: 'We used to have on the wall of our kitchen a chart extending to six weeks ahead . . . if one or another of us was hooked up to do a meeting we filled in that day and we had to arrange a baby-sitter.'[95] Supportive of the women's movement and his wife's activism, Richard Kuper was also keen to take on childcare. He and his wife routinely took their children along to meetings, reflecting his commitment for the organisation to improve female participation.[96] IS baby-sitting rotas and the conference crèches that began gradually to emerge from the mid-1970s provided little to help members cope with the sheer pressure of demands which the organisation placed on their time. Remembering the 'nightmare' that activism created for his personal life after the birth of his children, Alan Watts spoke of the prevailing ethos that discouraged men from voicing the pressures they felt: 'It's not a hospital, they said.'[97] Ian recalled: 'Just the sheer pressure of time; trying to do a full-time job, and raise a family, and be a professional revolutionary meant a lot of demands on your time and it did cause tensions in relationships. I would come home at one a.m. after speaking somewhere and have to prepare my teaching for the next day and get to bed at three to five a.m. quite often.'[98] Such pressures were typically not felt by IMG activists until the end of the decade, when only then did many begin to have children. By then, the waning of the Left saw many winding down their activities as they turned their attention to new activities around the Labour Party or invested energies in jobs and relationships outside politics.

In the early 1970s, however, the reticence with which many IS and IMG men responded to the new politics rested upon an undercurrent of uncertainty and anxiety about how to reconcile the competing roles they faced as political and private beings. Coming to political and emotional maturity within the organisation, by the early to mid-1970s their immersion in class struggles had imprinted a masculinity that reinforced the early social practices of home and school subordinating the personal. Within this landscape, learning how to accept challenges to long-held social and cultural patterns entailed a longer, gradual psychic process that conflicted with the organisational shifts that were beginning to occur in response to the economic downturn of the late 1970s.

Notes

1 Alan Johnson, '"Beyond the Smallness of Self": Oral History and British Trotskyism', *Oral History*, 24, Spring, 1996, pp. 39–48.
2 I. Birchall, *Tony Cliff: A Marxist for His Time* (London: Bookmarks, 2011), p. 301.
3 Interview with John Rose.
4 Interview with Steve Jefferys.
5 Interview with Laurie Flynn.
6 Interview with Phil Hearse.
7 Interview with David Carter.
8 Interview with Wenda Clenaghen.
9 C. Harman, *The Fire Last Time: 1968 and after* (2nd edn, London: Bookmarks, 1998), p. 223.
10 Interview with Dave Lyddon.
11 Interview with Mike McGrath.
12 Tebbutt, *Being Boys*, p. 233.
13 Interview with Mike McGrath.
14 Interview with Sandy Irving.
15 Interview with Sabby Sagall, London, 12 March, 2009.
16 Interview with John Charlton.
17 Interview with Sandy Irving.
18 S. Rowbotham, 'Travellers in a Strange Country: Responses of Working-Class Students to the University Extension Movement – 1873–1910', *History Workshop Journal*, 12, Autumn (1981), p. 66.
19 Interview with Sabby Sagall.
20 Interview with John Charlton.
21 I. H. Birchall, 'Building "The Smallest Mass Party in the World": Socialist Workers Party 1951–1979', p. 8 [consulted at www.marxists.org/history/

etol/revhist.otherdox/smp/smp2.html (11 March, 2008)]; Circular letter from D. Hallas, IS National Secretary to IS members, 14 May, 1971, MRC, Papers of the International Socialists: internal documents, MSS. 128/158.

22 Interview with John Rose.

23 Interview with Nigel Coward.

24 Interview with John Charlton.

25 Interview with Nigel Coward.

26 Beckett, *When the Lights Went Out*, p. 471; paper detailing the October 1971 pay agreement at Cowley's Morris factory, MRC, Papers of Alan Thornett, MSS.391/3/28.

27 Interview with Dave Lyddon.

28 R. Linhart, *The Assembly Line* (translated by Margaret Crosland, London: Calder, 1978), p. 49.

29 Interview with Dave Lyddon; interview with Steve Jefferys.

30 T. A. Bull, 'The White Collar Worker and Trade Union Consciousness', p. 5; 'National IS Committee Minutes', 23 May, 1970, p. 1. Both MRC, Papers of the International Socialists: internal documents, MSS. 128/158.

31 Interview with Alan Watts.

32 Interview with Roger Cox.

33 Interview with Alan Watts.

34 Interview with Roger Cox.

35 IS Industrial Conference Paper, Birmingham, 1970, MRC, Papers of the International Socialists: internal documents, MSS. 128/158; 'Editorial [Industrial Relations Bill], *International Socialism*, No. 46, February/March, 1971, p. 1.

36 Interview with Roger Cox.

37 Interview with Bob Light.

38 F. Lindop, 'Unofficial Militancy in the Royal Group of Docks, 1945–67', *Oral History*, 11:2 (1983), pp. 21–33.

39 Interview with Bronwen Davis.

40 Interview with Gilda Peterson.

41 Interview with Sheila Hemingway.

42 P. Summerfield, *Reconstructing Women's Wartime Lives: Discourse and Subjectivity in Oral Histories of the Second World War* (Manchester: Manchester University Press, 1998), p. 30.

43 Letter from Di Parkin to Annie Hewitt, n.d., 1974, DPA.

44 Booklet on the IS in Scotland, No. 4, March, 1970, p. 9, MRC, Papers of the International Socialists: internal documents, MSS. 128/158.

45 Interview with Joan Smith.

46 Notice about the formation of the North London IS Women's Group by Margaret Renn, Hazel French and Anna Paczuska in MRC, Papers of Richard Hyman: International Socialists, MRC, MSS. 84, Box 1; interview with Anna Paczuska.

47 A. Paczuska, 'Comment', IS Women's Newsletter, No. 3, April 1971, MRC, Papers of Richard Hyman: International Socialists, MSS. 84, Box 1.

48 A. Paczuska, 'Comment', IS Women's Newsletter, No. 3, April, 1971, p. 1; A. Paczuska, 'IS Women's Groups', IS Women's Newsletter, No. 2, December, 1970, pp. 1–2; Gill Simms (Harrow IS), 'Comments on the discussion of women at the annual conference'; K. Ennis (Southampton IS), 'Women's Liberation and the Revolutionary Party', IS Women's Newsletter, No. 3, April, 1971, p. 6. All items MRC, Papers of Richard Hyman: International Socialists, MSS. 84, Box 1.
49 Interview with John Charlton and Sandy Irving, Newcastle-upon-Tyne, 2 June, 2009.
50 Interview with Anna Paczuska.
51 Interview with Dave Lyddon.
52 Interview with Sabby Sagall.
53 Simms, 'Comments on the discussion on women at the annual conference'.
54 Interview with Di Parkin.
55 Interview with Sheila Hemingway.
56 Interview with Gilda Peterson.
57 Rowbotham, *The Past is Before Us*, pp. 68–9.
58 Interview with Jacqueline Thompson, 10 February, 2009.
59 *International*, Vol. 1, No. 6, September/October, 1971, p. 6.
60 *The Times*, 31 January, 1972, pp. 1–2.
61 *Socialist Woman*, Vol. 1, No. 2, March/April 1969, pp. 1–8.
62 A. Black, 'Why a Socialist Women's Committee?', *Socialist Woman*, Vol. 1, No. 2, March/April, 1969, p. 1; *Socialist Woman*, Vol. 3, No. 4, July/August, 1971, p. 14.
63 Interview with Hilary Wainwright.
64 Robinson, *Gay Men and the Left*, p. 98.
65 'Don't Call US Birds!', *International*, 1968, p. 7.
66 Letter from C. Singh to J. King, Lancaster, 9 June, 1971; Minority Report from the Commission Set Up to Investigate the Socialist Woman Affair, 18 June, 1971, Appendix 2, pp. 2–3. Both items MRC, Socialist Woman Papers, MSS. 128/95.
67 Appeal to the National Committee from the Nottingham Tendency Members, 3 January, 1972, pp. 1–6, MRC, Socialist Woman Papers, MSS. 128/95.
68 Callaghan, *British Trotskyism*, p. 131.
69 Interview with Jacqueline Thompson.
70 Letter from Di Parkin to Annie Howells, Oxford, n.d., Spring, 1973, DPA.
71 Interview with Di Parkin.
72 Interview with Prue Chamberlayne.
73 P. Chamberlayne and D. Parkin, 'Women, Sex and Revolutionary Politics', European Social Science History Conference, International Institute of Social History, Amsterdam, March, 2006, p. 11.
74 Interview with Sheila Hemingway.
75 Letter from Di Parkin to Annie Howells, Canterbury, 1972, in DPA.
76 M. Jolly, *In Love and Struggle: Letters in Contemporary Feminism* (New York: Columbia University Press, 2010), p. 3.

77 Letter from Di Parkin to Annie Howells, Oxford, 14 March, 1974, in DPA.
78 Interview with John Rose.
79 Interview with David Carter.
80 Interview with John Palmer, London, 22 June, 2009.
81 Interview between Ronald Fraser and respondent C896/18, p. 21, Ronald Fraser Interviews: 1968 A Student Generation in Revolt, British Library Sound Archive.
82 Interview with David Carter.
83 Interview with Dave Lyddon.
84 Interview with Roland and Claire Muldoon, London, 10 December, 2009.
85 Interview with Jacqueline Thompson.
86 Interview with Julia Fairchild, London, 11 August, 2009.
87 Interview with Richard Kuper.
88 Interview with Carole Reagan, London, 20 August, 2009.
89 Interview with Dave Lyddon.
90 Interview with Anna Pacuska.
91 Interview with John Palmer.
92 Interview with Alan Watts.
93 Interview with John Palmer.
94 *Spare Rib*, January, 66 (1978), p. 8.
95 Interview with Ian Birchall.
96 Interview with Richard Kuper.
97 Interview with Alan Watts.
98 Interview with Ian Birchall.

Conclusion

Young Lives on the Left has explored the memories and subjectivities of young men and women who joined the two main far-left organisations and the 'non-aligned' left milieu that grew out of the VSC from 1968 to 1969. The stories of activist life do not, of course, end at the point at which we left them in the closing chapter. Stories of self-realignment between political, social and psychic life continued to permeate the second half of the seventies, before Thatcherite retrenchment curtailed the extra-parliamentary space necessary for grass-roots change. Representations of seventies activism have traditionally painted a darker and more fractious picture in contrast to the utopianism of the preceding decade. This is epitomised by accounts of Women's Liberation that place emphasis on internal divisions, with the ascendancy of separatist revolutionary feminists and the movement's demise after the final national conference of 1978.[1] Certainly, the second half of the decade created challenging economic and political conditions for activists to operate in. In 1975–76 the impact of world recession and the doubling of unemployment deflated the militant confidence of trade union leaders that had characterised national strikes between 1972 and 1974.[2] Workers' reluctance to resist Labour's wage controls, and the general move to the Right, prompted internal shifts within the IS and IMG that brought a series of political realignments, personal ruptures and renewal, raising new questions for members about what it meant to be a revolutionary.

In IS, internal changes designed to respond to the declining impetus of rank-and-file groups, and the downturn in the organisation's fortunes, brought personal as well as political turmoil for the men and women in this book. From 1974 to 1975 the launch of the IS Opposition signalled the beginning of the end for a number of interviewees; this internal body of members came together in 1975 under a platform championing internal democracy, the independence of the rank-and-file movement and a more coherent approach to the Labour government.[3]

In the IMG some members followed the earlier forays of IS activists by making their own industrial turn, through entry into factories to take up work on assembly lines. From 1977, belief that the time had come for the revolutionary Left to join forces also saw attempts by the organisation to field Socialist Unity candidates in by-elections, supported in 1978 by the revolutionary grouping Big Flame.[4] In 1982 this new political direction would lead IMG members back to the organisation's roots inside the Labour Party.

Although activists were confronted with bleak prospects for revolutionary upsurge, the late 1970s did not represent an end-point in their trajectories; nor were these years of individual or collective despair. The changing political climate instead opened up new spaces in which activists could realign or shape new political and personal selves. In the short term, the intense pace of organisational life continued unabated, with renewed emphasis on trade union struggles concentrated inside the factory, school or college in which members worked. These were also the years of renewed campaigns; for the IS/SWP (Socialist Workers Party), the Right to Work campaign and the Anti-Nazi League; for the IMG, the Socialist Unity electoral challenge. For many women the arrival of motherhood brought renewed perspective, and commitment to the women's movement through activism in the NAC, from 1977 in the Reclaim the Night campaign and, for IS women, in *Women's Voice*, the organisation's female journal. However, the climax of bitter internal disputes also saw some men and women deciding to break from the organisations that had absorbed and shaped them from adolescence. The decision to leave was often considered incredulously by those who remained; in the IS, members referred to the process, in semi-religious terms, as 'going into the wilderness'.[5] Casting off the organisational identity and the familial network that accompanied it was likened to purgatory. The experience brought an uncomfortable consciousness of the ties between identity and politics as former members took stock of life and self outside the organisation. In some cases the ruptures brought added grief when the severing of formal revolutionary ties was accompanied by ruptures in friendships and long-term loving relationships. Anna Paczuska described her decision to leave IS as a 'double divorce', from comrades within the organisation as well as from her husband: 'As soon as people found out that you were no longer in the party they stopped being your mate.'[6] Yet Richard Kuper was relieved to discover that leaving 'wasn't the wilderness, because I met so many people on an everyday basis with whom I talked politics, just not organisationally focused politics.'[7] Roger Cox, who remained in the SWP, remembered how the slowing pace of activist life opened up new opportunities to pursue neglected leisure activities such as cycling, even decorating, as well as allowing more time for his wife and children.[8]

Narratives of activist life in the Trotskyist organisations in the late 1970s provide rich oral sources for a follow-up study to shed new light on this transitional political period. Testament to the commitment and affective ties interviewees retained to the Left and to a network of former comrades, the picture defies the pessimistic tenets that have defined previous accounts of this period.[9] Andy Beckett has reminded us that, far from being the 'hangover after the sixties', the seventies represented a decade 'when the great sixties party actually got started'.[10] Whilst it may be rather far-fetched to apply his interpretation to the latter end of the decade, he certainly highlights the potential for understanding how far-left men and women subjectively responded to the political and personal challenges the New Right presented in the early 1980s, what have traditionally been depicted as dismal days for the Left.

For 'non-aligned' activists too, this book has presented a limited picture. In many respects the seventies represented the high point of the libertarian milieu as far as their political evolution and membership growth was concerned. *Young Lives on the Left* has focused attention on the transitional experiences of a small cohort of men and women attempting to live out the new politics. These were the young activists who had been drawn into this world through the VSC network. The book has not attempted to address the experiences of activists, for example, who joined libertarian organisations like Big Flame. Further research is needed to more fully understand the political and private stories of 'non-aligned' activism as it developed over the course of the 1970s and 1980s; men's and women's political experiences and relations in local community campaigns; Women's Liberation childcare projects, tenants' disputes, trade union and council struggles and private relations inside collective households.

Efforts to understand the impact of Women's Liberation as a new female political authority call for historians to read male and female experiences of public activism and private life against each other. Chapter 5 revealed the crisis in masculine left identity that some 'non-aligned' men experienced in the early 1970s. Their testimonies suggest the potential of the anti-sexist men's movement as a historical source to complement studies of the WLM and its impact upon female political and affective life. By 1973, several men in that chapter were participating in men's consciousness-raising groups as part of their commitment to living out the new politics. They were members of a male network encompassing London, Brighton, Birmingham, Leeds and Manchester. This new movement sought to reconstruct a white, masculine politics of gender rooted in softer feelings and a capacity for empathy, honesty and compassion. In the midst of wider societal changes concerning the roles of women and men and the shape of the family, pro-feminist men confronted personal dilemmas of male identity as biological, single and surrogate fathers, as workers and as sexualised beings which they saw as having wider social purchase beyond the immediacy of the activist milieu. The story of the men's movement offers to bring the gendered study of 'non-aligned' selfhood full circle. Considered alongside recent perspectives on the WLM, it suggests possibilities for understanding the impact of the new politics on gendered subjectivity, political and social roles and hetero- and homo- social and sexual relationships in the 1970s and 1980s.

This book set out to provide an integrated account of the shaping of radical left cultures and activist selves that took place during the post-war years of British society, between roughly 1945 and 1975. Ultimately, it has perhaps told a story of England's private 1968. To conclude, this final section will address some of the main themes that emerge from the stories told; questions about social and cultural changes occurring both inside the activist terrain and in wider post-war English society. It is to the relationship between the private stories of 1968 and these two social worlds that we finally turn.

First, however, I wish to address the inevitable disappointments that will accompany the hopes and expectations that some interviewees may well have attached to this study. Throughout my research I have been aware of the responsibility I have felt towards interviewees who have entrusted private, sometimes intimate and previously hidden memories, feelings and reflections. I have often wrestled with anxiety and guilt about how to respect the form with which they told their stories without also eschewing my instincts as a historian to search for deeper meaning in gaps, silences and subterranean layers. This has been my own struggle with representation, politics, desire and selfhood. A letter one interviewee wrote to me after the interview left me feeling decidedly uneasy. He was puzzled by my interest in his social life and felt experience inside the far Left, and wondered why I did not seem to be so concerned with the political campaigns themselves. His comments told much about the way in which he had invested himself in IS as a young man – 'the aspect of social cement was less than the importance of implementing the next immediate decisions (this sale/that contact/the other demo . . . etc)'.[11] They also conveyed much about his *expectations of memory*', tied up with his political ideas about what should and should not be remembered or represented in historical accounts of six-ties activism.[12] During the interview he showed me a letter he had written to *Socialist Worker*, the SWP journal, in February, 2008, in which he had praised an article by a former comrade who had criticised the cultural misrepresentations of 1968 as 'a year of sex, drugs, and rock n' roll – and "student riots"'.[13] In this letter he expressed as 'sick-ening' the 'flower power' images of hedonism the media continued to perpetuate as a dominant narrative of the period, and offered the same political narrative he sought to portray in the interview, emphasising his activism in the London West India docks during the period of the Devlin Report.[14] He was one of four other respondents (all former IS and IMG members) who had initiated contact with me in response to notices I had placed in various left journals seeking potential inter-viewees. Clearly, he had sought to use the interview as an opportunity to offer a narrative of England's 1968 that would privilege the world of industrial left politics he and others felt had been written out of the histories. His agenda reflected Stuart J. Hilwig's arguments about the way in which the methods of oral history prompt interviewees not only to draw from their personal and collective memories but also to his-toricise the events, in the knowledge that the interviewer will record their testimony for historical posterity in a printed text.[15] He was one of several IS and IMG interviewees who communicated expectations that my historical account should accord with their remembered frame of class-based, industrial struggles. For these men and women the pol-itics of youth had carried on into the present to shape a 'politics of memory' around England's own relationship to 1968.[16]

Interviewees' doubts about the personal focus of this study raised important ethical questions about how to historicise these remembered stories: who may claim to speak for a neglected culture and what are the implications for the ability of political and social actors to achieve psychic composure, to resolve 'the-past-in-the present'?[17] The issue of authorial power, representation and responsibility will be set aside for now, since it raises deeper questions about the relationship between oral historian, politics and interviewee that may be better addressed elsewhere. For example, to what extent should the politics of the oral historian mirror that of the interviewee? For some of my interviewees, my own politics was one of the first questions they asked of me. How far should the oral historian write him or herself into the final narrative to acknowledge the interactive process of shaping selves? However, the questions of psychic composure, memory and 'the past-in-the-present' relate directly to the theme of self-realignment that brings this study full circle.

Throughout the life journey, from post-war child to adult activist, what tied these stories together was the search for belonging. Young sixties activists sought to make sense of themselves in relation to families, localities and contradictions they discerned between processes of change and modernisation (the post-war vision of prosperity, full employment, welfarism and the opportunities of expanding secondary and higher education) and older lived patterns of class, social relations and mentalities that penetrated the radical landscape. If the memories that informed this account were less concerned with a search for national healing and national identity (witnessed in post-war European efforts to come to terms with a fascist or Nazi past), they nonetheless told personal stories of political, social and emotional struggle, of the search for new forms of selfhood. In the late 1960s young activists shaped new political, social and sexual selves as complex responses to the dominant political and social patterns marking post-1945 English life. But in doing so, they found themselves negotiating a multilayered political and social landscape. The effort to realise liberated subjectivities meant realigning older radical histories, ways of seeing and being, with the new political and cultural impulses being transmitted on a national as well as a global scale. For them as young adults and post-war subjects it also meant realigning entrenched social roles and gendered models, which called for psychological as well as political and social change. Against this background authentic modern selfhood became problematic. It entailed the dual challenge of mediating between mainstream and radical discourses and representations. As husbands and wives, lovers, friends and parents, workers and activists, young sixties activists struggled to verify the self-liberation they desired and strived for. Their struggles for authentic selfhood may be seen as constituting the more widespread private post-war self-exertions that scholars have drawn attention to, of English men and women negotiating the gulf between discourse, representation and daily felt experience.[18]

This brings us back to the relationship between cultural discourse and the self, and to Rowbotham's question about why men and women in her radical world sought each other in new ways. In their search for belonging and psychic ease, young activists strove to make sense of the past and the present. The conflict between the self and the social, the emotional and the political that echoed throughout these histories signalled repeated tension between continuities and fractures within both the mainstream and radical landscapes in which they were socialised and politicised from child to adult. Young English activists shared the collective international subjectivities discernible across the globe as they found affective solidarity with liberation struggles being played out from Alabama and Berkeley to Berlin, Paris and Haiphong. Yet, private daily struggles over subjectivity related to more specifically English attempts for these young men and women to situate themselves within a radical world that was itself caught between older political, cultural and social patterns, change and renewal. The book has highlighted the symbolic significance of the family punctuating interviewees' narratives. Recurring tropes of fathers and mothers spoke of the contradictory gendered order of post-war English culture and society, which also crossed over into the extra-parliamentary world. They signalled young men and women's efforts to immerse themselves inside older Trotskyist, labour and New Left communities that had been shaped by men from a pre-war realm of political and social experience. Entry into the early left milieux offered young activists a way of translating childhood and adolescent feeling and perception into concrete ways of seeing and understanding hypocrisy and contradiction. The Marxist framework they discovered enabled them to bridge the gulf that by the early 1960s had opened up between the Communist, New Left and Labour Left world of their parents. In this context the trope of the father symbolised a traditional masculine authority that continued to shape political subjectivity, social conduct and culture in the early left spaces. Just as Frank Mort has recently argued that it is possible to speak of a *longue durée* of social and sexual relations during Britain's post-war years, so it is equally possible to identify a *longue durée* of social and political relations on the Left, which held implications for the subjectivities young men and women shaped as activists in the early and mid-sixties.[19]

Familial tropes denoted the affective, alternative kinship ties underlying the early political communities. Their presence denied a complete generational rupture between post-war parents and children that made theirs a much more complex, contradictory relationship. Young sixties activists consciously searched for ways in which to reinvest the left sensibilities of fathers, mothers and other family members into a post-war world in which older patterns of class jarred against the social and cultural transformations accompanying Cold War politics. The paternal trope signified the attempts of the young left man striving to make a new political self in the image of the Communist father, the apprentice finding emotional and intellectual connections between IS speakers and his anonymous work-a-day, blue-collar world, and the inspiration New Left intellectuals Thompson, Samuel, Williams, Hall and others provided to student activists through face-to-face meetings and mentoring friendships. It also denoted the daughter's rupture from the middle-class Communist mother; assuming a masculine model of left subjectivity and conduct, the daughter sought to reclaim the mother's abandoned radical youth. Within radical journals and newspapers occupying activist basements and bedrooms, repeated articles about historical revolutionary models showed that young men and women were consciously drawing upon older radical models for inspiration. From their earliest days in the YS and CND, to the VSC and the activities surrounding it, they drew lessons from older Marxist figures. The subjective connections were also present in the utopian impulses between 1970s 'non-aligned' socialists and the networks of nineteenth-century New Life fellows; both lived out a quest to formulate more egalitarian human relationships and cultural patterns, and both strove to make personal connections by transcending class boundaries.[20]

In the activist landscape the emphasis on community, though not peculiar to England, drew upon New Left discourses that related directly to laments for a utopian working-class world of local kinship ties, now fragmented by new media technology and post-war re-housing schemes. Yet it was in the search for belonging, for connection between self and culture, that older left impulses recurred inside the network.[21] It can be seen in the veneration activists attached to worker-intellectuals they came across in mining and dockland communities as well as in the imaginary community CMPP members conjured up during their weekly activities and gatherings at Camden Town market and Parliament Hill Fields. Attempts to recreate an imaginary socialist image of the past-in-the-present found its strongest expression in the People's War activity CMPP held between 26 April and 1 May, 1971. Through a series of film-showings, stories and activities, members sought to involve the citizens of Camden in efforts to re-enact the wartime spirit of community and social belonging that was bound up in the post-war idealisation of wartime national cohesion.[22] In their eyes, the Blitz spirit offered a model for the social renewal they sought to inspire within their small collective and the wider Camden community, whereby 'the war in fact satisfied for many the need to be a wanted member of society, encouraged spontaneity, and gave fuller self-expression'.[23] The event is notable for what it suggests about the relationship between the activist communities and selves that emerged in post-war England. Where their wartime parents might have found individual purpose and collective belonging through mobilising activities, inside the extra-parliamentary milieux young men and women found similar emancipation and personal realisation in late-sixties struggles: in demonstrations over local rent rises, national industrial disputes, the Ford Sewing Machinist strike, the Industrial Relations Bill, national coal, dock and building worker strikes and the Pentonville Five affair. Their participation in these English disputes occurred alongside the international liberation campaigns from Vietnam, Cambodia and Portugal.

Activist communities, real or imagined, existed at macro, micro and interior subjective levels and functioned as various sites of renewal and refuge, aiding adult self-making. However, New Left circles also facilitated divisions from the parental home. Young activists actively rejected Victorian prejudices they heard in the family, school and in local working-, lower- and middle-class communities. They displaced older prevailing mentalities, related to issues of class, race and sexuality, with a New Left identity as another form of modern reflexive, authentic selfhood. As sites of refuge, from their earliest beginnings in the mid-sixties, the activist communities spoke of the internal disquiet of these post-war youngsters. Once one was inside extra-parliamentary communities, belonging was derived from the collective self-identity that came from feeling oneself part of a radical minority. Sue Crockford explained how radical belonging and self-identity was heightened by the everyday experience of negotiating 'the system':

> There weren't that many of us. There really weren't, and you were having to invent it on the hoof, and when anyone complained . . . I went to lecture at Hammersmith School of Art because I ran out of money for my MA. I had a scarlet winter coat. I was told by my head that was provocative. Vietnam time. I had an NLF bag. He said 'Don't bring that again.' Came in next week, and he saw it again. I said 'They're breeding.' But you had people in positions of authority over you who saw a scarlet winter coat as an act of defiance.[24]

Her testimony indicates how, as students, citizens, workers and parents, young activists maintained one foot in mainstream society, shaping how they lived and felt every day. New Left circles not only bolstered collective political hopes and ideals, but sheltered individuals against everyday incidents and remarks that confirmed prevailing inequalities and prejudices yet to be defeated. In the same way as the libertarian collective household offered single mothers like Jo Robinson, Lynne Segal and Alison Fell refuge and succour, so far-left organisations performed a similar role for men and women like Dave Lyddon, David Carter, Di Parkin and Sheila Hemingway, through the masculine camaraderie and revolutionary identities that made everyday private life easier to bear. Within these communities the familial tropes denoted the interpersonal network of affective bonds that created enduring collective identities and enabled individuals to more easily negotiate post-war social contradictions.

On the 'non-aligned' Left the family assumed direct political significance when, from 1971 to 1972, women and men began consciously to dismantle the post-war family and to reshape it in the collective image of New Life socialists and Russian communards. Underlying these projects, the notes of subjective belonging assumed political meaning as men and women embarked on what Lynne Segal termed a process of 'making families, from whatever comes to hand'.[25] Alongside her 'gang' of socialist feminists and pro-feminist male comrades, Lynne attained 'a certain confidence' as a political being and single mother. Collective selfhood performed a psychological as well as a political purpose to bolster a fragile individual sense of self.[26]

However, the social and emotional release which left spaces offered young activists could be deceptive. Belonging and self-realisation were disrupted by dislocations between political culture and subjectivity. The emotional pressures of subordinating the self to the political were perhaps most visible in the 'non-aligned' communities of the 1970s, where liberating the self meant re-thinking every aspect of social life so that even love acquired new meaning. Realising the new collective life actively engaged the heart as well as the head, as the practice of shaping selves and scrutinising subjectivities became a political project. Dislocations between interiority and outward culture arose because young activists were not simply seeking to reject the established society and to shape an alternative. Political culture inside the extra-parliamentary Left was inextricably interwoven with dominant social and cultural patterns and, as such, efforts to reconcile Old and New Left ways of seeing and being brought them into conflict with the subterranean psychic depths of Victorian inequality that continued to dominate post-war society. The politics of the late sixties engendered angry impulses from the young, impatient with the tired, myopic practices of old-world political leaders. Yet, even as they held up old political, social and sexual models for account, psychically and socially, consciously and unconsciously, they carried traces of these models into the radical Left. The result was a radical social and cultural scene wrought with contradictions between continuity and discontinuity, and alive with the social and emotional tension these could create for relationships and subjectivity. Although young activists looked up to older left individuals as role models, ruptures also occurred, discernible in the gulf between the first New Left and younger left activists, who in 1968 abandoned all hope in the parliamentary Left as an avenue for change.[27] It was also evident in the old masculine culture of far-left organisations, as young women especially found old social and emotional models incompatible with the freer, more authentic models of womanhood that Women's Liberation offered as possibilities.

The widening gulf between the left generations reflected the rapidity of the political transition that took place on the English extra-parliamentary

Left in the years between 1968 and 1972. The moment mirrored the longer-term 'moment of crisis and opportunity' that occurred elsewhere on the Left, in 'northern European states', and that was especially pronounced in 'Mediterranean Europe'.[28] On the English scene, subjective experiences of self-realignment played out against a background in which the demise of the VSC initiated a paradigm shift across the network. Whereas the VSC had, from 1966 to 1969, served as a prism for an all-encompassing New Left scene, incorporating far-left groups and non-aligned communities alike, in its wake emerged a demarcated extra-parliamentary Left, characterised on the one hand by an exclusively 'non-aligned' libertarian New Left, and on the other hand by a Trotskyist milieu that increasingly displayed the centralist tendencies of far-left organisations evident elsewhere in northern Europe.[29] Despite the cross-over of personnel that was visible on national demonstrations throughout the 1970s, the new personal politics of Women's Liberation informed a post-VSC New Left in which 'non-aligned' libertarian communities came to be defined by loose associations of feminists, gay liberation activists, socialists and anarchists committed to forming local alliances with squatters, tenants' associations, claimants, single parents and mental health patients. Inside this New Left, activists' attention to living their politics in everyday personal, social and emotional life responded to a new political authority that from the early 1970s began to reshape political and social subjectivity along new gendered lines. On the far Left, in contrast, increasing commitment to building the revolutionary party saw centralising power structures occur in tandem with an exclusive, externally focused politics that revolved around industrial class struggles. Within this milieu a traditionally masculine authority retained a dominant presence, denying political legitimacy to internal affective life. Yet, in the transitional years in which this political and cultural mutation began to occur, in both the post-VSC New Left and the far Left, activists who had come of political age at the height of the VSC struggled to negotiate the still fluid political and personal, public and private boundaries to realign themselves as political beings. During these years of rapid political change left subjectivity remained a pre-eminently mutable, often uncertain affair.

Situated at the point between two competing social worlds, young activists struggled to relinquish traditionally gendered models of self-hood as familial cultural patterns and childhood structures of feeling found echoes in private radical life. In this respect the prevalence of parental tropes also carried turbulent undertones, as they signalled the competing presence of old and new male and female subjectivities. Attempts to break away from longstanding social models were thwarted by the enduring psychic imprint of gendered and emotional models that activists transplanted into their activist lives and selves; the image of the good woman, mother, wife and dutiful public activist; the scholarship boy, public revolutionary and hidden, private man. In the mid- and late sixties the bonds of comradeship, shaped in the best traditions of post-war mixing, offered women and men a way of mediating the gendered contradictions between equality and difference. Assuming the masculine model of political authority prevailing around the VSC, young women displayed a social mobility and sexual self-determination that in sixties society remained for the most part the preserve of men. That women struggled to reconcile this masculine subjectivity with their internal female not only confirms the cautious, darker picture of sixties permissiveness but also tells of the longevity of post-war social conservatism shaping gendered roles, cultural discourse and male and female selfhood.[30] Although female experiences within the Trotskyist organisations presented far from a uniform picture of social subordination or sexual exploitation, even the public life of the revolutionary woman sat uneasily with the internal image of the post-war girl and mother, shaping contradictory identities that confirmed the prevalence of the mantra 'equal but different'. Inside the activist terrain, women's narratives confirmed the apparent impossibility of being active just like a man.

Yet men's stories of the private experience of activist life have also shown that the process of forming a left identity and finding a self within Trotskyist and 'non-aligned' circles was far from straightforward. Here too older masculine models proved often difficult to relinquish and the competition on which public revolutionary models rested allowed little space for vulnerable feeling or insecurity to find a voice. The testimonies of men from CMPP show that, prior to the emergence of Women's Liberation, unease with the competitive militancy of the street politics around VSC was not a solely female concern, and the political precursors of the new politics were also being mutually developed in an intimate group modelled on North American pre-figurative politics. However, alongside women, the arrival of the new politics also saw men struggling to remake activist selves and to reconcile previously separate public and private, political and personal lives. The new female political authority often sat uneasily with the internal activist man because of the way in which it challenged longstanding discourses of public and private masculinity that continued to prevail in English society. The men's stories call for further research into the little-understood relationship between cultural discourses and representations of post-war English masculinity and subjective experience. The attempts of 'non-aligned' left men to reconfigure personal and political life, and to internalise the New Left women's politics, suggest a valuable starting-point for interrogating important social and emotional sites of middle-class male life.

Ultimately, for both men and women, the search for belonging in the extra-parliamentary Left was a life-shaping, gendered process ongoing to the present day. For some individuals, as we have seen, it remained elusive, within sight, but never actualised; for others, belonging arrived only through activism in later movements. IS member James Hinton explained how:

> My comfort zone was a middle-class politics, and that is probably why I can't remember why I went into IS, because of the guilt, and why I was very involved in CND in the 1980s, because I came home. Suddenly my spontaneous reactions to things were the right ones . . . that gulf between theory and practice haunted me. I remember that vividly at Cambridge and then along comes END [European Nuclear Disarmament] in the 1980s. Edward [Thompson] provides the theory. It is called Exterminism, that's fine, it's not perfect, but it'll do, and I provided the practice. I was good at it.[31]

To that end, the stories underlying this book also told of another stage of self-making. This was the attempt for interviewees to recompose themselves as political, social and gendered subjects in the wake of the changes brought about since Thatcher and Blair. For many, the interviews provided opportunities to reflect on the cultural transformations on the Left and to try to make sense of themselves in relation to these. For some former IS and IMG members, the demise of England's old industrial heartlands and its integrated world of trade union class politics had left them discomposed as revolutionary beings. For some male interviewees this discomposure was an inherently gendered process. In their minds, the demise of the industrial heartland of the factory, the docks and the union shop floor had become intertwined with the feminisation of politics and the cultural appropriation of a masculine political sphere in which, as young men, they had served out an activist apprenticeship and discovered a left selfhood. In a joint interview with Sandy Irving and his former SWP comrade, John Charlton, for example, Sandy provided telling commentary about his past and present understanding of his IS activism and his place within its culture. I had invited him to reflect on how he had felt in the mid-1970s when chairing an important meeting with the socialist republican Irish Bernadette Devlin:

> I think the question what does it mean to you doesn't quite capture what motivates me . . . About seven 'o clock I had organised the meeting. The

crowd went to see Bernadette Devlin. It was not what it means to me personally, it was just a great event, but I feel on a selfish note I was glad I was there. But I didn't go there thinking what am I going to get out of it. This is this touchy-feely stuff which irritates me inside the Green Party for example.[32]

For Sandy, the identity politics of the late 1970s had represented 'the stick' beginning to be 'bent too far the other way'. He cited the motto 'the personal is political, the political is personal', referencing also the 1979 *Beyond the Fragments* discussions he remembered of socialist-feminists Sheila Rowbotham, Lynne Segal and Hilary Wainwright.[33] His motivation for engaging in the oral history interview seemed to reflect his desire to reclaim a legitimate space for his past and present revolutionary selves within what he perceived to be the feminised discourse which had displaced the traditional masculine framework of industrial class politics.[34] Detailing the cultural minutiae of IS politics, he responded to me as a young woman who had come of age in the wake of second-wave feminism, not because he entirely rejected the discourse of the 'new man' (he saw the responsibility of caring for children to lie equally with men and women, and disapproved of the neglect towards children he had occasionally witnessed during his years in the organisation), but because the effort to recall the conduct of meetings, the tactics concerning paper sales and recruitment related to his effort to resurrect his revolutionary self:

> There would be the routine of branch life. There was the routine of the branch meeting that was being the main focus . . . There was the sale of *Socialist Worker*, but then there was the planning of the next meeting so you would look around for the next public speaker, someone you have got some faith in who will a) turn up and b) do a good platform performance . . . I actually did enjoy this. I miss it actually, I really do miss it.

Yet, this mourning for the old left world of class struggles was not exclusive to men. Di Parkin's story illustrated how individuals' attempts to make sense of wider social and cultural changes on the Left could be interwoven with more intimate life events. In her oral history interview and her written memories of activist life she sought to provide an account of herself as a revolutionary woman and to see that account represented in the public domain. Her self-narrative expressed a need to recapture the validation she had felt as a young Trotskyist woman for the purposes of psychic composure. Di's was an identity that had shifted over time in response to political and personal events in her life. Although no longer a member of a far-left organisation (she had left the Spartacist League in 1981), she retained powerful psychic connection to the fifteen-year-old revolutionary self she had formed on joining the Wimbledon YS in 1962. The affective ties she continued to feel with former comrades informed this self-continuity:

> The image of my people, like when we go on a demonstration and they've all got banners and placards and stuff, and they are my people ... I still am part of those people and will go on ... I went on the last big, not this year but a year, against the cuts and a demonstration against pensions or I went along to the Occupy thing, and I'm still part of that movement, and sometimes I describe myself as a lapsed Trotskyist (laughs). It's like it might come back ... I am still she even if it's only still going to the radical history group. But, so I feel as if my sense of self has been consistent throughout my life.[35]

This self-reflection and moment of self-renewal came at the end of Di's interview. As shown in Chapter 6, hers was a story of self-recrimination and guilt as a mother as well as of self-discovery and actualisation as an activist. Her written reflections and her eagerness to engage in two separate interviews spoke of a need to recompose herself as a revolutionary woman. Her story represented an attempt to come to terms with the loss of a political landscape that had shaped her adult self, and the loss of her close IS comrade, Annie, whose friendship had been formative to her social and emotional life as a revolutionary woman. It was a dual elegy for Annie, her other self, and her identity as a revolutionary woman and single mother in a period when political and personal change had felt truly possible. Di's need to revisit the past, and to locate herself within the correspondence between her and Annie, was an attempt to resurrect her friend once again and to come to terms with her identity in a world inexorably changed beyond class politics. Her written reflections on the women's correspondence explained: 'Now I find it a comfort to return to those days of how we were ... I seek to climb back into that time; if I go back there, then she'll be there.' Like other interviewees, she mourned the loss of a sense of the possible, and her narrative spoke of her difficulty in situating herself in the present:

> We stood then on our tiptoes, we danced, stretching our lithe arms towards all kinds of futures, our banners fluttering. We had the world to win and knew we would win it. Yet, here now, we stand beyond our losses, beyond Thatcher (even Blair now stale and older) ... many of us creaking and broken, trying for optimism beyond the defeats.[36]

Yet, alongside the desire for former activists to narrate their stories, to celebrate and confirm their young lives on the Left, fractured narratives and silences also spoke of the desire to forget or keep hidden memories that remain raw, capable of wounding others as well as themselves. Several 'non-aligned' men declined my request for interviews; their silence suggests a number of possible conclusions. For some, perhaps, silence was an act of self-preservation; the possibility of conjuring memories of buried identities threatened to disturb present composure. It may also have reflected the wish to protect other comrades from possible hurt or undesired disclosure. Yet the men's silence told much about their own expectations or ideas about what should or should not be remembered or forgotten about their activism. For such men the private world of the 'non-aligned' left man remained a subject for forgetting or at least protecting. How far it is for the historian to contradict her subject's judgements about what should or should not be memorialised for historical posterity remains open to debate. The personal, subjective history of England's own '68 remains incomplete, sensitive and contested terrain where the politics of memory and activist selfhood is still being individually and collectively assembled and reworked.

Notes

1 Setch, 'The Women's Liberation Movement in Britain', p. 14.
2 Harman, *The Fire Last Time*, p. 268.
3 Shaw, 'The Making of a Party', pp. 28–9.
4 Callaghan, *British Trotskyism* (Oxford, 1984), p. 161.
5 Interview with Richard Kuper.
6 Interview with Anna Paczuska.
7 Interview with Richard Kuper.
8 Interview with Roger Cox.
9 Callaghan, *British Trotskyism*, pp. 118–21, pp. 161–2; Shipley, *Revolutionaries in Modern Britain*, pp. 148–50.
10 Beckett, *When the Lights Went Out,* p. 209.
11 Correspondence from Nigel Coward to the author, 9 April, 2009, p. 1.
12 J. Foot, 'Looking Back on Italy's "Long '68". Public, Private and Divided Memories', in I. Cornils and S. Waters (eds), *Memories of 1968: International Perspectives* (Oxford: Peter Lang, 2010), p. 109.
13 I. Birchall, '1968, the Power of the Masses', *Socialist Worker*, 19 January, 2008 [consulted at www.socialistworker.co.uk/art.php?id=14022 (8 April, 2009)].
14 N. Coward, 'Lessons from the Struggles of 1968', *Socialist Worker*, 2 February, 2008 [consulted at www.socialistworker.co.uk/art.php?id=14022 (8 April, 2008)].
15 S. J. Hilwig, 'An Oral History of Memories of 1968 in Italy', I. Cornils and S. Waters (eds), *Memories of 1968: International Perspectives* (Oxford: Peter Lang, 2010), p. 225.
16 Foot, 'Looking Back on Italy's "Long '68"', p. 111.
17 Schwarz, 'Not Even Past Yet', p. 103.

18 Hinton, *Nine Wartime Lives*; Langhamer, *The English in Love*.
19 Mort, *Capital Affairs*, p. 5.
20 Rowbotham, *Edward Carpenter*, p. 4.
21 S. Rowbotham, 'Introduction', in *Threads through Time: Writings on History and Autobiography* (Harmondsworth: Penguin, 1999), p. 3.
22 Geoff and Marie Richman and Tony Wickert, Pamphlet accompanying 'The People's War Event, 26 April–1 May, 1971', pp. 3–26, GRA.
23 Ibid., p. 3, GRA.
24 Interview with Sue Crockford.
25 Interview with Lynne Segal.
26 Ibid.
27 Rowbotham, *Promise of a Dream*, p. 201.
28 Horn, *The Spirit of '68*, pp. 228–9.
29 Ibid., pp. 160–1.
30 Mort, *Capital Affairs*, p. 5.
31 Interview with James Hinton.
32 Interview with John Charlton and Sandy Irving, Newcastle-on-Tyne, 2 June, 2009.
33 S. Rowbotham, L. Segal and H. Wainwright, *Beyond the Fragments: Feminism and the Making of Socialism* (London: Merlin, 1979).
34 For discussion of narrative constructions of masculinity in the wake of second-wave feminism, see H. Young, 'Hard Man, New Man: Re/Composing Masculinities in Glasgow, c. 1950–2000', *Oral History*, 35, Spring (2007), pp. 71–81.
35 Interview with Di Parkin, Warwick, 23 December, 2012.
36 D. Parkin, 'Remembering the 1970s: Two Women Revolutionaries', September, 2005, pp. 1–2, DPA.

Select bibliography

Oral history interviews

Interview with Ian Birchall, London, 4 November, 2008.
Interview with Caroline Bond, Leeds, 5 April, 2009.
Interview with Caroline Bond and Gilda Peterson, Leeds, 5 April, 2009.
Interview with Sue Bruley, London, 14 May, 2009.
Interview with David Carter, Middlesbrough, 1 June, 2009.
Interview with Prue Chamberlayne, London, 8 May, 2009.
Interview with John Charlton, Newcastle-upon-Tyne, 2 June, 2009.
Interview with John Charlton and Sandy Irving, Newcastle-upon-Tyne, 2 June, 2009.
Interview with Wenda Clenaghen, London, 22 January, 2009.
Interview with Lee Comer, Leeds, 3 June, 2009.
Interview with Nigel Coward, London, 7 April, 2009.
Interview with John Cowley, London, 22 January, 2009.
Interview with Roger Cox, London, 24 March, 2009.
Interview with Sarah Cox, London, 24 March, 2009.
Interview with Sue Crockford, London, 30 September, 2009.
Interview with Geoffrey Crossick, London, 21 April, 2009 and 23 June, 2009.
Interview with Bronwen Davis, Llanishen, 17 June, 2009.
Interview with Julia Fairchild, London, 11 August, 2009.
Interview with Max Farrar, Leeds, 5 June, 2009.
Interview with Alison Fell, London, 8 June, 2010.
Interview with Laurie Flynn, London, 23 December, 2009.
Interview with Val Graham, Chesterfield, 17 October, 2009.
Interview with Phil Hearse, London, 23 December, 2009.
Interview with Sheila Hemingway, Wakefield, 7 June, 2009.
Interview with Judith Herren, London, 5 March, 2009.
Interview with James Hinton, Coventry, 20 November, 2008.
Interview with John Hoyland, London, 19 November, 2008 and 4 March, 2009.
Interview with Wisty Hoyland, London, 21 January, 2009.
Interview with Sandy Irving, Newcastle-upon-Tyne, 2 June, 2009.
Interview with Steve Jefferys, London, 13 November, 2008.
Interview with Richard Kuper, London, 31 March, 2009.

Interview with Bob Light, London, 28 March, 2009.
Interview with Fred Lindop, Wareham, 13 January, 2009.
Interview with Dave Lyddon, Keele, 15 July, 2009.
Interview with Elizabeth Mansfield, London, 8 July, 2013.
Interview with Mike Martin, Warwick, 15 June, 2010.
Interview with Mike McGrath, Leeds, 3 June, 2009.
Interview with Stephen and Alicia Merrett, Wells, 16 December, 2009.
Interview with Anita Merryweather, London, 10 October, 2009.
Interview with Judith Milner, London, 2 December, 2008.
Interview with Roland and Claire Muldoon, London, 10 December, 2009.
Interview with Mica Nava, London, 20 November, 2009.
Interview with Sue O'Sullivan, London, 19 January, 2010.
Interview with Anna Paczuska, London, 4 January, 2010.
Interview with John Palmer, London, 23 June, 2009.
Interview with Di Parkin, Totnes, 27 April, 2009 and Warwick, 23 December, 2012.
Interview with Sarah Perrigo, Leeds, 4 June, 2009.
Interview with Gilda Peterson, Leeds, 4 June, 2009.
Interview with Chris Ratcliffe, Hebden Bridge, 6 June, 2009.
Interview with Chris Rawlence, Chipping Norton, 29 August, 2012.
Interview with Carole Reagan, London, 20 August, 2009.
Interview with Mike Reid, Sheffield, 12 July 2013.
Interview with Margaret Renn, London, 4 January, 2010.
Interview with Jo Robinson, London, 18 January, 2010.
Interview with John Rose, London, 30 October, 2008.
Interview with Sabby Sagall, London, 12 March, 2009.
Interview with Lynne Segal, London, 30 January, 2010.
Interview with Martin Shaw, Brighton, 15 January, 2009.
Interview with Joan Smith, 20 March, 2009.
Interview with Jane Storr, Leeds, 4 June, 2009.
Interview with James Swinson, London, 2 February, 2010.
Interview with Jacqueline Thompson, 10 February, 2009.
Interview with Martin Tompkinson, London, 6 November, 2009.
Interview with Stephen Trafford, London, 8 July, 2013.
Interview with Rita Vaudrey, 2 September, 2009.
Interview with Hilary Wainwright, London, 26 November, 2009.
Interview with Alan Watts, London, 20 March, 2009.
Skype interview with Tony Wickert, 31 May, 2010.
Interview with Alan Woodward, London, 2 January, 2009.
Skype interview with Henry and Sheli Wortis, 1 September, 2009.

Private correspondence

Correspondence from Ian Birchall to the author, 20 October, 2008 and 9 September, 2010.

Correspondence from Nigel Coward to the author, 9 April, 2009.
Correspondence from Ann Hunt to the author, 20 December, 2009 and 31 January, 2010.
Correspondence from Tony Wickert to the author, 21 April, 2009.

Unpublished primary sources

British Library sound archive
Ronald Fraser interview with respondent C896/03, 4 April, 1984, Ronald Fraser Interviews: 1968 – A Student Generation in Revolt.
Ronald Fraser interview with respondent C896/18, 9 October, 1984, Ronald Fraser Interviews: 1968 – A Student Generation in Revolt.
Ronald Fraser interview with respondent C896/30, 17 June, 1984, Ronald Fraser Interviews: 1968 – A Student Generation in Revolt.
Ronald Fraser interview with C890/06, 20 April, 1984, Ronald Fraser Interviews: 1968 – A Student Generation in Revolt.

London School of Economics
Papers of the International Marxist Group, International Marxist Group 4/1/2.

Hull University archives
Papers of Lt Commander Edgar Philip Young, RN and Amicia More Young, DYO, University of Hull Archive.

Modern Records Centre, University of Warwick, Coventry
Papers of Colin Barker: International Socialists, MSS. 152.
Papers of Alan Clinton, MSS. 539/2/2/14.
Correspondence with Chris Davison (International Socialists and Secretary of the London Industrial Shop Stewards Defence Committee, 1966–67), MSS. 152, Boxes 6 and 9.
Papers of Richard Hyman: International Socialists, MSS. 84.
Papers of the International Marxist Group, MSS. 128.
Papers of the International Socialists: internal documents, MSS. 128/158.
Papers of Steve Jefferys: International Socialists, MSS. 244.
Papers of Richard Kuper: International Socialists, MSS. 250 Box 9.
Socialist Woman Papers, MSS. 128/95.
Papers of Alan Thornett, MSS. 391.

The Women's Library, London Metropolitan University
Papers of Sheila Rowbotham, 7SHR.

Private collections
'Children's Community Centre: our experiences of collective child care', pamphlet written by members involved in running the project, c. 1972, Private archive of Sue Crockford.

Connell, E. 'The Day I Asked: Are We Going To Die at Three O'clock Mum?', *News on Sunday*, 15 November, 1987, obtained with the permission of Chris Ratcliffe.

Chamberlayne, P. and D. Parkin, 'Women, Sex and Revolutionary Politics', European Social Science History Conference, International Institute of Social History, Amsterdam, March, 2006.

Reid, M., 'Mix Café: Laurieston Hall, 1972–77', unpublished account, 2008.

Private papers of Prue Chamberlayne.

Private papers of Geoffrey Crossick.

Private papers of John Hoyland.

Private papers of Mica Nava.

Private papers of Di Parkin.

Private papers of Geoff Richman.

Private papers of David Robinson.

Private papers of Andrew Tolson.

Newspapers and periodicals

Agitator (the magazine of the LSE IS Socialist Society)
Black Dwarf
Brixton's Own Boss
Campus (Warwick University newspaper 1967–73)
Community Newspaper of West Kentish Town and Gospel Oak
Daily Telegraph
Guardian
Hackney Gutter Press
International
International Socialism
Islington Gutter Press
Labour Worker
Morning Post
North Kensington Area Paper
Peace News
Red Camden
Red Mole
Red Rag
Sanity
Shrew
Socialist Woman
Socialist Worker
Spare Rib
The Sunday Times
The Times
The Week
Woman's Voice
Women's Voice

Contemporary articles, books, pamphlets and speeches

Abrams, P. and A. Little, 'The Young Activist in British Politics', *British Journal of Sociology*, 16:4, June (1965), pp. 315–33.

Abrams, P. and A. Little, 'The Young Voter in British Politics', *British Journal of Sociology*, 16:2, June (1965), pp. 95–110.

Ali, T., *Street Fighting Years: An Autobiography of the Sixties* (2nd edn, London: Verso, 2005).

Ashbolt, A., 'The American New Left and Community Unions', *Illawarra Unity*, 8:1, 2008, pp. 37–42.

Authors' Collective (ed.), *Storefront Day Care Centres: The Radical Berlin Experiment* (English translation by Catherine Lord and Renée Neu Watkins, Boston, 1973, of orig. edn, Cologne, 1970).

Birchall, I., '1968, the Power of the Masses', *Socialist Worker*, 19 January, 2008 [consulted at www.socialistworker.co.uk/art.php?id=14022 (8 April, 2009)].

Book, T. and L. Flynn, 'Celebration of the Life of Basker Vashee and of the 40th Anniversary of the LSE Student Sit-in', April, 2007 [consulted at www.lse.ac.uk/collections/alumniRelations/reunionsAndEvents/2007/0420.htm (11 May, 2008)].

Bowlby, J., *Child Care and the Growth of Love* (Harmondsworth: Penguin, 1953).

Campbell, B., 'A Feminist Sexual Politics: Now You See It, Now You Don't', *Feminist Review*, 5 (1980), pp. 1–18.

Cliff, T., *The Employers' Offensive: Productivity Deals and How to Fight Them* (London: Pluto Press, 1970).

Cohen, P. (ed.), *Children of the Revolution: Communist Childhood in Cold War Britain* (London: Lawrence and Wishart, 1997).

Comer, L., *Wedlocked Women* (Leeds: Feminist Books, 1974).

Coward, N., 'Lessons from the Struggles of 1968', *Socialist Worker*, 2 February, 2008 [consulted at www.socialistworker.co.uk/art.php?id=14022 (8 April, 2008)].

Cowley, J., 'The Politics of Community Organising', in J. Cowley, A. Kaye, M. Mayo and M. Thompson (eds), *Community or Class Struggle?* (London: Stage 1, 1977), pp. 222–42.

Curtis, H. and M. Sanderson (eds), *The Unsung Sixties: Memoirs of Social Innovation* (London: Whiting & Birch, 2004).

Dickinson, M. (ed.), *Rogue Reels: Oppositional Film in Britain, 1945–90* (London: British Film Institute, 1999).

Diski, J., *The Sixties* (London: Profile Books, 2009).

Douglass, D. J., *Geordies – Wa Mental* (Hastings: Read 'n' Noir, 2002).

Douglass, D. J., *The Wheel's Still in Spin: A Coal Miner's Mahabharata* (Hastings: Read 'n' Noir, 2009).

Dunn, N., *'Talking to Women'* (London: Pan Books, 1965).

Friday, N., *My Mother/My Self: The Daughter's Search for Identity* (3rd edn, London: Harper Collins, 1994).

Gorer, G., *Sex and Marriage in England Today* (London: Thomas Nelson, 1971).

Green, J. (ed.), *Days in the Life: Voices from the English Underground, 1961–1971* (London: Pimlico, 1998).

Heron, L. (ed.), *Truth, Dare or Promise* (London: Virago, 1985).

Higher Education, Report of the Committee appointed by the Prime Minister under the Chairmanship of Lord Robbins 1961–1963, Cmnd. 2154, Parliamentary Papers xi–xiv, 1962–63.

Hoggart, R., *The Uses of Literacy* (Harmondsworth: Penguin, 1961).

Home Office, *Report of the Tribunal to Inquire into the Vassall Case and Related Matters*, Cmnd. 2009 (London, 1963).

Hoyland, J. (ed.), *Fathers and Sons* (London: Serpent's Tail, 1992).

Ingham, M., *Now We Are Thirty: Women of the Breakthrough Generation* (London: Eyre Methuen, 1981).

Jackson, B., *Working Class Community* (London: Routledge, 1968).

Jackson, B. and D. Marsden, *Education and the Working-Class* (Harmondsworth: Penguin, 1969).

Kaplan, J. and L. Shapiro (eds), *Red Diapers: Growing Up in the Communist Left* (Chicago: University of Illinois Press, 1998).

Keables, K. (ed.), *London Recruits: The Secret War against Apartheid* (London: Merlin, 2012).

Linhart, R., *The Assembly Line* (translated by M. Crosland, London: Calder, 1978).

Macrae, D. G., 'The Culture of a Generation: Students and Others', *Journal of Contemporary History*, 2:3 (1967), pp. 3–13.

Maitland, S. (ed.), *Very Heaven: Looking Back at the 1960s* (London: Virago, 1988).

Marris, P., *The Experience of Higher Education* (London: Routledge, 1964).

Mead, M., *Culture and Commitment: A Study of the Generation Gap* (London: Bodley Head, 1970).

Ministry of Education, *The Youth Service in England and Wales* (the Albemarle report) (1960).

Musgrove, F., *Youth and the Social Order* (London: Routledge, 1968).

Newson, J. and E. Newson, *Patterns of Infant Care in an Urban Community* (Harmondsworth: Penguin, 1965).

Nuttall, J., *Bomb Culture* (London: Paladin, 1970).

Osborne, J., *Look Back in Anger!* (London: Faber, 1957).

Osborne, J., 'They Call It Cricket', in Tom Maschler (ed.), *Declaration* (London: Macgibbon & Kee, 1957), pp. 61–84.

Parkin, F., *Middle Class Radicalism: The Social Bases of the British Campaign for Nuclear Disarmament* (Manchester: Manchester University Press, 1968).

Ratcliffe, C., 'May Days in Paris' [consulted at www.essex68.org.uk/may68-p.html (10 November, 2010)].

Roberts, E., *Women and Families: An Oral History, 1940–1970* (Oxford: Blackwell, 1995).

Roberts, M., *Paper Houses: A Memoir of the '70s and Beyond* (London: Virago, 2007).

Rose, J., 'Debate Sparked by Six Day War 1967 Transformed a Generation', *Socialist Worker*, 2054, 9 June, 2007 [consulted at www.socialistworker. co.uk/art.php?id=11874 (14 October, 2008)].

Rowan, J., 'Achilles Heel and the Anti-Sexist Men's Movement', *Psychotherapy and Politics International*, 3:1 (2004), pp. 58–71.

Rowbotham, S., *Woman's Consciousness Man's World* (Harmondsworth: Penguin, 1973).

Rowbotham, S., *Dreams and Dilemma: Collected Writings* (London: Virago, 1983).

Rowbotham, S., *Threads Through Time: Writings on History and Autobiography* (Harmondsworth: Penguin, 1999).

Rowbotham, S., *Promise of a Dream: Remembering the Sixties* (London: Verso, 2000).

Rowbotham, S., L. Segal and H. Wainwright, *Beyond the Fragments: Feminism and the Making of Socialism* (London: Merlin, 1979).

Samuel, V. (ed.), *Darling Alicia: The Love Letters of Alicia Kaner and Stephen Merrett* (Leicester: Matador, 2009).

Schofield, M., *The Sexual Behaviour of Young People* (Harmondsworth: Penguin, 1965).

Schofield, M., *The Sexual Behaviour of Young Adults* (London: Allen Lane, 1973).

Segal, L., *Making Trouble: Life and Politics* (London: Serpent's Tail, 2007).

Segal, L., *Slow Motion: Changing Masculinities, Changing Men* (London: Virago, 1990).

Segal, L., 'Who Do You Think You Are: Feminist Memoir Writing', *New Formations*, 67 (2009), pp. 120–33.

Seidler, V., *Rediscovering Masculinity: Reason, Language and Sexuality* (London: Routledge, 1989).

Thompson, E. P., *The Making of the English Working Class* (3rd edn, London: Gollancz, 1980).

Tolson, A., *The Limits of Masculinity* (London: Routledge, 1987).

Tynan, K., 'The Angry Young Movement', *Curtains: Selections from the Drama Criticism and Related Writings* (London: Longmans, 1961).

Wandor, M. (ed.), *The Body Politic: Writings from the Women's Liberation Movement in Britain 1969–1972* (London: Stage 1, 1972).

Wandor, M., *Once a Feminist: Stories of a Generation* (London: Virago, 1990).

Kate Weigand interview with Barbara Winslow, Williamstown, Massachusetts, 3–4 May, 2004, Voices of Feminism Oral History Project, Sophia Smith Collection, 2004 [consulted at www.smith.edu/libraries/libs/ssc/vof/transcripts/ Winslow.pdf (24 October, 2009)].

Widgery, D. (ed.), *The Left in Britain 1956–68* (Harmondsworth: Penguin, 1976).

Wilson, E., *Mirror Writing* (London: Virago, 1982).

Wilson, S., 'The Poster Workshop' [consulted at www.posterworkshop.co.uk/aboutus.html (3 November, 2010)].

Wright Mills, C., *The Sociological Imagination* (2nd edn, Oxford: Oxford University Press, 2000).

Young, M. and P. Willmott, *Family and Kinship in East London* (Harmondsworth: Penguin, 1957).

Young, M. and P. Willmott, *Family and Class in a London Suburb* (London: New English Library, 1960).

Zweig, F., *The Student in the Age of Anxiety: A Survey of Oxford and Manchester Students* (London: Heinemann, 1963).

Published secondary sources

Abrams, L., *Oral History Theory* (Abingdon: Routledge, 2010).

Alexander, S., *Becoming a Woman: and Other Essays in 19th and 20th Century Feminist History* (London: Virago, 1994).

Alexander, S., 'Room of One's Own: 1920s Feminist Utopia', *Women: A Cultural Review*, 11:3 (2000), pp. 273–88.

Allport, A., *Demobbed: Coming Home after the Second World War* (London: Yale, 2009).

Ashbolt, A., 'The American New Left and Community Unions', *Illawarra Unity*, 8:1 (2008), pp. 37–42.

August, A., 'Gender and 1960s Youth Culture: The Rolling Stones and the New Woman', *Contemporary British History*, 23:3 (2009), pp. 79–100.

Beckett, A., *When the Lights Went Out: What Really Happened to Britain in the Seventies* (London: Faber, 2009).

Bhambra, G. K. and I. Demir (eds), *1968 in Retrospect: History, Theory, Alterity* (Basingstoke: Palgrave Macmillan, 2009).

Bingham, A., *Family Newspapers? Sex, Private Life, and the British Popular Press 1918–1978* (Oxford: Oxford University Press, 2009).

Birchall, I. H., 'Building "The Smallest Mass Party in the World": Socialist Workers Party 1951–1979' [consulted at www.marxists.org/history/etol/revhist.otherdox/smp/smp2.html (11 March, 2008)].

Birchall, I. H., 'History of the International Socialists – Part 1', *International Socialism*, 76, March (1975) [consulted at www.marxists.de/intsoctend/birchall/theoprac.htm (22 May, 2009)].

Birchall, I. H., *Tony Cliff: A Marxist for His Time* (London: Bookmarks, 2011).

Birmingham Feminist History Group, 'Feminism as Femininity in the Nineteen-Fifties', *Feminist Review*, 3 (1979), pp. 48–65.

Black, L., *Redefining British Politics: Culture, Consumerism and Participation 1954–70* (London: Palgrave Macmillan, 2010).

Black, L., H. Pemberton and P. Thane, *Reassessing 1970s Britain* (Manchester: Manchester University Press, 2012).

Bourke, J., *Working-Class Cultures in Britain 1890–1960* (London: Routledge, 1994).

Breines, W., *Community and Organization in the New Left, 1962–1968: The Great Refusal* (New York: Praeger, 1982).

Brooke, S., 'Gender and Working Class Identity in Britain during the 1950s', *Journal of Social History*, 34:4, Summer (2001), pp. 773–95.

Brooke, S., *Sexual Politics. Sexuality, Family Planning and the British Left, from the 1880s to the Present Day* (Oxford: Oxford University Press, 2011).

Brooke, S., '"Slumming" in Swinging London? Class, Gender and the Post-War City in Nell Dunn's *Up the Junction* (1963)', *Cultural and Social History*, 9:3 (2012), pp. 429–49.

Brown, C. G., *The Death of Christian Britain: Understanding Secularisation 1800–2000* (London: Routledge, 2001).

Brown, C. G., 'Sex, Religion and the Single Woman, c. 1950–75: The Importance of a "Short" Sexual Revolution to the English Religious Crisis of the Sixties', *Twentieth-Century British History*, 22:2 (2011), pp. 189–215.

Brown, T. S., '"1968" East and West: Divided Germany as a Case Study in Transnational History', *American Historical Review*, 114:1, February (2009), pp. 69–96.

Browne, S. F., '"A Veritable Hotbed of Feminism"? Women's Liberation in St Andrews, Fife, c. 1968–c. 1979', *Twentieth Century British History* 23:1 (2012), pp. 100–23.

Callaghan, J., *British Trotskyism: Theory and Practice* (Oxford: Blackwell, 1984).

Carroll, S., 'Danger! Official Secret: the Spies for Peace: Discretion and Disclosure in the Committee of 100', *History Workshop Journal*, 69, Spring (2010), pp. 158–76.

Caute, D., *Sixty-Eight: The Year of the Barricades* (London: Hamilton, 1988).

Cesarani, D., *Justice Delayed: How Britain became a Refuge for Nazi War Criminals* (London: Phoenix, 1992).

Charlesworth, S. J., *A Phenomenology of Working-Class Experience* (Cambridge: Cambridge University Press, 2000).

Charlton, J., *Don't You Hear the H-Bomb's Thunder? Youth and Politics on Tyneside in the Late 'Fifties and Early 'Sixties* (Pontypool: Merlin, 2009).

Clark, M., *Narrative Structures and the Language of the Self* (Columbus: Ohio State University Press, 2010).

Claussen, D., '"Chiffre 68"', in Dietrich Harth (ed.), *Revolution and Mythos* (Frankfurt: Fischer, 1992).

Cohen, P., 'Sub-cultural Conflict and Working Class Community', *Working Papers in Cultural Studies*, 2, Spring (1972), University of Birmingham, pp. 5–51.

Collins, M., *Modern Love: An Intimate History of Men and Women in Twentieth-Century Britain* (London: Atlantic, 2003).

Conekin, B., F. Mort and C. Waters (eds), *Moments of Modernity: Reconstructing Britain 1945–1964* (London: Rivers Oram Press, 1999).

Cook, M., '"Gay Times": Identity, Locality, Memory, and the Brixton Squats in 1970's London', *Twentieth Century British History*, 24:1 (2013), pp. 84–109.

Cook, H., *The Long Sexual Revolution: English Women, Sex and Contraception, 1800–1975* (Oxford: Oxford University Press, 2004).

Cooper, R., S. Fielding and N. Tiratsoo (eds), *The Wilson Governments, 1964–1970* (London: Pinter Publishers, 1993).

Coote A., and B. Campbell, *Sweet Freedom* (Oxford: Blackwell, 1982).

Cornils, I. and S. Waters (eds), *Memories of 1968: International Perspectives* (Oxford: Peter Lang, 2010).

Darlington, R. and D. Lyddon, *Glorious Summer: Class Struggle in Britain 1972* (London: Bookmarks, 2001).

Davis, A., 'A Critical Perspective on British Social Surveys and Their Accounts of Married Life, c. 1945–1970', *Cultural and Social History*, 6:1 (2009), pp. 47–64.

Davis, A., *Modern Motherhood, Women and Family in England, c. 1945–2000* (Manchester: Manchester University Press, 2012).

Davis, B., W. Mausbach, M. Klimke, and C. MacDougall (eds), *Changing the World, Changing Oneself: Political Protest and Collective Identities in West Germany and the US in the 1960s and 1970s* (Oxford: Berghahn Books, 2010).

Dawson, G., *Soldier Heroes: British Adventure, Empire and the Imagining of Masculinities* (London: Routledge, 1994).

DeGroot, G. J. (ed.), *Student Protest: The Sixties and After* (Essex: Longman, 1998).

DeGroot, G. J., *The 60s Unplugged: A Kaleidoscopic History of a Disorderly Decade* (London: Macmillan, 2008).

Donnelly, M., *Sixties Britain: Culture, Society and Politics* (Harlow: Pearson, 2005).

Dorey, P. (ed.), *The Labour Governments, 1964–1970* (London: Routledge, 2006).

Dyhouse, C., *Girl Trouble: Panic and Progress in the History of Young Women* (London: Zed Books, 2013).

Eaden, J. and D. Renton, *The Communist Party of Great Britain since 1920* (Basingstoke: Palgrave Macmillan, 2002).

Eley, G., *Forging Democracy: The History of the Left in Europe, 1850–2000* (Oxford: Oxford University Press, 2002).

Eley, G., 'The Family is a Dangerous Place: Memory, Gender, and the Image of the Working-Class', in R. Rosenstone (ed.), *Revisioning History* (Princeton: Princeton University Press, 1993), pp. 17–43.

Ellis, C., 'The Younger Generation: The Labour Party and the 1959 Youth Commission', *Journal of British Studies*, 41:2 (2002), pp. 199–231.

Evans, M., *A Good School: Life at a Girl's Grammar School in the 1950s* (London: Women's Press, 1991).

Evans, S., *Personal Politics: The Roots of Women's Liberation in the Civil Rights Movement and the New Left* (New York: Vintage Books, 1979).

Feely, C., 'From Dialectics to Dancing: Reading, Writing and the Experience of Everyday Life in the Diaries of Frank P. Forster', *History Workshop Journal*, 69, Spring (2010), pp. 90–110.

Finch, J. and P. Summerfield, 'Social Reconstruction and the Emergence of Companionate Marriage, 1945–59', in G. Allen (ed.), *The Sociology of the Family: A Reader* (Oxford: Blackwell, 1999), pp. 12–35.

Fink, C., P. Gassert and D. Junker (eds), *1968. The World Transformed* (Cambridge: Cambridge University Press, 1998).

Fisher, K., *Birth Control, Sex, and Marriage in Britain 1918–1960* (Oxford: Oxford University Press, 2006).

Fowler, D., *Youth Culture in Modern Britain, c. 1920–c. 1970* (Basingstoke: Palgrave Macmillan, 2008).

Francis, M., 'Tears, Tantrums and Bared Teeth: The Emotional Economy of Three Conservative Prime Ministers, 1951–1963', *Journal of British Studies* 41:3 (2002), pp. 354–87.

Francis, M., 'A Flight from Commitment? Domesticity, Adventure and the Masculine Imaginary in Britain after the Second World War', *Gender and History*, 19:1 (2007), pp. 163–85.

Francis, M., *The Flyer: British Culture and the Royal Airforce 1939–1945* (Oxford: Oxford University Press, 2008).

Fraser, F. (ed.), *1968: A Student Generation in Revolt: An International Oral History* (London: Chatto & Windus, 1988).

Frazier, L. J. and D. Cohen (eds), *Gender and Sexuality in 1968: Transformative Politics in the Cultural Imagination* (New York: Palgrave Macmillan, 2009).

Freedman, M., 'From "Character-Training" to "Personal Growth": The Early History of Outward Bound 1941–1965', *History of Education*, 40:1 (2011), pp. 21–43.

Freeman, M., *Rewriting the Self: History, Memory, Narrative* (London: Routledge, 1993).

Giddens, A., *Modernity and Self Identity: Self and Society in the Late Modern Age* (Cambridge: Polity Press, 1992).

Giddens, A., *The Transformation of Intimacy: Sexuality, Love and Eroticism in Modern Societies* (Cambridge: Polity Press, 1992).

Gildart, K., 'From Dead-End Streets to "Shangri Las": Negotiating Social Class and Post-War Politics with Ray Davies and the Kinks', *Contemporary British History*, 26:3 (2012), pp. 273–98.

Gildea, R., 'The Long March of Oral History: Around 1968 in France', *Oral History*, 38, Spring (2010), pp. 68–80.

Gildea, R., J. Mark and A. Warring (eds), *Europe's 1968: Voices of Revolt* (Oxford: Oxford University Press, 2013).

Gledhill, J., 'White Heat, Guide Blue: The Girl Guide Movement in the 1960s', *Contemporary British History*, 27:1 (2013), pp. 65–84.

Grant, M., *After the Bomb: Civil Defence and Nuclear War, 1945–68* (Basingstoke: Palgrave Macmillan, 2010).

Green, A., 'Individual Remembering and "Collective Memory": Theoretical and Presuppositions and Contemporary Debates', *Oral History*, 32, Autumn (2004), pp. 35–44.

Hajek, A., *Negotiating Memories of Protest in Western Europe: The Case of Italy* (London: Palgrave Macmillan, 2013).

Halbwachs, M., *The Collective Memory* (translated by L. A. Coser, London: University of Chicago Press, 1992).

Hall, S. and T. Jefferson (eds), *Resistance through Rituals: Youth Subcultures in Post-War Britain* (2nd edn, London: Routledge, 2006).

Harman, C., *The Fire Last Time: 1968 and After* (2nd edn, London: Bookmarks, 1998).

Hebdige, D., *Subculture: The Meaning of Style* (London: Routledge, 1995).

Hennessy, P. and G. Brownfeld, 'Britain's Cold War Security Purge: The Origins of Positive Vetting', *Historical Journal*, 25:4 (1982), pp. 965–74.

Hewison, P. *Too Much: Art and Society in the Sixties, 1960–75* (London: Methuen, 1986).

Hinton, J., *Protests and Visions: Peace Politics in Twentieth-Century Britain* (London: Hutchinson Radius, 1989).

Hinton, J., 'Middle-Class Socialism, Selfhood, Democracy and Distinction in Wartime County Durham', *History Workshop Journal*, 62, Autumn (2006), pp. 116–41.

Hinton, J., *Nine Wartime Lives. Mass-Observation and the Making of a Modern Self* (Oxford: Oxford University Press, 2010).

Hopkins, A. G., 'Rethinking Decolonisation', *Past and Present*, 200, August (2008), pp. 211–47.

Horn, G-R., *The Spirit of '68. Rebellion in Western Europe and North America, 1956–76* (Oxford: Oxford University Press, 2007).

Houlbrook, M., '"A Pin to See the Peepshow": Culture, Fiction and Selfhood in Edith Thompson's Letters, 1921–1922', *Past and Present*, 207 (2010), pp. 215–49.

Hudson, K., *CND: Now More Than Ever. The Story of a Peace Movement* (London: Vision Paperbacks, 2005).

Jobs, R. I., 'Youth Movements: Travel, Protest and Europe in 1968', *American Historical Review*, 114:2 (2009), pp. 376–404.

Johnson, A., '"Beyond the Smallness of Self": Oral History and British Trotskyism', *Oral History*, 24, Spring (1996), pp. 39–48.

Jolly, M., *In Love and Struggle: Letters in Contemporary Feminism* (New York: Columbia University Press, 2010).

Kaplan, C., *Sea Changes: Culture and Feminism* (London: Verso, 1986).

Kenny, M., *The First New Left: British Intellectuals after Stalin* (London: Lawrence & Wishart, 1995).

King, L., 'Hidden Fathers? The Significance of Fatherhood in Mid-Twentieth-Century Britain', *Contemporary British History*, 26:1 (2012), pp. 25–46.

Klimke, M. and J. Scharloth (eds), *1968 in Europe. A History of Protest and Activism, 1956–77* (Basingstoke: Palgrave Macmillan, 2008).

Kushner, T., 'Anti-Semitism and Austerity: The August 1947 Riots', in P. Panayi (ed.), *Racial Violence in Britain 1840–1950* (Leicester: Leicester University Press, 1993), pp. 149–68.

Kynaston, D., *Austerity Britain 1945–51* (2nd edn London: Bloomsbury, 2008).

Kynaston, D., *Family Britain 1951–57* (London: Bloomsbury, 2009).

Langhamer, C., 'The Meanings of Home in Post-war Britain', *Journal of Contemporary History*, 40:2 (2005), pp. 341–62.

Langhamer, C., 'Adultery in Post-War England', *History Workshop Journal*, 62, Autumn (2006), pp. 86–115.

Langhamer, C., *The English in Love: The Intimate Story of An Emotional Revolution* (Oxford: Oxford University Press, 2013).

Lewis, J., *Women in Britain since 1945* (Oxford: Blackwell Publishing, 1992).

Lewis, P. M., 'Mummy, Matron and the Maids: Feminine Presence and Absence in Male Institutions, 1934–63', in M. Roper and J. Tosh (eds), *Manful Assertions: Masculinities in Britain since 1800* (London, 1991), pp. 168–90.

Linde, C., *Life Stories: The Creation of Coherence* (Oxford: Oxford University Press, 1993).

Lindop, F., 'Unofficial Militancy in the Royal Group of Docks 1945–67', *Oral History*, 11:2 (1983), pp. 21–33.

Long, P., *Only in the Common People: the Aesthetics of Class in Post-War Britain* (Newcastle: Cambridge Scholars, 2008).

Lovell, T., 'Landscapes and Stories in 1960s British Realism', *Screen*, 31, Winter (1990), pp. 357–76.

Lowe, R., *Education in the Post-War Years: A Social History* (London: Routledge, 1988).

Luckett, M., 'Travel and Mobility: Femininity and National Identity in Swinging London Films', in J. Ashby and A. Higson (eds), *British Cinema Past and Present* (London: Routledge, 2000), pp. 115–33.

Marwick, A., *The Sixties. Cultural Revolution in Britain, France, Italy, and the United States, c. 1958–1974* (Oxford: Oxford University Press, 1998).

McIlroy, J., N. Fishman and A. Campbell (eds), *The High Tide of British Trade Unionism: Trade Unions and Industrial Politics, 1964–79* (Aldershot: Ashgate, 1999).

McKibbin, R., *Classes and Cultures: England 1918–1951* (2nd edn, Oxford: Oxford University Press, 2000).

McRobbie, A., *Feminism and Youth Culture* (Basingstoke: Macmillan Education, 1991).

Mica, N., *Visceral Cosmopolitanism: Gender, Culture and the Normalisation of Difference* (Oxford: Berg, 2007).

Mort, F., 'Scandalous Events: Metropolitan Culture and Moral Change in Post-Second World War London', *Representations*, 93:1 (2006), pp. 123–32.

Mort, F., 'Social and Symbolic Fathers and Sons in Postwar Britain', *Journal of British Studies*, 38:3 (1999), pp. 353–84.

Mort, F., *Capital Affairs: London and the Making of the Permissive Society* (London: Yale University Press, 2010).

Mort, F., 'The Ben Pimlott Memorial Lecture 2010: The Permissive Society Revisited', *Twentieth Century British History*, 22:2 (2011), pp. 269–98.

O'Malley, J., *The Politics of Community Action: A Decade of Struggle in Notting Hill* (Nottingham: Spokesman Books, 1977).

Osgerby, B., *Youth in Britain since 1945* (Oxford: Blackwell, 1998).

O'Sullivan, S., *I Used To Be Nice: Sexual Affairs* (London: Continuum, 1996).

Passerini, L., *Autobiography of a Generation*, Italy 1968 (translated by Lisa Erdberg, Middletown: Wesleyan University Press, 1996).

Philips, D., 'The Women's Liberation Movement at Forty (review)', *History Workshop Journal*, 70, Autumn (2010), pp. 293–7.

Ponting, C., *Breach of Promise: Labour in Power, 1964–1970* (London: Hamish Hamilton, 1990).

Portelli, A., *The Battle of Valle Giulia: Oral History and the Art of Dialogue* (Madison: University of Wisconsin, 1997).

Pugh, M. *Women and the Women's Movement in Britain, 1914–1959* (Basingstoke: Macmillan, 1992).

Radstone, S., 'Reconceiving Binaries: the Limits of Memory', *History Workshop Journal*, 59, Spring (2005), pp. 134–50.

Radstone, S. and B. Schwarz (eds), *Memory: Histories, Theories, Debates* (New York, 2010).

Rees, J., 'A Look Back at Anger: the Women's Liberation Movement in 1978', *Women's History Review*, 19:3 (2010), pp. 337–56.

Rees, J., 'Are you a Lesbian?': Challenges in Recording and Analysing the Women's Liberation Movement in England', *History Workshop Journal*, 69, Spring (2010), pp. 177–87.

Robertson, G. I. M., 'The Generation Gap and the Defence of Britain', *Contemporary Review*, 242 (1983), pp. 71–7.

Robinson. L., *Gay Men and the Left in Post-War Britain: How the Personal Got Political* (Manchester: Manchester University Press, 2008).

Roper, M., 'Between Manliness and Masculinity: The "War Generation" and the Psychology of Fear in Britain, 1914–1950', *Journal of British Studies*, 44:2 (2005), pp. 343–62.

Roper, M., 'Re-remembering the Soldier Hero: The Social and Psychic Construction of Memory in Personal Narratives of the Great War', *History Workshop Journal*, 50, Autumn (2000), pp. 181–204.

Rose, N., 'Assembling the Modern Self', in R. Porter (ed.), *Rewriting the Self: Histories from the Renaissance to the Present* (London: Routledge, 1997), pp. 224–48.

Rose, N., *Governing the Soul: The Shaping of the Private Self* (London: Free Association Books, 1990).

Ross, K., *May '68 and its Afterlives* (Chicago: University of Chicago, 2002).

Rowbotham, S., *Edward Carpenter: A Life of Liberty and Love* (London: Verso, 2008).

Rowbotham, S., *The Past Is Before Us: Feminism in Action since the 1960s* (London, 1989).

Rowbotham, S., 'Travellers in a Strange Country: Responses of Working-Class Students to the University Extension Movement – 1873–1910', *History Workshop Journal*, 12, Autumn (1981), pp. 62–95.

Samuel, R., *The Lost World of British Communism* (London: Verso, 2006).

Sandbrook, D., *Never Had It So Good: A History of Britain from Suez to the Beatles* (London: Abacus, 2005).

Sandbrook, D., *White Heat: A History of Britain in the Swinging Sixties* (London: Abacus 2006).

Sandbrook, D., *State of Emergency: The Way We Were, 1970–1974* (London: Abacus, 2011).

Sangster, J., 'Telling Our Stories: Feminist Debates and the Use of Oral History', in R. Perks and A. Thomson (eds), *The Oral History Reader* (London: Routledge, 1998), pp. 87–100.

Savage, M., 'Affluence and Social Change in the Making of Technocratic Middle-Class Identities: Britain, 1939–55', *Contemporary British History*, 22:4 (2008), pp. 457–76.

Savage, M., *Identities and Social Change in Britain Since 1940* (Oxford: Oxford University Press, 2010).

Schwarz, B., 'Not Even Past Yet', *History Workshop Journal*, 57, Spring (2004), pp. 101–15.

Setch, E., 'The Face of Metropolitan Feminism: The London Women's Liberation Workshop, 1969–79', *Twentieth Century British History* 13:2 (2002), pp. 171–90.

Shaw, M., 'The Making of a Party? The International Socialists 1965–76', in R. Miliband and J. Saville (eds), *The Socialist Register* (London: Merlin Press, 1978), pp. 100–45.

Shipley, P., *Revolutionaries in Modern Britain* (London: Bodley Head, 1976).

Sinfield, A., *Literature, Culture and Politics in Postwar Britain* (Oxford: Basil Blackwell, 1989).

Snow, D. A., S. A. Soule and H. Kriesi (eds), *The Blackwell Companion to Social Movements* (Oxford: Blackwell, 2007).

Stanley, J., 'Including Feelings: Personal Political Testimony and Self-Disclosure', *Oral History*, 24, Spring (1996), pp. 60–7.

Stedman Jones, G., 'History and Theory: An English Story', in *Historien: European Ego-histoires: Historiography and the Self, 1979–2000*, vol. 3 (2001), pp. 103–24.

Steedman, C., *Strange Dislocations: Childhood and the Idea of Human Interiority, 1790–1930* (London: Virago, 1995).

Steedman, C., 'The Peculiarities of English Autobiography: An Autobiographical Education, 1945–1975', in *Plurality and Individuality. Autobiographical Cultures in Europe* (ed. Christa Hammerle), IFK Internationales Forschungzentrum, Kulturwissenschaften, Vienna (1995), pp. 86–94.

Steedman, C., 'Writing the Self: The End of the Scholarship Girl', in J. McGuigan (ed.), *Cultural Methodologies* (London: Sage, 1997), pp. 106–25.

Steedman, C., *Landscape for a Good Woman: A Story of Two Lives* (London: Virago, 1986).

Stephens, J., 'Our Remembered Selves: Oral History and Feminist Memory', *Oral History*, 38, Spring (2010), pp. 81–90.

Summerfield, P., 'Culture and Composure: Creating Narratives of the Gendered Self in Oral History Interviews', *Cultural and Social History*, 1, January (2004), pp. 65–93.

Summerfield, P., *Reconstructing Women's Wartime Lives: Discourse and Subjectivity in Oral Histories of the Second World War* (Manchester: Manchester University Press, 1998).

Taylor, C., *Sources of the Self: The Making of the Modern Identity* (Cambridge: Cambridge University Press, 1989).

Taylor, C., *The Culture of Confession from Augustine to Foucault: A Genealogy of the 'Confessing Animal'* (London: Routledge, 2009).

Taylor, R. and C. Pritchard, *The Protest Makers: The British Nuclear Disarmament Movement of 1958–1965, Twenty Years On* (Oxford: Pergamon, 1980).

Tebbutt, M., *Being Boys: Youth, Leisure and Identity in the Inter-War Years* (Manchester: Manchester University Press, 2013).

Thane, P. 'Introduction: Exploring Post-War Britain', *Cultural and Social History*, 9:2 (2012), pp. 271–5.

Thomas, N., 'Challenging Myths of the 1960s: The Case of Student Protest in Britain', *Twentieth Century British History*, 13:3 (2002), pp. 277–97.

Thomas, N., 'Protests against the Vietnam War in 1960s Britain: The Relationship Between Protesters and the Press', *Contemporary British History*, 22:3 (2007), pp. 335–54.

Thomas, N., 'Will the Real 1950s Please Stand Up?: Views of a Contradictory Decade', *Cultural and Social History*, 2, June (2008), pp. 227–36.

Thomson, A., *Moving Stories: An Intimate History of Four Women Across Two Continents* (Manchester: Manchester University Press, 2011).

Thomson, M., *Psychological Subjects: Identity, Culture, and Health in Twentieth-Century Britain* (Oxford: Oxford University Press, 2006).

Thompson, P., 'Family Myths, Models and Desires in the Shaping of Individual Life Paths', in D. Bertaux and P. Thompson (eds), *International Year Book of Oral History and Life Stories: Between Generations: Family Myths, Models and Memories*, Vol. 2 (Oxford: Oxford University Press, 1993), pp. 14–37.

Thompson, W. and M. Collins, 'The Revolutionary Left and the Permissive Society', in M. Collins (ed.), *The Permissive Society and Its Enemies: Sixties British Culture* (London: Rivers Oram Press, 2007), pp. 155–68.

Thorpe, A., *A History of the British Labour Party* (Basingstoke: Palgrave Macmillan, 2008).

Todd, S., 'Affluence, Class and Crown Street: Reinvesting the Post-War Working Class', *Contemporary British History*, 22:4 (2008), pp. 501–18.

Turner, A. W., *Crisis? What Crisis? Britain in the 1970s* (London: Aurum, 2008).

Veldman, M., *Fantasy, the Bomb, and the Greening of Britain: Romantic Protest 1945–1980* (Cambridge: Cambridge University Press, 1994).

von der Goltz, A. (ed.), *'Talkin' 'bout my Generation': Conflicts of Generation Building and Europe's '1968'* (Göttingen: Wallstein, 2011).

Walker, D., 'The First Wilson Governments, 1964–70', in P. Hennessy and A. Seldon (eds), *Ruling Performance: British Governments from Atlee to Thatcher* (Oxford: Blackwell, 1987), pp. 172–98.

Waterman, P., 'Hopeful Traveller: The Itinerary of an Internationalist', *History Workshop Journal*, 35, Spring (1993), pp. 165–83.

Waters, C., '"Dark Strangers in Our Midst": Discourses of Race and Nation in Britain, 1947–1963', *Journal of British Studies*, 36:2 (1997), pp. 207–38.

Webster, W., *Englishness and Empire, 1939–1965* (Oxford: Oxford University Press, 2007).

Weeks, J., *Sex, Politics and Society: The Regulation of Sexuality since 1800* (London: Longman, 1989).

Weeks, J., *The World We Have Won* (London: Routledge, 2007).

Williams, R., 'Culture is Ordinary', reprinted in A. Gray and J. McGuigan (eds), *Studying Culture: An Introductory Reader* (London: Arnold, 1993), pp. 5–14.

Wilson, E., *Only Half-Way to Paradise: Women in Postwar Britain, 1945–1968* (London: Virago, 1980).

Young, H., 'Hard Man, New Man: Re/Composing Masculinities in Glasgow, c. 1950–2000', *Oral History*, 35, Spring (2007), pp. 71–81.

Unpublished papers and theses

Abrams, L., 'Mothers and Daughters: Negotiating the Discourse on the "Good Woman", in 1950s and 1960s Britain'.

Browne, S., 'The Women's Liberation Movement in Scotland, c. 1968–1979' (Unpublished PhD thesis, Department of History, University of Dundee, September, 2009).

Ehrlich, A. Z., 'The Leninist Organisations in Britain and the Student Movement, 1966–1972' (Unpublished PhD thesis, University of London, 1981).

King, L., 'Fatherhood and Masculinity in Britain, c. 1918–1960' (Unpublished PhD thesis, University of Sheffield, September, 2011).

Setch, E., 'The Women's Liberation Movement in Britain, 1969–1979: Organisation, Creativity and Debate' (Unpublished PhD thesis, University of London, Royal Holloway, July, 2000).

Thomas, N., 'The British Student Movement 1965–72' (Unpublished PhD thesis, University of Warwick, December, 1996).

Young, H., 'Representation and Reception: An Oral History of Gender in British Children's Story Papers, Comics and Magazines in the 1940s and 1950s' (Unpublished PhD thesis, University of Strathclyde, 2006).

Index